KT-166-142

Virginia Cowles

Looking for Trouble

faber

This edition first published in 2021
by Faber & Faber Limited
Bloomsbury House
74–77 Great Russell Street
London WC1B 3DA

This paperback edition published in 2022

First published in the USA in 1941
by Harper & Brothers, New York

Typeset by Ian Bahrami
Printed and bound by CPI Group (UK) Ltd, Croydon, CRO 4YY

All rights reserved
© Virginia Cowles, 1941
Foreword © Christina Lamb, 2021
Map by ML Design
Inside cover printing imagery © *The Sunday Times* / News Licensing

The right of Virginia Cowles to be identified as author of this work
has been asserted in accordance with Section 77 of the Copyright,
Designs and Patents Act 1988

Looking for Trouble was first published in 1941. The language in these pages is a
reflection of the historical period in which the book was originally written

*This book is sold subject to the condition that it shall not, by way of trade
or otherwise, be lent, resold, hired out or otherwise circulated without the
publisher's prior consent in any form of binding or cover other than that in which
it is published and without a similar condition including this condition
being imposed on the subsequent purchaser*

A CIP record for this book
is available from the British Library

ISBN 978-0-571-36755-9

FSC
www.fsc.org
MIX
Paper from
responsible sources
FSC® C171272

2 4 6 8 10 9 7 5 3 1

For

MY SISTER MARY

with all my love

Contents

Foreword
by Christina Lamb

One of my favourite Virginia Cowles anecdotes concerns Lloyd George reading her article on the Spanish Civil War in the *Sunday Times* and being so impressed that he quoted it in Parliament, before asking Winston Churchill's son Randolph to bring the author to lunch in the country. The piece had no byline, and when this glamorous young American stepped out of the car, he was blindsided.

'The old man regarded me with surprise that almost bordered on resentment,' Cowles wrote afterwards. 'I suppose it was a nasty shock to find that the eminent authority he had quoted was just a green young woman.'

In the end he recovered, showing her his chickens, pigs and cows – 'sloshing through the fields like an ancient prophet with his green cloak and long white hair blowing in the wind' – and sending her home with a jar of honey and a dozen apples.

This is classic Cowles: self-deprecatory, while revealing her impressive list of contacts, bordering on name-dropping, as well as possessing an eye for the telling detail.

As a female war correspondent who grew up devouring the work of trailblazers such as Martha Gellhorn, Lee Miller and Clare Hollingworth, whose reporting of the Second World War paved the way for my generation, I have to admit it took a long while for their contemporary, Virginia Cowles, to come onto my radar, even though she had worked for my own paper. Reading this book after meeting her daughter, Harriet, I was blown away. First, by the image of Cowles as a twenty-six-year-old debutante from Boston arriving at the Spanish Civil War in hat, tailored suit, fur jacket and heels, with a typewriter and a suitcase containing three wool dresses. 'I had no qualifications as a war correspondent except curiosity,' she writes.

Curiosity is, of course, important, as is determination, which she had in spades – she would go on to be one of the only reporters to cover the Civil War from both sides. What Cowles also had, as this book reveals, was an astonishing ability to paint a scene and transport the reader there. It's hard to think of a more compelling account of the Nuremberg rallies than her description of 'the huge burning urns at the top of the stadium, their orange flames leaping into the blackness . . . the steady beat of drums that sounded like the distant throb of tom-toms . . . a shimmering sea of swastikas', and her own growing claustrophobia as she watches Hitler working people up into a frenzy of delirium.

Then there is the fact that she seemed to know everyone. A few days after that rally, she attends a tea party for Hitler. There, she witnesses his bizarre friendship with twenty-four-year-old Unity Mitford, who tells her over supper about Hitler's love for gossip and his impersonations of Goering, Goebbels and Mussolini, claiming that if he was not Führer, he could have made a fortune in vaudeville. Breezily, Unity assures her he won't go to war. 'The Führer doesn't want his new buildings bombed,' she says.

On returning angry from a doom-laden Czechoslovakia following the September 1938 Munich Conference, in which Britain and France allowed Germany to annex the country's Sudetenland borderlands, believing this would avoid a major war, she is invited to dinner with one of its architects, Neville Chamberlain. Hitler is 'beginning to lose his power', he assures her.

Cowles's encounters with all the key players have led some to describe her as the Forrest Gump of journalism. Another Sunday lunch is with Winston Churchill, who, after searching his pond for his lost goldfish, shows her his paintings and launches a diatribe against Chamberlain for failing to realise the threat Britain is facing. Then there is a series of lords and aristocrats who turn up conveniently with planes just when she needs them. Perhaps we shouldn't be surprised: after all, Cowles had started off as a 'society girl columnist' in New York, writing in *Harper's Bazaar* about fashion, debs and the death of romance.

Indeed, her own story was as remarkable as the subjects she covered. It was the tragic premature death of her mother Florence from appendicitis in 1932, when Cowles was just twenty-two, that set her off on the road to foreign reporting. Florence had left an insurance policy worth $2,000, which Cowles persuaded her sister they should spend on travelling the world, in honour of their mother's memory.

She pitched the idea of a travel column to Hearst Magazines, and over the next year wrote a series of pieces, stretching from Tokyo to Rome, where, of course, she gets an interview with Mussolini, just days after he has launched his invasion of Abyssinia. So nervous is she that she can't eat lunch. 'My knowledge of foreign affairs was negligible . . . I hadn't the faintest idea how one went about an interview.' She needn't have worried. When she enters the medieval Palazzo Venezia, guarded by Blackshirts greeting her with the Fascist salute, Il Duce lectures her about Italy's right to have an empire.

She soon gets a crash course in foreign affairs and front-line journalism after persuading her editors to let her head to Spain, where volunteer soldiers were flocking from around the world to join the fight against Franco's Fascist forces. Her first time under fire, while walking along Madrid's Gran Via, captures the war exquisitely: 'I heard a noise like the sound of cloth ripping . . . gentle at first, then it grew into a hiss; there was a split second of silence, followed by a bang as a shell hurtled into the white stone telephone building at the end of the street. Bricks and timber crashed to the ground and dust rose up in a billow . . . Everyone started running, scattering into vestibules and doorways, like pieces of paper blown by a sudden gust of wind.'

Most wars have their great journalist hotels, and in Madrid it was the Hotel Florida, which she memorably describes as peopled by 'idealists and mercenaries; scoundrels and martyrs; adventurers and *embusqués*; fanatics, traitors and plain down-and-outs. They were like an odd assortment of beads strung together on a common thread of war.' Among the resident correspondents were Tom Delmer of the *Daily Express*, whose room became a gathering point, Beethoven's Fifth blaring from his gramophone to drown out the artillery, and Ernest Hemingway, who would hold court in his second-floor room, with a young American bull-fighter as his sidekick. Cowles sounds unimpressed, describing him in his 'filthy brown trousers and torn blue shirt'. By all accounts it was mutual, Hemingway regarding this ingénue, with her gold bracelets and high heels, with disdain. Even so, they go for lunch, running into 'a fastidious-looking man dressed from head to toe in dove grey . . . [with] bright marble-brown eyes' who turns out to be the grand executioner of Madrid. He joins them for a carafe of wine, and as they leave, Hemingway warns her, 'Now remember, he's mine,' later quoting him in a play.

She goes window-shopping with Hemingway's lover, her fellow American Martha Gellhorn, staring at furs and perfumes, after which they drink afternoon cocktails in the Miami bar. I love her description of how, beneath the camaraderie and drinking, the correspondents 'studied each other like crows'. Cowles was regarded as particularly suspect, because unlike most, who were partisan, sympathising with either the Republicans or the Communists, she reported from both sides.

Though she may not have had the righteous anger of Gellhorn, she clearly cared, and like her compatriot she focused on the human cost of conflict. She quickly showed an ability to charm information from anyone and a journalist's luck to be in the right place at the right time. At one point she gets lost driving out to one of the fronts where the International Brigades are fighting and finds herself at the divisional headquarters for the Russians who are training the Republicans, which was supposed to be secret. The Russian general is hostile but clearly captivated, sending his car to Madrid to bring her back and plying her with champagne and wild strawberries, as well as the principles of Marxism. He sends her off with a red rose.

After Spain, Cowles would jump at the sound of a car backfiring or a vacuum cleaner, but it didn't put her off. Instead, she goes back and forth through a Europe on the verge of war, the lights going out in one country after another. She wears her courage lightly, yet takes incredible risks: to cover the destruction of Poland she zig-zags across the Channel in a boat for fourteen hours to escape the German U-boats. Eventually, she makes it to Romania, where she runs into her friend, Lord Forbes, who in his own plane flies her to the border, where she finds a hotel full of dazed Polish refugees fleeing the German tanks and bombs. Among them are three children sitting on suitcases, waiting for parents who will never come.

From there she heads to Finland for the little-remembered Winter War. After their country was invaded by the Soviet Union in November 1939, the Finns stunned everyone with their bravery, small numbers of soldiers on skis 'sliding like ghosts through the

woods' and beating back the initial offensive. After female correspondents are blocked from the front, following an allegation of
sexual harassment, she works her contacts and manages to get to
the remote city of Rovaniemi, near the Arctic Circle, this time clad
more adequately. She is taken to a spot where a few weeks previously the Finns had annihilated two Russian divisions. It is 'the
most ghastly spectacle I have ever seen', four miles of roads and
forests strewn with the bodies of men and horses, some 'frozen as
hard as petrified wood'. It was, however, all for nothing, the lack
of international support forcing the Finns into a peace agreement
that ceded more than ten per cent of their territory.

By June 1940, the German forces were moving on Paris.
Desperate to be there for what she imagines will be a protracted
French defence of their capital, she flies to Tours and takes what
turns out to be the last train to Paris. She arrives to find everyone is leaving. Somehow she manages to find a taxi and gives a
lift to a girl who turns out to be a prostitute, but discovers that
the hotels are all closed and her friends all gone. Eventually, she
hooks up with Tom Healy from the *Daily Mirror*, who has a sports
car, and together they drive along the Seine and south out of the
city. They are met by astonishing scenes of 'noise and confusion,
of the thick smell of petrol, of the scraping of automobile gears,
of shouts, wails, curses, tears . . . Anything that had four wheels
and an engine was pressed into service, no matter what the state
of decrepitude; there were taxi-cabs, ice-trucks, bakery vans, perfume wagons, sports roadsters and Paris buses, all of them packed
with human beings. I even saw a hearse loaded with children.'

She ends up back in London, reporting on the Blitz and the
Battle of Britain, writing from Dover: 'You knew the fate of civilisation was being decided fifteen thousand feet above your
head in a world of sun, wind and sky.' She moved out of town to

write *Looking for Trouble*, ostensibly a memoir of her journalistic exploits, but equally an exhortation for her own country to join the war.

Always fascinated by Britain, she would make it her home, and after the war married journalist and MP Aidan Crawley, with whom she had three children. She went on to write a play with Martha Gellhorn about women war reporters, as well as twelve other books on some of her rich acquaintances, such as the Astors and the Rothschilds, and a number of historical biographies.

If today there are almost as many women as men reporting from war zones, it is thanks to women like Cowles, who showed what is possible. It's a mystery to me that she doesn't receive the same recognition as Gellhorn.

Looking for Trouble was a bestseller when it was published in 1941, and I hope that its re-release will introduce her to a whole new generation.

Rovaniemi ↑ Ⓔ

Kajaani

FINLAND

Sortavala

Turku
Helsinki Ⓓ
Hanko
Leningrad
kholm
ESTONIA

ⁱⁱᶜ Sea
LATVIA
Moscow

ZIG LITHUANIA

GERMANY

Warsaw

POLAND
Kiev

UNION OF

SOVIET SOCIALIST

REPUBLICS

LOVAKIA

NGARY
Odessa

ROMANIA

Bucharest
Black Sea

GDOM OF
OSLAVIA

BULGARIA

ALBANIA

TURKEY

GREECE
IRAQ
SYRIA

Ⓐ Rhineland, remilitarised by Germany, 1936

Ⓑ Sudetenland, annexed by Germany, 1938

Ⓒ Austria annexed into Germany by the Anschluss of 1938

Ⓓ Mannerheim zone

Ⓔ Great Arctic Highway

| 0 | 100 | 200 | 300 | 400 | 500 miles |
| 0 | 200 | | 400 | 600 | 800 kilometres |

Prologue

On that November evening (Armistice Night), the three men at
the head of Great Britain, the United States and France seemed to
be the masters of the world. Behind them stood vast communities
organised to the last point, rejoicing in victory and inspired with
gratitude and confidence for the chiefs who had led them there.
In their hands lay armies of irresistible might, and fleets without
whose sanction no vessel crossed the sea upon or beneath the
surface. There was nothing wise, right and necessary which they
could not in unity decree. And these men had been drawn together
across differences of nationality and interest and across distances
on land and sea by the comradeship of struggle against a dreaded
foe. Together they had reached the goal. Victory absolute and
incomparable was in their hands. What would they do with it?

The World Crisis: The Aftermath
Winston S. Churchill, March 1929

Here is a full moon shining down on London and overhead you
can hear the drone of German bombers. The streets are deserted,
but every now and then the stillness is broken by the wracking
explosions of the guns.

On nights like this you wonder if future historians will be able to
visualise the majesty of this mighty capital; to picture the strange
beauty of the darkened buildings in the moonlight; the rustle of the
wind and the sigh of bombs; the long white fingers of the searchlights and the moan of shells travelling towards the stars. Will they
understand how violently people died: how calmly people lived?

Long ago Britons set out to master the sea for fear it would
imprison them on their island. Today the same sea holds them

secure against their enemies, and, so long as the great water high-ways remain in their control, their land can be attacked only from the air.

So far, the air has not proved decisive. The terror of the night-bomber is combated by the robust spirit of the people, and the accuracy of the day-bomber destroyed by the fierce onslaught of the Royal Air Force.

The air battles fought over the English coast have been more spectacular than any battles history has seen before. When German planes, in mass formation, approached the cliffs of Dover they were met by a shattering barrage of anti-aircraft fire, and then by the swift, angry whine of fighters. Many of these battles were fought over the sea. I have often stood in the sunshine on top of Shakespeare Cliff, a mile from the town, and watched the twisting, turning planes with a feeling of unreality. Somehow it was always difficult to grasp that these were the actual combats on which civ-ilisation depended; that although modern armies were counted in terms of millions, the sea had immobilised their strength and the issue was being decided by a handful of men above.

Of all the days I spent at Dover I remember August 15th the best. On this day the Royal Air Force shot down a record number of one hundred and eighty planes. I drove down from London with Vincent Sheean and from the cliff we tried to piece the drama together like a jigsaw puzzle. In almost the whole range of the sky there was action. To the right we could see a plane falling like a stone into the sea, leaving a long black plume against the sky; to the left, one of the great silver balloons in flames; and directly above, a fighter, diving down on one of the bombers and suddenly a tiny fluttering parachute as one of the pilots baled out; and all the time the crackling noise of the anti-aircraft guns' fire and the white bursts of smoke against the sky.

During one of these battles I looked through a pair of field-glasses at a small trawler anchored in the harbour below. The crew had evidently accepted the fierce encounters above them as part of their daily routine, for no one was paying much attention. One of the men was lying on the deck fast asleep, another was doing his washing, and a third was reading a paper. A few hours later the little trawler hoisted up its flag, got up steam, and went paddling nonchalantly down the Channel. It had an arrogant air as though it were saying: 'Hands off; this sea is ours.'

We watched the battle for some time, then Vincent turned to me and said, 'It's funny to think all this business started down there.' He nodded towards the mists.

'Down there?'

'In Spain.'

Undoubtedly future historians will puzzle over the lessons that were never learned from the first world war; they will shake their heads that the three great democracies refused to join hands and accept their responsibilities as the guardians of world peace. They will trace the causes of the present conflagration to the break-down of the League of Nations, pointing to Manchuria in 1931 and Abyssinia in 1935. But they will have to turn to Spain in 1936 for the first rumble of gunfire to break the stillness of the European continent; and it is in Spain that my story begins.

I saw the villages of Spain burning and followed the flames across the map of Europe. They spread upwards, scorching the woods of Bohemia, ravaging the plains of Poland, and even searing the ice-bound forests of the Arctic. Then the evil winds of conquest blew them to Norway. They swept through Holland and Belgium and burnt the rich fields of France black, so that now there is no life stirring.

The part I have seen is small in the picture history will record, but it has shown me that the war today is not only an issue between nations. It is a struggle to keep justice and mercy on the earth, and to preserve the very dignity of man.

London, May 1941

Part I

REPUBLICAN SPAIN

1

Trip to War

If you look back over the newspapers of March 1937 you will recall a number of things: that the *Normandie* beat the record for the Atlantic crossing; that King Leopold visited London; that Neville Chamberlain succeeded Stanley Baldwin as Prime Minister of England; that the lost diary of Dr Samuel Johnson was found; that Queen Marie of Romania was gravely ill; and that Noël Coward was resting.

You will also read that General Franco launched an offensive. On March 10th the newspapers reported that he had broken through the Madrid defences and on the following day the correspondent of the London *Daily Telegraph* wrote:

> The Nationalists have advanced eighteen miles in two days.
> They are now fifteen miles from Guadalajara. The defenders
> of Madrid realise that the battle of Guadalajara will decide the
> fate of the capital.

A few days later the story began to trickle out and the world learned that not only was Madrid still standing, but that Franco's Italian Legionaries had broken and fled, and the Nationalist offensive had been turned into the first (and what proved to be the last) major victory for the Republic.

It was a week after the battle of Guadalajara that I made my first trip to Spain. I stood at the Toulouse aerodrome at five-thirty in the morning waiting for an aeroplane to take me to Valencia. It was pitch black and bitterly cold. The frost on the ground shimmered through the darkness like a ghostly shroud, and the small red bulbs outlining the airfield had an eerie glow. My heart began to sink at the prospect of the trip.

I had no qualifications as a war correspondent except curiosity. Although I had travelled in Europe and the Far East a good deal, and written a number of articles, mainly for the 'March of Events' section of the Hearst newspapers, my adventures were of a peaceful nature. In fact, after a twelve-month trip from London to Tokyo in 1934, I had written an article for *Harper's Bazaar* which soon dated sadly. It was entitled: 'The Safe, Safe World'.

When the war broke out in Spain, I saw an opportunity for more vigorous reporting; I thought it would be interesting to cover both sides and write a series of articles contrasting the two. I persuaded Mr T. V. Ranck of the Hearst newspapers that this was a good proposition and happily set off for Europe. I knew no one in Spain and hadn't the least idea how one went about such an assignment, so waited until reaching Paris before mapping out a plan of campaign. And then the battle of Guadalajara took place. I read about the heroic resistance of beleaguered Madrid, and decided that Madrid was obviously the place to go.

Friends in Paris were not encouraging. They warned me if I didn't dress shabbily I would be 'bumped off' in the streets; some suggested men's clothes; others rags and tatters. I finally took three wool dresses and a fur jacket.

They also filled me with atrocity stories and gloomily predicted that if I was not shot down on the flight to Valencia I would surely be bombed on the road to Madrid. I had paid no attention to their forebodings, but now, as I stood on the aerodrome, a procession of terrible pictures filtered through my mind. I went into the waiting room to have a cup of coffee and took comfort from the fact that no one seemed impressed by the imminent departure of a plane for the perils of 'war-torn' Spain. There were only a half-dozen people in the room; some reading yesterday's evening papers, some sleeping with their heads on the tables. It was so cold the French mechanics were pacing up and down, stopping every now and then to warm their hands over a small stove. At last the door opened and a man announced the plane was ready to leave. I paid my bill, and as I got up an old man in a black beret who had been sitting quietly by the fire walked over to me, clasped my hand, and in a voice trembling with emotion said: *'Bonne chance, mademoiselle, bonne chance.'* I stepped into the aeroplane with a feeling of doom.

It took us only an hour to reach Barcelona. Most of it was spent in flying over the Pyrenees. The mountains were covered with snow and at first they looked grey and remote; then the dawn came up and they were swept with a fiery pink. When we circled down to a landing and I walked into the airport waiting room, I remember the surprise I felt at my first picture of Spain. The scene was so peaceful it was almost incongruous. A woman sat behind the counter knitting a sweater, two old gentlemen in black corduroy suits were at a table drinking brandy, and a small girl sprawled on the floor with a cat. They greeted the French pilots cordially, but when the latter commented on the war and asked for the latest news, one of the old men shrugged his shoulders uninterestedly, and said: 'The war has nothing to do with Catalonia. We don't want any part of it; all we want is to be left alone.'

We had a cup of coffee, our baggage was inspected by an indifferent customs officer, and an hour later we were in Valencia.

Valencia was a mass of swarming humanity. It was the temporary seat of the Government and its population of four hundred thousand had swollen to over a million. People poured through the streets, crowded the squares, clustered the doorways, thronged the beaches and flowed endlessly through the markets, to the shops and cafés. Everything was noise and confusion. Horse-drawn carts clattered over the cobblestones, and automobiles, with official stickers pasted on the windshields, raced dangerously down the main thoroughfares honking their horns wildly. The buildings were plastered with garish posters showing the mangled bodies of women and children and inscribed with the single word: 'Fascism!' Down the street a gramophone blared out gaily: 'I can't give you anything but love, Baby.'

I was deposited at the Air France office on the main street and regarded the scene with bewilderment. I asked the way to the best hotel and the clerk told me a mile or so 'down the road'. It was impossible to get a porter or a taxi. I only had one suitcase and a typewriter, so I started to walk. All the people on the streets were working-class people and everyone was dressed in black: the women wore black cotton dresses and shawls over their heads, and the men black suits and berets. Some of them paused to stare darkly at me and at first I thought it was because I was the only person wearing a hat; then I suddenly realised that the red and yellow bands painted inadvertently on my suitcase were General Franco's colours.

A street car came by and I climbed on nervously, but I had to get off at the next stop, for I had no Spanish money and I couldn't make the conductor understand that by accepting a ten-franc note he was driving a good bargain.

I finally reached the Hotel Bristol and found it packed. People were even sleeping in armchairs in the lobby. I left my bags and went into the dining room for lunch. The restaurant was crowded with a strange assortment of characters: few of them looked like Spaniards, and I later learned that this was the Valencia back-wash – businessmen, *agents provocateurs*, social workers, spies and racketeers. I asked the waiter if any American or English correspondents were staying in the hotel, and he told me Mr Kennedy of the Associated Press was sitting at a table across the room. I sent him a note telling him of my predicament and asking him to help me.

Mr Kennedy was a tough young American reporter, with an efficiency for which I was deeply thankful. Within an hour he had browbeaten the manager of the hotel into finding me a room, and introduced me to the foreign press chief, who arranged for me to go to Madrid by car in two days' time.

I remember pressing Kennedy with questions about the war, and in order to have a place to talk we took a dilapidated carriage and drove around the town. It was pleasant on the outskirts; the crowds thinned out, the Mediterranean stretched peacefully before us, and, in the fields behind, long rows of orange trees glowed in the sun. I was at a loss to understand how much of the general confusion of Valencia was due to the war, how much to the revolution, and how much to Spain.

'All three,' said Kennedy. 'God, how I wish I were back in the USA.'

I told him I thought Spain was exciting and he gave me a sour smile.

'Listen, sister, I'm too fed up with red tape and censorship trouble and not even a healthy American cigarette to smoke or a decent-looking dame to take out to dinner, to think of this any longer as a great big adventure. You'll learn.'

I must have looked crestfallen, for a moment later he added: 'Of course, Madrid isn't so bad. You get shelled every day and the food's rotten, but at least there's something to do besides arguing with a bunch of people who only know how to say *mañana*. There are lots of correspondents there and you can get out to the front when you want and see some action. Not like this burg; half of them don't even know there's a war on.'

I had noticed that the squares of Valencia were filled with young men of military age who seemed to have nothing better to do than stand in the sunshine picking their teeth. With the war at a critical stage it seemed strange, and Kennedy replied that as Valencia hadn't yet been attacked (the port had occasionally been shelled from the sea, but that was all), many of the people regarded the war as a local affair confined exclusively to Madrid. We drove past the beach and saw three gendarmes threading their way through the crowds; every now and then they stopped and questioned a group of men and scribbled in their notebooks. Kennedy explained that this was the usual method of rounding up loafers for the army.

That night we had dinner at the hotel with Captain 'Pinky' Griffiss, the American air attaché, and two French aviators known only as 'Jean' and 'Henri'. They were the black sheep of respectable French families.

Professional pilots were highly paid by the Spanish Government and they had joined up to earn enough money to pay off their gambling debts. They spent the evening regaling us with their exploits at the battle of Guadalajara. I later learned their activities were confined to patrol work over Valencia and the stories purely imaginary. Nevertheless, they were good company and the next day we all went to the bull-fight.

The bull-ring was in the centre of the town and it shone in the sunshine like a huge half grapefruit. It was noisy and crowded and the air was heavy with sweat and the rich smell of tobacco. There was none of the picturesque elegance of former days, for the crowd was a drab sweep of black, sprinkled with the khaki of the militia.

The matador, however, wore the traditional tri-cornered hat, the pink stockings and buckled shoes, and an elaborate but shabby blue-brocaded uniform. He received a loud ovation and the show was on.

I had never seen a bull-fight before and the sight of the bull pawing the ground with the blood streaming down his sides was nauseating to me. Most of the time I couldn't look. The small, dark Spaniard next to me complained loudly but not for the same reason. He explained that the fight was no good because the big bulls were bred in the south, and the south belonged to Franco. 'Curse the war,' he grumbled, 'and look at that matador. He ought to be fighting a cow.'

The matador was clumsy and the crowd booed; hats and orange peels sailed into the ring. Then a drunken militiaman climbed over the fence, careened into the arena and grabbed the cape from the matador. The latter shouted angrily at him and indignant officials ran out to drag him back. But before they could reach him he gave an expert flip of the cloth and sent the bull charging after them. They fled for the safety of the barrier and the crowd screamed with delight.

For twenty minutes the militiaman fought the bull. Five times the officials tried to pull him back and five times he sent the animal snorting after them. Suddenly the bull charged him. Its right horn hooked the soldier's belt and lifted him high in the air. The crowd rose breathless, but the man was unhurt. His belt broke and he went sprawling to the ground while the bull thundered across the ring. This gave the officials their chance to drag him back. He held his trousers up with one hand and protested comically with the other, but he was returned to his seat in the midst of wild applause. Even the disgruntled Spaniard on my right felt he'd had his money's worth.

* * *

Early on Monday morning I left for Madrid in a small car packed with boxes of food, sweets and cigarettes. It was driven by a Spanish anarchist chauffeur, and the other passengers were an American woman, Mellie Bennett (who worked in the propaganda department), and a Catholic priest.

I was astonished by the presence of a priest in a community bitterly hostile to the Church, and wondered why he was free. He was an old man, with a sly face and fingers stained yellow by nicotine. We hadn't driven far before he opened a polite conversation in bad French.

'You, I presume, are an anarchist?'

'No,' I said.

'A Communist?'

'No.'

'A Trotskyist?'

Here Mellie Bennett intervened. 'Tell the old devil to shut up.'

I was afraid he could understand, but she said she had crossed his track before and he didn't speak any English. 'I know the old humbug: he's a show-piece. He goes around France doing propaganda lectures – saying the priests are well treated in Republican Spain. He's made a packet.'

Mellie Bennett had a monkey-like face and wore thick horn-rimmed spectacles. She had a strong provocative personality and I liked her at once. She had come from Moscow, where she had worked for several years on the *Moscow Daily News*. She had left-wing convictions, but on this particular morning her outlook was sour and she criticised conditions freely.

'Look at this road,' she said. 'It ought to be crowded with trucks taking food up to Madrid, but a fat lot the politicians care.'

The narrow asphalt road wound for miles through a barren, rolling countryside. The railroads that led from the coast to Madrid had been bombed, and now this was the only line of communication linking the capital with the outside world. There were few cars on the road and during the whole two hundred miles to Madrid we counted only twenty trucks. This was due partly to lack of petrol, but, as I later learned, also to lack of organisation.

About a hundred miles from Valencia we stopped at a small village and went into a restaurant for lunch. The room was dark and a frowsy woman in a blue dress flicked dead flies and pieces of bread off the table with a cloth. She gave us an omelette, bread and wine.

The anarchist chauffeur sat down at the same table and the Catholic priest patted him on the back and said he was a good boy; he had been wounded fighting on the Aragon front. He had a bullet-hole in his thigh and it hadn't yet healed, but as soon as he was well enough he was going back to the front. Mellie Bennett explained (in English that neither could understand) that he had fought with an anarchist regiment which had gone to war with no officers. Most of them had been wiped out.

The anarchists were opposed to organisation of any kind. They believed that people, left to themselves, were instinctively good, but that an organised society always resulted in evil. Hence they had gone into battle with no leaders. We soon had an example of this idealistic but impractical creed, for a few miles further along the road we passed a car that had run out of petrol. Our chauffeur stopped and obeyed his good instincts by funnelling off some of our petrol. The result was that an hour later our car gave a nasty cough and we were in the same predicament. Mellie said: 'Now, do you understand the philosophy? We simply wait for another anarchist to come along.'

We sat by the roadside in the hot sun for nearly an hour. A 'comrade' finally appeared, gave us some petrol and once more we were on our way.

The priest was consumed with curiosity about my political faith and once again made an attempt to tabulate my views. This time he tried to wheedle them out. 'Perhaps you have, let us say, Trotskyist *leanings*? It is impossible to be nothing; no one comes to Spain without an *idée fixe* . . .'

Mellie cut into his conversation again and he finally lapsed into silence.

About forty miles from Madrid we were stopped by sentries who told us we would have to branch off on a side road and swing around by the village of Alcala de Henares. The main road to Madrid was under enemy fire from this point on. It was growing dark and we were warned to be careful about our lights. The country roads were bad, but fortunately there was a new moon which helped a little.

At nine o'clock we swung down the Gran Via, Madrid's main thoroughfare. The city was blacked out and the streets were deserted and still. The silence was oppressive and there was a strange atmosphere of foreboding. Suddenly the quiet was broken by the distant rumble of artillery. I had never heard the sound of war before and my heart beat fast.

The others were unperturbed, and when we reached the Hotel Florida, Mellie went inside to get a porter to carry out the food. While she was gone the priest bent down quickly, slit open one of the packages with a penknife and stole three packages of Chesterfield cigarettes. He smiled at me, put a yellow-stained finger over his lips, and said: 'Shhh!'

2

High Explosives

My room, on the fifth floor of the Hotel Florida, stamped me as an amateur: knowledgeable people lived as close to the ground as possible as a precaution against aerial bombs. The hotel was crowded, however, so the best the manager could do was to switch me to a large outside room on the fourth floor; but this, too, had its disadvantages. It faced a broad square and overlooked a jumble of grey roof-tops that dwindled into a distant landscape of rolling green hills. And these hills belonged to the enemy. Although this placed me in the direct line of shell-fire, the desk clerk refused to let me move. He said the inside rooms were dark and stuffy, and, besides, the hotel was not a military objective, so if a shell went through my room it would only be a mistake.

Madrid, dark and gloomy at night, was transformed into a new world with the daylight. The sun was shining and the air resounded with the clatter of humdrum business. I leaned out of the window to find the square thronged with people. Khaki-clad militiamen with red ties around their necks threaded their way into a café across the street, while black-shawled housewives with children tagging after them hurried off to do the day's market-ing. A trio of peroxide blondes swayed along the rough pavement on high-heeled shoes to the intense interest of a group of young men in dark blue berets who stood in the sun prodding their teeth with toothpicks. Donkey-carts rumbled across the cobblestones, newspaper-sellers shouted their wares, and from a movie house half a block away came a lively melody from Al Jolson's *Casino de Paris*. For a city subjected to daily bombardments, Madrid seemed as unreal as a huge movie set swarming with extras ready to play a part.

The telephone rang with a message from Sefton (Tom) Delmer of the London *Daily Express*, who offered to show me the sights of Madrid. I had often heard of Tom, who was noted for his quick wit and had the reputation of being one of the shrewdest journalists in Europe. He was a large bulk of a man with a smiling face. He greeted me by asking hopefully if I had brought any food from France. The fact that I hadn't I soon realised was an unforgivable oversight.

We strolled down the streets and Tom told me he had covered the war on the Nationalist side until he made the mistake of writing the story of Knickerbocker's trip to Burgos. The latter's plane had been mistaken for an enemy machine and fired upon by anti-aircraft guns. Tom pointed out in his story that Knickerbocker had been unaware of the episode until he was informed of it by the aerodrome authorities. The Nationalists claimed this was an attempt to cast reflection on their anti-aircraft defences and Tom was thereby expelled. Since then he had been covering the news from Madrid: 'All Spaniards are mad,' he said, 'but the people over here are less dangerous to England.'

We walked along the main streets and passed dozens of holes blasted out of the pavements where shells had fallen; many buildings bore jagged wounds, and on the Castellana a huge stone lion stared gloomily into space as though it knew its nose had been chipped off by shrapnel.

There was a good deal of traffic on the streets. Ministry of War cars, evacuation lorries, bicycles and ambulances all raced past us, and once a despatch rider on a motorcycle roared by headed for the front. Parked on a side street we saw a brown and green camouflaged truck bearing proud white letters that said: 'Captured from the enemy at Guadalajara.'

At many of the corners stone barricades were erected across the streets – barricades that had been built in November when Franco boasted that his generals would soon be drinking in the Puerta del Sol. 'If Franco takes Madrid,' said the people, 'he'll have to fight for it inch by inch.'

And yet the atmosphere of the city was not one of war. Although it had become transformed into a village behind the front, bombs and shells had been unable to erase the daily routine of life. It was this that lent the city its curious air of theatre. Bright yellow tram-cars rattled peacefully down the avenues; shop windows displayed Schiaparelli perfume, silver fox furs, jewellery, gloves and ladies' hand-made shoes; movie houses advertised Greta Garbo in *Anna Karenina* and the Marx Brothers in *A Night at the Opera*. A store on the Gran Via held a gala exhibition of war posters; they were ultra-modern posters, screaming out in reds, oranges and blues for the people of Spain to defend the Republic against Fascism. There was a small jagged hole in the ceiling where a shell had come through; beside it a card had been tacked: 'Art as practised by General Franco'.

The shell-holes, the camouflaged trucks and the stone barricades seemed as unreal as stage props; the sun was too warm, the people too nonchalant for war. Only the queue lines carried a sense of tragedy. On a side street a procession of women and children were lined up before a grocery store, with empty baskets over their arms. Some leaned wearily against the building, others sat on the curb staring into space with a strange Oriental impassiveness. All over Madrid these queue lines were formed. The city's main diet was beans, bread and rice, but food was so scarce that only a limited number could be served. Tom said that often the lines waited from midnight till noon the next day.

We crossed the Puerta del Sol and Tom stopped at a small shop to look at some cavalry cloaks which he was thinking of taking back to England as presents. We had to step over an old peddler woman who was selling red and black anarchist ties and small tin ornaments made in the shapes of tanks and aeroplanes which she had carefully spread over the pavement.

The proprietor welcomed Tom warmly and brought out an assortment of capes of different lengths and cuts with a variety of brightly coloured linings. They discussed them for some time and Tom decided to come back again. When we said goodbye he asked the proprietor how his business was going and the man sighed and shook his head: 'It is very difficult, Señor. There are so few gentlemen left in Madrid.' Outside, Tom said: 'It is obvious where *his* sympathies lie.'

As we were walking down the Gran Via on the way back to the hotel I asked Tom how often the city was shelled, and he stopped and looked meditatively at his watch. 'It's past noon now. They usually drop a few before lunch.' Scarcely a moment later I heard a noise like the sound of cloth ripping. It was gentle at first, then it grew into a hiss; there was a split second of silence, followed by a bang as a shell hurtled into the white stone telephone building at the end of the street. Bricks and timber crashed to the ground and dust rose up in a billow. A second shell plunged into the pavement thirty yards away and a third hit a wooden block of flats on a corner. Everyone started running, scattering into vestibules and doorways, like pieces of paper blown by a sudden gust of wind.

Tom and I took cover in a perfume shop and the explosions continued one every minute. My heart pounded uncertainly; the crash of falling bricks and breaking glass and the thick dust that rose up to blot out the sunshine seemed like some fearful Bible plague tuned up and mechanised for the twentieth-century appetite. The proprietress of the shop, however, appeared to be far more concerned with the preservation of property than possible death.

She hastily began removing the perfume bottles from the window and laid them in neat rows on the floor. With each explosion she broke into a fresh flow of expletives. Tom explained she was afraid the windows would break. And glass, she said, was very dear.

The bombardment lasted about half an hour. When it was over we walked down the street: the pavements were strewn with bricks and shrapnel and a telephone pole leaned drunkenly across one of the buildings, the wires hanging down like streamers. The second floor of a hat shop had a gaping hole and at the corner an automobile was a twisted mass of steel. Nearby, the pavement was spattered with blood where two women had been killed.

Desolation hung over the thoroughfare, but the loudspeaker was still screaming a tune from the *Casino de Paris*. Trucks rolled up and men got out and began to clear up the debris, the music ringing in their ears as they worked. Groups of people gathered on the corners and little boys ran out to collect pieces of shrapnel as souvenirs, newspaper-sellers drifted back to their boxes, the bootblacks called for customers and the shopkeepers rearranged their wares. Two hours later the rubble was in neat piles along the curb. Automobiles hooted their way over the cobblestones, and once again people sauntered arm-in-arm in the sunshine. That, I learned, was Madrid. Mr Hyde had vanished and Dr Jekyll once more had control of the city.

I had never before felt the sort of fear that sends the blood racing through your veins. As intense an emotion as it was, I was surprised to find that with the passing of danger it disappeared so completely it was difficult even to recall the sensation. More curious still, it left no hangover of apprehension. In between bombardments you literally forgot about them. Why this was I don't know; nature, I suppose, taking its course. At any rate, the whine of a shell never failed to come as an utter surprise, and, to my way of thinking, a very nasty one at that. I greatly admired the indifference, often bordering on nonchalance, with which the Spaniards accepted these bombardments.

Strategically, Madrid was a third-line trench and the population had received their training. Civilian ears had become so acute that the ordinary man or woman could judge the proximity of a shell by the sound of the whistle. When shells fell at four- or five-minute intervals it indicated that only one battery was firing and there was always 'a safe side' of the street. But if the explosions came fast it meant a cross fire – then there was nothing to do but take cover and trust to luck. During innumerable shellings I never once saw a sign of panic. People conducted themselves as coolly as trained soldiers; narrow escapes became so much a part of daily life they were not even major topics of conversation.

I soon discovered that food was much more of a preoccupation than danger. Occasionally, when a donkey-cart, filled with lettuces or bread, moved through the streets, a crowd gathered and tagged it breathlessly to its destination. In spite of this terrible shortage of essentials, the cognac and gin supplies had held up well and every afternoon the cafés were crowded. One of the most popular cafés was on the Puerta del Sol. A bomb had gone through the top of the building and you could see chunks of sky through the roof, but the ground floor did a thriving business.

The two gayest meeting places, however, were the once fashionable Chicote's and Molinero's. Although these cafés were on the Gran Via, the most frequently bombarded street in Madrid, every afternoon they were crowded with soldiers with guns dangling from their hips and platinum blondes whose hair was growing out very black due to the fact that all the peroxide had been confiscated by the hospitals.

At Molinero's you found a last lingering badge of class-conscious Spain. The waiters were the same waiters who used to serve the wealthy Madrileños, and they were dressed in the conventional uniform of black suit and white shirt. Some pushed their way through the noisy, singing throngs with obvious disdain; others took advantage of the *camarada* spirit and served you with unshaven faces and cigarettes hanging from their mouths.

The owners of Chicote's and Molinero's and most of the big shops and hotels had either been shot, were in gaol, or had fled from the city. Their concerns had been taken over by the Trades Unions and many were run collectively by the employees. Palaces and country villas were used as ministries and headquarters. Often journalists went to get their permits from officials in sweaters and leather jackets, reclining in sixteenth-century chairs in rooms with carved walls and priceless tapestries. More than once interviews were brought to a halt while the 'comrade' proudly insisted upon your making an inspection of the books and paintings, and even the statues in the garden.

During those first few days in Madrid, it all seemed like a strange carnival to me. It was only at night when the capital was swallowed up in a suffocating darkness that the atmosphere took on a note of grim reality. The buildings jutted up so blackly the sky looked almost white, and as you threaded your way along the pavement, guards moved noiselessly out of the doorways and asked to examine your credentials.

Everything was deserted and still. The only noise was a distant one: the noise of fighting on the Casa del Campo, a mile and a half away. You could hear the dull thud of trench mortars like far-off thunder, and the thin crack of rifles like sheets snapping in the wind. And as you walked through the night, stumbling over shell-holes, you wondered whether this was just the beginning and how long it would be before the lights went out somewhere else.

3

The Press

The foreign journalists gathered for lunch and dinner in a basement restaurant on the Gran Via, the only restaurant open in the whole of Madrid. It was run by the Government and had a restricted clientele made up mostly of officials, police agents, army officers and prostitutes.

The room was always noisy and crowded and blue with smoke. Once during a bombardment a group of militia raised their wine glasses and toasted each crash with shouts and bursts of song. When a six-inch shell smashed through the pavement in front of the door, twisting the steel frame of the awning, the waiter drew a tumult of applause by offering everyone a drink on the house.

The door of the restaurant was heavily guarded by armed sentries, and often I saw women crying and begging to be let in, but no one was allowed to enter without an official pass.

Once inside, the food was meagre and at times scarcely eatable. The routine menu was salami and a plate of rice for luncheon, more salami and a plate of beans for supper. Once we had a three-day run of eggs, but they had a queer taste and word spread around quickly that they were bombed eggs from Cordoba. Exactly what shape a bombed egg took on I never discovered.

We always left the restaurant hungry, and although I'd never experienced discomfort from lack of food before, our lot was so much better than the average Spaniard's that we seldom passed through the guarded door without a guilty feeling, as though we had no right to be there.

Some of the journalists had managed to bring in food supplies from France, and Tom Delmer's sitting room in the Hotel Florida became a popular meeting place. Tom had equipped the room with electric burners and chafing dishes. A ham was suspended from a coat-hanger on the cupboard door and the table was littered with crackers and sardine tins. Every night from eleven on, the press gathered: there was Herbert Matthews of the *New York Times*; Ernest Hemingway of North American Newspaper Alliance; 'Hank' Gorrell of the United Press; Thomas Loyetha of the International News Service; Martha Gellhorn of *Collier's*; George and Helen Seldes, Josephine Herbst, and many others. Although the food was distributed gingerly, there was always plenty of beer and whisky and the gatherings seldom broke up before the early hours of the morning.

When the room got hot Tom used to switch out the lights and open the windows. He often turned on the gramophone and played Beethoven's Fifth Symphony. Between the chords of music we could hear the distant rumble of artillery; it was always a strange mixture.

Tom's parties came to an abrupt end when a shell plunged into his room and turned the chafing dishes and furniture into pulverised debris. Fortunately no one was there at the time. I came into the hotel lobby shortly afterwards and found the hotel manager sitting at his desk, poring over his accounts as though nothing had happened. When I asked him what damage had been done, he regarded me coldly and denied the hotel had been hit. Only a gas main had broken, he said. Although the gaping hole in Tom's room was there for everyone to see, he stubbornly clung to his story for fear his guests would grow alarmed and leave.

One guest did leave. He was a nameless American aviator who had come to Madrid on a few days' leave. He was in the corridor

near the room when the shell hit and was knocked down by the
blast. He was a little tipsy anyway, and came swaying down the
stairs, shouting: 'A fine type of relaxation. For fun, I'll do my own
bombing!'

* * *

The newspaper men filed their stories each night from the
Telephone Building on the Gran Via. It was the tallest building in
Madrid and from the top floor you could see the Casa del Campo
and the University City battlefields. As it was frequently used as an
observation post, it was a legitimate military objective, and during the time I was in Madrid received over eighty direct hits. The
building was made of steel and concrete, however, and the walls
proved too solid for six-inch explosives, so little damage was done.
Once a three-inch shell made a hole in the roof of the telephone
room, but none of the operators was hurt.

All newspaper stories were telephoned to London and Paris and
from there cabled on to various parts of the world. There was a
good deal of competition between the agencies as to who got the
first call through. As there were only two outside lines it sometimes
took four or five hours to establish connections. The majority of
special correspondents were working for morning papers, which
meant that the greatest rush came at nine o'clock in the evening;
there were several cots in the telephone room, and some of them
went to sleep there until their 'urgents' came through.

All stories had to be submitted to the censor and each page
approved by an official stamp. When they were read over the telephone an operator sat beside the journalist ready to cut the line if
anything was inserted not included in the approved copy. There
were frequent attempts 'to beat the censor' by employing American
slang expressions, but this came to an end when a Canadian girl

joined the staff. The International Brigades were not allowed to
be publicised; no reference could be made to Russian armaments;
and buildings and streets which suffered bombardments could
not be identified.

It was only in the realm of the human interest story that the
journalists had a free hand. They could describe bombardments to
their hearts' content. It was dramatic to sit in the darkened room
at night and listen to versions of the day's news being sent over the
wires in German, French, Spanish and English, to be relayed to
the most remote corners of the earth. The despatches were always
varied, for some described the bombardments with indifference
and others with fevered intensity. I began to realise that much
depended on where the writer had been when the shells fell. In
the darkness of the beleaguered capital it seemed odd to think of
the telephone wires running through the misery of Spain into the
free fields of France and across the Channel to the sleepy peace of
London. After listening to some particularly moving eye-witness
account, I was usually jerked back to reality by a journalist shouting, 'Ne coupez pas, Madame. Listen, Eddie, how about sending
some more dough . . .?

* * *

I was not covering daily news so I worked out an outline for a
series of articles. One of the first things I wanted to do was to go
to the front. Now this was not difficult. Although journalists were
supposed to get a proper authorisation, few of the Spanish sentries
could read and almost any bit of paper (no matter how far out of
date) would do. When you wanted to go to the front, you just got
into a car and went.

The most convenient front, however, ran through the Casa del
Campo and the University City, only two miles from the main

shopping district of Madrid. You took a tram halfway, walked the
other half, and you were there. The two armies had been stale-
mated at this point ever since the previous November, when
the Republican International Brigades had halted the Franco
advance and at the eleventh hour saved Madrid. Neither side had
been able to dislodge the other and for the past five months the
soldiers had sat in opposite trenches, breaking the monotony by
machine-gunning each other and lobbing grenades and mortars
back and forth.

I didn't have to wait long for an opportunity to visit the Casa
del Campo. A few days after I arrived in Madrid I met Professor
J. B. S. Haldane, an English scientist and former don at Cambridge
University, who was lunching at the Gran Via restaurant. 'Think
I'll hop down to the battlefield and have a look round,' he said
casually. 'Do you want to come?'

An hour later I found myself walking along a street on the outskirts of the city. The Professor cut an eccentric figure in a pair of
breeches too tight for him and a tin hat with a broken chin-strap,
left over from the Great War, which he'd brought from England. As
it was the only tin hat in the whole of Republican Spain, it attracted
a good deal of attention from passers-by, and twice sentries saluted
us respectfully, obviously impressed. Although Haldane had come
to Spain to advise the Government on antidotes for gas, he liked
to pass himself off as a joke character. When anyone asked what
he was doing in Madrid, he always replied, 'Just a spectator from
England. Enjoyed the last war so much I thought I'd come to Spain
for a holiday.'

We walked down a long avenue with stone barricades built
across the intersections. Guards in sweaters and corduroy trousers,
with rifles propped up beside them, said *Salud* and asked to see
our passes. Most of them could not read, and some even held the

papers upside down, but they all studied them with knitted brows, raised a clenched fist in the Popular Front salute, and let us pass.

At the end of the avenue the streets grew desolate and blocks of houses were gutted and empty. Some had only the frames standing where bombs had plunged through the middle; others looked like stage sets with whole fronts ripped off. High up on one was a table all set for dinner, napkins in place, chairs pulled up, but for a wall it had only a piece of blue sky.

It was ghostly and sad with the wind whistling through the window frames, and doors high above banging back and forth on empty caverns, but the Professor's spirits were high. He was just remarking on how fine the weather was when there was a loud whistle. A shell hit the brick house on the corner and another plunged into the pavement. We stumbled into a doorway and stood against a dark wall while several more passed overhead. After a few minutes the Professor decided it was safe to continue. 'Anyway,' he added, with all the disdain of the World War veteran, 'they are only little shells, so come along.'

My confidence in the Professor was shaky. I thought he was making too light of the situation, and the prospect of the front was growing more alarming every minute. However, at this stage there seemed little else to do but follow.

The communication trenches started at the park at the end of the street. They were narrow, dirt trenches with a row of sandbags at the top. As they were only five feet high we had to bend down to keep under cover. The lines twisted and curved through the fields and as we crawled along, the mud slopping over our shoes, the guns grew louder. Bullets passed over our heads with an angry ring, some of them hitting the sides of the parapet with staccato cracks. From somewhere to the right was the rumble of artillery and the dull thud of mortars.

The Professor called out to me cheerfully and asked how I liked it. I said, not much, and he seemed to resent this, for he yelled back that in the last war women were not allowed within six miles of the front lines. 'You ought to be grateful for the privilege,' he shouted.

Suddenly the trench turned and we found ourselves in the front line. Long streams of soldiers were firing through the openings in the sandbags. Their faces were unshaven and their jackets and khaki trousers were smeared with grease and mud. Some looked not more than sixteen or seventeen years old.

I should think we must have been a strange pair, but they didn't seem surprised to see us. They smiled warmly and the greeting *Salud* echoed up the line. One of them put down his rifle and pulled out a wooden box for me to sit on. Another, with a hand in a dirty bandage, offered us a package of dark brown cigarettes; then they all talked at once in eager Spanish. I couldn't understand, but it didn't matter, for someone suddenly opened up with an ear-splitting rattle of machine-gun fire. I put my hands over my ears and wondered how anyone ever got used to the noise.

One of the soldiers handed me a rifle and asked if I did not want to take a shot at *los facciosos*, and then a young boy with pink cheeks and large brown eyes stepped up and held a periscope over the trench so I could see the enemy lines. They were a jumble of stones and grass only fifty yards away. On the no-man's land in between lay three twisted bodies.

'*Los muertos nuestros*,' the boy said softly.

The Professor squinted through the sandbags but said he didn't like the view. He explained that he wanted to get a look at the Clinico (a building in which the enemy was entrenched) and that we could probably see better from another position, so once again we started crawling along the line. There were forks to the right and left, and once he called out that he hadn't the foggiest idea where we were. 'Hope we don't land up with the Fascists,' he said cheerfully, and just then the trench came to an abrupt halt. Directly ahead was a small green slope.

Haldane scratched his head and said that in his opinion the other side of the hill ought to prove a better vantage point; but he didn't know what was on the other side and therefore might be wrong. Stray bullets were passing overhead and I refused to move until he found where he was going. As there was nobody in sight, I admit it offered a problem; nevertheless, I was unprepared for the Professor's quick solution. 'You wait here,' he said, and before I could stop him he ran up the slope and disappeared down the other side.

I stood alone in the trench and wondered why I had ever come to Spain. I could hear the long swish of shells overhead and the explosions as they fell in the distance. Bullets whined past and I ducked my head again and again, although I'd been carefully instructed that when you hear the whine, you're safe.

The sun had gone behind a cloud and it was getting cold. I looked up and down the deserted line and wondered if the Professor would ever find his way back. Suddenly there was an explosion and twenty yards in front of me the earth shot up in a fountain. I went down on the ground as dirt and stones sprayed the air. When I found I was still intact I got up and tried to wipe the mud off my clothes with a handkerchief. Just then I heard someone whistling a tune and I looked up to see an officer approaching. He was a jaunty little man with a forage cap tilted over one eye. He spoke Spanish, but, when I said I couldn't understand, broke into a jumble of French.

'This is no place to stand, Mademoiselle. They are throwing trench mortars.'

I told him he'd never spoken a truer word and explained my predicament. He laughed and told me to follow him. 'Don't worry: I'll find your friend – dead or alive.'

He helped me over the slippery places with the air of a great cavalier and took my hand when we crawled through two dark tunnels; at last we came to a clearing. To the right of it was a white shack surrounded by trees and bushes and protected by a small hill.

The room inside was crowded with soldiers. The blinds were drawn and the only light was a feeble bulb suspended from the ceiling. The lieutenant explained that I was an American writer who'd got lost in the trenches, and told them to look after me while he tried to find my friend. The soldiers grinned and all talked at once in Spanish I couldn't understand. There was a small burner in the middle of the room, and one of them pulled a chair up and motioned me to dry myself beside the fire. I took off my shoes and someone wiped them with a rag. Another soldier pushed his way through the group and offered me a piece of stale bread; the others laughed and explained with empty hands it was all they had to offer.

Half an hour later the lieutenant reappeared and said he had found the Professor. While I was shaking hands all round they told the lieutenant to apologise for the poor hospitality, and one of them asked if I were going to write about them in an article. When I nodded, a tall soldier standing near the door, obviously an accepted wit, said to be sure to say that they liked fighting Fascists a good deal better than their grandfathers had liked fighting Americans. And did I think the United States would send some guns and planes to show what a fine new friendship it had turned out to be? Everybody laughed and I followed the lieutenant out of the door amid a farewell of *Salud*.

Once again we crawled through the trenches and finally came to a small dug-out. Inside, two soldiers were lying on a cot eating rice from a battered tin plate; a wireless operator sat at a wooden table with earphones on his head, and in the middle, crouched on a low wooden stool drinking a bottle of wine, was the Professor. 'Hullo,' he said affably, 'where have you been hiding?'

He seemed to take my reappearance for granted and enthusiastically described the splendid view he had had of the Clinico. Apparently, for him, at any rate, the trip had been a great success.

The lieutenant led us through the communicating lines and finally set us on our way down the avenue. Before he said goodbye, he drew a bottle of gin from his pocket, gave the Professor a swig, then took one himself. With a parting salute, he disappeared back into the trenches again, whistling as he went.

4

Life in Madrid

On looking back, I suppose Madrid was closer to being 'gay' that April than at any other period of the war. The Republicans had taken great heart at their Guadalajara victory, and now regarded the future with a robust optimism. They talked in terms of large-scale offensives and of the peace they would impose at the end of the war. Even to an inexperienced military observer like myself, all this seemed premature, but faith in victory had become a fierce necessity to soldiers and civilians who had suffered much during the cold winter months.

Now the spring had come to dry the ground and warm the houses, and the people had gathered new strength. The daily bombardments of Madrid had become a routine matter; it was always quiet at siesta time and the capital was seldom shelled at night. (For some unknown reason, after the first seven or eight months of the war, Madrid proper was never again bombed from the air.) There was an average of approximately fifty or sixty casualties a day, but as there were nearly a million inhabitants, proportionately this was not high.

As I have said before, the worst phase of Madrid life was the shortage of food. Although many of the surrounding villages were well supplied with vegetables, eggs and milk, there was no proper organisation for transporting food into the capital. Several times I saw crowds running after food-trucks, shouting at the drivers and imploring them to stop. And more than once people tried to storm the heavily guarded doors of the Gran Via restaurant.

I remember a scene in the restaurant when the Duchess of Atholl, a member of the House of Commons, visited Madrid. The manager had somehow managed to get a chicken which he served Her Grace for lunch. After she had left, one of the anarchists upbraided him fiercely for showing 'class distinction'. A group gathered around and the argument became many-sided.

'While the people starve, the Duchess eats chicken.'

'But, *camarada*, she is powerful in England and she is a friend of the Republic.'

'Then let her go hungry so that she can tell them better how we live. If she were not a Duchess, you would have given her rice.'

The manager was in danger of being denounced as a Fifth Columnist and he persisted heatedly, 'I am not interested in whether or not she is a Duchess. She is a friend. There can be nothing wrong in making an impression for the sake of the cause.'

The argument went on for some time until one of the journalists stepped in as a mediator, and the group dispersed. But that night the Duchess ate the ordinary fare of salami and rice.

* * *

The war atmosphere in Madrid was confusing to the newcomer. Although all the propaganda was concentrated on the German and Italian invasion of Spain, rather than on the class issue, the character of Madrid was distinctly revolutionary. Apart from a handful of Government officials, Madrid was proletarian with a vengeance. Almost without exception, members of the upper and middle classes had sided with General Franco. Many, of course, had been unable to escape from Republican territory and were in hiding; others were in gaol or had been shot. The hotels and cafés were run by the waiters and employees. All businesses and shops had been taken over by the Government and the profits

confiscated for the prosecution of the war. Only a few proprietors were allowed to continue the direction of their firms and
they were paid a weekly salary. Naturally, enormous disorgani-
sation had resulted in this upheaval and the problem of internal
re-orientation was almost as great as waging the war.

The Communists were by far the most powerfully organised
party in Spain and their influence was widely felt. Although they
declared vehemently that they were fighting to re-establish the
Republic, I found this difficult to believe. Anyone who really did
believe in a republic and was hostile to a dictatorship of the proletariat was instantly branded as Fascist. The fact that I was not a
Communist immediately stamped me as suspect. Although at that
time they had orders from Moscow to support the democracies
against the Fascists, their efforts were entirely spent on spreading the Marxist doctrine. For this reason they insisted fiercely on
the system of political commissars in the army in order that they
might convert many of the men.

Certainly many Spaniards were not in sympathy with the
extreme Left. The *petits bourgeois*, whose small properties had been
confiscated, could not be counted as loyal supporters; neither could
the deeply religious people, even among the poor. I remember one
day Thomas Loyetha, the International News Service correspondent, taking Tom Delmer and me to a small flat for lunch, which
was kept by a middle-aged Spanish woman, who, before the war,
had been a procuress. Since all the wealthy young men were on the
Franco side, her livelihood had fallen off, and now she earned a few
pesetas as a cook. Somehow she always managed to get hold of a
few chickens and once a week Loyetha went there for a really good
meal. During lunch she showed us a small cupboard in which several crucifixes were hidden. She said that when the bombardments
came she took them out and prayed. There was little doubt where

her sympathies lay, and if the crucifixes had been discovered by the police she would have been imprisoned if not shot.

I also remember the surprise I had when I visited one of the gaols in Madrid. It was inside a hastily converted monastery. When I walked in I found the anarchist warden seated behind a huge oak desk with a background of dark red tapestries, hung with pictures of the Virgin. He led me through long corridors, with small rooms on either side, crowded with men. Some of the prisoners were scrubbing floors, others were wandering aimlessly along the corridors, and still others were standing in groups, talking and smoking. Most of them were ordinary working-class people, and it was then that I realised how deep the political cleavage had gone. Indeed, these people and the small middle-class proprietors were the section from which the executioner had taken the heaviest toll, for the aristocrats, through money and influence, had managed to bribe their way out and the majority escaped.

For this reason Republican propaganda was directed almost entirely against the foreign invader, and many Spaniards who varied on the class issue rallied to the call of the great posters picturing a peasant's foot crushing the iron swastika with the words: 'Madrid shall be the tomb of Fascism'.

Madrid was under strict martial law and on the whole life was orderly. Sometimes one of the soldiers who thronged into Chicote's bar in the afternoon drank too much and the air resounded with revolver shots, and occasionally the police reminded people of the blackout restrictions by shooting up at rooms whose lights were showing. Martha Gellhorn went back to the hotel one night to find a neat round bullet-hole in her window because the maid had forgotten to draw the curtains.

The city's streets were deserted at night and sentries were posted at the barricades on the corners. You could wander about without being molested, but if you rode in a car you had to know the password. When Tom Delmer first arrived he was not familiar with this regulation, and drove through the streets in a car with another journalist. A sentry accosted the pair: 'Halt! Who goes there?', and asked for the password with the sentence, 'Where are we going?' The answer was 'To Victory.' But Tom replied: 'To the British Embassy,' with the result that they achieved neither one, for they were promptly taken to headquarters for questioning.

Madrid was honeycombed with Fifth Columnists and spies, and the Republicans had a large secret police force working to combat the leakage of information. Dossiers were kept on thousands of suspects, including the entire foreign press, and garish posters pasted on the buildings warned the population of the dangers of spies even among friends. A favourite poster showed a green-faced man with a hand cupped to his ear and in front of him a *señorita* with fingers raised to her red lips, saying: 'Sh! Comrades, not a word to brothers or friends or sweethearts!'

None of us knew the full activities of the secret police or what went on behind the prison walls of Madrid. There is no doubt, however, that the Government was waging a desperate struggle against Fifth Columnists who were supplying the enemy with a steady stream of information by radio and courier. There is no doubt, either, that many thousands of innocent persons were dragged from their beds and shot without trial.

Although I never witnessed any 'atrocities' myself, there is one episode that stands out in my mind. I was having lunch at the Gran Via restaurant with Ernest Hemingway and Josephine Herbst when a bombardment started. Shells were dropping on the street outside the café and it was impossible to leave, so we sat lingering over our coffee. At the next table I noticed a fastidious-looking man dressed from head to toe in dove grey. He had the high forehead and long fingers of the intellectual and wore horn-rimmed spectacles which added to his thoughtful appearance.

'That,' said Hemingway, 'is the chief executioner of Madrid.'

Ernest invited him to join us and he accepted on the condition we would allow him to buy us a carafe of wine. His manner was ingratiating to the point of sycophancy, but I shall never forget the look in his bright, marble-brown eyes. Perhaps it was my imagination, but to me they mirrored all the traditional sadism of Spain. Hemingway was passionately interested in details of death and soon was pressing the man with questions.

'Have many people died in Madrid?'

'A revolution is always hasty.'

'And have there been many mistakes?'

'Mistakes? It is only human to err.'

'And the mistakes – how did they die?'

'On the whole, considering they were mistakes,' he said meditatively, 'very well indeed; in fact, *magnifico!*' It was the way he said it that sent a shiver down my spine. His voice rose on the last word to a note of rapture and his eyes gleamed with relish. He reached out for the carafe of wine and filled my glass. It gurgled into the tumbler, thick and red, and I could only think of blood.

When we got out of the restaurant, Hemingway said: 'A *chic* type, eh? Now remember, he's mine.' When I read his play, *The Fifth Column*, many months later, I was not surprised to find the following lines:

Philip: And, Antonio. Sometimes there must have been mistakes, eh? When you had to work in a hurry, perhaps. Or you know, just mistakes, we all make mistakes. I just made a little one yesterday. Tell me, Antonio, were there ever any mistakes?

Antonio: Oh, yes. Certainly. Mistakes. Oh, yes. Mistakes. Yes.
  Yes. Very regrettable mistakes. A very few.
Philip: And how did the mistakes die?
Antonio (proudly): All very well.

Hemingway was greatly admired in Spain and known to everyone as 'Pop'. He was a massive, ruddy-cheeked man who went around Madrid in a pair of filthy brown trousers and a torn blue shirt. 'They're all I brought with me,' he would mumble apologetically. 'Even the anarchists are getting disdainful.' Although he had been wounded four times in the World War, the trenches had a fascination for him. On days when the front was quiet, he used to prowl around trying to borrow cartridges to go out to the country and shoot rabbits.

His room on the second floor of the Florida shared honours with Tom Delmer's suite as a meeting place for a strange assortment of characters. I don't suppose any hotel in the world has ever attracted a more diverse assembly of foreigners. They came from all parts of the globe and their backgrounds read like a series of improbable adventure stories. There were idealists and mercenaries; scoundrels and martyrs; adventurers and *embusqués*; fanatics, traitors and plain down-and-outs. They were like an odd assortment of beads strung together on a common thread of war. Any evening you could find them in the Florida: Dutch photographers, American airmen, German refugees, English ambulance drivers, Spanish picadors, and Communists of every breed and nationality.

Hemingway's room was presided over by Sydney Franklin, a tough young American bull-fighter. He had often fought in the bull-rings of Spain and had a collection of rings and heavily embossed cigarette-cases which had been presented to him by various fans. When I asked him how he had happened to come to

Madrid, he said: 'Well, see, one day Ernest rings me up and says, "—'lo, kid, want to go to the war in Spain?" and I says, "Sure, Pop. Which side we on?"'

Then there was Lolita, a Spanish prostitute, with a round, innocent face, who, temporarily at least, was the mistress of a member of the secret police. Whenever he quarrelled with her he had her arrested and sent off to gaol for a few days, which always resulted in fearful agitation to get her out again. And there was Kajsa, a Swedish girl who dressed in men's clothes and wore her hair in a Greta Garbo bob. She had held jobs all over Europe ranging from governess to tourist guide, and had finally wound up in Barcelona as a marathon dancer. On the twelfth day of the dance war broke out and she went to the front as a nurse. She spoke seven languages fluently and her talents finally had been employed by the Press Bureau, who appointed her as a semi-official interpreter for the foreign journalists.

The extraordinary personalities which became part of our daily life all held decided opinions, and there were endless and fierce discussions on the issues of the day. The Communist 'intellectuals' provided a cosmopolitan atmosphere, for their activities were not confined to Spain. The world was their battlefield and the political evolutions of Léon Blum, Neville Chamberlain and Franklin Roosevelt were of more interest to them than the immediate leadership of Largo Caballero.

Of all the Communists, Claud Cockburn, who wrote under the name of Frank Pitcairn for the London *Daily Worker*, was the best raconteur. He had a wealth of 'inside' stories dealing with banking scandals, international conspiracies and corrupt politicians. The world I had always found so innocent suddenly became alive with hideous melodrama, and for hours I sat enthralled. The solution for all panaceas lay, of course, in the theory of dialectical materialism. I was surprised to find that so ardent a champion of Marx had never visited the Soviet Union, but Claud explained it by saying: 'Russia is fixed; I am not interested in watching revolutions; my job is *making* them.' Most of the Communists were confident that the world uprising was not far distant. Fascism, they declared, would put the issue to a test and out of the chaos of a world conflagration the workers would rise.

Few of us went to bed before the early hours of the morning. We rose late and did most of our work in the afternoon. Martha Gellhorn was writing articles for *Collier's*, so we often visited prisons and hospitals together, collecting data and interviewing officials. On looking back over the meagre notes I kept, I find a few paragraphs marked 'Sunday, April 11th', which was perhaps a routine day. Here it is:

Woke up at eight o'clock starved from lack of food. Went downstairs to the lobby and found George and Helen Seldes talking to a newly arrived journalist who had a package of butter and honey. George had some tea, so I quickly attached myself to the party; we went upstairs and ate a luxurious breakfast.

About eleven, walked down to the Puerta del Sol with Tom Delmer, who wanted to buy some wine, but instead got caught in the middle of a bombardment. I thought it was our guns that were firing until everyone started running for cover. The only people who refused to move were the women standing in a queue line outside a bread shop. I suppose a quick death is preferable to starvation.

We started home but my shoe hurt, and instead of going around the long way we walked down the Gran Via, which was a very foolish thing to do as the shells were whistling over every few seconds. Tom said he had written so often about the inaccuracies of rebel gunfire it would be ironical to have one of them put an end to his promising career.

At the hotel we ran into Martha Gellhorn and Hemingway and arranged to meet at twelve to go to a festival for the benefit of the FAI and hear Pastoras sing. Pastoras never sang and the show was bad; a tap dancer in tails and top hat, a very old *flamenco* singer and a skit between a priest and a housewife, both of whom kept their backs turned squarely on the audience so that no one could hear what they said. Everyone cheered a lot, so it was evidently a success.

In the afternoon joined Herbert Matthews and Hemingway at the Old Homestead, to watch the battle on the Casa del Campo. The Republicans are trying to take three houses in which the Rebels are entrenched. We watched them shelling the houses, then saw two tanks come down a narrow path. One of them caught fire and turned into a sheet of flames and the other turned back. Herbert thought we might see a big offensive, but nothing doing, so finally went back to the hotel.

The battle we watched was an offensive launched by the Republicans; it extended from Las Rozas, on the Escorial road, through the Casa del Campo to Carabanchel. It lasted three days and in the end was repulsed with heavy casualties. The Old Homestead was a house which Hemingway found on the outskirts of the capital. The front had been ripped away by a bomb, so it provided an excellent vantage point from which to watch the battle. I was surprised to find how banal war became from a distance. Against the wide panorama of rolling hills the puffs of smoke were daubs of cotton and the tanks children's toys. When one of them burst into flames it looked no bigger than the flare of

a match. Against the great sweep of nature, man's struggle became
so diminutive it was almost absurd.

Hemingway, however, followed the moves eagerly. 'It's the nas-
tiest thing human beings can do to each other,' he pronounced
solemnly, 'but the most exciting.'

We heard footsteps coming up the stairs and looked around to
find Professor J. B. S. Haldane. He greeted us with his usual cordiality and looked round for a place to sit. The house was gutted
with pulverised furniture, old clothes and broken pictures. From
the debris he dragged a dilapidated red plush chair, placed it in
the middle of the room, and sat down in full view of the battlefield. He put his elbows on his knees and adjusted his field-glasses.
Hemingway warned him it was dangerous to remain exposed, but
Haldane waved him aside. A few minutes later Hemingway spoke
again: 'Your glasses shine in the sun; they will think we are military observers.'

'My dear fellow, I can assure you there isn't any danger here in
the house.'

Ten minutes later there was a loud whistle as a shell plunged
into a flat next door. Two more screamed overhead and we all went
down on the floor – all except Haldane, who scrambled down the
stairs and disappeared. We were shelled for fifteen or twenty minutes, and when at last we got back to the Florida we found him
sitting in the lobby, drinking beer.

'Hallo,' he called amiably, 'let's have a drink.'

We did; and more than one.

When the fighting was over the Republicans had a total of
nearly three thousand dead and wounded. The two largest hotels
in Madrid, the Palace and the Ritz, which had been turned into
hospitals, were both crowded. I went into the Palace and I shall
never forget the sight. The steps were spattered with blood and

the lobby was crowded with wounded men on stretchers waiting to be operated on. By mistake I went through the wrong door and found myself in the operating room. The nurses were not dressed in uniforms and went drifting in and out as though it were a smoking lounge. Most of them were peroxide blondes with dirty hands and nails painted vermilion. I learned that the nursing profession had been almost entirely restricted to the nuns; since they were on the Franco side the doctors had been forced to use whatever help they could find.

* * *

Do not imagine that hardship and suffering had tamed the natural high spirits of the Spaniard. Bitter trials had drawn them together and the atmosphere was quick and friendly. Everyone was *camarada* and everyone was fighting the Fascists. I took a great liking to the Spanish people; temperamentally, they were as quick and changing as the country they lived in, with its great mountains and its arid plateaux, its bitter cold and its tropical heat. If they cried one day, they laughed the next.

Even in their darkest hours they retained a sense of humour and a zest for living. Anyone who travelled through the country could scarcely fail to be shocked by the miserable living conditions in the villages. The houses were dilapidated and filthy, and often there were no sanitary arrangements of any kind. Children with sores on their faces and bodies sprawled in the dust like animals. I soon began to understand the grievance against the Church, for in many of these villages cathedral spires rose splendidly over scenes of unforgettable squalor – spires fashioned by the money of the peasants.

The hospitality of the poor was touching. They welcomed visitors eagerly and insisted on sharing whatever food and wine they had in the house. If you offered them payment, they were offended. Their spirits were exuberant and they took a passionate interest in the lighter side of life. One day I visited a small village about forty miles outside Madrid with Sydney Franklin, the American bull-fighter. One of the peasants had seen him fight in Seville and the word spread through the village like wildfire. People stared at him admiringly and children tagged after him when he walked down the road; the mayor of the village came out to shake his hand and made him promise that when the war was over he would come back and put on a show for them.

I think it was this natural buoyancy of spirit that kept the morale in Madrid so high during the long months of bombardment and semi-starvation. Their courage did not consist in bearing their burden patiently, but in ignoring it. Indifference to danger was almost a matter of honour to a nation that had long worshipped the courage of the bull-fighter. Once I sat in a café while a bombardment was going on outside. One of the journalists had left his car and chauffeur waiting for him, and when we went out we found the driver slumped over the wheel. We ran up to him thinking he had been injured, but he sat up, rubbed his eyes, and apologised for having fallen asleep.

To the average Spaniard the struggle for daily bread was far more worrying than shell-fire. A few days after Tom Delmer's suite had been hit the hotel was struck again. This time I found the manager having a tantrum in the lobby, denying that anything had happened. 'Lies, lies, lies!' he cried excitedly. 'You will give my hotel a bad name and ruin my business.'

Poor little man, I'm afraid that is exactly what did happen, for after I had left Spain I heard that the Florida had been struck again, and if you went to Madrid the place to stay was the Palace Hospital.

5

Civilian Army

During the month of May 1937 the two armies of Spain were deadlocked over a vaguely defined nine-hundred-mile front. The stubborn Republican defence had forced Franco to abandon his immediate drive to the capital and now he was preparing for a major offensive in the north. At many points along the north front opposing battalions faced each other from trenches only a few hundred yards apart. During periods of inactivity they lobbed grenades and mortars back and forth and broke the monotony by shouting insults across the short no-man's land; other times they sang *flamenco* love songs and occasionally, in the quiet of the night, the enemy picked up the chorus.

No one who saw the Republican troops could fail to be moved by the odds against which they fought. They were a ragged, unkempt lot. Their army numbered about six hundred thousand, but few had had any previous military experience. They were untrained, unequipped and badly fed. Many had learned how to fire a rifle in the front line and many had paid for it with their lives. Few had uniforms; they wore an odd assortment of sweaters and jackets, corduroy trousers and rubber-soled shoes. They were peasants drawn from the villages of Spain to fight Europe's first war against totalitarianism.

I made many trips to the front. I saw soldiers in the trenches at Escorial, in the mountains of Guadarrama, and in the rolling fields of Guadalajara. As there was only a handful of officers to train the men, it became necessary to recruit them from the ranks. Since few of the peasants could read or write, an accomplishment essential for officers, schools were opened at many headquarters and education became a feverish part of military life. At one of the barracks on the Casa del Campo I saw a roomful of grown men struggling over a children's primer entitled: 'Canuto el soldado bruto' ('Canute, the stupid soldier'). On the wall was a sign that said: 'Beat Fascism by learning to read and write'.

Although the Republican troops had endured great hardships, their spirits were usually high. Foreigners who went to the front were smothered with hospitality and the soldiers demonstrated their guns and tanks with childish delight. The wretched visitor was often subjected to terrifying experiences. When I went to the Guadarrama front with Ernest Hemingway, it was considered a friendly gesture to take us for a drive in an armoured car and run us down a road which was under enemy fire in order that we might hear the bullets cracking up against the steel sides.

This particular front consisted of a series of strong points scattered through the mountains and woods. One of the positions was at the top of a hill, and I shall never forget the scene that met us as we approached it. Behind a jagged boulder, jutting up against the sky, stood a group of ragged soldiers. One of them was sitting on a wooden box playing a guitar and the others stood around clapping their hands to the steady beat of the music. The guitar-player threw back his head and broke into a Spanish love song; his voice cut through the afternoon air in a mournful and passionate cry. Suddenly there was the sharp retort of machine-gun fire. Some of the bullets cracked up against the boulder and others went overhead with a sing-song whine. But the soldiers kept on beating a steady clap-clap to the time of the music.

When we got to the top of the hill they shook hands warmly and offered us cheese and wine. They made us look through an opening in the sandbags and told us the white house sixty yards away at the foot of the hill belonged to the enemy. Far to the right was another house which belonged to the Colonel of the Republican Brigade.

Then one of the soldiers came forward and said he was sure the lady would like to see how a trench-mortar worked. It was impossible to stop him and soon several of them had begun a minor offensive against the enemy position. It seemed only logical that the latter should retaliate and I waited, terrified, for the battle to develop. A moment later we heard the burst of machine-gun fire but not directed towards us – the enemy had mistaken our position and opened fire on the Colonel's house. The soldiers considered this an enormous joke and many of them laughed until they had to hold their sides.

The commander of this particular battalion, in boots and breeches and green turtle-necked sweater, had a forage cap pulled rakishly over one eye. In peace-time he had driven a truck in Madrid, but now his swagger and bravado had won him the name of El Guerrero. He had fought all winter in the mountain passes of Guadarrama and although his battalion had been wiped out on several occasions he had managed to get more replacements, and, fighting a desperate guerrilla warfare, had prevented the enemy from moving their columns along the narrow roads. At headquarters he introduced us to a girl who had fought side by side with them during the winter months. She had plucked eyebrows and rouged lips and was wearing a man's uniform. El Guerrero proudly told us his wife had also fought with them, but he had had to send her back to Madrid a few weeks before as she was expecting a baby.

El Guerrero's men were the toughest of the tough. They were few against many and their chances of survival were limited. Most of their work consisted of surrounding enemy positions

in the night and launching desperate surprise attacks. Besides
the danger of war they had to endure the rigorous mountain cli-
mate, inadequately clothed and badly fed. Knowing all this, I was
surprised to find many of the soldiers in this tough band of desperadoes were gentle boys with a wistful look in their eyes. One
nineteen-year-old peasant, who had thrown a grenade among
twelve sleeping men the night before, blushed as he handed me a
bunch of wild flowers; another, who had held a machine-gun position single-handed for forty-eight hours, showed me a poem he
had written extolling the beauties of nature. They talked about the
war with great optimism, saying that soon their army would be
strong enough to take the offensive and that before Christmas the
Republican flag would be flying in every village in Spain. Bright
visions of victory and a final lasting peace had kept their morale
high through all the long winter months. I left, thinking what a
strange mixture of emotions war produces; the more exalted man's
ideals, the more savage the battle becomes.

* * *

One of the most interesting trips I made was to the front where the
International Brigades were fighting. This was on the Morata front
where they were defending the Madrid–Valencia road, the last
link between the capital and the outside world. Although Franco
had launched fierce and repeated attacks, and the Republicans had
suffered heavy loss of life, the lines had held. In May, this front
was regarded as the most important sector in Spain, and was com-
manded by a Soviet General.

In spite of it being common knowledge that the Russians had
sent nearly two thousand staff officers, technicians, airmen and
tank experts to train the Republican Army, the subject was taboo.
Journalists were not allowed to come into contact with them and

the headquarters from which they operated was shrouded in secrecy. By accident I visited the Morata headquarters and was 'detained' there by the Soviet General for three days.

It happened in an odd way. One afternoon I drove out to Morata with Kajsa, a Swedish girl, and Jerome Willis of the Agence d'Espagne. We got lost and instead of reaching Brigade headquarters wound up before a ramshackle old mill which we discovered was serving as Divisional headquarters. The sentry led us into a garden where we were confronted by the commanding officer, a middle-aged man with a broad Slavonic face and sullen green eyes. He had an interpreter with him and spoke a language I thought was Hungarian. His manner was cold and hostile and he curtly cut off our attempts at conversation.

'Have many Fascist planes been over here?' Jerome asked.

'They fly.'

'Do you think the enemy will make another drive soon?'

'Who knows?'

We explained that we hoped to talk to some of the American and English soldiers fighting in the Brigade but received a blunt refusal. 'No visitors are permitted at the front.' Although we argued that several journalists had been taken through the lines a few days before, it was to no avail. As we were leaving he walked over to one of the rose bushes, snapped off a spray of flowers and handed them to me, saying, with a studied sarcasm apparent even through the mouth of the interpreter, 'You can write your story from the garden. No one will know the difference; and here is a souvenir to remind you of your adventure at the front.'

I replied by passing the flowers to a surprised sentry and walking angrily out to the car. On the way home I asked Kajsa if the officer was a Hungarian, and she nodded; but the rest of the trip she was unusually quiet.

I thought no more about the incident until a week later, when I was lunching in the Gran Via restaurant. A tall, serious-faced soldier spoke to me in English, introduced himself as 'Santiago', and asked if I had paid a visit to Morata a few days previously. I nodded, and he said: 'The commanding officer wishes to offer his apologies and says that perhaps you will come to lunch one day.' I was surprised by the invitation and wondered what had caused the officer's sudden change of heart. I wasn't particularly anxious to go, but as it was my only chance to visit Brigade lines I accepted; the following noon Santiago arrived in the pouring rain to drive me out.

Santiago was a quiet, melancholy man of Hungarian birth. I later learned he was the black sheep of a powerful family who had disinherited him when he joined the Communists and took part in the Bela Kun uprising; since then he had been wandering forlornly round the world as an agitator. During the drive he told me that the commanding officer was also a Hungarian but that he had lived in Russia since childhood. He had taken part in the Revolution, continued a military career, and was now a general in the Soviet Army. He had arrived in Spain in January and, although it was not officially admitted, he was in charge of the entire Central Command. I told Santiago I had taken a dislike to him, and he replied, 'You mustn't judge him too quickly. He has never been out of Russia before and his manners are rough, but he is a good soldier.'

The General's manner was scarcely more cordial than before. He received me with a salutatory smile and led the way to the mess hall. The room was shabby and the paint was peeling off the walls: there was a leak in the ceiling and the raindrops dripped slowly into a large tin placed on the floor. Standing around a long table in the centre were about a dozen officers: eight blond-haired Russian staff officers, two Hungarians, two Spaniards and a Russian-born American, David Jarrett, who acted as interpreter. I was introduced all round, but as only Santiago and David could speak English, my conversation was limited.

We sat down to a lunch of partridges, fresh vegetables, bread and butter and wild strawberries. There was an air of great formality and I had a feeling everything had been carefully arranged, even to the large bowl of flowers in the middle of the table. I sat next to David Jarrett, a clean-cut man with a pleasant smile. He spoke eight languages fluently and told me that he had given up a job in New York as a court interpreter to come to Spain. General Gal (whether or not this was a pseudonym I don't know) didn't address me until lunch was nearly over, then he instructed David to translate the following remark: 'I may take you to the front this afternoon, but first you will have to remove those gold bracelets you are wearing. The enemy would be sure to spot them.'

Everyone laughed and I seized the opportunity to press home the point about the front. 'You are too soft,' he replied. Then he looked disapprovingly at my black suede shoes. 'You would get tired and want someone to carry you.'

He was deliberately provocative, but I managed to keep a civil tongue, and an hour later, much to my surprise, my request was granted. The General, David and I got into a car and started for the front.

The front was about three miles away; it was raining hard, and as we neared the lines the woods on either side of the road became alive with tanks half hidden among the wet trees. Field-kitchens and first-aid stations were set up in the clearings, and when we swung around a bend we passed a large truck with a container on top that looked like a gasolene tank; this was 'the bath truck' that went up to the front once a week with gallons of hot water.

The noise of gunfire grew louder and every now and then the dull grey sky lighted up with a flash as a shell travelled through the rain somewhere in the distance. At the bottom of a long slope our car stopped. The lines ran along the top of a hill and the ground between was scarred with shell-holes and mortar pits. There was the constant crack of rifle-fire and the bullets whined over our heads like angry wasps. The General explained that the climb up the hill involved a risk and told us to walk as quickly as possible. It was certainly one of the most uncomfortable experiences I have had; several shells burst near us and the only thing that kept me from bolting in the opposite direction was fear of the General's contempt.

When at last we reached the trenches we found them ankle-deep in mud. They were deep, carefully constructed lines that twisted and turned for four miles through the rolling fields. Men were standing at intervals firing through the openings in the sand-bags. None were equipped with mackintoshes or tin hats, but wore an assortment of sweaters and jackets with mufflers tied round their necks. Most of them were soaked to the skin. The General led the way through the mud and we passed soldiers of every creed and nationality: Germans, Slavs, Jews, Frenchmen, Italians, Englishmen and Americans. They were each formed into their own companies and as we went along the General shook hands with them, patted them on the back and made light remarks that David translated into half a dozen languages.

The men looked strained and sick and I learned they had been in the front line for seventy-four days without a break. Most of them had been recruited by the Communist parties of the world and they struck me as a pathetic group. They had none of the swagger of the traditional legionnaire who fought for the joy of adventure; they were idealists and down-and-outs, many of them ill-suited for soldiering. They had fought bravely but already half their thirty thousand had been buried on the plains and plateaux of Castille.

When we reached the American section the men crowded around eagerly and pressed me with questions about 'the States'. One of them was an American negro who had arrived at the front only a day or two before. The General asked him how he liked it and his dark face broke into a wide smile. 'Ah appreciates de glory, suh, but to tell de truth ah was puffickly satisfied in de rear.'

There were factory workers from Massachusetts, miners from Pennsylvania and farmers from Mississippi. Their manners were light-hearted but their faces lined and worn. 'You might suggest to the General we get a vacation,' said one. 'Not that we have any kick about the neighbourhood, but the view is getting monotonous.' I left wondering how many would ever see the American continent again and a few weeks later heard that three-quarters of them had been wiped out in a fresh attack.

When we reached headquarters again I tried to dry my shoes and get the mud off my clothes, then went to Santiago to arrange about starting back to Madrid. He looked embarrassed and said, 'I don't think you can go back tonight.' I told him I was leaving for Valencia in a few days, but he replied that the General had given orders that I was to remain. I thought this was only a polite way of extending an invitation, but Santiago explained, 'When you came out here the other day with Kajsa and Willis, the authorities telephoned from Madrid that you were on your way to Brigade lines and warned us to be careful what we showed you. You are not a Communist and you are suspect. That's why the General gave you the reception he did. He now says that since you are here, you must stay for three days and learn what we are fighting for.'

I argued heatedly, but Santiago told me it was no use, the General had made up his mind. 'He wants to convert you,' he explained.

There was no way for me to get in touch with anyone in Madrid, so I accepted the situation with as good grace as possible. I was given a small room with no windows, and the only furniture a hard cot with filthy blankets. David brought me some toothpaste and Santiago provided a comb and a bottle of eau-de-Cologne. I had left Madrid in such a hurry that I had told no one where I was going and wondered what they would think of my sudden disappearance.

My education began at dinner. It was a strange setting with candles on the long wooden table throwing a pattern against the dilapidated walls and the babble of voices talking in four languages at once. The officers eyed me curiously, no doubt wondering how long I intended to be a visitor, but the General seemed highly amused by the situation. Once or twice I caught him staring at me, and David explained that I was the first American he had ever met. Halfway through dinner he made a remark to the waiter that caused surprise. There was a flurry of excitement as thick tumblers were distributed round the table, and, finally, three bottles of champagne produced. When the glasses were filled, the General gave a toast: 'Here's to the bourgeoisie! May we cut their throats and live as they do.' He watched me as David translated the words and looked disappointed when I raised my glass. Then he asked, with sudden childishness, 'Did you ever think you would find yourself drinking champagne with a Red Army general?' I shook my head, and he said: 'I suppose in your bourgeois world you were taught that Bolsheviks were lacking in culture. It is untrue. We often drink champagne in Moscow.' The Russian officers smiled and one of them made a remark that everyone laughed at. David said: 'He says champagne is good but vodka is quicker.'

Coffee was served and the General motioned the mess waiter to pull up a chair and join us. He filled the soldier's glass with champagne and turned to me: 'In the Soviet Army all men are equal. The comrade here is in no way inferior because of his rank. We don't believe in the rigid caste system the democracies impose on their fighting forces.' The Russian officers nodded and David explained that two of them were political commissars with the function of interpreting to the men the orders given by the officers.

They were husky, blond-haired boys in their twenties and after dinner one of them pulled a snapshot out of his pocket and showed it me. It was a picture of a woman lying on a rug with a rose in her mouth. She had heavy black curls and a knee-length skirt. It was so much a caricature of the 1920 vamp I thought it must be a joke, but David explained it was the boy's wife. The General examined the picture over my shoulder and said that the Soviet Union need not be ashamed of its women folk. The boy looked pleased and tucked it back in his pocket.

After dinner we went out and sat in the garden. It was hot and the smell of flowers was heavy. One of the soldiers played the ukelele and the Russians lay under the trees humming softly. Every now and then the sky lighted up and the quiet was broken by the rumble of artillery. Sometimes we could hear the shells like a deep, far-away sigh. There were footsteps on the garden path and a soldier came up through the darkness and saluted the General. He talked in Spanish, and when David translated everyone laughed: 'The enemy want to borrow some books and magazines.'

The General shook his head and David explained they never granted any requests at night, for at night it was apt to be a trick. In the daytime, however, they had often sent books and papers across. They flew a white flag while an officer and man from each side met in the middle of no-man's land. Sometimes they stood talking for ten or fifteen minutes, but generally wound up by insulting one another. On the last occasion, the Republican soldier had pulled a fifty-peseta note out of his pocket and handed it to the Rebel, telling him to buy some food for his half-starved brothers who were fighting to keep the rest of Spain in the same bedraggled condition that they were.

During the next two days I passed away the time by going out to the shooting-range while the men had machine-gun practice and talking to the Brigade soldiers billeted in the mill. One of the soldiers was an Englishman, a dock labourer from Newcastle, and he told me his main reason for coming to Spain was a love of travel: 'Just got bored with the missis, that's all,' he said cheerfully. Since his arrival, however, he had acquired a great admiration for the Spaniards and showed me a diary he was keeping. The incident that had impressed him the most was the Spaniard who had stood in the middle of the street during a bombardment, nonchalantly picking his teeth with a match.

In the afternoons I went to the village while Santiago ordered supplies for the mess. The town was always teeming with activity, a mêlée of soldiers, trucks and donkey-carts. The supply depot was in a large church in the middle of the town. The stone floors were stacked with tinned food, sugar, flour, oranges and enormous bins of bread. The walls were grey and bare where the paintings had been stripped away and the statues removed from the niches; and the altar, with its white and gold brocaded cloth, was used to weigh the butter on.

At night the General liked to talk, and after the others had left the table, David and I stayed while he filled our glasses with champagne and gave me lessons in Marxism. He told me he had hitherto considered it a sin to speak to anyone who did not share his views, but in my case he felt that perhaps I had been misled by a bourgeois education and might yet see the error of my way. He was fond of rolling phrases and told me he had sworn eternal enmity to the privileged classes of the world. 'My life,' he said, 'is dedicated to the Revolution and my destiny will lead me to the far parts of the world. Before it sets I will see it rise in the splendid awakening of the working-classes.' He asked me if I had ever read any of the great Russian writers, and when I mentioned the names of Tolstoy, Dostoevsky and Chekhov, he replied indignantly: 'Not our old-fashioned writers. Our great revolutionary writers.' Here he mentioned a series of Bolshevik journalists that I was forced to admit I had never heard of. I gathered he lived a fairly comfortable life in Moscow, for he told me proudly a motor-car was 'constantly at his disposal'. His family had moved to the Ukraine when he was a child and he had been brought up in miserably poor circumstances. When he talked of the days before the Revolution, he said bitterly: 'I used to live like an animal. Now I live like a human being.'

He lost no opportunity to impress me with his views and prophesied that the Revolution was spreading so rapidly, in another year he would be in America. He cautioned me to be on the right side when the day came. David interpreted these long conversations, but on one occasion he deserted me for nearly half an hour and I was left staring helplessly at the General. The silence grew so awkward I dug into my bag and drew out an ivory charm which I had got in India. It was a carved ornament of Ganesh, the elephant god of luck, and one of my most prized possessions. I showed it to the General, thinking it would amuse him.

He smiled and put it in his pocket, and I suddenly realised he thought it was a gift. Later I told David what had happened and he said he would try to recover it. He went to the General but found him proudly showing it to his officers and did not have the heart to explain the mistake. I daresay he has it to this day.

The General evidently thought his instructions in Marxism had been effective, for when at last the three days were up and I went to say goodbye to him, he gave me some final advice: 'Read the works of Lenin, all thirty-seven volumes. When you are well instructed, join the party, but conceal your views from your family. You will be useful as an undercover agent.' He walked over to the bowl of flowers, picked out a red rose and handed it to me: 'This flower was stained in the blood of the Revolution. Be faithful to it.' I thanked him, and as I started for the door he made a remark that David translated. 'He says he is sorry you are leaving; you may return when you wish.' I thanked him again and as we were walking down the steps he flung another remark after us and David laughed. 'He says he understands women. You won't return, but you will boast to your friends that a Red Army general took a fancy to you.'

A few months later I was told he had returned to Moscow. Whether he escaped the many purges that continued to sweep the Soviet Army, I never heard.

6

Exit Visa

When I got back to Madrid I found that my disappearance had caused a turmoil of excitement. The Press Bureau had been unable to discover any trace of me until a few hours before my return, when someone casually remarked I had last been seen driving out of Madrid in a car with Santiago. As Soviet headquarters were forbidden to journalists, alarm turned into deep suspicion, and when I arrived at the hotel I found a message to ring up Ilse Kulczak, one of the censors. She asked me where I had been, and when I told her, her voice grew menacing: 'The authorities are greatly displeased. You will hear more from us.' There was a sharp click at the other end of the line.

I repeated this brief conversation to Tom Delmer and was surprised to see he took a serious view of it. 'Whatever you do,' he warned me, 'don't drive to Valencia in a car by yourself. I think they have an idea you are a spy, and if they have, they won't hesitate to act ruthlessly. Road accidents are often the best way of settling an account.'

I thought Tom was being unduly pessimistic and, since I had already arranged to drive to Valencia with Sydney Franklin, thought no more about it. On the morning of our departure a Danish journalist asked if he could have a lift and the three of us set off together.

The journalist's real name I never discovered, for he was known in Madrid as 'The Trembling Dane'. Although he had been in the capital only three days, the bombardment had completely unnerved him. He had been unlucky, for everywhere he went a shell seemed to fall, and once a dozen people were killed a few yards from him in the main square. He had locked himself up in his room at the Florida and refused to go outdoors until Kajsa persuaded him that it wasn't as bad as he thought. She took him to Chicote's bar to restore his morale, but he hadn't been inside more than ten minutes before two soldiers got into an argument and one of them pulled out a gun and shot the other. After this incident his one idea was to leave Madrid as quickly as possible. As we neared Valencia he sighed with relief at the thought of a peaceful night. He was so grateful to Sydney and me for having given him a lift, he offered to take me to an interview he had arranged with Del Vayo, the Foreign Minister.

I don't remember much about the interview; it took place at eight o'clock in the War Ministry, and Del Vayo made the usual plea for more support from the democracies. But as it was over and we were walking down the broad stone stairs, we heard a whistle and a crash. The building shook, the lights went out and glass broke over the floor. There were several more crashes and people came streaming out of their offices and crowded down the stairway. At first I didn't realise what was happening, but the Dane grabbed my arm and screamed, '*Les avions.*' His voice carried through the halls and caused considerable panic. I tried to calm him but he went on shouting in French, '*Où est la cave?*' and tried to push his way through the crowd to the stairs. As this was the first serious air-raid Valencia had ever had, and there were no shelters to go to, everyone was at a loss what to do. Most of the people managed to make their way to the ground floor and stood silently in the hallway. The Trembling Dane squeezed into a corner and when he lighted a cigarette I saw that his face was bathed with perspiration.

The bombardment lasted only seven or eight minutes. There were a few more thuds and then silence. I suggested to the Dane that we try to find our way to the Press Bureau a few blocks down the street, but he stood against the wall moaning and refused to leave the building. I finally started off by myself.

It was an eerie scene: the dark forms standing huddled in doorways, the sound of women crying, and the dust still rising in the blackness where a bomb had fallen opposite the British Embassy two blocks away. The deserted streets were beginning to resound to the clang of ambulances and the shrill sirens of the police cars, and already men with flares had run to dig out bodies from the debris.

In spite of the atmosphere of terror and destruction, life was quick to regain a normal bent, for even as I stumbled along the desolate streets a small Spaniard approached me and said hopefully, 'Good evening, Señorita, how would you like a boyfriend?' When I told him that I had an *amigo* waiting for me at the Press Bureau, he sighed, then gallantly escorted me the rest of the way down the street, bent low over my hand and bade me goodnight with a flourish.

The next day we learned that the casualties amounted to about a hundred killed and wounded; Valencia had at last been baptised in the war that swept the rest of Spain. In the morning The Trembling Dane came over and said goodbye. He seemed badly shaken and told me he had stayed in the Ministry hallway all night.

My plane was not leaving until the following day. With all the excitement I had completely forgotten Tom Delmer's warning. That afternoon, however, I had a message that someone in the lobby wished to speak to me. He was a man I had never seen before. He was a German Communist who worked for the secret police. He asked me to come across the street and have a drink and I followed with a sinking heart, wondering if it would end in arrest. It was a disjointed conversation, for he told me my dossier had arrived from Madrid that morning and it showed I had spent a good deal of time at various army headquarters. 'I want to know,' he said, 'why you are leaving Spain so soon after these trips?' I told him I had only intended to stay in Madrid a couple of months as I had a series of articles to write in Paris. 'We have a nice new gaol at Albacete,' he smiled, showing a flash of white teeth. 'You could write them just as well from there.'

I replied lightly, as though I thought he were joking, and when I got up to leave he made no move to stop me. The next morning I flew to France.

Not until a year later, when I returned to Barcelona, did I discover from Ilse Kulczak that my arrest had been touch and go; the secret police were instructed to follow me in Valencia while the Madrid authorities debated whether or not to detain me. Even though the Press Bureau was convinced I was a spy, they had finally decided the amount of publicity given to the arrest of an American journalist would do more harm than good. I didn't know these things at the time; nevertheless, with a sigh of relief, I stepped on to the aerodrome at Toulouse and once again breathed the air of a country at peace.

Part II

NATIONALIST SPAIN

1

Frontier Interlude

It is odd how one's subconscious mind reacts to danger long after danger has passed. For weeks, in Paris, the sound of a car back-firing, or the drone of a vacuum cleaner, gave me a foolish start. I wrote my articles in a flat off the Champs-Élysées belonging to the Baroness X, a French woman I had known for several years. It was peaceful there with the sun streaming through the balcony windows and the only noise the early morning chatter of the concierge bargaining with the baker. Spain had left a deeper mark than I had realised; from a distance the war seemed more tragic than when I had been in the midst of it. In Madrid, life had moved so fast there had been little time to think. Now, memories were more vivid than actual happenings. Fleeting, half-forgotten scenes crowded into my mind: a particular expression on someone's face, a tone of voice or a casual sentence, that at the time had seemed to make little impression.

I had no 'line' to take on Spain as it had not yet become a political story for me. I was much more interested in the human side – the forces that urged people to such a test of endurance and the paradoxical mixture of fierce and gentle qualities their suffering produced. I was still surprised at how impersonal war was. All the old clichés about war starting with the beat of a drum and people surging to the colours in an emotional wave of hatred seemed to me untrue. Men killed from conviction, not passion; even in Spain, a man shot his brother not because he disliked him, but because he disagreed with him.

I wrote about the things I had seen and heard but did not try to

interpret them. Although it was not my war, I dreaded the thought
of visiting the Franco side and plunging into an atmosphere where
triumph meant disaster for the people I had left. On the other
hand, I was curious to hear the Nationalist point of view and felt
that until I did I would not have a proper perspective.

I was told I didn't stand a chance of getting a visa for Nationalist
Spain; the press censorship was strict and no journalist who had
been tainted by the Republic had ever been allowed to cross to
Franco's side. Nevertheless, I decided to try it and was told that
my best hope was to go to the French frontier and put in an application there.

My sister had come to Europe for the summer. After making a trip through Holland, Germany and Czechoslovakia, she
joined me and we went to Italy for a few weeks' holiday, and then
to Saint Jean-de-Luz, a small town on the French Basque coast
twelve miles from the Spanish border. The British Ambassador to
Spain, Sir Henry Chilton, had a house a few miles away. We had
known his daughter, Anne, in New York, and through them I met
Franco's agent, the Conde de Mamblas. On looking back I suppose
I took an unfair advantage of the Count, for he was an aristocrat
of the old school whose view on the war was confined to the simple philosophy that General Franco had the support of 'ladies and
gentlemen'. Having met me under the auspices he did, I suppose
he bracketed me as 'safe'. He didn't reply that my request was out of
the question, but said thoughtfully: 'After the chaos of Red Spain
the contrast would give you the valuable material for articles.' He
told me I would have an answer within two weeks.

My sister and I settled down to enjoy ourselves. Although Saint
Jean-de-Luz had once been a popular resort, in the summer of
1937 it lay too close to the Franco–Spanish frontier and now it
had an air of desertion. Pleasure-seekers had drifted away, the

hotels were half empty, and the smart shops were boarded up. The beach, usually crowded with gay umbrellas, had only a sprinkling of people, and the atmosphere of summer frivolity was replaced by a dozen sleek British warships anchored in the harbour for patrol duty along the Spanish coast. In spite of the outwardly quiet atmosphere, life was not dull. The Bar Basque, a small restaurant on the main street of Saint Jean-de-Luz, was a popular meeting place, and every afternoon and evening it was crowded with journalists, naval officers, diplomats, Spanish agents and aristocrats who sighed for the restoration of the old regime. My sister and I made friends with Geoffrey (Tommy) Thompson, the British First Secretary, and we often met Anne Chilton and her fiancé, Tom Dupree, an honorary attaché at the Embassy, at the Bar Basque for parties. On Saturday nights there was a three-piece orchestra and everyone danced in the crowded rooms until the small hours of the morning. At twelve o'clock the news was switched on and a sharp Spanish voice cut through the din: '*Ar–rriba, España!!*' and then the bulletin followed, always consisting of a series of brilliant successes by '*nuestros gloriosos soldados*'. At the end of these broadcasts the Nationalist anthem was played and the Franco supporters in the room stood rigidly at attention, their arms outstretched in the Fascist salute. One night after the news bulletin one of the journalists persuaded the French orchestra to play 'Valencia'. They swung into the tune with gusto: half the people joined hands and went rollicking around the room, while the other half shook their fists and protested angrily. Finally, the manager stopped the music. Someone accused him of being pro-Franco, but he replied that he was not interested in the war – 'Only in keeping my clientèle,' he said. 'People's views are no concern of mine.'

This was the general attitude about Spain that summer. Apart from the extremists (the supporters of Bolshevism and Fascism), most people refused to take sides in a conflict which seemed to them a purely internal affair. 'Just a lot of damned Spaniards cutting each other's throats', was the popular summarisation; the fact that Germany was sharpening her claws on Spanish soil had not yet caused alarm to many Englishmen and Frenchmen, who regarded it chiefly as a crusade against the Bolshevik menace.

One of the few exceptions was Tommy Thompson. I think his original antipathy for Franco's supporters started with the Englishman's instinctive dislike of uniforms and military display. The clicking of heels and the Fascist saluting in Nationalist Spain, the ubiquitous posters of Hitler, Mussolini and Franco, caused him particular irritation, not to mention the grandiose talk of future conquests. Long before anyone else was taking the situation seriously, he was sounding a grave note of warning; to him, the Spanish Civil War was taking the shape of a fight against England.

The Chancery of the British Embassy was established in a small grocery shop in Hendaye, overlooking the International Bridge. At one end, the French tricolours fluttered in the breeze and at the other flew the red and yellow stripes of Franco's Spain. The barriers on both sides were shut and few cars passed over, but somehow there was always an air of drama. The French guards paced up and down with an important stride while the Spanish Guardia Civil in their shiny patent-leather hats stood in clusters, smoking cigarettes and gazing curiously at the outside world. It gave me an odd feeling to see the soldiers of Franco's army. These were the people that I had thought of for three months as 'the enemy'. These were the people whose machine-gun fire we had ducked, whose shells we had cursed, and whose planes we had run from.

The American and French Embassies were also near the frontier. They had followed the lead of the British Embassy and now all three were in the peculiar position of being accredited to

Republican Spain, but firmly established in France with their main source of information derived from the opposition. I don't know how much the fact that the three democracies had no direct ambassadorial contact with the Republic affected the course of the Spanish war; for two years, however, most of the work of the ambassadors was limited to making futile representations on the subject of non-intervention and trying unsuccessfully to arrange for the exchange of prisoners.

Tommy Thompson refused to be done in by the situation and managed to gather a good deal of information from journalists back from the front. Handicapped as he was, he had an accurate appreciation of the situation and gave his Government a forecast of future events which has since been borne out.

During the next three weeks I received no word from Nationalist headquarters. Franco's northern campaign was in full swing. His troops had smashed the iron ring at Bilbao in June, and now it was rumoured that he would soon begin a push against Santander. The British Navy had been evacuating thousands of refugees from the stricken areas and the officers came back with pathetic stories of the misery and confusion. One of the warships had picked up a man in a rowboat; he had been hiding in the mountains for over a year and had built the boat himself in order to escape to Franco territory. They told us they had kept him aboard until they sighted the *Jupiter*, a Nationalist warship, and then turned him over. They said that they got most of their war news by intercepting the journalists' despatches radioed from Spain to London; the crew of the *Royal Oak* (which has since been sunk by the Germans) were highly indignant at being described by a *Daily Express* reporter as 'nursemaids' to the refugees.

I had begun to fear that my visa for Nationalist Spain would never arrive. One night I drove over to Biarritz for dinner with

Tommy Thompson. We went to Sonny's bar, and while we were having a cocktail, a young Englishman, Rupert Bellville, came in. Rupert had spent several years in Spain, where he had taken an interest in bull-fighting, and at the beginning of the war had joined Franco's army and fought for a few months with a Falangist regiment. I had met him in London, and when I told him I was waiting for permission to go to Spain, he suggested that I come with him. He had his own aeroplane and was planning to fly to San Sebastián on the following day. I replied that I hadn't yet got a visa for Spain, but he waved it aside as an unnecessary formality. He said he knew the authorities well and could guarantee there wouldn't be any trouble. He added that he would fly me to different parts of the country so that I could see how much the Italians and Germans were doing in the way of building aerodromes.

The proposition sounded slightly mad, for it seemed odd that a private individual should be allowed to fly at random around a country at war. On the other hand, Spain *was* slightly mad. Having given up hope of getting a visa, I decided this might be the only chance I would have to see the Nationalist side. Sir Henry Chilton and Tommy Thompson warned me strongly against the trip, but in the end I went.

Tony Mackeson, an English businessman and a friend of Rupert, was another passenger, and the three of us left the Biarritz aerodrome the following afternoon. When we got off the ground and headed towards San Sebastian, Rupert picked up a gin bottle, took a swig, and said: 'We may get shot at by the anti-aircraft batteries. Shall we fly high or fly low?' Tony replied: 'Keep low. We won't have so far to drop.'

In spite of this beginning, the flight was peaceful and took over twenty minutes. Rupert, an expert pilot, flew only a few hundred feet above the mountains that ringed San Sebastian. Not wishing to attract anti-aircraft fire by circling round the aerodrome, he cut his engine and side-slipped on to the field in a remarkable if precarious landing.

Tony and I drew a breath of relief and got out of the plane to find half a dozen officials running towards us. Rupert stepped forward and showed his papers, but instead of being welcomed by a hospitable flow of Spanish ('*Ruperto, mi amigo!*'), he was told his plane would be confiscated and that all three of us were under arrest. The commander of the aerodrome said we had no right to enter a military zone without the proper credentials and the case would have to be investigated. Rupert finally persuaded him to let us stay at the Maria Cristina Hotel in San Sebastian until the matter was cleared up.

For the next twenty-four hours we were kept under strict surveillance by the secret police. Rupert telephoned numerous friends in Salamanca, but none of them had sufficient authority to intervene. We drove down to the International Bridge to try to get back to France, but learned that for the last twelve hours all traffic had been suspended as the push to Santander had started. Through an American friend who chanced to pass, I sent a message to Tommy Thompson, but wasn't very hopeful about his getting it.

I can't say I enjoyed myself much. The only visas on my passport were stamped – Madrid, Valencia and Barcelona; I realised if we were sent to gaol I would find an explanation difficult. Although Rupert ran into several bull-fighters in Chicote's bar and settled down to enjoy himself, I spent most of the time in the hotel. What little I saw of San Sebastian offered a startling contrast to the shabbiness of Valencia. The Maria Cristina was filled with well-to-do Spaniards: young girls with their *duennas* and smiling officers in well-cut uniforms with neatly polished boots. There were expensive cars in the streets and the restaurants were crowded with smartly dressed women. General Franco's portrait hung in all the cafés with Monarchist flags crossed above it. Music and dancing were forbidden by the Church, so there was little for people to do but sit in the cafés. There seemed to be no shortage of food, for with the exception of two meatless days a week, the menus in the hotel were long and elaborate.

Most of the time I was too worried to take any interest in my surroundings, and when at last I got a message from the porter saying that Señor Thompson was in the lobby, I felt like a convict with a dim hope of escape. Tommy, who was accompanied by a Mr Goodman, the British Vice-Consul at Saint Jean-de-Luz, was in a bad temper and mumbled something about thank God Europe wasn't full of woman journalists. He said that he and Mr Goodman had had an unpleasant half-hour with the Military Governor at Irun, but had finally persuaded him to let us out. Rupert, however, was still optimistic; he didn't want to leave without his plane and Tony decided to stay with him. This made Tommy madder than ever.

When I got back to Saint Jean-de-Luz I looked for my sister to tell her about the trip. I found she was in no mood to listen, for she had just been to a bull-fight in Bayonne with Major Yeats-Brown, the author of *Bengal Lancer*. She had been badly shaken by the experience and had taken three aspirin tablets and gone to bed. The horses weren't padded and their insides had spilled over the ring. 'And do you know what the Major kept saying?' she asked indignantly. '"Don't worry, my dear, the horses are not unhappy – their ears are still standing up!"'

A few days later my sister left for America and I went back to Spain. This time everything was done in the proper way: a long examination by the customs officials at the bridge at Irun, photographs taken, and fingerprints made. At ten o'clock I was in a sleeping-car bound for Salamanca.

2

The Fall of Santander

German and Italian flags flew from one end of Insurgent Spain to the other. Although it was apparent that the polite exchange of notes between London, Berlin and Rome on non-intervention was a farce, I was not prepared for such an open flaunting of the Fascist alliance. In Salamanca, the quiet old university town, which General Franco had chosen as his headquarters, hotels, bars and restaurants blazed with swastikas and the colours of Savoy. Shops bore signs that said, '*Mann spricht Deutsch*', and many of the buildings were scrawled with '*Viva il Duce*'. The Gran Hotel was decorated with posters of the Dictators, odd in the contrast they offered: Mussolini in a steel helmet with his chin thrust out was stern and belligerent, while Hitler stared wistfully into space, calling on Europe to defend itself against Bolshevism.

The scene of the hotel lobby was a cosmopolitan one. German colonels sat solemnly drinking café-au-lait while Spanish general staff-officers, with bright blue sashes tied round their waists, strode importantly across the marble floor. Italians, booted and spurred, usually with a girl on each arm, came jingling down the stairs, and Foreign Legionaries in green shirts, their caps tipped jauntily to one side, argued with the desk clerk for rooms. It was difficult to get rooms at the Gran Hotel as most were occupied by the Germans. The top floor was used as German headquarters and guarded by Guardia Civil in shiny hats and with long rifles. I wandered up there by mistake and a German officer hustled me quickly down the stairs, telling me that my presence was strictly *verboten*.

The atmosphere of the hotel lobby was one of boredom and suspicion. Newcomers were eyed warily, and on the wall was a sign
which said, 'Sh! Spies!' It added that if anyone attempted to discuss
the military situation you should denounce them immediately
and thus save your country. The military situation, however, was
discussed twenty-four hours a day; passionately by the Spaniards,
boastfully by the Italians and ponderously by the Germans. Every
night at midnight crowds gathered in the great square where loudspeakers broadcast news of the front in half a dozen languages. The
spectacle was varied, for there were Requetés in bright red berets,
Falangistas in dark blue uniforms with red tassels swinging from
their caps, and Moors, some in dirty puttees and turbans, others
in red fezzes and sky-blue robes that swept the ground as they
walked. A calm descended on the square when the bulletin was
read and at the end the Nationalist anthem was played with the
crowd at attention, their hands raised in the Fascist salute. There
was complete confidence in a Franco victory. So much so that a
notice in one of the English newspapers stating that the odds were
'slightly' in favour of Franco was the cause of great amusement.

At this period, August 1937, there was every reason for Nationalist jubilation. Franco's northern campaign was going well, and
when it was finished a hundred thousand men would be released
and a large supply of artillery, tanks and aeroplanes to bolster his
army on the Aragon. With these new forces it was predicted that
he would be able to drive through Catalonia, separate Barcelona
from Valencia, and in all likelihood bring the war to an end by the
spring.

Italian forces, however, and the help of the German Air Force
and staff, were indispensable to him, and for this reason Great
Britain's attempts at non-intervention were reviled as the blackest
treachery. Somewhat paradoxically, Spaniards enjoyed speaking

cynically of Italy's fighting ability, but the fact remained that it was Italian and German aircraft that had smashed the iron ring at Bilbao and that three regular Italian army divisions were now pressing the northern campaign to a close.

General Franco was well aware of these facts and Italian and German diplomats were treated with marked esteem. I arrived in Salamanca on the same day that the new Italian Ambassador presented his credentials, and that night there was a large demonstration in the square. The buildings were lighted with torches in the same fashion as in the Piazza Venezia at Rome, and hundreds of blue-shirted Falangist soldiers formed a cordon to hold the crowds back. The Ambassador in a black Fascist uniform, a tassel swinging from his cap, made a speech from a central balcony; it was climaxed by a startling demonstration of Moorish cavalry who came thundering through the square, their white robes flying in the moonlight.

As the drive to Santander was the first major role the Italians had played since their ignominious defeat at Guadalajara, they were jubilant with success. Three days after I arrived in Salamanca, Pablo Merry del Val, the chief of the Foreign Press Bureau, rang up and said the city would fall within twenty-four hours. Most of the journalists were already in the north and he had arranged for me to meet them and cover the triumphal entry.

I left Salamanca in the afternoon in a car driven by Ignacio Rosalles, a Barcelona millionaire, who spoke English fluently and had volunteered his services as a press officer. We had hoped to reach Santander in the early hours of the morning, but when we had gone about a hundred miles we were stopped by sentries and told there was an unconfirmed report that fighting was still going on along the main road, somewhere in the vicinity of Reinosa. They advised us to swing round by Bilbao and travel along the coast. As this meant we wouldn't reach Santander until the next afternoon, I suggested taking a chance on the other, but Rosalles refused, saying he couldn't endanger my life. When I argued with him, he turned on me accusingly: 'That's the trouble with you American correspondents. If you get captured, nothing happens to you, but I'm a Spaniard – if I'm caught, I'm shot.'

This put me in a poor position to argue and we arrived in Bilbao the next morning to find that the press cars had left for Santander several hours before. No one was authorised to give us the necessary safe conduct papers to follow, but after a long conversation with the police it was thought that permits might be produced in an hour or so. Precious minutes were slipping away, but I was familiar enough with Spanish red tape to know there was nothing to do but wait.

Rosalles was upset, for he had never been a press officer before and it looked as though his first assignment was going to be a flop. He racked his brains to give me something to write about and finally conceived the idea of driving to Guernica, a few miles from Bilbao. The town had been destroyed several months before and was the subject of bitter controversy; the Republicans claimed that the Nationalists had bombed it and the Nationalists claimed that the Republicans had burnt it. Each side played it up as one of the great atrocities of the war. Rosalles asked me if I had been subjected to the lying Valencia propaganda and said: 'Now you can see for yourself.'

We arrived in Guernica to find it a lonely chaos of timber and brick, like an ancient civilisation in process of being excavated. There were only three or four people in the streets. One old man was standing inside an apartment house that had four sides to it but an interior that was only a sea of bricks. It was his job to clear away the debris which seemed a life's work, for with each brick he threw over his shoulder, he stopped and mopped his forehead. Accompanied by Rosalles I went up to him and asked if he had been in the town during the destruction. He nodded his head and, when I asked what had happened, waved his arms in the air and declared that the sky had been black with planes – '*Aviones*,' he said: '*Italianos y Alemanes.*' Rosalles was astonished.

'Guernica was burned,' he contradicted heatedly. The old man, however, stuck to his point, insisting that after a four-hour bombardment there was little left to burn. Rosalles moved me away. 'He's a Red,' he explained indignantly.

We returned to Bilbao and to our surprise found the permits ready. We learned that Franco's troops were entering the city at that very moment. As it was only seventy miles away, with any luck, we could still arrive in time to see the 'celebration'. Franco's northern army totalled about thirty thousand men, the spearhead of which was three Italian divisions (the Black Flames, the Black Arrows, and the Twenty-third of March Division) numbering about eighteen thousand; the rest was made up of two battalions of Moors, two battalions of Requetés and six or seven mixed squadrons of Spanish and Moorish cavalry. The bulk of the troops were entering Santander from the south, so that for the first half of our journey the road was fairly clear. The retreating army had blown up most of the bridges, however, and we had several precarious crossings on temporary structures thrown hastily over the river-beds.

The countryside was desolate and sad. We passed innumerable farmhouses wrecked by bombs and shells and a straggling stream of refugees heading for unknown destinations. One family had all their worldly possessions piled high on the back of a cow; others had wheelbarrows and donkey-carts, and still others trudged wearily along with their bundles tied to a stick carried over their shoulders. Many of the villages had been deserted; the doors were locked, the shutters drawn and the only sign of life a few half-starved dogs. Rosalles explained that the Reds forced the people to evacuate in order to immobilise the villages for the Nationalist troops. I regarded this sceptically, for I had heard enough on the Republican side to know the terror with which the ordinary people regarded a Fascist or Moorish occupation.

Further on we had a small illustration of Moorish discipline when we detoured into a small town off the main road to find thirty or forty of them looting an abandoned village. They were coming out of the houses, their arms filled with an odd assortment of knick-knacks: one soldier had a kitchen stool over his shoulder and an egg-beater in his pocket; another, a child's doll and an old pair of shoes. Several Moors were sitting on the curb, bending around a packet of playing cards, admiring the brightly coloured queens and knaves.

Further along, the main road became more congested. We passed a long line of Italian army lorries and a demolished tank turned upside down. One of the drivers was standing on the running-board tipping back a bottle of wine. As we went by he raised the bottle and shouted, 'Viva il Duce.' Rosalles flushed a little and said sourly, 'They don't often get a chance to celebrate.'

About twenty miles from Santander we turned a bend and came upon several hundred Republican Army prisoners, crowded together in a clearing at the side of the road. Their faces were unshaven and grimy and their clothes in rags. They looked half-starved and many of them had their arms and legs done up in dirty bandages. A Fascist truck was standing by the side of the road and the officers began to distribute bread and tins of meat and sardines. There was a scramble for the food; the men opened the tins with their knives and began to eat ravenously. They offered a pitiful contrast to the last Republican soldiers I had seen. Gone were the exuberant spirits and the virile hatred of Fascism; now there was only exhaustion and subservience and a future that lay in the grim confines of a prison camp.

We finally reached Santander to find that the Italians were holding a victory parade. Although the parade had been going on for three hours and the main part of it was over, tanks, trucks and armoured cars were still thundering through the squares. A bewildered population lined the streets and watched with open mouths while pictures of Mussolini were plastered on the buildings and black-plumed Italians on motorcycles roared down the streets followed by several battalions of steel-helmeted troops.

Santander presented an amazing spectacle. The main squares had been badly bombed and the debris had turned many of the streets into dump yards. It was hot and dry and as the lorries rolled by, pillars of dust rose into the air and hung over the crowd like a grey pall. All variations of human emotion seemed to be thrown together in a crazy conglomeration: there were half-starved refugees, vociferous Italians, wretched prisoners, rejoicing Fifth Columnists, excited children and weeping women. The city was in an appalling condition. The water mains had been destroyed and most of the food supplies exhausted for over ten days. Shops and restaurants were boarded up and the population had lived on a limited ration of rice. The entrance of the conquering army, with their guns and motorcycles gaily decorated with flowers and wreaths, struck an almost sinister note.

At every turn there was a sharp and almost horrifying contrast. Already Franco's troops were wandering about the town, pulling down the Republican flags. Hundreds of Nationalist supporters who had been trapped in the city for more than a year crowded the streets, laughing and crying. Dozens of balconies had become alive with red and yellow mantillas, forming the

Monarchist colours; posters crying '*Viva Franco*' blotted out the faded Republican call to arms. Groups of girls ran into the streets and hugged the Nationalist officers and a band of street urchins shouted at the passers-by and gave them the Fascist salute.

But the other side of the story was a desolate one. You had only to wander along the wharves to see the thousands of refugees sitting in a litter of debris, their bundles and bags piled up beside them, gazing on the celebration with tears running down their cheeks; or into the empty markets and deserted hotels to see the hostile stares of the street vendors or waitresses; or by the gaols to see the long columns of women and children patiently waiting for news of the prisoners. One of the most ironical sights was the hospital that stood in the main square: watching from the windows were dozens of wounded Republican soldiers, with a grandstand view of the celebration.

I suppose there were many hundreds of people who wished only to be left in peace and who changed their loyalties overnight to whichever side was in power. When we were standing on the crowded pavement watching the parade, Rosalles moved away to speak to a friend and I turned to the Spaniard next to me who was cheering loudly and said, falteringly: '*Cómo le gustan los Italianos?*' ('What do you think of the Italians?') 'Oh, we like them,' he replied. Then he winked and said, '*De otra manera . . .*' ('If we don't . . .'), and here he drew his finger suggestively across his throat.

We had another illustration of this when we drove down to the garage to get some petrol. When the tank was filled, the garage attendant absent-mindedly gave us the clenched-fist greeting of the Popular Front. In the middle of it his face turned red with embarrassment, his arm went forward and his hand opened into the flat palm of the Fascist salute.

Rosalles had a summer-house on the outskirts of the town which he hadn't seen for a year. After wandering about the streets for several hours, he suggested we drive out there and try to find something to eat. It was a large villa by the sea; when we reached the drive, the caretaker's wife recognised Rosalles and called excitedly to her husband. Both ran out and flung their arms around him, hugging him with joy. They told us that during the last month the house had been occupied by Aguirre, the Basque President, who used it as his headquarters. He had left Santander only the day before in a private plane, and twelve hours later General Davilla, the Commander of the Northern Army, had moved in with his staff.

The only food in the house was half a loaf of bread and a few tins of Russian meat which Aguirre had left behind. While the care-taker's wife was preparing it we went inside and talked to Davilla's staff officers. They were tall, good-looking Spaniards who spoke enthusiastically of the victory and predicted the end of the war by the spring. One of them said he had heard that America was anti-Franco and prophesied that unless the United States mended its ways the sickle and hammer would soon be flying over the White House. 'There's only one way to treat a Red,' he said, 'shoot him.'

Rosalles described our drive along the coast and told them of the incident at Guernica. 'The town was full of Reds,' he said. 'They tried to tell us it was bombed, not burnt.' The tall staff officer replied: 'But, of course, it was bombed. We bombed it and bombed it and bombed it, and *bueno*, why not?'

Rosalles looked astonished, and when we were back in the car again heading for Bilbao, he said: 'I don't think I would write about that if I were you.'

The drive home was more congested than on the way down, and we again had countless detours to make. At one bridge we were stopped for over an hour. At this particular spot the main bridge had been destroyed and the narrow dirt road leading down to the river-bed, where there was a temporary structure, was blocked by a heavy truck. The driver was unable to swing the machine round the narrow turn in the road. Faced by a steep cliff in front, he had no alternative but to back up the hill again. A road gang of prisoners were sent to his aid, but the engine spluttered, the wheel slipped in the mud, and the only result was a good deal of cursing.

After a wait of twenty minutes, a long black car, preceded by a motorcycle escort, swung up beside us, and the Italian Ambassador stepped out to watch the operations. Dressed in a magnificent black uniform with rows of medals across his chest, his appearance caused the Spaniards considerable excitement. The orders grew louder and more violent, but the wheels still whirled helplessly in the mud.

It was considered such discourtesy, however, to keep an Italian Ambassador waiting, that the officer in charge finally solved the problem by ordering the road gang to push the truck over the cliff. With the engine still running, the men heaved, and with a deafening roar the truck fell three hundred feet to the ravine below; the Ambassador gave the Fascist salute and climbed back into his car.

A small Spaniard standing near me became pale with indignation. 'A hundred thousand pesetas,' he moaned. 'Who's running this country, anyway?' That, of course, was the question.

When we had crossed the bridge and were on the main road, Rosalles said once again: 'I think it is better not to write about that.'

The day came to a climax when we reached Bilbao and went into a café for supper. Rosalles ran into a friend who had just heard an amusing story. He laughed so much he had difficulty telling it, but the gist was that two Englishmen had flown to Santander in a private plane to greet the victorious army. They had arrived too soon, however, and when they stepped out of the plane shouting, '*Viva, Franco! Arriba, España!*', the Red officers still in charge of the aerodrome had promptly arrested them. They forced the owner of the plane to fly several Government officials to the town of Gijon and then placed him in gaol.

'Do you know the name of the Englishman?' I asked.

The Spaniard shook his head, but I already knew the answer: Rupert Bellville.

3

Salamanca

Over the porter's desk, on the wall of the Gran Hotel in Salamanca, was a faded travel poster that said: 'Visit Madrid'. It was strange no one had torn it down, for 'Red' atrocity stories were on everyone's lips and hatred for the Madrileños approached fanaticism. Word spread quickly that I had 'visited Madrid' and I was often accosted in the lobby by strangers eager for news of relatives believed to be prisoners on the other side.

Each had his own version of conditions in Red Spain and I found it dangerous to make contradictions. One woman, the wife of an official in the Foreign Office, asked me how I dared walk along the streets of Madrid. She had heard there was so much sniping from the windows that bodies were piled up by the curbs and left to rot in the gutters. When I denied this her tone became hostile, and I later learned she had denounced me as suspect. Another man asked if I had seen the Reds feeding prisoners to the animals in the Zoo. I told him the Zoo had been empty for months, and his manner froze. Still another, Pablo Merry del Val, the head of the foreign press, admired a gold bracelet I was wearing: 'I don't imagine you took that to Madrid with you,' he said, smiling. When I replied I had bought it in Madrid he was greatly affronted and from then on bowed coldly from a distance.

If I had been a Spaniard, these remarks, innocent as they were, would have landed me in gaol. Objectivity was not tolerated. During the weeks I spent in Salamanca, the vilification of the enemy, even by responsible officials, was so extreme that it was almost a mental disease. I could understand and sympathise with Spaniards who had become embittered by tragic experiences. Many had escaped from Republican territory only after weeks of terror and misery, and many more were in mourning. But what I couldn't understand was that everyone seemed to have forgotten that General Franco had launched the war. They argued Franco had been forced to rebel in order to forestall a Bolshevik uprising scheduled for a week or two later. Considering that the Communist Party had numbered only a few thousand at the outbreak of the war, and that the arms and equipment on the Republican side were still pathetically inadequate, this scarcely seemed logical. They also claimed that if the elections of 1936 had not been corrupt, the Right Wing parties would have swept the country; but, in view of the fact that it was taking General Franco nearer two years than two weeks to accomplish his rebellion, it was difficult to believe Republican resistance was entirely forced.

The Nationalist war propaganda was concentrated exclusively on the fight against Bolshevism. Just as on the Republican side the people were called upon to resist a foreign invasion, the Nationalists rallied the peasants against the domination of Moscow. I found, however, that Bolshevism was an elastic word, for it included democrats as well as Communists; in fact, everyone who did not support a totalitarian regime was lumped together as Red.

This detestation of free government gave me an understanding of the difficulties that the Republic had had to deal with. In many instances, the claim that the Republic had failed to maintain discipline was true. But, on the other hand, it was equally true that ever since the Republic had first been established in 1931, Right Wing groups had plotted its downfall. Many of the terrorist acts in Spain were instigated by these groups and at no time did the legitimate Government receive their support. Proof of this lay in the fact that officials who had failed to resign when the Republic was established, and maintained friendly relations even for a limited period, were regarded as suspect. Count Florida, a prominent official in Salamanca, summed up the situation to me in a single sentence: 'In Spain,' he said, 'no *gentleman* would ever dream of supporting a Republic.'

Franco propaganda had drawn much attention to the strange companions who were fighting side by side under the Republican flag. Although the incompatibility of Republicans, Anarchists, Communists and Socialists banded together in a Popular Front was emphasised repeatedly, I found in Salamanca that the discords in the Franco ranks were just as deep and bitter.

From one end of Nationalist territory to the other there were two predominating uniforms: one was the Carlists (or Requetés) with their khaki shirts and bright red berets, and the other, the Fascists (or Falangistas) in navy blue with crimson tassels swinging from their caps. These two groups, although united into a single party to win the war and bound together by a common detestation of parliamentary government, held views stubbornly and bitterly opposed.

The Carlist Party, organised in 1830 and supporting Don Carlos, pretender to the Spanish throne, had now, with the backing of clergy and aristocracy, grown into a strong political force, advocating what in Spain was known as 'Traditionalism', but what in reality was nothing less than a return to the feudal system. With these reactionary views they considered the Fascists a dangerous and radical organisation. This feeling was not hard to understand, for the Fascist programme threatened the power of bishops and grandees. It favoured a supreme centralised government, stood for land reform and the separation of Church from state.

I heard Carlists argue that the peasant should stay on the clod of land on which he was born; that his happiness did not lie in

education but in the security that the great landowner could give
him. A Fascist leader commenting on these remarks, shook his
head emphatically. 'That is the way they talk,' he said. 'But when
the war is over, there won't be any great landowners.'

The Carlists were uncompromising in their attitude towards
Republican prisoners, demanding that they be placed into road-
building gangs and forced to restore the bridges and towns which
they had destroyed. The Fascists, on the other hand, insisted that
efforts be made to convert the enemy to their way of thinking. I
remembered how the Fascist food-trucks had rolled up to feed the
prisoners on the road to Santander, and later learned that thousands of these men had been given uniforms and drafted into the
ranks. In spite of the humanitarian appeal, it was part of a determined programme to expand the Fascist power. When I discussed
this subject with Count Florida, he replied vehemently that half
the Fascists were nothing but Reds. In indignation, he added that
in the north many of them were giving the Popular Front salute
and talking about their brothers in Barcelona.

Although Franco had made persistent efforts to bring the two
parties together, each continued to maintain its own flag and its
own national anthem, and at times hostilities became so bitter
that street fighting broke out in Saragossa and San Sebastian. It
was apparent even then, however, that the Fascists held the upper
hand. Already they numbered about three million as compared
with the Traditionalists' eight hundred thousand.

Needless to say, the internal affairs of Spain were being carefully manipulated by the Nazis, via tactics that now have become
familiar the world over. Although the Italians were playing a more
prominent part on the battlefield, there were over ten thousand
Germans in Spain, innocuously described as 'technicians'. Their
object, under the cloak of anti-Bolshevism, was to build up a Fascist

party which would one day fit into Hitler's grandiose scheme for world conquest. Many of these Germans were trained as air pilots, artillery officers and engineers; others directed the railroads, operated the radio and telegraphs and undertook the organisation of newly conquered territory. Most important of all, however, was the German infiltration into almost all departments of state administration. Through their influence they were able to see that Fascist sympathisers secured important bureaucratic jobs, thus establishing key men throughout the fabric of the Government.

They carried on a violent and intensive propaganda campaign against the democracies. In fact, this campaign was often a great deal more bitter against Great Britain and France than Republican Spain. The British plan of non-intervention had been condemned by the Communists in Madrid as a Fascist attempt to prevent arms from reaching Republican Spain: here in Salamanca it was attacked as a Communist plot to weaken Franco by excluding foreign aid. The fact that Great Britain was the only great power actively interested in the humanitarian aspect of the war received no thanks. Although the British Navy had evacuated over a hundred thousand refugees from both sides in Spain, and the Embassy had worked untiringly to effect the exchange of prisoners, they had only succeeded in arousing the hatred of both, who considered that those not for were against. On the soapboxes of Salamanca and Burgos, Fascist orators denounced the democracies as decadent and corrupt and boasted that the Axis powers would establish a new order throughout the world. It was made clear even then that Fascism was not a philosophy for internal consumption alone. I heard one orator at Salamanca proclaim that under Fascism Spain would rise to retrieve all her ancient glories. Gibraltar, North Africa, would mark a humble beginning; South America was to be the glittering prize.

As for internal conditions, it was difficult to make a fair comparison between the two sides. I took a good many trips throughout Nationalist territory: to Avila, Talavera, Toledo, and to the outskirts of Madrid, where I stood on a hill and saw with a start how large and white the Telephone Building looked and what easy targets the streets were that we had wandered about so freely. Many of the villages outside the military zone had undergone little change and in some it seemed doubtful that the people even knew that a war was going on. There was plenty of food, the market squares were crowded, and black-robed priests threaded their way along narrow streets crowded with donkey-carts, as though unaware that their fate was being sealed on the battlefields. The food situation was understandable, as the richest agricultural districts lay within Franco's control and he had no cities of any great size to feed. The lack of dislocation was also understandable, for the people had little to fear from aerial bombardments by a Republican air force that was almost negligible. Franco's chief headquarters, Burgos, was never bombed during the entire war. Salamanca, Valladolid, Seville and other Nationalist cities only suffered a few attacks.

In the realm of brutality there was probably little to choose between the two sides, but the spirit of revenge in Salamanca was far more virulent than that in Madrid. With a system that encouraged people to denounce their neighbours, suspicions had become so unbalanced that harmless remarks were often twisted out of recognition. Needless to say, the atmosphere was guarded: there was always the fear of dictaphones and eaves-droppers and conversation was generally limited to banalities.

The gaols were overflowing, and the executions reached staggering figures. As soon as the Nationalists occupied a town they set up military courts and the trials began. I got a small idea of the situation when I drove back to Santander a few weeks after the Nationalists had taken over and visited one of the tribunals. There were five judges. I had met one of them in Bilbao, an amusing young army captain by the name of Seraglio, who had been seconded for this particular duty. I went to the courthouse accompanied by a press officer and heard the cases of four men who were tried in one group.

Three were army officers (two lieutenants and one colonel), and the fourth was a civil servant, the secretary to the town treasurer. The trial took about fifteen minutes. The prosecution called for the death penalty on the grounds of treason, and the defence begged for leniency, arguing that the soldiers had been conscripted into the army and that the civil servant had committed no crime while in office. The court was cleared for the verdict, but when it adjourned for lunch I met my friend the Captain in the hallway and asked him what the sentences had been. He replied that they had been condemned to death. I asked what the standard was for the death penalty, and he answered: 'All officers, all government servants and all men and women who have denounced Whites.' He said they had heard sixteen cases that morning and fourteen had been condemned to death. Several weeks later in Salamanca an official bulletin was published stating that out of four thousand prisoners tried, only thirty-five had been given the death penalty. I could scarcely believe, however, that I had happened to choose the one morning that nearly half these sentences had been imposed.

I have often thought of the scene as the Captain and I walked down the courtroom steps into the open. Standing in front of the building was an open lorry filled with men. As we got closer I saw they were the prisoners who had just been tried. The sky was blue and the sun was streaming down, which made the death sentence seem all the more unreal. Some of them sat with bowed heads, but as we came closer they recognised the young captain as one of the judges, and for one brief second I suppose they had a glimmer of hope that he might save them. They stared at him like bewildered animals, then scrambled to their feet and saluted. It was a pathetic and terrible sight, but the young captain saluted back casually, took a deep breath of fresh air, and said, gaily: 'Let's go down to the café and have a drink. Conditions have improved since you were last here.' As we walked down the hill I could hear the truck starting up, and I wondered whether it was heading for the execution ground then and there. It rattled past us and the Captain said: 'Filthy town, this. When the war is over you had better come back to Spain and we will show you some real fun.'

Tribunals were going on all over Spain. Even in Salamanca, removed as it was from the military zone, the small gaol was crowded with prisoners awaiting trial. One day news spread around that hundreds of Russian prisoners had arrived. The story sounded incredible, but I got hold of a White Russian whom I had met in the hotel, a strange character named Mr Petroff, and persuaded him to go down to the gaol with me. We argued with the warden, Captain Costello, and he finally gave us permission to go in and talk to them. The number of Russians totalled three; all aviators who had been shot down at the battle of Brunete. I only talked with two and the first was a man of about thirty, hollow-chested and thin, with sad, melancholy eyes. He said he had come to Spain because he had been offered fifteen hundred roubles a month, six times his normal pay. He had no idea what the war was about but had always longed to travel, and it seemed to be his only opportunity. When I asked him how much flying experience he had, he replied: 'Six months'; he claimed the battle of Brunete was the first operation he had taken part in. Both mentally and physically he seemed a man of inferior quality for an air-force pilot. It was impossible to know whether he was speaking the truth, but there was something genuinely touching in the naïveté of his replies. He had never been out of Russia before, and when I asked him what had impressed him the most, he said: 'To see the people smiling. We had been taught that the world outside Russia was sad and terrible. In France, people were laughing. I think we have been badly deceived.'

France seemed to have made a deep impression upon him; he told me that whereas in his village in Russia they threw their cigarette stubs on the floor, in Paris they had been given little china trays to put them in. I asked him whether his salary in Russia was large enough to afford him any luxuries. 'Oh, no,' he said, shaking his head gloomily. 'It has always been my ambition to own a bicycle, but I have never been able to have one.' Somehow the idea of a bomber pilot hankering after a bicycle seemed slightly irrational.

The second Russian was in the hospital. Landing by parachute, he had broken his leg; he didn't seem to mind as he had become a focal point of attention. He was a different type from the first pilot: a big blond-haired peasant without a nerve in his body, who kept up a steady stream of laughter and conversation. He, too, claimed he had come to Spain only because of the money, but now he was homesick and longed to get back to Moscow. He said Russia was the finest place in the world; he seemed very much at home and Captain Costello told me he had become a show-piece. The Spanish nurses had never seen a Russian before and all day long an endless stream of them tiptoed into his room, stood at the foot of his bed, and stared curiously at him. Some months later I heard that the Russians had been released from gaol. Whether or not this was true and what happened to them afterwards, I never learned.

During the next two weeks in Salamanca I talked with everyone I could find, piecing scraps of information together and trying to make a composite picture out of the whole crazy pattern. I could understand the mentality of the upper-class Spaniards who were fighting for homes, property and old-time privileges; I could also understand the peasants, who had joined Franco's army because their masters had bid them to, and even the Germans, who probably did not think at all beyond the fact that the Führer's orders were sacred. But I was curious about the Italians. I wondered what they thought Mussolini had sent them to Spain for. I talked with several in the Embassy and Press Bureau but their comments were guarded and I longed to hear the point of view of someone in the fighting forces. By chance, I had an opportunity one day when I went into a café to meet a friend; while I was waiting, an Italian aviator came up and sat down at my table. He was a young man of about twenty-five, with a row of medals which he had won in Abyssinia. He opened a conversation and when I told him I was an American, smiled warmly, and said: 'I love American jazz.' With some difficulty I got him off this subject and on to the war. I asked him why the Italians were fighting in Spain, and he replied gaily: 'We must destroy the Bolsheviks.'

'Is that really why you are here?'

'Well,' he smiled, 'the two things coincide. You see, Italy is a very poor country. If we can kill Reds and get raw materials at the same time, it is a very fine combination. This is the age of expansion.'

I asked him if Italy couldn't manage any other way but war, and he said: 'War is not so bad; sometimes it is fun to drop bombs. The trouble with you Americans is you're too sentimental; and you're sentimental because you're too smug. You've got everything you want. Perhaps we Italians wouldn't go to war if there were any new lands to discover. Now, of course, if Cristoforo Colombo had hung on to America . . .'

Just then my friend arrived, and I never had a chance to hear this theme developed.

4

March through the North

During the month of September Franco's army advanced through the rugged province of Asturias, bringing his northern campaign to a close. Although the Republican troops were doomed in the slow squeeze, they were putting up a fierce and stubborn resistance.

I was in Santander at the time and a Spanish officer, Captain Aguilera, the seventeenth Count of Alba y Yeltes, offered to drive me to León where the base of the attack was taking place.

Captain Aguilera (who spoke English fluently) was booted and spurred, with a blue tassel swinging from his cap; he had a pale yellow Mercedes car, and in the back seat were two large repeating rifles, and a chauffeur who drove so badly he was usually encouraged to sleep.

We swung along the coast but the going was bad; the road was crowded with soldiers and Italian army trucks, and all along the way came a steady stream of refugees. The refugees had fled before the advance, but, cut off on the other side, were returning now to their homes.

Aguilera liked to drive fast, so he cursed a good deal at the carts and animals. 'You never see any pretty girls,' he grumbled. 'Any girl who hasn't got a face like a boot can get a ride in an Italian truck.'

A few minutes later, however, two girls with red and blue kerchiefs tied over their heads motioned frantically and we pulled over to the side of the road. They ran up to the car and in an excited flow of Spanish told us the retreating army had taken away their cows. Some of the animals had escaped along the way, so they'd gone out to search for them, but they hadn't found them and now they were tired and wanted a ride back home. We gave them a lift a few miles down the road and drove on to Llames.

Llames was a sea of uniforms. Italian soldiers crowded the pavements, some of them squatting by the roadside opening tins of meat with their bayonets; others eating bread and cheese and gulping down bottles of red wine. The main street was blocked by supply trucks filling up with petrol, and around a bend a crowd of children and housewives were gazing curiously at a large Russian tank which had been captured two days before. Outside the town we passed a six-inch gun being dragged along by a team of mules. The Captain shouted at one of the crew and asked if the road to Infiesto was clear. One of the soldiers replied: *'Ich weiss nicht. Ich bin hier fremd.'* ('I don't know. I am a stranger here.') Even then the word 'stranger' had a sour ring. Aguilera said: 'Nice chaps, the Germans, but a bit too serious; they never seem to have any women around, but I suppose they didn't come for that. If they kill enough Reds, we can forgive them anything.'

It grew colder as we drove along, for now we were in the foothills of the Picos de Europa, some of the highest mountains in Europe. The dark hills seemed to squeeze in on us as the road narrowed and began to twist and turn through the gorges. Soon it started to rain, but the Captain drove faster than ever, until it seemed we would surely end up skidding over the precipice. Round a turn we came upon a line of soldiers on muleback. They made a long, silent procession winding through the mountains; the only noise was the hoof-beats of their animals sloshing in the mud, and at the head of the procession the jingle of teams dragging light artillery and anti-aircraft guns.

The front was close now. They were fighting in the mountains about a mile away. Every now and then there was a dull, rumbling noise; if we hadn't known we might have thought it thunder. Coming into a tiny village we found the main street blocked by three long, grey cannon, with the ends wrapped in black cloth. The royal colours of Spain, guarded on either side by German and Italian flags, had been placed above the door of a dilapidated blacksmith's shop, while high above, half washed away by rain, was a frayed poster which said: 'Vote for the Popular Front'.

Several dirty children stood at the side of the road, gazing on the scene in bewilderment, while a very old lady, her eyes bright with interest, peered timidly through the window of a ramshackle mountain cabin. It seemed an extraordinary accident that this tiny village, isolated from the world by its great mountain barrier, should have found itself on the route of the retreat of one army and the advance of a second.

A girl in a calico dress came round the corner carrying a bucket of water. I asked her what she thought of it. What she thought of it, she repeated, a puzzled look in her eyes – thought of what? 'The armies,' I said. 'One army moving out, the other moving in.'

'Oh,' she said, 'that. Well, we haven't had much food.'

Food. That was to the point. That's what war meant. Lack of food and loss of cows, and houses with bomb-holes in them.

Aguilera climbed out of the car to see what the trouble was, and a few minutes later came back with the news that a bridge was down, with little chance of being repaired before the following day. We would have to go back to Torrelavega and try to get through on another road.

It was cold and dark now. Torrelavega, which had been captured only a few days before, had a curious air of stillness about it. There was a small hotel in the main square, but we walked in to find it deserted. The dining room was bare; some of the table-covers lay on the floor, and the only light was a dim bulb. Aguilera stamped and shouted, and a few minutes later a very fat Spanish woman came stumbling breathlessly up the stairs. When we asked if there was any food to be had, she threw her arms into the air and launched into a passionate explanation. They were cleaned out, she said; the army had taken everything; they had even taken her coffee-grinder. She could understand the food all right, but she didn't see why they'd had to take the coffee-grinder: it was a fine coffee-grinder that had come all the way from America.

We drove on to Corrales, where we finally got some dinner. The hotel dining room was crowded with German and Italian officers, and at first the concierge said he couldn't feed us. But Aguilera argued with him, and soon we had an enormous dinner of soup, fish, meat and vegetables. The Germans in the room were solemn and polite, and the Italians loud and vociferous, frequently bursting into song. They were just the way Italians and Germans ought to be, so we left with a feeling of satisfaction.

Our problem now was to find a place to sleep. Cutting across country, the roads were bad, but the Captain raced along at high speed, until it seemed that every spring had broken. At the first medium-sized town we came to he pulled up before the hotel and banged on the door. It was dark and still, so the sound of the engine and the shouts and knocks soon drew forth a rattling of windows; but as for a place to sleep we met with no success, for the concierge's voice rang out to say that the Government troops had taken all the mattresses. He suggested that we drive to the next village, about twenty miles away, but when we reached it we found that over eighty people had been turned away from the one and only inn; that it was swarming with officers who were even sleeping in armchairs in the lobby.

It was nearly midnight now and the Captain was growing bad-tempered. The ruts in the roads were so deep he was forced to slow down, and at one of the temporary bridges we were held up nearly half an hour by an army truck stuck in the mud. The main bridge, which had been blown up by the retreating Asturians, was lighted by flares with over five hundred men working on the reconstruction. German engineers in khaki uniforms and black ties were directing the labourers, most of whom were prisoners who had been captured at Santander.

'*Bueno*,' said Aguilera, 'it's good to see them building up what they've destroyed. The only thing the Reds like to do is destroy. You must emphasise that in one of your articles. The joy of destruction.'

'Yes,' I said, 'but the army was in retreat. If they blow up the bridges it holds up the advance, doesn't it?'

Aguilera gave me a hostile look. 'You talk like a Red.' From then on the atmosphere was strained. Fortunately, the trip soon came to an end, for an hour later we succeeded in getting lodgings in a little village called Aguilar de Campo.

The next morning the sun shone down on a serene countryside. We were out of the military zone now, and soldiers, guns, trucks and confusion seemed to have passed away with the blackness like a strange dream. Driving towards León, there were no flags or uniforms to suggest that a war was being fought. Just donkeys plodding along the roads, peasants tending their crops, lazy little villages, and ragged children playing in the dust.

'Blast the Reds!' said Aguilera suddenly. 'Why did they have to put ideas into people's heads? Everyone knows that people are fools and much better off told what to do than trying to run themselves. Hell is too good for the Reds. I'd like to impale every one and see them wriggling on poles like butterflies . . .' The Captain paused to see what impression his speech had made, but I gave no reply, which seemed to anger him. 'There's only one thing I hate worse than a Red,' he blazed.

'What's that?'

'A sob sister!'

* * *

Franco's troops were closing in on the Republican army like a nut-cracker. They were close to Gijon, the last big port on the coast, and with its capitulation the northern campaign would be over. At the hotel in León there was a group of fifteen or twenty journalists who were making daily trips to the front. Among the American and British were Richard Sheepshanks of Reuter's, Reynolds Packard of the United Press, and, if I remember correctly, William Carney of the *New York Times*, Harold Cardozo of the *Daily Mail*, and 'Kim' Philby of the London *Times*.

The trips to the front were like a mad tea party from the pages of a bellicose *Alice in Wonderland*. First there was the press chief, Major Lombarri (in peace-time, an artist on *Vogue*), who fluttered around like a Sunday-school teacher trying to assemble press cars, journalists, and lunch-boxes all at the same time. The lunch-boxes were prepared by the hotel and filled with potato omelettes, a few slices of cold meat, cheese, fruit and bottles of red wine. This gave the outing a picnic air and everyone set off in holiday spirits.

I made the first trip in a car with Dick Sheepshanks. We followed Major Lombarri's lead and drove for about an hour along winding mountain roads, until the noise of gunfire grew loud and we came to a clearing where two batteries were firing. At one side twenty or thirty pack mules were tethered to ground stakes and nearby hundreds of soldiers lay stretched out on the grass taking an afternoon siesta. To the right there was a small slope which Major Lombarri decided would be a pleasant spot for lunch. He bustled about, spreading out rugs and opening lunch-boxes, and then said, graciously: 'Now sit down and enjoy yourselves.'

The scene was incongruous. While the press officers were opening their potato omelettes and gulping down their wine, the guns
shuddered and split the air, coughing out blue fire as the shells went
moaning across the countryside. It took the explosives twenty-five
seconds to reach the Republican stronghold, a mountain-top
about two miles away; then there was a muffled crash and shrapnel rained down upon the hill like black soot. Each time the guns
fired, the mules brayed hysterically, but no one seemed to mind
the noise. The soldiers went on sleeping and the press officers went
on drinking their wine and chaffing each other about the fun they
would have in Paris when the war was over.

As I sat there in the sunshine I had a feeling of revulsion; when
the gunner pulled the lanyard I automatically counted twenty-five
and wondered for whom the sands were running out. According
to one of the officers there were about a thousand men on the hill.
Their ammunition had given out several days before, and it was
only a question of time before they surrendered – if there were any
left to surrender.

The inequality of the two armies was striking. Besides being
better equipped, Franco's troops were better organised and dis-
ciplined. Of the Republic's six hundred thousand soldiers, there
were probably less than four thousand who had ever had any previous military experience. The majority of the twenty thousand
international volunteers were not trained soldiers but ordinary
working-class men recruited by the Communist parties of the
world. The Russians were estimated at about two thousand, consisting of air pilots, staff officers, gunners and technicians. To me,
it seemed extraordinary that they had been able to hold out as
long as they had against the Nationalists' trained forces.

Aside from Franco's civilian conscription, he had eighty thousand Italians, which included three regular army divisions; he had

an experienced Foreign Legion, hard-fighting Moorish regiments, the Guardia Civil, the regular Spanish Army, and ten thousand German 'technicians' and pilots.

As I sat on the hill, I wondered what Spaniards thought of foreigners slaughtering their countrymen. The officer in charge of the batteries was an Italian. He was smartly dressed in a turtle-necked sweater and high polished boots, and each time he gave the signal to fire he lifted his cane gracefully as though he were conducting a symphony orchestra. He came over to talk to us and commented on the enemy, saying: 'Stubborn devils! They don't know when they are beaten.'

'Of course not,' retorted Major Lombarri proudly. 'They're Spaniards.' Somehow it all seemed slightly confusing.

Suddenly we saw a long line of men with picks and shovels come around a bend in the distance. Captain Aguilera interrupted us excitedly: 'Red prisoners, captured at Santander. I hear they built one of the mountain roads in eight days. Not much chance for sleep, eh? That's the way to treat them. If we didn't need roads I would like to borrow a rifle and pick off a couple.'

Lunch was finally over. Major Lombarri collected the picnic-boxes and threw them down the far side of the slope, then said he would take us to where the Commandant was directing operations. He shepherded Captain Aguilera, Dick Sheepshanks and me into his car and drove us over a road that spiralled for several miles through the mountains. At the bends the chauffeur honked the horn loudly, but jammed on his brakes when he was suddenly confronted by a large Italian truck. Everyone got out and argued as to whether or not there was room to pass. The Italians said it was easy, but when they pulled past they hit one of our mudguards. We were on the outside and our rear right-hand wheel tilted over the edge. The driver accelerated loudly and, fortunately, the car leapt back on the road. The Major was furious and shouted after the Italians: 'Try killing the enemy for a change.'

We left the car in a clearing and went the rest of the way on foot. Hundreds of soldiers were sprawled on the ground on either side of the narrow path. Some of the men were repairing machine-guns, some brushing down mules, and others just sleeping. When we reached the top of the hill we found the Commandant having lunch in a small dug-out with two officers. He was a plump, middle-aged man who greeted us warmly and insisted that we all crowd into the tiny space. Although we told him we had finished lunch, he produced a bottle of Malaga wine, some chocolate cookies and a plate of tinned American pineapple. He winked and said he was sympathetic to Americans because he was not one to forget that America had quite a slice of Spain. His name was Pablo, or Paul, he said, and what was mine? When he heard it was Virginia, he was delighted. 'Paul and Virginia,' he repeated. And had I read the book?

Just then one of the soldiers came in and said a message had been received that a squadron of aeroplanes was on its way to machine-gun the enemy positions. We went outside and soon we saw six small specks swoop down over the hill like birds of prey. They went backwards and forwards for nearly an hour, and occasionally, when the wind was right, we could hear the far-away rattle of bullets.

At last we started home. As we threaded our way down the hill past men, mules and machine-guns, I asked Major Lombarri what the ordinary soldier would say if he were asked why he was fighting. 'Oh, they know all right,' he said. 'We will stop and ask one.'

We questioned a boy of about nineteen who was lying in the grass gnawing a piece of bread and cheese. He was a peasant from Seville, and when the Major put my question to him, he replied:

'We are fighting the Reds.' I asked what he meant by the Reds, and he said: 'The people who have been misled by Moscow.' Why did he think they had been misled? And he answered: 'They are very poor. In Spain it is easy to be misled.'

Captain Aguilera, who had been standing next to me, interrupted. 'So you think people aren't satisfied?'

The boy looked frightened. 'I didn't say that, Señor.'

'You said they were poor. It sounds to me as though you are filled with Red ideas yourself.'

Dick and I walked away and Captain Aguilera and the Major came after us. 'That's the sort of thing we must stamp out,' said Aguilera.

'Oh, well,' sighed the Major, 'it is all very confusing. When the war is over, I'm going back to *Vogue*.'

* * *

I decided that I had had enough of Spain. I asked Major Lombarri for a car to return to Salamanca, but he said there wouldn't be one available for several days. In the meantime, he suggested that I take a trip to Oviedo, a town in Asturias, that had been captured by General Franco in the early days of the war. The mountains surrounding it were still held by the Republicans, and for over a year it had been subjected to constant artillery and aerial bombardment.

I was anxious to compare it with Madrid, but when I heard that the party (which consisted of two German and Russian photographers) was to be conducted by Captain Aguilera, I hesitated. Ever since my unfortunate remark about the Republicans blowing up the bridges not merely for the joy of destruction but to slow down the enemy advance, Aguilera had regarded me as Red, and our relationship was far from friendly. Nevertheless, I finally decided it was foolish to let personal animosity stand in the way and agreed to go, determined to get on with him as best I could. Before the trip was over I realised I had made a mistake.

It took about five or six hours to get to Oviedo, as most of the drive was through the mountains. The road leading down to the old town, which lay in a valley, was under continuous shell-fire; as it was the only road open, food-trucks and official cars were forced to run the gauntlet daily. The driver accelerated and we made a hectic dash down the hill – to my way of thinking much more in danger of breaking an axle on the shell-holes in the road than from receiving a hit. From the top of the hill Oviedo had presented an ordinary appearance, but when we drove into it, it was hard to believe anyone could still be living there. It looked as though it had been struck by a hurricane. Not a single building or house had escaped damage; some of them looked like stage sets with the walls pulled off; others like birthday cakes with holes scooped out of the centre.

Although the normal population of thirty thousand people had been evacuated, there were about fifteen hundred civilians who still clung to their homes. Most of them lived in the basements of ruined buildings, scurrying in and out of their retreats as though they had been accustomed to it all their lives. The main café was open, but as the window-glass had long ago been shattered, the wind whistled through the room, and customers sat drinking their coffee with coat-collars wrapped tightly round their necks.

All day long there was the dull thud of shells dropping sporadically into the town, but no one seemed to mind: bands of ragged children played games in the middle of the street, a bootblack stood on the curb shouting for customers, and at the corner an old lady argued with the butcher over a cut of beef.

The hotel I slept in (a hotel in the main street, the name of which I have forgotten) had been hit by shells sixteen times. There were only three rooms left, but the proprietor was still doing business. He was an agreeable little man who insisted that 'the lady must have the best room'. He led me into it, apologising for the jagged shell-hole over the bed. There was no electricity, so he left the candle and said that if the bombardment got bad in the night to come down to the cellar. He added that when the war was over he had plans for a better hotel; he hadn't the money to build it, of course, but that would have to take care of itself. With peace, he said, everything would come.

I was learning that to the civilian population of a country, war was seldom interpreted in terms of military strategy and high-sounding 'isms'. War meant soaring prices, lack of food, and houses with bomb-holes in them. Their opinions were influenced largely by the effect it had on their personal lives. Government officials answered you in terms of politics, soldiers in terms of strategy, and civilians in terms of domestic upheaval.

We spent only one night in Oviedo. Captain Aguilera took us to dinner with the Colonel, and the room we dined in had a gaping shell-hole, covered by strips of brown paper, in the wall. The blinds were tightly drawn and two candles flickering on the table provided the only light. I don't remember much about the evening except that the Colonel seemed pleased to have visitors and gave us a surprisingly elaborate dinner. I talked to one of the officers, who said the war would soon be over and prophesied that Franco would spend Easter in Barcelona. As we sat there we heard the sound of explosions outside; the wind moaned eerily through the gap in the wall and it all seemed like a strange dream.

Aguilera and I had not had any conversation since the trip began, but the following morning I received a message telling me to be ready to leave at eight-thirty. After a breakfast of coffee and dry bread we got into the car and drove to the outskirts of the city. The

chauffeur pulled up at the corner of a small shopping street, not far
from where the communication trenches started which marked the
beginning of the Nationalist trenches. Aguilera conferred with the
photographers in German, then turned to me and said they wanted
to take some pictures and would return in ten minutes. They disappeared round the corner and came back two hours later. The
street was almost deserted save for an empty grocer's shop and a
small pâtisserie which did not seem to be doing much of a business.
All morning long there was the crash of shells falling into the town.
No one stayed in the open more than they could help, and people
scurried along the streets, every now and then darting into doorways for cover. As the minutes turned into hours I suspected that
Aguilera had left me in the car on purpose; as, I suppose, a form
of reprisal. When he came back he didn't apologise, but said: 'Now
we will say goodbye to the Colonel and return to León.' We drew
up before the Colonel's house, but I told Aguilera he would have
to pay my respects for me. He received this indignantly, as it was
obviously to his advantage to present a genial and smiling party to
his superior officer. I refused to go in with him, however, and when
he came out his face was still red with anger. 'You have insulted the
Nationalist cause,' he said. 'You will hear more of this later.'

I realised that our feud had reached a climax and knew that
he was not an enemy to take lightly. However, as I was planning
to return to France, I wasn't particularly worried until I reached
Salamanca and went in to see Pablo Merry del Val. When I told
him I wanted to leave Spain and asked for the necessary travelling
permits, he replied coldly that no press cars were available and it
was impossible to grant me permission to travel by train. 'You will
remain here,' he said, 'until you hear further from us.'

I guessed that Aguilera had already sent in a report against
me. I knew he wouldn't hesitate to launch any accusation that

suited him, however serious. As two American correspondents, H. R. Knickerbocker and Webb Miller (not to mention several English journalists), had already seen the inside of a Spanish gaol, I knew my passport would be of little use if the authorities pointed out that I had been on the Republican side and chose to launch a spy charge against me.

I realised it was dangerous to remain in Salamanca and decided to try and make my own way to Burgos, then on to San Sebastian. As it was impossible to travel in Nationalist territory without a government authorisation, I was at a loss as to how to go about it. Luckily I ran into the Duc de Montellano, a friend of Rupert Bellville, whom I had met in San Sebastian; when I told him I wanted to go to Burgos, he replied that his wife and sister-in-law were leaving by car in an hour and would take me with them.

The Duchess was an amiable little woman; she told me that before the war her house in Madrid had been leased to the American Ambassador, Claud Bowers. Although none of the dip-lomats were there it was still used as an Embassy, and she was delighted to hear that her paintings and furniture were safe. We were stopped several times along the road by sentries, but they were satisfied with the car permits and waved us on. We reached Burgos in the afternoon and I said goodbye to them in the Hotel Norte y Grande. I remember the hotel well, for on the wall was a large poster advertising a bull-fight. It pictured Domingo Ortego, the famous matador, killing a particularly gory bull. Beneath was the sentence: 'For the benefit of the Red Cross'.

I discovered that the city was overflowing and not a room to be had anywhere. There was no American or British Consulate and I had neither friends nor acquaintances to go to. I went to a café to think out a plan; in the back of my mind I remembered some-one remarking vaguely that Count Cosme Churrucca, a Spaniard whom I had met in the Philippines several years before, was on the general staff in Burgos. I wrote him a note and sent the hotel porter over to the War Ministry with it. I didn't expect any results. I felt it would be too good a stroke of luck to find him there, and was racking my brain for an alternative when to my astonishment he came through the door wreathed in smiles. I explained I was stranded and he told me he was going to San Sebastian in the morning and would take me with him. For the night he offered me a room in his sister-in-law's flat.

So far I had been incredibly lucky, but I realised even in San Sebastian the difficulties would be only half over. I sent Tommy Thompson a telegram suggesting lunch, hoping he would take the hint and come across the frontier to meet me.

When I had last known Cosme Churrucca he was an amiable, care-free man who lived a pleasant life in Manila. Now I found he had been transformed into an excitable Fascist. He talked heatedly about the decadence of the democracies and asserted fiercely that when the war was over, Germany, Italy and Spain would fall on France and divide her into three parts: the north for Germany, the Riviera for Italy and the Basque coast for Spain. Leaving Paris for the French, he added, because they ran it so well.

On arriving at San Sebastian I went directly to the Maria Cristina Hotel. I had the good fortune to run into Eddie Neil of the Associated Press (who was killed at the front a few weeks later with Dick Sheepshanks when a shell hit their car), who took me to Chicote's bar for a cocktail. It was noisy and gay and seemed so far removed from the bitterness of war I was beginning to wonder whether perhaps I hadn't imagined the trouble in Salamanca, when a Dutch journalist came up to me and said: 'What a surprise! I thought you were in gaol.' He explained he had heard a rumour in Saint Jean-de-Luz that I had been arrested.

This didn't indicate a very friendly atmosphere and that night I slept uneasily, half expecting to hear footsteps along the corridor, a knock on the door, and the voice of the police. The morning came with no such spectacular developments and, to my great relief, about twelve-thirty I had a message that Tommy was downstairs. He, too, had heard from Philby of *The Times* the rumour of my arrest. When he got my telegram, he called at the office of the Military Governor at Irun and was told that I could leave Spain if I had a permit from GHQ. That, of course, was the hitch! He thought that to ask for one would probably only serve to call official attention to the fact I was in San Sebastian without authority. Once again the frontier was closed, and after discussing the situation for some time, he decided the only solution was to take a chance and to drive out in his car in the hope that the sentries would let us go through without trouble.

I shall never forget approaching the International Bridge. The Union Jack was fluttering bravely from the radiator cap, and when the Spanish guards stopped us, Tommy handed them his *salvo conducto*. They inspected it carefully and I waited for the terrible moment when they would turn to me. It never came; they nodded with a satisfied air, handed back the paper and saluted. The barriers rose slowly, Tommy stepped on the gas, and we dashed across the bridge to freedom. I have never been back to Nationalist Spain since, and have often wondered whether Pablo Merry del Val was surprised by my strange disappearance. Whether or not I really escaped from the clutches of the police, I have never discovered. But I certainly enjoyed my cocktail at the Bar Basque.

* * *

The orderly life of France with its peaceful villages seemed like a different world after the chaos of Spain. It was here that I heard the story of Rupert Bellville. He had flown to Santander with a young Spaniard by the name of Ricardo Gonzalles. When they got out of the plane, crying '*Viva Franco!*', they had promptly been arrested by Republican officers who were still in charge of the aerodrome. As the town was about to capitulate, Rupert was forced to fly two officials to the safety of Gijon. Once there, he was put in gaol. In the meantime, his friend Ricardo had been placed under the custody of two young army officers. He pretended to be an Englishman and said he couldn't understand Spanish. He then had the unpleasant experience of listening to them debate whether or not to shoot him. According to Ricardo's story, they were still arguing when a soldier dashed up on a motorcycle and announced that Franco's vanguard was marching into the city. One of the officers turned to him, ripped the insignia off his own coat, and said dramatically: 'It is not you who will die today.' Then he took out his revolver, went to the other side of a hill, and shot himself.

The British Embassy at Hendaye made representations on Rupert's behalf and, finally, after a good deal of argument, the anarchist Governor of Gijon agreed to release him on the condition that a British warship picked him up.

Rupert had been shaken by his experience. From one day to the next he hadn't known whether he was going to be shot, and several times, when Gijon was bombed, angry crowds had mobbed the gaol and shouted for the blood of the 'Fascist' prisoners. When Rupert landed in France he was met by a barrage of reporters and the *Evening Standard* paid him five hundred pounds for an exclusive story. He lost it the same night gambling in the casino at Biarritz.

I heard later that the Governor of Gijon had entrusted Rupert with a letter, painstakingly typed in English, saying he would accept the assurance of the British Embassy that the prisoner he was releasing was not a spy but merely an 'irresponsible'. The letter went on to add that Rupert was being given his freedom unconditionally; nevertheless, he would venture to mention the names of certain prisoners – friends of his – who were in the hands of the Nationalists, in case it should be possible to arrange an exchange. Months later Tommy told me representations had been made to the Franco authorities but without success.

Although the anarchist governor was only a name to me, I have often wondered how his story ended.

Part III

SPRING SHADOWS

1

London

On Christmas Day, 1937, my taxi-cab crawled down Piccadilly in a fog so thick the driver kept the car in low gear, every now and then jamming on the brakes as objects loomed up eerily a few inches ahead. I had been in London fogs before, but never in a black one. This was like a cloud of dark, suffocating smoke. It smothered the street lamps and even rolled into the houses, throwing a gloomy shroud over the Christmas trees. It hung over the whole capital like a dark angel that had spread its wings with a terrible prophecy for the future. This was the Christmas before the German occupation of Austria; the last Christmas that the rights of sovereign states were to be respected on the European continent.

Living in London that winter, and hearing the sound and fury across the Channel, was like sitting too near an orchestra and being deafened by the rising crescendo of the brass instruments. But apart from the threat of world events, I found London perilous in itself. The lack of central heating, the fogs, the left-hand traffic, and the crooked, twisting streets offered hazards almost as great as the international situation.

Although my contract with the Hearst papers had ended, I decided to settle down in England for a few months before returning to New York, and took a small flat in Eaton Mews, in which a dog named Pickles and a caretaker named Mrs Sullivan were included. Mrs Sullivan came every morning to cook my breakfast, left at noon, and returned in the afternoon to get tea. She was an enormous woman, weighing over fourteen stone, and during the whole time I knew her, never once took off her hat. Even when she brought my tray in the morning, a black felt creation with a red rose was perched firmly on top of her head. No matter what the weather was like (and the sun rarely shone), she always came in with Pickles barking at her heels, saying: 'It's a fine day, miss. Nothing to grumble about.'

Mrs Sullivan used to do exactly as she wished, and on rainy days didn't appear at all. I never reprimanded her, for a few days after I arrived I realised she was not a woman to quarrel with. One morning she came in with breakfast and told me she had just strangled her neighbour, 'Until she was black as your dress, miss.'

Startled out of my sleep, I learned the row had started over hanging out the washing. 'She inferred that I wasn't respectable,' said Mrs Sullivan indignantly. 'She even insinuated I earned my money off the streets.'

With Mrs Sullivan's portentous appearance, this almost could have been accepted as a compliment, but she regarded it as the gravest insult. I asked her if she wouldn't get into trouble for prosecuting the matter herself, but she replied gleefully that the unfortunate neighbour kept lodgers in the basement, which was against the law. 'I've got the upper hand, miss. She won't dare make any complaints.' After that, Mrs Sullivan ran my flat as she saw fit.

I loved London. I had a number of English friends who were very kind (particularly Sir Philip and Lady Chetwode, whom my sister and I had met in India), and soon found myself on a round of lunches and dinners. From a journalist's point of view I had arrived at an opportune moment, for there was a pressing demand for articles on Spain; conversationally, the war was almost an obsession. It was like a crystal that held all the shades of the rainbow; you turned it to the light and chose the colours that suited you. The issues were argued passionately on widely different grounds: Democracy versus Fascism; Fascism versus Bolshevism; Bolshevism versus Religion; Religion versus the Republic; the Republic versus the Aristocracy; the Aristocracy versus Bolshevism.

Everyone had an opinion, but save for Left and Right extremists (who advocated immediate intervention), it was the opinion of the onlooker. The mass of people supported Great Britain's policy of non-intervention, and one London paper (I think it was the *Express*) advocated that all Spaniards should be evacuated so that the foreigners could fight it out.

My own views on Spain had become clearly defined. Although my sympathies lay with the struggle of the Republic against the military and landlord class, rebelling to recapture their old-time privileges, I couldn't believe that democracy would emerge from the war, no matter who won. In Republican Spain I felt the Communist Party had grown too strong ever to relinquish its hold. Vincent Sheean, in his book *The Eleventh Hour*, wrote that it had become 'the most powerful single party in Spain', but somehow reached the surprising conclusion that the Communists were not fighting for Communism but to re-establish a bourgeois republic. I was unable to accept this reasoning, but even so felt that from an international point of view the Communist menace was far less dangerous than the Fascist menace.

I wrote this in an article which appeared in the London *Sunday Times*, emphasising that the Germans and Italians were far less concerned about fighting 'Bolshevism' than in preparing the ground, politically and strategically, and training their armies for the day when they could expand at the expense of Great Britain and France.

A few days before the article was published, I gave a copy to Tommy Thompson (then on short leave from Spain), who sent it to the head of the News Department, Rex Leeper, and the following morning I had a telephone message asking me to come to see Sir Robert Vansittart, who was then the permanent Under-Secretary of State for Foreign Affairs.

I had often heard of Sir Robert, but visualised him as a mysterious figure whom no one ever met. His name was not well known to the general public, but he wielded more influence than most members of the Cabinet. As the head of the Foreign Office, reports flowed into his desk from all over the world, and it was his job to piece them together and advise the Foreign Secretary on the proper course to adopt. He rarely appeared in the limelight, but his views were speculated on as instrumental in shaping British policy.

In spite of the aura of mystery that shrouded Vansittart, he was one of the most simple men I have ever met. Perhaps I expected a slightly sinister character; at any rate, I was completely taken aback by a tall, handsome man in his early fifties with a carnation in his buttonhole, a pair of keen brown eyes and a charming smile. When his secretary led me into his office he looked almost as surprised as I, for he told me later that from my article he had expected a middle-aged woman with flat-heeled shoes and a man's tie.

We talked about German and Italian intervention in Spain and it wasn't difficult to gauge what Vansittart thought of the policy of appeasement. 'They're trying to lead the world back to the Dark Ages. And if we don't wake up in time, here in England, they may succeed in doing it.' Sir Robert had over thirty-five years' experience in diplomacy and it wasn't difficult for him to recognise Nazi Germany as a grave menace to the British Empire. But apart from this, he abhorred the philosophy of National Socialism and expressed his views vigorously – which reminded me of the comment Webb Miller, the United Press correspondent, had made after talking with Vansittart and Major Attlee on the same afternoon.

Webb had left with a puzzled air. 'They seem to have switched their roles,' he said, 'for Attlee was as reserved as a diplomat while Sir Robert spoke like the Leader of the Opposition.'

Vansittart was already courageously bucking the tide of appeasement, but the current was growing too strong. He watched with anxiety the increasing lawlessness on the continent and I remember an ironical comment he made on the contempt with which treaties and promises were already regarded. Somehow or other, we got on to the subject of the archives in the Foreign Office and he told me that not only were official documents treated with respect, but even scrap paper made a dignified exit. Every evening a man came along the corridors wheeling a bin marked 'Confidential Waste'. The scraps were then taken under escort to an incinerator and burned. One day, Sir Robert said, something went wrong with the incinerator and the papers blew up the chimney and scattered all over London. For weeks, aged gardeners and conscientious taxi drivers were picking up formidable reports marked 'This document is the property of His Britannic Majesty's Government' and returning them to the sanctity of the Foreign Office. 'Just as treaties are now blowing over Europe,' he added ironically. 'Except that nobody bothers to pick them up.'

This was the beginning of a friendship with Sir Robert and his wife Sarita; during the next three years I lunched and dined with them often. If Vansittart's warnings and prophecies should ever be published, they will chronicle the events of the past few years with astonishing accuracy. Unfortunately, his opposition to the increasing aggression of Germany made him one of the first sacrifices on the altar of appeasement, and shortly after that black, gloomy Christmas of 1937, he was removed as the chief of the Foreign Office and replaced by Sir Alexander Cadogan. Although Sir Robert was given the post of Chief Diplomatic Adviser to the Government, and remained in contact with the affairs of the office, Mr Chamberlain and Lord Halifax rarely sought his advice. Winston Churchill, however, was a close personal friend.

* * *

Churchill was appeasement's most vigorous opponent. The official opposition in the House of Commons, the Labour Party (which at the General Election in 1935 had used the slogan 'Armaments Mean War – Vote Labour') discredited itself by urging firm action against the dictators, yet refusing to vote for more arms. The only effective opposition, therefore, was Mr Churchill, who believed not only in strong words but in the capacity to appear formidable. That autumn the names Chamberlain and Churchill became identified with two conflicting schools of thought on foreign policy.

Now, British foreign policy has often been presented in a Machiavellian light, but on looking through the pages of history, few policies have been so consistent. It has always been shaped for one purpose and one purpose only: to maintain and ensure the safety of the Empire. Both Churchill and Chamberlain held this interest in common, but their conceptions of how best it could be guarded bore little resemblance. Whereas Mr Chamberlain believed security lay in a compromise between the four great powers of Europe (England, France, Germany and Italy), Mr Churchill turned to the lessons of the past. Through centuries, England's security had been based on maintaining a balance of power; she had always been the friend of the second strongest power on the continent.

This formula was expressed in 1907 by Sir Eyre Crowe, a member of the Foreign Office, who wrote:

The only check on the use of political predominance has always consisted in the opposition of an equally formidable rival or a combination of several countries forming a league of defence. The equilibrium established by such a group of forces is technically known as the Balance of Power, and it has been a historical truism to identify England's secular policy with the maintenance of this balance by throwing her weight now on this scale, now on that, but ever on the side opposed to political dictatorship of the strongest single state or group of states at a given time.

If this view of British policy is correct, the opposition to which England must inevitably be driven by any country aspiring to such dictatorship assumes almost the form of a law of Nature . . .

In all the wars of history England had followed this policy. When Napoleon threatened Europe she lined up with Prussia, and when Prussia threatened Europe she lined up with France. Now once again Germany threatened to establish a hegemony, and Churchill knew that England must inevitably oppose her.

Unfortunately, Chamberlain was in power and Churchill was not. Although both men claimed the courses they advocated were the only courses which, in the final analysis, would prevent war, Mr Chamberlain received the backing of the majority in the House of Commons who had not yet grasped the fact that the ears of the dictators were immune to the murmur of the conference tables, and the only noise that could penetrate was the roll of guns and the roar of planes. It is true both men favoured rearmament, but whereas Churchill advocated it, wholeheartedly, to make his policy *succeed*, Chamberlain advocated it, halfheartedly, in case his policy *failed*. That was the difference; and, as John Kennedy wrote in *Why England Slept*: 'A boxer cannot work himself into proper psychological and physical condition for a fight that he seriously believes will never come off. It was the same with England.'

* * *

Churchill's voice rang through the House of Commons with little effect and Chamberlain quietly set out to appease. First, Lord Halifax went to Berlin on the pretext of viewing a hunting exhibition and opened conversations with Hitler at Berchtesgaden; then a month or two later, Lady Chamberlain (widow of Sir Austen) went to Rome to feel Mussolini's pulse and to report on the likelihood of an Anglo–Italian agreement. Meanwhile, everyone in London society discussed the moves with passionate interest. Dinner tables and drawing rooms became far more controversial than Parliament, for in private people could be as rude as they liked.

What surprised me most about these gatherings was that everyone seemed to have known everyone else since childhood. When they argued it was like a huge family wrangling among itself, each delighted to score at the other's expense, yet underneath bound by a strong bond of loyalty. Opponents who crossed sharp swords politically played golf together over the weekends; Chamberlainites and Churchillites made bridge foursomes, and the pro-Hitler Mitford family were cousins and friends of the pro-Churchill Churchill family. All this was peculiar to the English parliamentary system, which, as John Gunther says, is played in the grand manner. 'After an election the opposing candidates shake hands exactly as if it had been a game of tennis. When Baldwin became Prime Minister for the first time, one of the first things he did was to call on Lord Oxford, his most eminent adversary, to ask advice.'

It all seemed like an exciting game (dangerously removed from the grim reality of the continent) and even the women forsook social gossip for political speculations. In the morning there were long telephone conversations. 'But, darling, Mussolini *can't* like Hitler. It's simply not on.' When the rift between Eden's Foreign Office policy and Chamberlain's appeasement policy had reached breaking point, Lady Abingdon rang me up, remonstrating indignantly: 'I've just talked to Bill Astor, and do you know what he says? He says, if our foreign policy ever gets into the hands of the Foreign Office, we're sunk. Now, fancy that!'

The only rest from political conversation was Mrs Sullivan, who was far more interested in her neighbours' opinions than those of Herr Hitler. One morning I asked her what she thought of the Prime Minister, and, to my surprise, she replied: 'Now, what's 'is name, miss? Sir Samuel 'Oare, is it?'

In the end she disappointed me, for one day she came in with news that had a slight political tinge, declaring that Lord Halifax (who lived in Eaton Square) had pensioned off one of his housemaids because she drank too much. According to Mrs Sullivan, the woman refused to leave: 'She just sits up in the attic all day drinking gin and moaning. Sounds a bit queer in the head, doesn't she?' What worried Mrs Sullivan the most was the fact that the maid owed her five shillings. A few days later she succeeded in collecting it and then her interest waned. I never heard the end of the drama, but I could never see Lord Halifax's serene countenance without wondering whether she was still there, moaning in the attic.

* * *

When the study of the pre-war House of Commons is written, the name of Captain David Margesson, former Chief Whip of the Conservative Party, will assume a prominent position. It was his job to keep the House in line with the Prime Minister's policy, and he did it so thoroughly that he won its members an unenviable place in the annals of history. Suave and good-looking, Captain Margesson was bitterly attacked by the Opposition and referred to by the press as the 'Himmler' of England. The first time I met him he protested to me, saying: 'Where do the press get all these idiotic ideas? I'm only a humble Whip. I have no authority. I only do as I'm told.' His modesty was unwarranted, for Margesson's power lay not only in the fact that he controlled the patronage lists (by which the faithful were rewarded with knighthoods and peerages), but chiefly because Chamberlain was known to accept his advice on political appointments. Recently, when asked what he regretted most in his career, he replied: 'Not pressing for Churchill's inclusion in the Cabinet when Lord Swinton resigned.'

However, the truth of the matter was that Margesson's authority lay not so much in his own activity as in the inertia of the House of Commons. At any time, Tory MPs could have insisted upon more vigorous rearmament; at any time the public could have made itself felt. But the fact was that the general mass of people in England (like the mass of people in America today) refused to be aroused by words. War was still an unreal bogey to them, and in spite of the persistent warnings of Mr Churchill it took events, and events alone, finally to awaken them.

There were always heated assertions that the general lethargy of this period was due to a self-imposed censorship of the press. It is true that each newspaper interpreted the news, either playing it down or building it up according to the views of the publisher, but the 'Press Lords' represented a wide variety of opinion. The scale ranged from the Conservative *Times* to the Communist *Daily Worker*; of the two 'popular' dailies, the *Mail* prophesied horrible havoc by the German Air Force, while the *Express* cheerfully asserted that sunny days lay ahead. Every morning the *Express* ran a streamer across the front page, saying: 'There will be no war.'

When I asked Lord Beaverbrook why he took such a firm stand on so shaky a limb, he replied: 'Other people can be wrong a dozen times. But I can be wrong only once.'

Of all the 'Press Lords', Beaverbrook (the leading advocate of 'Splendid Isolation') had the most striking personality. He was a small, gnome-like man who lived in a large and solemn house near St James's Palace. Born in Canada, a poor boy, he was reputed to have made over a million dollars before he was thirty. He had come to England shortly before the war and in 1918 bought the *Daily Express* and raised the circulation from three hundred and fifty thousand to two and a half million – the largest daily circulation in the world. His brilliant, hard-headed business sense was combined with a strange, almost feminine, curiosity in human beings. When I first arrived in England I worked on his *Evening Standard* for a few weeks, and several times the telephone rang for me in the afternoon with Beaverbrook's voice at the other end: 'Wal! What are you doing now?' Then he would suggest that I come over to Stornoway House for a cup of tea. I always arrived to find him surrounded by papers, dictaphones and secretaries. Tea was usually interrupted half a dozen times by messages and telephone calls, but he seemed to enjoy the general state of confusion, which he punctuated by a series of surprising questions flung across the room at me: 'What people *don't* you like in England? Why did you come here, anyway? Who are you in love with?'

Beaverbrook enjoyed being provocative. Complacency was as tempting to him as a balloon to a small boy with a pin. He liked to draw out antagonisms among his guests, until they all fell wrangling among each other, then sit back and watch. But he was provocative not only at other people's expense. You often picked up one of his newspapers and read an audacious paragraph about himself; it was always under the signature of one of his feature writers but reputedly dictated by 'the Beaver' for the pleasure he got from the astonishment it caused. To give you a small idea: one day I picked up the *Sunday Express*, to read under Peter Howard's signature the following paragraph:

> Strange, is it not, that so few newspaper peers have lifted up their voices in the House of Lords? So far as I can discover, my Lords Camrose, Kemsley, Iliffe, and Southwood have yet to make their maiden speeches in the Upper Chamber. Lord Rothermere has spoken there, Lord Beaverbrook also is maiden no more, so far as the House of Lords is concerned. He is the only newspaper peer who has engaged in prolonged political controversy on the debating floor of the House of Lords. Lord Beaverbrook is always complaining about others that they want their palm without the dust. This is exactly his own condition. He wants power without working for it. He imagines himself to be ill. He walks out of the arena and takes his place in the grandstand. From there he wishes to continue to take a part in the game. Lord Baldwin once said of him that he desired to exercise power without responsibility, the prerogative of the harlot throughout the ages . . .

* * *

One of my colleagues on the *Evening Standard* was Randolph Churchill, the son of Winston. I had known Randolph in New York; he was a fiery young man of twenty-seven who had wanted to fight the Germans ever since their occupation of the Rhineland in 1936, and who bitterly attacked the policy of appeasement at any opportunity, whether given or not given. I greatly admired the courage with which he launched his views; nevertheless, going out with him was like going out with a time bomb. Wherever he went an explosion seemed to follow. With a natural and brilliant gift of oratory, and a disregard for the opinions of his elders, he often held dinner parties pinned in a helpless and angry silence. I never knew a young man who had the ability to antagonise more easily. When I once told him he ought to be less tactless, he replied: 'Nonsense! My father used to be even ruder than I am. These pusillanimous Chamberlainites – they need someone to give it to them!'

Randolph was charming with people whose views he considered 'sound'. One of these was Sir Robert Vansittart, and occasionally we lunched there together. Another was Lloyd George, and one day Randolph drove me down to his house in the country. My article on Spain, published in the *Sunday Times*, had been quoted by Lloyd George in the House of Commons; it was unsigned and he had referred to the writer in the masculine gender. Randolph didn't tell him anything about me, merely that he was bringing the 'author' to lunch, and when I stepped out of the car the old man regarded me with surprise that almost bordered on resentment. I suppose it was a nasty shock to find that the eminent authority he had quoted was just a green young woman.

At any rate, lunch was delicious, provided entirely from his own farm. Afterwards he took us around showing us his chickens, pigs and cows, and as he sloshed across the fields he looked almost like an ancient prophet with his green cloak and his long white hair blowing in the wind, his blue eyes sparkling, and his cheeks pink from the cold.

At tea he argued with Randolph on the international situation; he picked up a stick and pointed to a huge map on the wall, declaring that England had never before been in such a desperate strategic position as she was at the present time. He was in favour of immediate help to the Spanish Republic, and when Randolph asked him why he had become such an active partisan, he replied with a twinkle: 'I always line up on the side against the priests.'

By the time we left, he seemed to have forgiven me for not being a general, and presented me with a jar of honey and a dozen apples from the farm. Mrs Sullivan was impressed. Not at first, but after her husband had explained to her who Lloyd George was. When she appeared the next morning, she said brightly: 'My old man says Mr Lloyd George 'as got more fire in 'im than all the others put together. They ought to stop 'im growing apples and get 'im back in the Government. But I say it would be an awful pity. I don't know *when* I've seen such fine big apples.' I told her to help herself and she went off humming a tune.

Randolph had begun compiling a collection of the speeches his father had made in the House of Commons, which were later published under the title *While England Slept*. His flat was cluttered with Hansards, and he worked feverishly, prefacing each speech with appropriate dates, and quotations giving the background. Needless to say, he had an enormous admiration for his father, and one Sunday drove me down to the Churchills' country house, Chartwell, where I met his family for the first time.

We arrived to find Mary Churchill, his fourteen-year-old sister, in the stable inspecting a newly born lamb; Mrs Churchill in the garden talking to her neighbour, Miss Henrietta Seymour; and Mr Churchill down by the pond, in a torn coat and a battered hat, prodding the water with a stick, looking for his pet goldfish, which seemed to have disappeared.

The most endearing thing about the Churchill offspring was the deep affection they showered on Winston. It was understandable, for everything about him had a human touch that drew one to him instantly. When we walked back to the house he said to Randolph: 'Oh, I forgot my galoshes. Now, don't tell Clemmie or she'll scold me!'

Clemmie was Mrs Churchill. She was a tall, handsome woman, obviously adored by her husband; you caught him looking at her to see whether his jokes had gone down well. During lunch there was a general discussion of the topics of the day, and Mr Churchill spoke critically and sadly of the Government's inability to see the rising storm on the continent. 'They can't seem to understand that we live in a very wicked world,' he said. 'English people want to be left alone, and I daresay a great many other people want to be left alone, too. But the world is like a tired old horse plodding down a long road. Every time it strays off and tries to graze peacefully in some nice green pasture, along comes a new master to flog it a bit further down the road. No matter how much people want to be left alone, they can't escape.'

After lunch we walked down to the cottage on the estate where Mr Churchill kept his paintings. (The cottage, incidentally, had been built by himself. He had worked on the job with a professional bricklayer until he had learnt to lay a brick a minute, then, in 1928, had created a sensation by joining the Amalgamated Union of Building Trade Workers as an 'adult apprentice', paying an entrance fee of five shillings. This created considerable controversy in the Trade Union world, which considered it 'humiliating and degrading buffoonery'; nevertheless, bricklayer he was and bricklayer he remained.)

Painting was Churchill's favourite hobby, and there were thirty or forty pictures in the cottage – mostly landscapes done in oils. He said he regretted the fact that lately he had been too busy to go on with it. 'With all the fascinating things there are to do in the world,' he reflected, 'it's odd to think that some people actually while away the time by playing Patience. Just fancy.'

Since that day, Hitler has learned that 'Patience' is not one of Mr Churchill's vices.

2

The Policy of Appeasement

I walked into the Ritz in Barcelona (past a block of flats demolished by a bomb) to find the lobby thronged with soldiers and girls in cheap dresses who had come for the Sunday afternoon tea dance. I was pushing my way through the crowd, looking for a telephone box, when I heard a voice say 'Hello,' and looked around to find a young Spaniard, Ignacio Lombarte, whom I hadn't seen since I was in Madrid nearly a year before.

He looked older than when I had last seen him; he had been wounded at Teruel and come to Barcelona on a few days' leave. 'It's good to see you again,' he said. 'Are you enjoying yourself?'

Now 'enjoyment' was the last word I would have associated with Spain that February 1938. Franco's troops were driving towards the sea, and the morale of Catalonia was almost at breaking point. During the last few days I had found little besides starvation, terror and misery. At the Hotel Majestic the waiters scraped the food plates for scraps to take home to their families, and in the country people bartered soap, coal and clothes with the peasants for enough to keep them alive. I talked with a girl who was elated to have exchanged a bag of coal for two pounds of chocolate.

But even worse than hunger were the air-raids. On a three-day drive along the coast to Valencia and back I had passed hundreds of refugees fleeing from their homes to more secure spots in the interior. Scarcely a town had escaped. All along the way there were ghastly ruins; and even in the desolation there was no relief, for every few hours the countryside resounded with the wail of sirens as more bombers appeared from their bases in Majorca. The inability to hit back and the rumour that Italy and Germany were increasing their supply of planes to Spain had filled many people with despair.

I heard my friend, Ignacio Lombarte, repeating his question, 'Are you enjoying yourself?' and I nodded, not knowing what to say, and told him I had come for only a week and was returning to London in the morning. 'You have other things to do?' he asked. Then, without waiting for a reply, 'I understand. Soon new things will be happening. We are only the first.'

I thought of his words, 'We are only the first', when I reached London, for the stage hands were already setting the scene for the second phase of the European drama. You could read the cues in your morning papers, for in that month of February Hitler took control of the German Army, Herr von Ribbentrop became the Foreign Minister, Anthony Eden resigned from the British Cabinet, and Mussolini introduced the goose-step (*passo Romano*) into the Italian Army. Finally, the set was ready and Herr von Schüssnig, the Austrian Chancellor, was summoned to Berchtesgaden.

The world waited fearfully and a month later the curtain rose. Hitler's planes circled over Vienna and his troops poured across the Austrian frontier. In London, the tension rose to a higher pitch than at any time since the Great War. Silent crowds gathered in Downing Street to watch the Cabinet ministers leaving their hastily summoned meeting, while newsboys cried out to a cold, grey world: 'Germany on the march again.'

The fear of immediate war hung in the air like poison gas. Worried speculation ran the gamut from saloons to fashionable London drawing rooms. There was a general rush of volunteers to ambulance services and air-raid precaution organisations, and hundreds of young businessmen signed up with the Territorial Army. Everywhere there was a cry for more arms.

The tension, however, was like a high-voltage wire. Mr Chamberlain succeeded in turning down the current by declaring with renewed (and inexplicable) confidence that there was little likelihood of a conflict in which England would be involved; *The Times* ran leading articles emphasising the enthusiasm with which thousands of Viennese welcomed the Nazi regime; and the Archbishop of Canterbury rose in the House of Lords to say that Hitler should be thanked for preserving Austria from a civil war.

'Why all the gloom?' cried Lord Beaverbrook, and the catchword stuck. 'Why all the gloom?' echoed the public, and settled back in its comfortable illusion of peace.

This complacency was difficult to understand. Great Britain's prestige was lower than at any time since Napoleon. Her ships were bombed and her ultimata ignored; her Government was excoriated and her people pronounced effete. The aggressor nations had pulled off one successful coup after another. During the past three years, Mussolini had conquered Abyssinia, Hitler had occupied the Rhineland and absorbed Austria, Japan had seized the Yangtse, threatening vast sums of British capital, and in Spain General Franco, with the aid of the dictator powers, was on the verge of establishing a regime which showed every indication of affiliating itself with the Rome–Berlin Axis. Although only nineteen years before, the peace of Versailles was signed, and, under the Covenant of the League of Nations, the world seemed to be approaching a genuine international understanding, Europe was now split into irreconcilable camps. The air was charged with the drone of aircraft, while a militant spirit more fierce and ruthless than ever before was trampling half the continent.

To understand British policy at that time, however, it must be emphasised that the Government did not accept the situation at its face value. Chamberlain was banking on the following beliefs: first, that although the procedure might be a lengthy one, it would be possible to detach Italy from the Rome–Berlin Axis; second, that although General Franco was sympathetic to Italy and Germany, he would eventually be forced to London for a loan; and, third, that although Germany might wish to dominate Central Europe, she had no fundamental quarrel with England.

Working on these hypotheses, Chamberlain had not been idle. Although Great Britain still recognised the Government of Republican Spain, she had sent permanent representatives to Burgos. Although she had demanded that Italy withdraw her troops from Nationalist territory, she had overlooked Mussolini's refusal to do so, and hurriedly signed an Anglo–Italian agreement declaring her willingness to recognise Abyssinia. Although Germany had forcibly occupied Austria and shocked the world by her brutal treatment of the Jewish minority, England had warned the Czechoslovakians that they must be careful to treat the German minority with every consideration.

Mr Churchill had little faith in the success of these moves and pled desperately for more vigorous efforts at rearmament, pointing out that the situation had no parallel in history. The Empire had been menaced four times in four successive centuries: by Philip II of Spain, by Louis XIV, by Napoleon and by the German Kaiser. On all these occasions England had emerged victorious through the predominance of her sea power. This predominance enabled her to protect her island from invasion and at the same time send money and arms abroad and to form allied leagues against her enemies. Even when Napoleon dominated half of Europe and declared sanctions against England, boycotting her goods from all the ports beneath his control, Britain's command of the seas enabled her to develop an enormous smuggling trade, and to form four successive coalitions against him until he met defeat, first at

Trafalgar, finally at Waterloo. In the World War, once again it was British sea power, with its steady, persistent blockade, that finally crushed the German people.

But now England could no longer depend exclusively on her naval strength. When Blériot flew the Channel in 1909, the end of her impregnability was in sight, for the sea that had hitherto served as her guardian showed signs of transforming her into one of the most vulnerable nations of Europe. Her harbours and factories were open targets, and on these harbours and facto-ries her existence depended. Although she possessed the most powerful navy in the world, her General Staff was faced with the prospect of fighting on three fronts at once: in the Far East, in the Mediterranean, and in the North Sea. Even if the danger in the Orient were eliminated, her strategic position remained far graver than in 1914, for at that time the Mediterranean was blocked off, Spain was neutral, and Portugal and Italy her allies.

To fight, Britain needed more ships, arms and aircraft than ever before. The House of Commons undoubtedly agreed on this point, but who said Britain would have to fight? On every side one heard the phrase: 'Hitler doesn't want a war.' It was uttered with the same complacent conviction that one used to say: 'The French have the finest army in the world.' Some people claimed that Hitler's interest lay in the East – Russia was his real goal; others that he was only blowing the trumpet to recover his African colonies. Whatever the argument, a second war with Great Britain was unthinkable, and outsiders began to wonder if England would pass quietly away in a deep slumber.

I was in the House of Commons on March 24th, two weeks after the annexation of Austria, when Churchill made a dramatic and moving appeal. As I looked down from the Gallery, on the sea of black coats and white faces, he seemed only one man among many;

but when he spoke his words rang through the House with terrible
finality. He stood addressing the Speaker, his shoulders slightly
bent, his head thrust forward, and a hand in his waistcoat pocket.

For five years I have talked to the House on these matters –
not with very great success. I have watched this famous island
descending incontinently, fecklessly, the stairway which leads
to a dark gulf. It is a fine broad stairway at the beginning, but
after a bit the carpet ends. A little further on there are only
flagstones, and a little further on still these break beneath
your feet. Look back over the last five years. It is true that
great mistakes were made in the years immediately after the
War. But at Locarno we laid the foundation from which a
great forward movement could have been made. Look back
upon the last five years – since, that is to say, Germany began
to rearm in earnest and openly to seek revenge. If we study
the history of Rome and Carthage, we can understand what
happened and why. It is not difficult to form an intelligent
view about the three Punic Wars; but if mortal catastrophe
should overtake the British Nation and the British Empire,
historians a thousand years hence will still be baffled by the
mystery of our affairs. They will never understand how it was
that a victorious nation, with everything in hand, suffered
themselves to be brought low, and to cast away all that they
had gained by measureless sacrifice and absolute victory –
gone with the wind!

Now the victors are the vanquished, and those who threw
down their arms in the field and sued for an armistice are
striding on to world mastery. That is the position – that is the
terrible transformation that has taken place bit by bit. I rejoice
to hear from the Prime Minister that a further supreme effort

is to be made to place us in a position of security. Now is the time at last to rouse the nation. Perhaps it is the last time it can be roused with a chance of preventing war, or with a chance of coming through to victory should our efforts to prevent war fail. We should lay aside every hindrance and endeavour by uniting the whole force and spirit of our people to raise again a great British nation standing up before all the world; for such a nation, rising in its ancient vigour, can even at this hour save civilisation.

When Mr Churchill sat down there was a deep silence for a moment, then the show was over. The House broke into a hubbub of noise; members rattled their papers and shuffled their way to the lobby. Harold Balfour (now Under-Secretary of State for Air) came up to the Ladies' Gallery to take me to tea. I was talking with Sheila Birkenhead, and when we asked him what he thought of the speech, he replied, lightly: 'Oh, the usual Churchillian filibuster; he likes to rattle the sabre and he does it jolly well, but you always have to take it with a grain of salt.'

A grain of salt, while the German armies were beginning their march across Europe . . .

3

Dress Rehearsal in Czechoslovakia

On the afternoon of May 20th, four months before the Munich Agreement, I found myself hurtling through the Czechoslovakian countryside on the Istanbul–Berlin Express. I was only a 'local' passenger, for I had got on at Prague and was travelling no further than Aussig, a town ninety miles away, where the Sudeten Germans were holding their yearly election campaign. Hitler's annexation of Austria (two months before) had dealt Czechoslovakia a heavy blow, sending a wave of Nationalism sweeping through the German districts, and now the Nazi Party showed every sign of 'cleaning up' at the polls.

I had come to Prague to write an article for the London *Sunday Times*, and when Ralph Izzard of the *Daily Mail* suggested going to one of the Henlein rallies, I jumped at the chance. We were accompanied by Herr Ulrich, the press chief of the Sudeten Nazi Party, who seemed to regard the excursion as a holiday, for as soon as we settled ourselves on the train, he ordered half a dozen bottles of beer and said, 'Now we must enjoy ourselves.'

Herr Ulrich was a placid, mild-mannered little man who, until recently, had been the manager of a small firm near Reichenberg; now he had given up his job to devote all his time to party affairs. Without knowing his background you could picture his life: punctual at the office, kind to animals, paying his bills on time, and living in a respectable neighbourhood with an equally respectable wife. Everything about him was quietly suburban.

At first his conversation was limited to pleasantries, but the beer loosened his tongue and before long he was discussing the political events of the day. His voice grew shrill when he got onto the subject of Sudeten German autonomy and his quiet manner changed. Banging his fist threateningly on the table, he rolled off a series of well-worn phrases such as 'the destiny of the German race', 'the indignity of Slav rule', and the 'new order of Europe'. It was an extraordinary performance, like an actor rehearsing a part, for he was a good-natured little man and at heart bore no personal grievance against the Czechs – in fact, he had admitted to Ralph, in an off moment, that they were 'pretty good fellows'. It was as though he were cast in a role and had come to believe himself the character he was portraying. He was no longer Herr Ulrich, business manager, but Herr Ulrich, leader of destiny. Hitler had made him feel himself a link with history.

He went on talking about the Czechs and claimed they were already 'trembling in their boots'. He told us of an incident on the frontier near Warnsdorf where Czech soldiers had constructed granite barriers with an opening just wide enough for a single car to pass. The Germans, who were holding manoeuvres on the other side, built larger barriers, then, to illustrate their contempt, drove two tanks down the road and smashed them to pieces. 'Just to show the Czechs,' explained Ulrich, 'what to expect if they argue with Germans.'

The more beer Ulrich drank, the more he talked. Suddenly he said: 'I will tell you a secret. Henlein is with Hitler this very moment at Berchtesgaden. The German Army may cross the frontier at any hour.'

Ralph and I received the news with astonishment. When Hitler marched into Austria it was feared that his eyes were on Prague; but people with these misgivings had been branded by the appeasers as 'jitterbugs', and once again the world had settled down to complacency. Now, on a train hurtling through the Bohemian countryside, we were calmly being told that the German Army might cross the frontier at any hour. 'But that would mean a world war,' I protested lamely. 'Not at all,' replied Ulrich. 'It will all be over in a few days.' We reminded him of France's treaty with Czechoslovakia and added that England was bound to support France, but he shook his head. 'No one will fight for the Czechs.'

He went on to tell us that party headquarters were waiting for the signal, which might come at any moment. When Ralph asked him what he intended to do if war broke out, pointing out that Czechoslovakia wouldn't be a very healthy place for Nazi supporters, he answered lightly, 'Oh, I have a Czech friend who has promised to hide me until the fighting is over. I always help him with his income tax.' The fact that Ulrich was counting on a representative of an 'inferior race' to save him didn't seem to strike him as illogical.

When Ralph and I got to Aussig we immediately put in calls to London but were told there was an indefinite delay. We were only two miles from the German frontier and went off to the election meeting with an uneasy feeling, wondering if our evening would be interrupted by the rumble of tanks and the tramp of marching feet.

Our anxiety probably invested the rally with an exaggerated belligerency. But to me it was a nightmare of flags, swastikas, banners, photographs of Henlein, posters of Hitler, and earsplitting 'Heil's. It was held in the town hall, which was packed with over six thousand five hundred Germans. The crowded corridors were lined with uniformed Sudeten guards, who, Ulrich confided, were future SS men. Beer flowed and a German band struck up all the famous marches. The candidates made speeches, gesticulating and shouting, and when one of them said the Sudeten Germans were tired of being ruled by 'a race of émigré peasants' and referred to

Hitler and the power of the Reich, the crowd burst into a frenzy of cheering, chanting 'Sieg Heil' over and over again.

When the meeting was over we went back to the hotel and tried again to get through to London. The town had suddenly become so quiet, the possibility of a German invasion seemed unreal, and I wondered if the beer had gone to Ulrich's head and he had been talking nonsense. Nevertheless, I slept restlessly and about five in the morning heard the sound of aeroplanes. I got dressed and went outside. Six reconnaissance planes passed overhead, flying in groups of three. The town was still asleep and the streets deserted. I heard the sound of a train and walked down to the railroad station, a few blocks away, to find several hundred Czech soldiers spilling on to the platform. I went back to the hotel and sent a message to Ralph; obviously something was up, and after a consultation we decided to return to Prague, where we could get telephone communications.

Herr Ulrich came with us and suddenly seemed nervous and upset; he didn't talk much and I wondered if perhaps he was thinking for the first time what it would be like to have his backyard turned into a battlefield.

From the appearance of the Hotel Ambassador at seven o'clock in the morning it was hard to believe anything out of the ordinary could be happening: a charwoman was scrubbing the floors, the desk clerk sorting the mail, and the lift boy mulling over the morning paper. The restaurant was empty and we had coffee in solitary state. We put in calls to London, then rang the Foreign Office, but could get no confirmation of any activity, and once again began to wonder if the whole thing was in our imagination. However, about nine-thirty, Reynolds Packard of the United Press came dashing through the lobby in a state of excitement. I cornered him and (since I wasn't competition) finally succeeded in worming out the news: the Czech Army, fearing a lightning thrust from the Germans, had called up a hundred thousand reservists and ordered a partial mobilisation. My telephone call came a few minutes later and the calm voice of the telegrapher seemed from another world.

'Good morning,' he said amiably. 'How are you?'

'Not very well. The Czech Army is mobilising.'

'I say! Why are they doing that?'

'They think the German Army's coming across the frontier.'

'I say! Are you sure?'

'I'm sure the Czechs are mobilising.'

'I say! Fancy that. That *is* news.'

I left a message for Mr Hadley, the editor, saying I would cover the news story and would ring again that evening.

The rest of the day was one of fevered activity. Before noon the lobby of the Hotel Ambassador was swarming with journalists. Telephones were ringing from half the capitals of Europe, messenger boys dashing through the lobby with urgent telegrams, and the Czech porters scratching their heads and looking on in bewilderment.

The news of the mobilisation spread through the capital quickly: cafés became alive with speculation, and 'extras' were bought up as soon as they appeared in the streets. I rang up Major Lowell Riley, the American military attaché, and that afternoon we took a drive towards Tabor, a town in the direction of the Austrian frontier; but we passed only half a dozen lorry-loads of soldiers, for most of the men were being sent to the Czech 'Maginot Line' along the frontier. That night no one went to bed; crowds gathered on the boulevards shouting 'Long live Czechoslovakia!' and 'Down with Henlein!' Feeling was running high and policemen kept the throngs moving for fear of clashes between Czechs and Germans.

A few days later the crisis blew over. The Germans indignantly denied that they had any 'dishonourable intentions' towards Czechoslovakia; British and French statesmen reprimanded President Benesch like a master reprimanding a mischievous schoolboy, and the Czech Army finally demobilised. But that was the beginning, not the end, for in that month of May the Czechs knew that sooner or later the issue would come to a showdown. From then on, living in Prague (as the Czech porter said) was like living with the sword of Damocles hanging over your head. It would fall – the only question was when.

The fact that Czechoslovakia's independence must be defended by flesh and blood was accepted as a grim fact. The powerful democracies took their freedom for granted, but the Czechs had enjoyed self-government for only twenty years; they guarded it with the hard possessiveness of a peasant people, whose bodies still bore the marks of chains. After the mobilisation, whenever the sight-seeing guide in Prague drove people to the old town hall, he stopped before the heavily enscrolled clock and said fiercely: 'This clock was built in 1499. We were a free nation then; we are a free nation now; and we will remain a free nation.'

At that time, Czechoslovakia had deep faith in her alliances with France and Russia, and even though fight she must, she was confident that in the end she would triumph. One night I went to a performance of *Libuse*, Smetana's opera, in which there was a prophecy that the Czech people would always survive final domination. When the curtain fell the normally phlegmatic Czech audience rose and cheered for twenty minutes.

Things soon drifted back to normal. But although the capital presented an outward calm, tension remained. If you spoke German in the shops, you quickly scratched beneath the placid Slav surface and were met with icy silence. Since few foreigners could talk Czech they were forced to adopt the method of beginning in English, then switching to French (neither of which could be understood), until German finally became a relief.

The antagonism between Germans and Czechs, inflamed by Hitler's rising star, was not difficult for the Nazis to capitalise on, for the rift between the two was an old one. For three hundred years the Czechs of Bohemia had lived under the domination of the Hapsburgs at Vienna, who treated them as a wholly inferior race. When the Great War broke out they reacted by deserting in hundreds of thousands to the Allied side, where they formed units and fought with the French, the Italians and the Russians.

Thus in 1918 the Czechs were representatives of a victorious cause, while the Sudeten Germans were among the vanquished. The incorporation of victor and vanquished under a single government offered sufficient difficulties in itself. But the fact that the old subject race – the Slav – was now the master of Bohemia (even though Bohemia was historically the Slavs' rightful land) was what the Sudetens most deeply resented; and the Czechs, jealous of their hard-bought independence, did not make it easier.

The Germans protested bitterly against discrimination and complained that their people were constantly subjected to irritations by officials who could speak only Czech. Many of these grievances were legitimate, but on looking back it seems astonishing that anyone could have solemnly argued the pros and cons of the German case, when the latter had already suppressed their own minorities with unequalled savagery.

What is even more astonishing, in the light of past events, is that the Henlein party, maintaining headquarters in Prague, was allowed to carry on propaganda that ate into the spinal column of the nation like a malignant cancer until the end. It was due, I suppose, to the Czechs' stubborn faith in democracy. But even in the relatively quiet month of May, Nazi headquarters struck a jarring note.

They were established in the office of the newspaper *Die Zeit*, over a large restaurant known as the Deutsches Haus. I remember the first time I went there – leaving a thoroughly Czech world with its sprawling, indistinguishable advertisements and posters, walking down an alleyway, and turning into a dark doorway. The restaurant was crowded with Germans heiling Hitler and giving the Nazi salute. The walls were decorated with pictures of Henlein and large red streamers predicting victory in the demands for autonomy. The outer halls were filled with German guards. The first day I went there, the German who issued my permit wrote down by mistake, 'Deutsches Reich', instead of 'Deutsches Haus'. When I showed it to the guards at the door they burst into laughter. '*Deutsches Reich! Das ist gut!*' They bowed delightedly and let me pass.

Frequently those days the windows of the Deutsches Haus were smashed by Czechs. As Czechs were not permitted in the building, I was astonished to see four men in Czech uniform strolling through the restaurant, smiling and bowing. I learned they were Sudeten Germans who were doing their two-year compulsory service in the Czech Army.

I went upstairs to the office of *Die Zeit*, pushed my way through a hall filled with unsmiling party workers (mostly boys in their early twenties) and asked for Herr Ulrich. I hadn't seen him since our trip to Aussig, and wanted to collect some material on the elections. But the man at the desk told me that he was away – 'indefinitely'. His whereabouts seemed to be a mystery, and I wondered if he had suddenly become frightened at the magnitude of the drama and decided to wash his hands of the whole affair. I never saw him again.

One afternoon, a day or so before I returned to England, Professor B, a Czech to whom I had been given a letter of introduction, took me to tea at an outdoor restaurant on a hill high above Prague. It was one of the most beautiful spring days I have ever seen. The slope in front of us was white with cherry blossoms, and to the left the ancient towers of Hradschin Palace rose towards the sky like a fairy palace; far below, the River Moldau glistened in the sunshine like a strand of golden hair.

The Czech professor talked about the difficult days we were living through, and expressed an almost childish faith that since democracy was *right*, it was bound to triumph. 'But, life will not be easy,' he sighed. 'I find myself staring at the cherry blossoms very hard this year, wondering whether I shall see them again next spring.' He lapsed into silence, then shook his head. 'I think not,' he said.

The following spring, shortly after the Germans marched into Prague, I heard he had been sent to a concentration camp.

4

Who Wants a War?

A few weeks after the Czech crisis, Martha Gellhorn (now Mrs Ernest Hemingway) and I went into a public house in Birmingham to try and get an idea of what the ordinary people in England were thinking. It was a typical English pub in the working-class district, with grey, colourless walls, a dartboard in one corner and two cheap racing prints over the bar.

It was about six o'clock in the evening and soon the room began filling up with factory workers, their wives and girlfriends. There was an air of reserve that made it difficult to get into conversation, but, finally, an elderly gentleman sitting in the corner, in a long, yellow dust-coat, made a comment on the weather and we eagerly jumped into the breach and told him we were Americans who were touring about England. 'Is that so?' he replied. 'I've never talked with Americans before.' We thought the ice was broken and sat back, eagerly waiting for him to ply us with questions, but he lapsed into silence and we suddenly realised the conversation had ended.

The public house grew crowded: everybody knew everybody else; it was 'Good evening, Bill,' and 'Nice to see you, Jim,' and then each retired to his own little group and talked in low, modulated voices. The calm was nearly upset, though, when the door opened and a stranger appeared carrying a large valise. He stood in the middle of the room, opened the suitcase, and took out an array of ties. Instantly the air was charged with hostility. The woman next to us said it was an outrage for salesmen to come and disturb people, when all they wanted was to be left alone to enjoy a nice, quiet drink. Fortunately, the barmaid intervened and told him to go away, and the room soon regained its normal composure.

By this time the atmosphere was thawing, and the group next to us allowed us to join in their conversation. We succeeded in turning the talk to politics, and the charwoman, who worked in a café, said she wouldn't live in a Fascist country, 'not for a thousand pounds a month'. In England, she explained, people respect each other's rights, but as far as she could gather, foreigners weren't the same. She had seen them in the moving pictures, with 'everybody in uniform, marching, and waving flags'. 'But if they like it,' she added, 'it's not up to us to criticise; we should stop at home and mind our own business.'

Her husband, an ex-sailor, backed her up in that. He said he had travelled all over the world, and England was the only place to live in. He longed to reminisce on his experiences in China, but his wife had evidently heard the stories before and kept the conversation well in hand. The British Government, she explained, was the best government in the world. 'No one would be foolish enough to start a war against us, because we always win.'

'That's right,' the sailor interrupted. 'Twist the lion's tail once too often, and you're for it.' The third man in the group, a worker in an electrical plant, shook his head morosely. 'When I read the papers,' he said, 'sometimes I have my doubts.' The other two were exasperated. 'Now, be sensible. Whoever heard of England getting beaten?' The little man shook his head and sank into silence, thoroughly squashed.

Martha and I motored through the Midlands as far north as Newcastle and back to London again. We picked our people at random – in pubs, tea shops, at ARP meetings and dockyard restaurants; we talked with farmers, factory workers, waiters, mechanics and shipbuilders. And always we got the same reaction.

'War! Who wants a war?' They seemed to take it for granted that 'foreigners' were always squabbling among themselves, but the fact that these squabbles might involve them wasn't even a possibility to be discussed. Malcolm Muggeridge summed it up in *The Thirties*, when he wrote:

> Public events, however portentous, trouble little the great mass of mankind, who feel with reason that they are powerless to influence them, and in any case must endure their consequences. An aching tooth is more woeful than Hitler, a cold in the head of greater concern to the sufferer than the annexation of Albania. What turns a Foreign Secretary grey and haggard in a few months, leaves unperturbed the half-million who assemble to watch the Derby.

Martha had come to England to write an article for *Collier's Magazine*. Her editor, three thousand miles away in New York, was alarmed; he saw a civil war raging in Spain; he saw the French Army manning three frontiers; the German Army elated after its absorption of Austria; and the Czech Army digging in its third line of defence only twelve miles from Prague. He saw the British Isles, once immune from attack, now transformed through the development of aircraft into one of the most vulnerable targets in Europe. 'What is the reaction of the British public?' he cabled. 'Are the people alarmed? What do they think of Fascism, or Aggression, or the possibility of war?'

Martha was at her wits' end. 'I can't cable back "War! Who wants a war?"' she said indignantly. And yet even in the armament manufacturing towns such as Sheffield and Newcastle, the people we saw showed no apprehension. Oh yes, they were making armaments and a fine thing it was for unemployment. But use them? On whom?

To direct questions, such as 'Would you fight for Czechoslovakia?', we received a confusion of replies. The waiters in a café in Leeds said they would fight if the Government had signed any obligations, but had the Government signed obligations? they asked. Several textile workers at a nearby table, all ex-servicemen, interrupted to say they wouldn't fight on foreign territory again; but this brought a sharp retort from an elderly waitress, who said it was a shame to give Americans such an impression. 'Of course the boys will fight,' she said, 'for King and Country.'

But it was all a far-away drama, and the reason it was far away seemed due to the extraordinary faith which the ordinary man appeared to have in the 'experts' who ran the country. Over and over again we had it carefully explained that it was difficult for outsiders to judge the situation, because negotiations were private. Things, we were told, were never as bad as they seemed in the papers, for the Government always had 'an extra trick up its sleeve'. People appeared to be confused as to why Mr Eden resigned, the general opinion being that he was 'a fine man with high ideals'. Mr Chamberlain was also a fine man because he was pledged to do everything to keep the country out of war, and Mr Churchill was fine because he made good speeches.

In fact, everything was fine that June 1938, three and a half months before the German Army crossed the Czechoslovakian frontier. Martha was infuriated by the complacency. A tall, blonde girl with a brilliant gift for writing and a passionate concern for the underdog, she refused to take the woes of the world lightly. The fact that the working man in England was not stung to fury (as she was) by the treatment of his brothers in Spain or the doom of his brothers in Czechoslovakia struck her as shameful.

Soon our trip began to take on the mild form of a lecture tour. The sentence 'War! Who wants a war?' became like a red rag to a bull, and with a burst of exasperation Martha told them about Adolf Hitler, his mighty armies and his hosts of bombers. But they only looked at her with mild surprise, as though she were a little queer in the head, and by the time we reached Lord Feversham's house in Yorkshire, on Sunday afternoon for tea, her indignation knew no bounds.

She had scarcely said hello before she was telling Sim Feversham (then Under-Secretary of State for Agriculture) that the people in the country could think of nothing else but racing and the weather.

Sim found it funny. To begin with, he thought our trip very odd. 'Fancy going round to the pubs and asking people what they think. You two are a couple of warmongers. Just trying to upset the country and stir up trouble.'

Martha said she was going to stir up more trouble by talking to his peasants. 'In England we call them farmers,' he said. 'I know,' retorted Martha. 'That's what you *call* them.'

An hour or so later we were tramping across the fields to one of the cottages on Sim's estate. The door opened and a very old man appeared.

'Good morning, Geoff,' said Sim amiably. 'How are you?'

The old man was delighted to see his master. 'Oh, good morning, m'lord,' he said, bowing several times. 'Good morning. Won't you come in?'

Sim shook his head. 'We've just walked over to ask you a few questions. These two girls have been driving around England warmongering. They think there's going to be a war. Now, you don't think there's going to be a war, do you, Geoff?'

'Oh no, m'lord. No, m'lord.'

'You think things are all right, don't you, Geoff?'

'Yes, m'lord. Yes, m'lord.'

'You don't think Hitler wants a war with England, do you, Geoff?'

'No, m'lord. No, m'lord.'

'In fact, you think all this talk is rather silly, don't you, Geoff?'

'Yes, m'lord. Yes, m'lord.'

Martha couldn't stand any more. She stamped back across the fields, Sim following behind, grinning from ear to ear. 'Just try coming to *my* country some day,' she exclaimed. 'You won't get all that bowing and scraping, and imagine putting those ideas into that poor old man's head! When the war *does* come, your corpse will be found bobbing about in the river and we'll know who did it. But you can rest assured *I* won't give him away.'

A year and a half later Geoff 'turned'. I ran into Sim just before he left with his regiment for Palestine, and he told me that soon after Munich, Martha's 'peasants' began to regard him with the gravest suspicion. When he said goodbye to Geoff, the old man remarked: 'It's too bad to see you in a uniform, m'lord,' then glared ferociously. 'But I suppose we must pay for our mistakes. Isn't that so, m'lord?'

Sim told me to be sure and inform Martha. 'It will please her a lot. Do you think she thinks we are going to get beaten?'

'No,' I said, 'I don't.' For I remembered how, on the way home, Martha, still infuriated, had remarked: 'And the worst part of it is, their skulls are so thick, you can't crack them. If the world comes to an end tomorrow, and there's only one person left, I know it's bound to be an Englishman!'

Part IV

BARGAIN TIME IN EUROPE

1

The Candles Start to Flicker

When you walked down the Champs-Élysées you noticed, suddenly, the way the sun streamed through the chestnut trees; you watched the fountains at the Rond Point shooting into the air like a stream of diamonds; and you wandered along the banks of the Seine, wondering, with a fear that clutched at your heart, how long the glow of Paris would stay undimmed.

Only a few days before, on August 15th, the news had been flashed around the world that the German Army was mobilising. Already the decorations, put up in July for the visit of the King and Queen of England, were being replaced by red, white and blue posters, calling on the people to prepare for the national defence – '*pour sauvegarder la patrie*'. Newspapers brought out extras every few hours and politics absorbed the minds of everyone from statesmen to couturiers. Peace was dying. In their hearts people knew it, but the actual fact was so appalling they clung desperately to hope. They kept a vigil in the death-chamber, clasping the patient's cold hands and refusing to admit, even to themselves, the growing pallor of her face.

The agony of that long illness was terrible to watch. It lasted over a year, but the anguish of Europe was never again so acute as during those summer months when every type of medicine – hope, treachery, idealism and compromise – was feverishly injected into her veins in a desperate attempt to keep her alive. Her recovery at Munich was an artificial one. After that she went into a coma and a year later died.

I had given up all idea of returning to America and joined the staff of the London *Sunday Times* as a permanent 'roving' correspondent. During the next year my job sent me to many countries and many capitals, and I watched the lights in the death-chamber go out one by one, until the sheets were pulled up over the corpse's head and the European continent reverberated to the roar of bombers. That pre-Munich August, when despair was sweeping France, I stayed once again with the Baroness X in her flat off the Champs-Élysées where I had written my Spanish articles.

The sun flooded the balcony and the shrill voice of the concierge broke the early morning stillness, just as it had the year before. The only difference was that now the concierge no longer spent her time bargaining; instead, she discussed the political situation. One morning I overheard her arguing with the baker. He was grumbling that France's internal affairs were a *mélange* of stupidity; no one ever seemed to agree, while Germany, on the other hand, made lightning decisions. This brought a sharp retort from the concierge, who said, naturally, it was bound to be so; Germany was Hitler, but France was a lot of people. She rebuked him for putting the blame on internal affairs. France's difficulty was not due to the falling birth-rate or the devaluation of the franc, or even the friction between Left and Right. France's difficulty, she said fiercely, was the same as it had always been: her geographical position. I couldn't hear the baker's reply. Probably he agreed, for it was the terrible repetition of history that haunted the French more than anything else. The scarred battlefields of the north had not even had time to heal and now the German Army was marching again.

I had never seen those battlefields and one morning I took a train to Amiens with Tommy Thompson, who had come to Paris on leave. We hired a taxi and drove to Vimy Ridge, and then to Bapaume and across the old Somme battlefield. I was startled to find how fresh the wounds of the last struggle had remained. For miles we drove through a battered and desolate countryside. With the world on the threshold of a new war, the old war seemed to move out of the pages of history like an angry skeleton. Along the main road there were still signs warning the public not to trespass beyond certain limits for fear of unexploded shells and grenades. Further on there were crumbling machine-gun emplacements and rusted barbed-wire stakes stuck in the ground as firmly as on the day when some hand had placed them there two decades ago.

Along Vimy Ridge the ground was pitted with shell-holes and gouged by huge mine craters. Over one hundred thousand men had died on the hill before it had finally been captured by the Canadians in 1917. It was grim walking up the Ridge, but when we reached the top the skeleton vanished and tragedy turned into a bitter comedy. It was a sunny day and the slope was crowded with sight-seers. Families had brought picnic lunches with them and settled themselves comfortably in shell-holes which offered shade from the sun. Guides were busy conducting parties of tourists into the damp, twisting underground tunnels where the soldiers had fought for five francs a head. Nearby, a luncheon-stand did a thriving business in beer and snacks.

Tommy got into conversation with our taxi driver, and discovered he had fought in the first battle of Vimy Ridge. He regarded the scene with a certain ironical amusement. It was all right for people to bring picnic lunches, he said. When he had been in the trenches he and his friends had often joked that one day people would pay money to see where they had fought. But what wasn't all right was that only twenty years later Europe should be standing on the brink of another war. But he shrugged his shoulders: 'It is always the same story; France against the Boches.'

For weeks that scene haunted me. The shrug of the taxi driver's shoulders and the look on his face was symbolic of the despair that swept the country. During the next two weeks I motored from Paris to Saint Jean-de-Luz, along the Spanish frontier and up the Riviera to the gay and noisy port of Marseilles. I talked with people all along the way, and on looking over my notes, the reaction was always the same: war must be prevented. Over and over again, people repeated the phrase that Hitler was only bluffing, and if France stood firm the catastrophe could be averted. I suppose one should have taken warning from this psychology. France must stand firm, not because France *was* firm, but in order to prevent a war. The whole policy of the country was built on the hypothesis that Hitler was bluffing. But what if Hitler wasn't bluffing, what then?

Every week French statesmen repeated their solemn assurances to Czechoslovakia; it was all part of the game. Most people, myself included, accepted this show of strength on its face value. When I got back to Paris I was shocked to hear Sir Charles Mendl, the press attaché of the British Embassy, say he didn't believe the French intended to fight for Czechoslovakia. 'But how can they go back on their pledge?' I protested. 'I don't know,' replied Sir Charles. 'But I've lived in this country for twenty-five years and it doesn't ring true. I don't believe they're going to fight.'

I thought Charles was cynical. When I left Paris for Berlin in August, I wondered if I would return to find it blacked out and the people of France at war.

* * *

Berlin offered a strong contrast to the beauty of the French capital. It was cold and windy and a feeling of menace hung in the air. The pavements were crowded with uniforms and the streets resounded to the sound of tanks and armoured cars. Even the sombre grey buildings had a forbidding look. I'd never been to Berlin before, and when I wandered about I had the same feeling of uneasiness as when I had first seen Franco's guards on the International Bridge at Hendaye. Instinctively, this was 'the enemy'. Although my country was three thousand miles away, the ideas for which it stood were threatened just as much as though its borders were contiguous with those of Czechoslovakia.

I tried to overcome this feeling and set to work to gather material for articles. I stayed at the Hotel Adlon on the Unter den Linden, which, during the last war, had been the social centre of Berlin. In 1914 the lobby had been crowded with multi-coloured Austrian, Hungarian and Prussian uniforms; now it was filled with the brown and black of the SA and the SS men. The bar of the Grill Room, however, was always crowded with foreigners; before lunch it filled up with journalists, diplomats, military attachés and businessmen, and was referred to affectionately as 'The Club'.

The German clerks and porters were polite and helpful, but there was the same uncomfortable atmosphere I had found in Spain: always guarded conversations and a feeling of being watched. Most of the telephones were tapped and you could often hear the click of the recording machines at the other end of the line. The telephone of the British military attaché, Colonel Macfarlane, was fitted with a wire that ran into the German War Office. This became known when the telephone went out of order and an engineer came to repair it. After labouring over it for several hours it still failed to work. The engineer looked at it stupidly, scratched his head, and said: 'I can't understand it. It's working all right at the War Office.'

The German press attack on Czechoslovakia was increasing in violence, and even in the hotel you saw signs of uneasiness. Several times I found a group of waiters clustered together outside my room, hastily reading the English papers before delivering them, and one night at dinner an old lady at the next table burst into tears, saying that it was like 1914 all over again. During the next few weeks the offices of the foreign correspondents were besieged by people begging to know 'what the situation really was'.

I presented my papers at the Foreign Office and the Ministry of Propaganda and started on a series of interviews. I visited schools, labour camps and welfare organisations. The Germans who took me round were agreeable and efficient and argued their case with conviction. But all the time I couldn't help thinking of the quotation from Stevenson: 'What you are speaks so loudly that I cannot hear what you say.' The soft words about social progress were drowned by the rumble of tanks on the streets of Berlin.

* * *

Every evening the foreign correspondents gathered at the Taverna, a small restaurant on the Courbierestrasse. The Taverna was first made popular by H. R. Knickerbocker and Edgar Mowrer, two American journalists who were expelled from Germany soon after Hitler came to power. (Edgar Mowrer was told to leave in 1933 after the publication of his book, *Germany Puts the Clock Back*. When he asked on what grounds he was being expelled, the Foreign Office official replied bluntly: 'The Führer didn't like your book.' To which Edgar is said to have replied: 'Oh, that's all right. Tell him I didn't like his either.')

The Taverna had continued to be a nightly meeting place, and although the room was usually crowded, a table was always reserved for the foreign press. The correspondents I saw the most of were Euan Butler of *The Times* and Edward Beattie of the United Press. Although *The Times* favoured appeasement, Euan and his colleague, Jimmy Holburn, managed to charge their despatches with a warning note which didn't endear them to the local authorities.

Euan believed that war with Germany was inevitable. One night at the Taverna he looked around the room at the young German soldiers and the SS men and remarked in a ringing voice: 'What a bore it's going to be to have to kill so many of these people.' At the height of the attack on Czechoslovakia he persuaded the slightly intoxicated piano-player to swing into the Marseillaise. Some of the Germans joined in the tune until it suddenly dawned on them it wasn't the proper moment for such a song, and the manager indignantly ordered the piano-player to change to a German march.

Most of the correspondents pooled their information, as there was small opportunity of getting a 'scoop'. There was little news apart from that given in official 'handouts', and for the most part, a journalist's job was limited to the interpretation he put on the events of the day. It wasn't difficult to form an accurate appreciation of the situation, for Berlin officials made no effort to conceal Germany's aims. This astonished me more than anything else. While the world was being assured that after a just settlement of the Sudeten German grievances, the Third Reich had no further ambitions, Nazi spokesmen in Berlin talked openly of the new world to come.

One night I had dinner with Herr von Strempel, a Foreign Office official, now in the German Embassy in Washington, who told me bluntly that Sudeten self-determination was only another name for Germany's passage to the Black Sea. On another occasion, I had cocktails with Dr Karl Silex, editor of the *Deutsche Allgemeine Zeitung*, who said, just as bluntly, that the whole of South-Eastern Europe must come under Germany's rule. Certainly there was no secret about it; if subsequent events came as a shock to British, French and American statesmen, it was not due to Nazi discretion.

There was not a foreign correspondent in Berlin unaware of the fact that the 'socialisation' of Germany was only another term for the militarisation of Germany; that chemists and scientists were experimenting to increase the country's war-time self-sufficiency, while armament factories worked on triple shifts; that school-children were being drilled on 'Racial Science', 'Eugenics' and 'Heredity', to prove that the superiority of the German race jus-tified Hitler's programme of expansion. After Czechoslovakia more countries would follow until Germany became so powerful that no nation would dare to accept her challenge. I doubt if even the great mass of Germans were taken in by the press campaign against the Czechs. Those who believed in the Führer accepted the doctrine of expansion as a matter of course.

One night at the Taverna, Euan Butler got into conversation with a waiter, who confided that his wife was going to have another child. 'It will be our sixth,' he said proudly. When Euan asked why he wanted such a large family, the man regarded him with mild surprise: 'Because Germany must advance.'

Meanwhile, the Ministry of Propaganda continued to assure the world of Germany's pacific intentions. Certainly no country has ever conducted a more effective sales campaign. The flood of material that went forth each day from the great white building on the Wilhelmstrasse affected the judgment and paralysed the will of thousands of people. Not only did it convince many pow-erful politicians of the justness of Germany's claims, but it sowed suspicion and fear and infected treachery into countries which have since fallen by the wayside. The propaganda was devised with cunning; no class was ignored. It attacked the capitalists to appeal to the working man; it attacked the Communists to appeal to the capitalists. It created dissension by excoriating the foreign press as 'Jewish controlled'. It jeered at freedom, coupling it with unemployment, and extolled National Socialism as a model eco-nomic system in spite of the fact that forty per cent of German labour was absorbed by the country's expanding war-machine. Today, it is no exaggeration to claim that out of the eleven countries smashed and overrun by Germany, half of them were destroyed, not by tanks, but by propaganda.

When I was in the Propaganda Ministry one day, I walked into the wrong room by mistake and found over two hundred German journalists gathered to receive their daily instructions. The room was noisy and crowded and blue with smoke. I was hustled out quickly and discovered later that I had invaded the holy of holies. The penalty for a German who revealed the instructions given at one of these conferences was death!

I never met the genius of the Ministry, Dr Goebbels, but just before I left Berlin I ran into him (literally) in the lobby of the Adlon. It was during the State visit of Admiral Horthy, the Hungarian Regent. A large military demonstration was given in the latter's honour. It took place at the Technische Hochschule, on the outskirts of Berlin. Hitler and Horthy stood in the reviewing box while shock troops goose-stepped past followed by a long procession of tanks, guns and armoured cars. The climax of the review came when a Big Bertha, a cannon of enormous dimensions, was dragged past the stand. The crowd looked at it in astonishment, then burst into a roar of wild and spontaneous cheering. Ed Beattie, who was standing next to me, gave a sour smile and remarked above the din, 'A dear little German reaction.' In the next box the military attachés scribbled notes on their cuffs and the agency correspondents made a dash for the nearest telephone box. The gun wasn't a new invention, only a show-piece; at any rate, it seemed to have the desired effect on the crowd.

After the review we went back to the hotel. Admiral Horthy had brought a large retinue with him and the lobby was crowded with brightly coloured uniforms, medals and decorations. In the midst of all the splendour stood a small man in a drab brown uniform, his back turned to me. He seemed out of place among the gay plumage and I remember thinking he was probably a humble aide-de-camp. About ten minutes later a telephone call came for me, and I pushed my way through the crowded lobby and made a dash round the corner to the public booth. I collided squarely with the small man in the brown uniform. I stepped back, apologising, and saw that he was no other than Dr Joseph Paul Goebbels. He smiled wryly and went off, rubbing his shoulder. That was my only contact with him. But on looking back, the events of the day seemed to fit into a neat pattern: the gun and Dr Goebbels; the sword and the pen; Germany marches on.

2

German Merry-Go-Round

I saw the spirit of Nazi Germany flowing through the ancient streets of Nuremberg like a river that had burst its dams. A million red, white and black swastikas fluttered from the window-ledges, and the town, swollen to three times its normal size, resounded to the ring of leather boots and blazed with a bewildering array of uniforms.

Although the vast regimentation of modern Germany was a phenomenon which only the machine age could produce, at night the medieval background became curiously real. The clock swung back to the Middle Ages. The long red pennants, fluttering from the turreted walls of Nuremberg Castle, shone in the moonlight like the standards of an old religious war; the tramp of marching feet and the chorus of voices chanting the militant Nazi hymns had all the passion of an ancient crusade. It was only when you heard the sudden whine of a silver-winged fighter, travelling at three hundred miles an hour, that you were jerked back to the grim reality of 1938.

That grim reality had cast a dread shadow over the Party Congress, for this was 'crisis week'. Never in history had a crisis been more cold-bloodedly manufactured. For days the world had known the exact form it would take, even the date of its culmination. It had watched the attack against Czechoslovakia growing in violence, and now, with the German Army mobilised, it waited for the crescendo to be sounded by Hitler's speech, dramatically planned for the last day of the Congress.

The very fact that the crisis was a manufactured one made it all the more to be feared, for its calculated ruthlessness. The faces of politicians, diplomats and journalists were strained and anxious. In the hotel lobbies, groups of people clustered together and talked in low voices. You saw Italian diplomats in earnest conversation with delegates from Nationalist Spain; German party leaders smiling at the Japanese; worried French statesmen cornered with the British. Newspaper correspondents from most of the capitals of Europe hurried through the lobbies, asking questions and exchanging information, while messenger boys dashed up with cables, and telephones rang continuously from Berlin and London and Paris.

There were only three large hotels in Nuremberg and most of the rooms were filled with German officials and favoured delegates such as the Italian, Spanish and Japanese. The foreign press was shunted off on to railway sleeping-cars outside the town. I was lucky enough to persuade the manager at the Hotel Wurttemberger Hof to give me a room, but my good fortune only lasted two days, for a fresh delegation of Japanese suddenly arrived and I was told to leave. Jules Sauerwein of the *Paris Soir* came to my rescue, and got me a room in a small pension where he was staying. The pension was run by a frowsy woman named Frau Fleischer, who took a passionate interest in the political situation. All day long she kept the radio going, and no charge against the Czechs was too outrageous for her to believe. She told Jules and myself that if the Kaiser had been in control of the country, Germany would have been at war long ago. But Hitler had patience. He would refuse to allow himself to be 'provoked'.

The rooms at Frau Fleischer's were dark and unswept, and breakfast was uneatable – watery coffee and a piece of black bread. Even so, I was lucky to be there, for not only were the hotels too full to accommodate the press, but even the foreign diplomats had been relegated to sleeping-cars. The ambassadorial trains were at a siding twenty minutes from the town. A fleet of cars was placed at the service of the diplomats, and a squad of SS men were on duty as aides-de-camp. Everything was done for their comfort; nevertheless, when you walked down the bleak platform and saw the ambassadors of the three great democracies – Great Britain, the United States and France – leaning out of the windows of a derailed restaurant car, it brought it home to you that affairs in Europe had taken a turn for the worse!

One morning I drove down to the train with Jules Sauerwein and Ward Price of the *Daily Mail*. They wanted to talk to their respective ambassadors and I was anxious to find Prentiss Gilbert, the American Chargé d'Affaires. We passed the black-uniformed SS men and walked down the deserted platform searching for the right car. Ward Price caught sight of Sir Nevile Henderson in the restaurant car, and further on, the French Ambassador, M. François Ponçet, poked his head out of the window and waved at Jules. I got on the train and walked through the passages until I finally came to a compartment marked 'The United States'. I knocked at the door and a voice said: 'Come in.' Inside, I found the American Ambassador, Mr Hugh Wilson, sitting alone, aimlessly drumming his fingers on the window-ledge. Obviously, he had nothing to do. It struck me painfully that this was significant of the role that the most powerful democracy in the world was playing at a time when civilisation was gravely menaced.

I exchanged pleasantries with Mr Wilson (who seemed glad to have company) and learned that Prentiss Gilbert had remained in Berlin. When I rejoined Ward Price and Jules, they were looking discouraged. Jules shrugged his shoulders and said, 'Some day I hope to find an ambassador who answers questions instead of asking them!'

The truth of the matter was that the diplomats knew even less than the journalists. Hitler had refused to receive any of them, and their contacts were even more limited than ours. Nevertheless, Ward Price had hoped to find out from Nevile Henderson the meaning of the article which had appeared in the London *Times* the day before (September 7th), suggesting that the Czechs solve their difficulties by ceding Sudetenland to Germany. The states-men who believed the policy of 'standing firm' could hold Hitler in check considered this a treacherous stab in the back. There was no doubt as to the buoying effect it had on German officialdom. Long faces became wreathed in smiles and minor Nazi leaders went about good-naturedly assuring everybody there wouldn't be a war. Dr Dietrich, the German press chief, explained that Hitler didn't want a war. Then added with a sly smile, 'He can get what he wants without.'

This smug conviction was widespread among the German people. The beer gardens rang with laughter and music and everyone merrily agreed that Hitler was clever enough to score by diplomacy alone. One afternoon I climbed the hill to the old city with Bertrand de Juvenel, a French journalist. We went into a small restaurant, crowded with SA men, drinking beer and eating sausages and sauerkraut. Somehow it was difficult to realise that the SA contingents in their heavy black boots and their khaki uni-forms, with the swastika pinned on the sleeve, were the ordinary citizens of Germany – the bus-drivers, the hairdressers, the garage mechanics and small shopkeepers. Nuremberg was a holiday for them. All day long they wandered about the town visiting exhib-ition halls, eating enormous meals, and having snapshots taken to send home to their girls. At night they filled the cafés and were always the last to leave.

The particular group of SA men in the restaurant were tall and blond with honest, scrubbed faces. There were no empty tables and they cordially invited Bertrand and myself to join them.

When they asked what nationality we were and Bertrand replied that he was a Frenchman, their eyes grew wide with interest.

The leader of the group, an older man, grasped his hand and shook it warmly; he said he had lived in France for four years. He added that the time had been spent fighting in the war, but, nevertheless, he felt he knew the country very well indeed. No one seemed to consider the conversation tactless when he tried to recall the names of the towns he had entered; then suddenly he broke off and assured Bertrand there wouldn't be another war. He had confidence that things would be settled in a peaceful way, for no one wanted a war, least of all Hitler.

His companions nodded in agreement, then all six raised their glasses and drank a toast to Germany, to France, and to Czechoslovakia. When they had finished, a small man at the end of the table, a blacksmith from Cologne, asked us what we thought of Germany; before we had time to reply he was telling us what a fine country it was. It wasn't like other countries, he said, for in Germany there was no unemployment. Bertrand nodded, but suggested that the unemployment was absorbed to some extent by the vast production of armaments.

This seemed to perplex the group. A silence fell until the leader suddenly proffered the theory that when the international situation was straightened out they would stop building guns and instead they would build stadiums and houses and fine new parks. Everyone seemed relieved at this explanation, and we left amid an elaborate flurry of '*Merci beaucoup*' and '*Au revoir*'.

When we got outside, Bertrand shook his head sadly. 'They're like children,' he said. 'Why anyone ever lets them play with explosives, God knows!'

More knowledgeable people were unable to share the ordinary German's complacency; to them the Nuremberg festivities went on like a gigantic fair removed from all reality. Would the merry-go-round suddenly stop and the lights go out? This speculation ran through the press room like a live current; meanwhile, the journalists were hustled about to endless speeches and reviews.

Every morning a bulletin was posted containing a long schedule arranged with typical German thoroughness – the time of the meeting, the hour the buses left and returned, the number that could be accommodated, and so forth. I went to a few of these gatherings. I heard Dr Dietrich attack the press, Hitler attack the Jews, Dr Rosenberg attack the Church, and Goering attack the Czechs, calling them 'ridiculous dwarfs backed by Moscow'. After that I preferred to wander about by myself.

Unfortunately, all the exhibition halls sounded the same note of hatred: National Socialist Germany against the Bolsheviks, the Jews and the world in general. The walls were decorated by enormous banners that said: 'The struggle of Germany is the struggle to preserve civilisation'. Below, maps of Europe showed the spread of Bolshevism; Czechoslovakia was painted the same dangerous red as Soviet Russia, while France dwindled into a vivid pink. (I have often wondered what happened to this vast array of maps and posters since the Russian–German alliance.)

The Jews were vilified by literature entitled 'Racial Science' and displays of genealogical charts and hideous photographs of 'Non-Aryan' types. Nuremberg, because its mayor was Julius Streicher, the notorious Jew-baiter, was one of the most rabidly anti-Semitic towns in Germany. Hundreds of shops and beer gardens bore signs: 'Jews not wanted', and in the old city near the market, small Streicher news-stands advertised anti-Semitic literature.

These stands contrasted strangely with the everyday life of the busy market, with its brilliant array of vegetables and its plump *Hausfrauen* with market baskets over their arms. And yet history

repeated itself, for it was in this very square in 1499 that proc-
lamations were posted ordering the expulsion of the Jews. The
campaign was waged by a monk named Capeistranus, and the hostile feeling lasted so long that it was not until 1800 that Jews were
again permitted in the city as free citizens. Now they were expelled
once more under another creed – the creed of new Germany.

'New Germany' was typified by a group of young men, hand-
picked for the Hitler Youth, to be trained as the future leaders
of the people. Every year a few hundred of them were chosen to
come to Nuremberg as the finest representatives of the nation.
One afternoon I visited their camp, the *Funker-lager*, a few miles
outside the town. I went with Herr von Lösch, a young Foreign
Office official, who had been educated in England. There was
nothing much to see when we got there, but a lean, brawny,
golden-headed German, about twenty years old, took us about,
showing us the tents in which the men ate and slept. Their training
lasted three years and most of it seemed to be devoted to physical exercises. The boy explained that they spent several hours
a day studying the tenets of National Socialism: 'Racial Science',
'Eugenics', 'Heredity', etc. But when I asked if they received any
other instruction, he shook his head. Formerly, he said, they had
had courses in history, literature and philosophy, but the profes-
sors had been unable to interpret their subjects from a National
Socialist point of view, so their lectures had been discontinued.
Even Herr von Lösch was embarrassed by this reply and we drove
him in silence.

A far more powerful factor in the new Germany than the appeal
of Hitler's doctrine, however, was the appeal of Hitler himself.
Many Germans believed that Hitler was actually endowed with
superhuman qualities. I remember Frau Fleischer telling Jules
Sauerwein and myself that in Germany there was no need for

people to have opinions; they had the Führer's opinions and the Führer was 'inspired'.

Certainly the idea of the superman was encouraged by the vast displays in Nuremberg. Everything that was done was done on a gigantic scale. The power of the spectacles lay not so much in their ingeniousness but in their immensity. The keynote was always repetition and uniformity. Instead of a few gilt eagles there were hundreds; instead of hundreds of flags there were thousands; instead of thousands of performers there were hundreds of thousands.

At night the mystic quality of the ritual was exaggerated by huge burning urns at the top of the stadium, their orange flames leaping into the blackness, while the flood-lighting effect of hundreds of powerful searchlights played eerily against the sky. The music had an almost religious solemnity, timed by the steady beat of drums that sounded like the distant throb of tom-toms.

One night I went to the stadium with Jules Sauerwein to hear an address Hitler was making to Nazi political leaders gathered from all over Germany. The stadium was packed with nearly two hundred thousand spectators. As the time for the Führer's arrival drew near, the crowd grew restless. The minutes passed and the wait seemed interminable. Suddenly the beat of the drums increased and three motorcycles with yellow standards fluttering from their windshields raced through the gates. A few minutes later a fleet of black cars rolled swiftly into the arena: in one of them, standing in the front seat, his hand outstretched in the Nazi salute, was Hitler.

The demonstration that followed was one of the most extraordinary I have ever witnessed. Hitler climbed to his box in the Grand Stand amid a deafening ovation, then gave a signal for the political leaders to enter. They came, a hundred thousand strong, through an opening in the far end of the arena. In the silver light they seemed to pour into the bowl like a flood of water. Each of them carried a Nazi flag and when they were assembled in mass formation, the bowl looked like a shimmering sea of swastikas.

Then Hitler began to speak. The crowd hushed into silence, but the drums continued their steady beat. Hitler's voice rasped into the night and every now and then the multitude broke into a roar of cheers. Some of the audience began swaying back and forth, chanting '*Sieg Heil*' over and over again in a frenzy of delirium. I looked at the faces round me and saw tears streaming down people's cheeks. The drums had grown louder and I suddenly felt frightened. For a moment I wondered if it wasn't a dream; perhaps we were really in the heart of the African jungle. I had a sudden feeling of claustrophobia and whispered to Jules Sauerwein, asking if we couldn't leave. It was a silly question, for we were hemmed in on all sides, and there was nothing to do but sit there until the bitter end.

At last it was over. Hitler left the box and got back in the car. As soon as he stopped speaking the spell seemed to break and the magic vanish. That was the most extraordinary thing of all: for when he left the stand and climbed back into his car, his small figure suddenly became drab and unimpressive. You had to pinch yourself to realise that this was the man on whom the eyes of the world were riveted; that he alone held the lightning in his hands.

* * *

The most fashionable gathering place in Nuremberg was the Grand Hotel. Here, the Parteitag's *Ehrengäste* were housed. Usually they consisted of prominent foreigners from all over the world, but this year the French were conspicuous by their absence and only twenty or thirty English people were present. They included a sprinkling of peers eager for an Anglo–German alliance, but for the most part were Fascist-minded Britons, members of the Mosley Party.

Outstanding in the English group were Lord and Lady Redesdale and their daughter, the Honourable Unity Valkyrie Mitford. Unity was a tall Junoesque girl, with shoulder-length blonde curls and large blue eyes. She worshipped Hitler with a schoolgirl passion and had persuaded her mother and father to come to Germany with her to see for themselves how wonderful he was.

Unity's brother, Tom Mitford, was a friend of mine in London, and I had met the Redesdales before, so I saw them several times during the week. It was their first visit to Germany, and they treated the whole affair as though it were as detached from their lives, or the future of their country, as a bizarre operetta. Lady Redesdale was a small, retiring woman who spent most of her time (when she was not at one of the reviews with Unity) in the corner of the hotel lobby sewing, while Lord Redesdale, a tall, handsome man with a large white moustache, wandered about with a bewildered air as though he were at a rather awkward house party where (curiously enough) no one could speak any English.

Owing to the fact that Unity was known to be a friend of Hitler, all week long Lord Redesdale was inundated with frantic letters begging him to use his influence to stop the war. One day he received a note from the Buchman Society, which was holding a conference in Geneva. The note begged him to show the Führer a letter which had been published in the London *Times* on September 10th (referring to the need for moral re-armament), declaring that it might 'change the Führer and alter the course of history'. His slightly petulant comment was: 'Dammit all, I haven't got a copy of *The Times*.'

Somehow it was all like a chapter from P. G. Wodehouse.

Besides bringing her family with her, Unity had also invited Robert Byron to Nuremberg. This gave the group an even more curious complexion, for there was certainly no more rabid an anti-Nazi than Robert. He was an Englishman in his early thirties, who had already established a reputation as a writer and expert on Eastern art. I had known Robert in London, and during the week we frequently wandered about the town and visited the beer gardens together. Robert had come to Nuremberg out of curiosity and was undecided as to whether the show was comic or sinister.

'These people are so grotesque,' he kept saying. 'If we go to war, it will be like fighting a gigantic zoo.'

Robert maintained a light vein but at times his indignation got the better of him. I remember one afternoon when we went into the Wurttemberger Hof for tea. The restaurant was crowded with officials, all of whom seemed in a very jolly frame of mind, laughing and talking loudly. Seated at the next table were Dr Silex, editor of the *Deutsche Allgemeine Zeitung*, Dr Dietrich, the press chief, Dr von Dircksen, the German Ambassador to London, and Herr von Lösch of the Foreign Office. They invited us to join them, and soon the conversation turned inevitably to the topics of the day. Dr Silex referred to the article in the London *Times* and said he was sure England would come to her senses before it was too late and realise that Czechoslovakia was not the concern of Britain but of Germany. I saw a red flush rising on Robert's neck and the next moment I heard him saying in a deadly voice, 'What happens on the continent is always England's concern. Every now and then we are unfortunate enough to be led by a Chamberlain – but that's only temporary. Don't be misguided. In the end we *always* rise up and oppose the tyrannies that threaten Europe. We have smashed them before, and I warn you we will smash them again.' A terrible silence fell, then Herr von Lösch laughed uneasily and suggested that we talk of 'less serious things'. The conversation was strained, and when we got up to leave no one urged us to stay.

* * *

All week long Hitler had appeared grave and preoccupied. He had refused to receive foreign diplomats and even to talk with his own advisers. But on Saturday afternoon he appeared at a tea which Herr von Ribbentrop, the German Foreign Minister, gave in his honour. Invitations were eagerly sought, but the guest list was limited to about seventy people, most of whom were diplomats and delegates. I was lucky enough to be included and at four o'clock the guests gathered at the Hotel Deutscher Hof. Ribbentrop, smiling and obsequious, stood at the door, receiving. The banquet hall was crowded with small tea tables, and on each one was a card saying: 'Please Don't Smoke In The Presence Of The Führer'.

Most of the leading German officials were present – Goering, Goebbels, Himmler, Heidrich, Hess, and many others. Unity Mitford was there, surrounded by officials who kissed her hand and bowed and scraped. She seemed rather embarrassed by their attention, left the group, and joined my table; a few minutes later the doors swung open and Hitler came in. Everybody rose to their feet and the German party leaders stood rigidly at attention, giving the Nazi salute.

I had never seen Hitler at close quarters before, and what struck me most was his lack of distinction. If he hadn't been Adolf Hitler he would have been lost in the crowd. There was nothing in his face, or his walk, or his smile that either attracted or repelled. He was just an ordinary and rather inconspicuous little man. On the other hand, this was provocative in itself and I found myself searching his face for some sign of the genius that had raised him to his giddy height.

He took his place at a table across the room at which there were about a dozen men, including two English peers: Lord Stamp and Lord Brocket. There was also Ward Price (of the *Daily Mail*) and Herr Henlein, the leader of the Sudeten German Nazi Party.

When everyone was seated, Hitler's gaze wandered over the gathering and his eyes suddenly lit on Unity. His face broke into a smile, he nodded, and gave her the Nazi salute. She saluted back and a few minutes later Captain Wiedemann, Hitler's ADC, came over to our table and whispered in Unity's ear, 'The Führer would like to see you. When tea is over he would like you to come to his suite.' Unity nodded. I couldn't help thinking how odd it was that, on the brink of war between Germany and Great Britain, the only person that the Führer would condescend to see was a twenty-four-year-old English girl.

During the rest of tea Hitler was in high spirits. He kept up a steady stream of conversation with Lord Brocket and several times threw back his head and laughed loudly. I had always imagined him a grave and melancholy man and was surprised by his animation. His glance continuously wandered to our table and I had the impression that he was showing off to impress Unity!

After the reception Unity had her talk with Hitler and came back to the Grand Hotel just before dinner. I hastily cornered her and asked what he had said and whether or not she thought there was going to be a war. 'I don't think so,' she smiled. 'The Führer doesn't want his new buildings bombed.'

She went on to add she had never seen Hitler in more exuberant spirits. 'He says it's very exciting to have the whole world trembling before him. He needs the excitement as other people need food and drink.' Somehow, it was profoundly disturbing to hear that Hitler was actually enjoying himself while people all over Europe tossed in their beds.

That night I dined with Robert Byron, Ward Price and Unity at a small restaurant in the old city. It was difficult to get across the town, as the Storm Troopers' parade was scheduled to begin at nine o'clock and no cars were allowed on the streets. Unity, however, arranged for one of the SS cars to drive us to the restaurant, and we soon found ourselves in a long, sleek black car racing through empty streets with crowds on either side. Unity sat in front with the black-uniformed chauffeur, her blonde curls streaming in the wind, like the Valkyrie after which she was named.

The restaurant was near the river and as we sat there we could hear the sound of tramping feet in the distance and voices rising into the chant of Nazi military hymns. It was a starlit night, but somehow the beauty of our surroundings seemed to add to a general feeling of depression.

Unity was the only one in gay spirits and talked at length about Hitler. 'The first moment I saw him,' she said, 'I knew there was no one in the world I would rather meet.'

That moment was in 1933 at the first Nazi Partietag, which she attended with her sister Diana (now Lady Mosley). Deeply impressed by Hitler's personality, she was determined to become acquainted with him. Since she couldn't speak German, she decided to master the language first. She studied in Munich for nearly two years, then tried to find someone to introduce her to him. For weeks she had no success. One night she went into a beer garden and found him sitting at a table with a group of friends. She watched him with admiring attention. He dropped a magazine and she sprang to pick it up. The following night she went back to the beer garden, and again found him there. Summoning her courage, she walked over to his table and stammered that she was the girl who had picked up his magazine, and asked if she could talk with him. He smiled and invited her to join him. From then on they were friends.

To Unity, National Socialism was a Left Wing revolution and Hitler the champion of the downtrodden masses. There was no doubt that the latter was flattered by her admiration and sincerely fond of her. He often telephoned her, gave her presents, and in public treated her with deference. Although the Nazi Party leaders fawned over her in public, in private they were jealous of the friendship. Tom Mitford told me that when Unity went to Germany they often refused to tell Hitler she had arrived. The only way she could get into communication with him was to wait in the street, sometimes for hours, hoping to catch his eye when he passed.

She seldom asked for favours and, in spite of the attentions thrust upon her during the week of the Party Congress, kept modestly in the background. She had a straightforward, friendly manner and a lively sense of humour. Her rather naïve observations on Hitler were at times strangely revealing. When I asked her what she talked with him about, she replied, 'Gossip.' He liked to hear the anecdotes his advisers were apt to overlook. For instance, when Madame de Fontanges, the French journalist, fired a revolver at Count de Chambrun, the French Ambassador in Rome, declaring that the latter had tried to thwart her romance with Mussolini, Unity related the episode to Hitler. She said he thought it very funny and laughed delightedly, saying what a narrow squeak it might have been for 'poor old Mussolini'.

According to her, Hitler had a sense of humour and liked company. He was a man who seldom read, but when he was at Berchtesgaden spent a good deal of time drawing up architectural plans for new housing settlements. 'But what he really likes,' she said, 'is excitement. Otherwise he gets bored.'

Somehow, the thought that world happiness hung on the *ennui* of one man was a frightening contemplation. But the remark that struck me most was her comment on Hitler's talent as an imitator.

She claimed that if he were not the Führer of Germany, he would make a hundred thousand dollars a year on the vaudeville stage. He often did imitations of his colleagues – Goering, Goebbels and Himmler – but, best of all, he liked to imitate Mussolini. This always provoked roars of laughter. 'And sometimes,' added Unity, 'he even imitates himself.'

Now this threw a new light on the character of the Führer. This was the personality of the showman, not the fanatic. No sincere crusader would laugh at his own expense. Perhaps, after all (to quote Hitler), he was 'an artist, not a politician'.

I didn't wait for Hitler's Nuremberg speech, scheduled for Monday night. I had done my article for the *Sunday Times* and decided to return to Paris where I could collect clothes and money, and leave for Prague if the situation grew worse. Just before the plane left, Robert Byron came to say goodbye to me. He said Lady Redesdale had lost her embroidery needle and Lord Redesdale was searching for it on his hands and knees in the middle of the Grand Hotel lobby, while a flow of heavily booted Storm Troopers and SS men strode past in every direction.

'Now, that's symbolic of England. You might almost say it was like looking for a needle in a sword-rack!'

3

The War That Didn't Happen

I listened to Hitler's Nuremberg speech in H. R. Knickerbocker's flat on the Quai de Bethune – the whining, cajoling, bullying voice that rose to a scream with the sentence: 'If these tortured creatures (the Sudeten Germans) cannot obtain rights and assistance by themselves, they can obtain both from us.'

On looking back it seems strange the speech should have left anyone in doubt, but it did. Optimists pointed out that Hitler hadn't committed himself to a 'definite' line of action. Perhaps this was the master bluff; if the democracies stood firm, he now might be forced to accept his first diplomatic defeat. On the other hand, could a dictator back down? Statesmen had not yet learned that clever words and subtle manoeuvres no longer fashioned policies; the only things that counted were guns, tanks and planes.

When the speech was over I drove to the Quai d'Orsay to see M. Comert, the French foreign press chief, with John Whitaker of the *Chicago Daily News*. He received us with a smile. 'It is better than we expected. Naturally, the picture isn't altogether rosy but it might have been worse. He didn't say he would *attack* Czechoslovakia.'

In that atmosphere of uncertainty and false hope, the only wise reaction we got was from the taxi driver who took us home. John asked him if he had heard the speech and muttered something about Hitler being a maniac. 'Ah, no,' said the taxi driver. 'That is not the right word. On the contrary. He is an ace for Germany and a disaster for France.' I often thought of those words and wondered how different the destiny of France might have been

if the taxi driver had been Minister for Foreign Affairs, instead of
M. Bonnet. (When Bonnet went to London to hold conversations
with the British Government, Randolph Churchill stood on the
street corner, and when his car passed, shouted at the top of his
lungs: 'Courage, Monsieur Bonnet, courage!')

John and Knickerbocker left for Prague the next morning and I
followed a day later. The speech had inflamed the Czechoslovakian
Germans and rioting had broken out all over Sudeten territory.
The Czechs had declared marshal law, and once again called up
their reservists. I arrived in Prague to find the capital chilled by
an air of menace, with the centuries-old buildings looking sad
and grey beneath an overcast sky. Everywhere there were signs
of feverish activity: workmen were digging air-raid shelters in
the park; women queuing up outside the shops to lay in stores
of food; children being fitted with gas-masks. Thousands of civilian recruits with suitcases and bundles were streaming into the
barracks, and all day long troop trains pulled slowly out of the station. Although there was an emergency censorship on the press,
extras appeared every few hours and were immediately sold out.
The cafés were crowded with people in anxious speculation, and
every now and then you overheard a grim snatch of conversation.
'Tonight. Do you think the bombers will come tonight?'

Yet, in spite of this hourly uncertainty, life went on in its normal swing. That was what always struck one most in a crisis: the
commonplace things that people did and said. Men having their
hair cut, women arguing with the grocer, children going to the
cinema. Even the porter in the Hotel Ambassador greeted me with
a polite, matter-of-fact smile, and said, 'I'm glad to see you back' –
as though I'd come for a holiday!

The hotel was already full of press correspondents, photographers and broadcasters. The telephones were ringing just as they

had rung in Nuremberg, Paris, Berlin and London, ready to relay the latest news from Prague.

I ran into Ed Beattie of the United Press, who had arrived that morning, and he told me that Knickerbocker and John Whitaker had gone into the Sudeten areas and were making their headquarters at Carlsbad. All sorts of reports were coming in about the fighting. The Germans were declaring that it had turned into a bloody civil war and the Czechs were denying it. Ed and I decided to drive through the territory and find out for ourselves.

We hired a car and left the next morning. A few miles outside Prague we passed three schoolchildren cycling down a dusty road, their pigtails flying in the breeze, with long grey cylindrical gas-masks slung carelessly over their handlebars. A little further on the Czech lines of defence started – neat rows of pill-boxes, camouflaged to look like haystacks, that stretched for miles across the fields. They were guarded by Czech soldiers with fixed bayonets and steel helmets, who seemed oddly out of place in the peaceful countryside; peasants in nearby fields went on working as though their presence was a matter of course.

It wasn't difficult to tell when we had reached the Sudeten districts, for the white posts along the road suddenly bloomed with swastikas vividly painted with red chalk. The telephone posts blazed with 'Heil Hitler's, and most of the sign-boards bearing Czech names had been mutilated and torn down.

We stopped at Carlsbad, one of the most popular health resorts in Europe, to find the great hotels, usually crowded with foreigners, forlorn and deserted. We went into the Grand Hotel Pup for tea, where we were the only people in the restaurant. A dozen waiters hung about idly, and our voices sounded so loud in the stillness that we began talking in embarrassed whispers. When I went into the dressing room, the maid, a middle-aged German woman, fussed over me as though she were starved for company. Suddenly she burst into tears and said the summer business had been ruined by the terrible talk of war. 'I don't know what has happened,' she cried. 'A few months ago we were living here peacefully. Now people suddenly seem to have gone crazy.' She said there were only two guests in the entire hotel: American schoolteachers who had come to Carlsbad for a cure and stubbornly refused to move.

Ed and I found, as we drove along, that apart from Nazi leaders and a few zealots, the ordinary people with whom we talked – like simple people anywhere – wanted to be left alone and in peace. Their tragedy was that they were pawns in a game too big and too complicated to understand. We had an example of this in the tiny village of Harbersbirk, where one of the most violent riots had taken place, when two thousand Sudeten Germans had stormed the doors of the Czech Police headquarters. Four Czech gendarmes had been killed and a flag fluttered from the roof-top at half-mast. Inside, the rooms were a debris of smashed furniture, and the floor stained with blood. On the wall, the glass frame over the picture of Thomas Masaryk, the founder of the Republic, bore a jagged crack.

Outside, two Germans wandered forlornly round the court-yard. One was a young Social Democrat who talked in excited tones and said because he had supported the Czechs in the riot the Nazi Germans accused him of being a traitor, and now he was afraid to go home. The other, an old man, a schoolteacher, stood quietly in the middle of the yard, shaking his head over and over again. He explained he was too old to take an interest in politics, but he couldn't understand why they had done it; surely, he said, pointing towards the smashed doors, that could not be the new German culture.

Ed and I drove about for several hours; the outbreaks could scarcely be described (as the German press claimed) as 'civil war'.

The quick action of the Czechs in declaring martial law had soon re-established order. Only a few districts still showed outward hostility. One of these was Eger, a town not far from the frontier. Here the Nazi machine was well organised and the community offered a grim picture of resistance.

We drove into the main square, which ordinarily hummed with life, to find it deserted. The Germans had pulled down their blinds, closed their shops, and now they refused to leave their houses. The streets were empty save for a few Czech gendarmes and stray groups of soldiers who stood forlornly at the corners. There was no traffic, only an occasional army lorry that came rattling through the square headed for some unknown destination. The Czechs had posted notices appealing to the people to resume their normal duties, but no one had responded. It was a weird experience to wander through the silent streets and to know the town was not deserted at all – that behind the drawn blinds the Germans sat waiting. We found one small restaurant open with no one in it except the proprietor, who lolled behind the counter in his shirt-sleeves. He stared at us suspiciously and when we asked for a cup of coffee, shook his head: 'Business is suspended.' Ed asked when he was opening up again and he thumped the counter angrily and replied, 'When the German Army marches in.' We enquired when that would be, and he said, 'Any hour.' He told us he had just heard over the radio that Henlein had issued a proclamation demanding the immediate surrender of Sudeten territory to Germany. 'Now the Reichswehr will come,' he said (still with a sort of angry triumph), 'and soon we will be liberated.'

Ed and I were startled by the news of the proclamation, and after a consultation decided to drive on to Asch, a frontier town which jutted deeply into the Reich and which had, for the past few weeks, served as Henlein's headquarters. Ed thought Henlein might be hiding there, and perhaps he would be lucky enough to get a story. We drove on, not knowing at any moment whether or not we might round a bend to find ourselves confronted by a long grey column of flashing steel. However, when we reached Asch we got a very different shock. Ed went into a hotel to ring up his Berlin office and came out with a startled expression. 'If you thought for a hundred years, you'd never guess what's happened now! It's a real brain-twister!'

He was right, for when he told me that Chamberlain was flying to Berchtesgaden I thought some overworked United Press correspondent's brain must have snapped. Ed was indignant that a British Prime Minister should fly halfway across Europe to court favour from Hitler, but gradually adopted a more hopeful view. 'If only Hitler will scream at him, perhaps it will cure him of any illusion about dealing with Germany.'

We had dinner at the hotel, then started in search of the Sudeten Nazi headquarters. Most of Henlein's supporters had either fled into Germany or were in hiding, and when we reached the address given to us by the porter, a small boy appeared and told us no one was there. He flashed a light in our faces and after a long and troubled hesitation finally gave us another address. An icy wind swept the streets, and it took us nearly an hour to find it; at last we stumbled down a dark alleyway and knocked on a door that was opened by two Nazi guards. They argued about us for a considerable time, but finally led us upstairs where we found eight men huddled round an oil-burner listening to the radio news from Leipzig.

The air was thick with tobacco smoke and they talked in low, strained voices. The windows were pasted with black paper, and one of them explained that it was necessary to take every precaution lest the Czech police should find them and close the building.

We asked if they knew Henlein's whereabouts and they stared at us suspiciously and shook their heads. Gradually they grew more talkative, and when we commented on the *Anschluss* proclamation, a tall man with a three-day beard shrugged his shoulders and said it was nothing new – it was merely the expression of an idea which every Henleinist had had from the beginning. The group then plunged into an account of wrongs done them by the Czechs. One man said he was sure Mr Chamberlain would come to an agreement with Hitler, and another added if he didn't the German Army would enter Sudeten territory anyway, and Asch, with its fortunate strategical position, would have the honour of being the first town incorporated in the Reich. The others nodded and assured us it could be captured in less than twenty minutes.

It was a strange scene: those grim, unshaven men living like outlaws, waiting hourly for the tramp of German feet to make them part and parcel of the Third Reich. I have often wondered if any of them changed their opinions once their desire was granted.

When Ed and I left, a man peered cautiously up and down the street to make sure no Czech policemen were hovering about, before letting us out. The following morning Ed took a train to Berlin and I drove back to Prague.

* * *

During the next few days, as the wires flashed news of one dramatic event after another, the hopes and fears of Prague swung back and forth like a compass needle in a fast-gathering storm. Chamberlain to Berchtesgaden, Daladier and Bonnet to London. What did it all mean? The destiny of Czechoslovakia lay in the hands of a few men; the mass of people had no part in the moves played across the international chessboard; all they could do was to wonder and to wait and to hope.

They waited uneasily, for they were becoming alarmed by articles in the leading English and French newspapers, which suddenly began to treat the Sudeten–Czech problem as though it were an isolated quarrel, arguing the pros and cons of the case on its face value and naïvely insisting that a solution must be found by a display of goodwill on both sides. To the Czechs, the problem was not a local one. The cession of Sudetenland didn't mean the convenient loss of an unruly population; it meant the loss of a fortified mountain frontier which would bring the borders of the Reich within thirty miles of Prague – little more than an hour for the mechanised units of an invading army; it meant the death of the Republic and the disruption of the country into a German corridor for the riches of the East.

Czechoslovakia was originally created as a buffer state to prevent this very thing from happening. The reason that the Sudeten Germans had been included in the Czech Republic was because they lived within the mountains which were Bohemia's natural lines of defence. But statesmen seemed to have lost sight of this fact and now the problem had become one 'which must be localised'. It was argued that the Sudeten Germans had many just grievances, and that (as *The Times* had pointed out on September 7th) the Czechs might be far better off freed of a disloyal population.

The Czechs countered these assertions stubbornly, but helplessly, insisting that Sudeten dissension had been deliberately provoked by German agents. They pointed to the fact that in 1933, after fourteen years of Czech administration, Henlein had made the following statement: 'By identifying ourselves with the Czechoslovak State we assent to the fundamental idea of democracy, and assess the Czech people, whose destiny is inextricably bound up with our own, as a cultural nation, equal in quality to any nation in Central Europe.'

But 1933 was the year Hitler came to power, and from then on corruption set in. Henlein's party steadily increased, and with the Austrian *Anschluss*, Czechoslovakia received a heavy blow. Nazi agents encouraged the wave of militarism that swept the German areas, and the Sudetens, swelling with the pride of nationalism, became openly pro-Hitler. They held Nazi rallies, decorated their houses with swastikas and formed their own SS guard. The Reich press campaign against the Czechs continued to inflame opinion and Hitler's Nuremberg speech fired it to open revolt. Only four months before Herr Ulrich had admitted the Czechs were 'pretty good fellows'; now a state of siege existed, entirely brought about by the cunning and relentlessness of the German propaganda machine.

The genius of Dr Goebbels was not yet recognised as Germany's most dangerous weapon. Today, after experience of Fifth Column activities in Norway, Holland, Belgium and France, it is not difficult to believe Czech assertions that the Sudeten revolt was engineered by Nazi agents. But in the summer of 1938, many people pointed to Czech 'stubbornness', arguing that had Dr Benesch given proper concessions to his minorities, the crisis might never have arisen. These arguments, pontificated so wisely, gravely and painstakingly, are ludicrous in the light of past events. To the Czechs, they seemed just as ludicrous three years ago.

My Czech friend, Mr B, the little professor who had sighed over the cherry blossoms and who believed so passionately that because democracy was *right* it was bound to triumph, came into the Hotel Ambassador on Sunday morning just after he had learned that a conference was being held in London to find a basis on which to open negotiations with the Germans. He was deeply distressed. 'If they force us to surrender,' he said with tears in his eyes, 'it will be the end of us. Why can't they understand? The only trouble with Czechoslovakia is that it lies in the way!'

* * *

On Sunday I decided to return to London. The fate of Czechoslovakia was being decided by British and French statesmen and no further developments were likely to take place in Prague until Chamberlain had his second talk with Hitler, scheduled for the following week. I had been away from England since July and wanted to make arrangements about my flat, and collect some warm clothes in case I should find myself spending the winter in Central Europe 'covering' a long war. I asked the porter to try and get me a ticket on the plane, but there were so many refugees leaving the country that there were no available seats. After making my plans to go by train, he suddenly rang back and said that a private plane was leaving for Paris at noon. It was making a landing at Nuremberg, but if I had no objection to stopping in Germany, the pilot would take me for the price of the ordinary fare.

It was one of the strangest trips I have ever made. The plane was an eight-seater Potez; there were two French pilots and a navigator, and I was the only passenger. I thought it odd that in spite of the feverish exodus from Czechoslovakia, there should be seven empty seats, but I put it down to the fact that the majority of refugees didn't care to enter German territory.

The three Frenchmen sat in the cockpit and I sat alone in the empty cabin. It took only an hour and a half to reach Nuremberg. When we landed I noticed that the pilots seemed nervous. They lit innumerable cigarettes while the German officials were inspecting our papers and made an exaggerated effort at conversation. We were detained for nearly half an hour and when at last we took off again and rose safely above the town, the navigator laughed excitedly and said, 'Thank God for that.' He must have noticed my perplexity, for he quickly added, 'It's always a relief to leave Germany, isn't it?'

I realised that something unusual was taking place, but couldn't imagine what – until we neared Strasbourg. Suddenly the plane swooped down to less than a thousand feet. The navigator came out of the cockpit, carefully shut the door, and took a seat beside me. He pointed out of the window. 'Look. We are flying over the Siegfried Line.' Below, we could see miles of roadway, crowded with trucks and swarming with workmen.

It suddenly dawned on me that I was in a reconnaissance plane. Obviously I had been taken aboard as a dupe passenger. The Frenchmen had cleared their papers at Nuremberg, probably calculating there was less likelihood of being shot down if properly registered than crossing the German frontier unauthorised.

I realised the pilots were undoubtedly taking photographs and gazed out of the window fascinated. So this was the line that Hitler had described as 'the most gigantic fortification of all time'. According to his own report, over half a million men were working on it, but it was by no means complete, although Goering had declared it 'already invincible'. We could see miles of steel and concrete blockhouses still under construction. It was interesting to reflect that although Hitler had repeatedly wailed that he was ringed by enemies (France, Czechoslovakia and Poland), this was the first defensive line he thought necessary to build.

Momentarily, I expected to hear the crack of anti-aircraft bullets, for we certainly must have been violating every international air code in flying so low; the pilots seemed to think it remarkable too, for when we finally reached Le Bourget aerodrome, they jumped out, wreathed in smiles, slapped each other on the back and shook hands with me warmly, saying what a pleasure it had been to have me as a passenger! I wished them luck; when I got into a taxi they stood on the steps and waved goodbye as though we were old friends.

Death by Strangulation

I was glad not to be in Prague during the next few days. When M. Bonnet, the French Foreign Minister, sent the Czechoslovakian Government the proposals agreed upon in London, and two days later (on September 21st) Dr Benesch accepted them, announcing he had done so only 'under unbelievable pressure', the Prague newspapers ran headlines 'Absolutely Forsaken', and people wept hysterically in the streets.

Besides the cession of the Sudeten districts to Germany, the proposals agreed that Czechoslovakia must be neutralised – her alliances with Soviet Russia and France abandoned for a four-power guarantee by Great Britain, France, Germany and Russia.

Now, from an international point of view, the second clause was even more of a German victory than the first. Not only had Hitler stripped Czechoslovakia of her fortified frontier, but had succeeded in reducing France, overnight, to a second-class power. France's prestige and security were based on two factors: first, her system of alliances throughout the continent; and second, her army. By surrendering her alliance with Czechoslovakia, the whole structure of her position had become untenable; the French dam carefully designed to hold German aggression in check had been allowed to break at Bohemia, and now German might was free to flow over the continent at will.

The *bouleversement* was so immense, it was difficult to grasp. What had happened? The press immediately seized upon Mr Chamberlain as the arch villain of the piece, claiming that the French had given way to British 'pressure'. This was furthered by

M. Daladier and M. Bonnet, who justified the proposals to the French Cabinet by explaining that 'the British Government, while in no way disputing the right of France to honour her treaty obligations to Czechoslovakia, had made it clear that they would not commit themselves in any way to military support of France, unless her integrity was threatened'.

This was a feeble justification. When all was said and done, it was France and not Great Britain who had a treaty with Czechoslovakia; and the reason France had a treaty with Czechoslovakia was to preserve her own (France's) frontiers from being overrun at some later date. However much she might deplore the fact that England had not also pledged direct aid to Czechoslovakia, she knew that if she went to war with Germany, Great Britain could not stand idly by.

France's diplomatic position was so strong that I found it hard to believe she had been merely a puppet in Mr Chamberlain's hands. I remembered Charles Mendl's warning, but it wasn't until I got to London on Thursday that I heard a true account of the story.

I dined with a Foreign Office official the night I arrived and learned from him that it was the French who had first caved in. On the evening of September 13th, M. Daladier, alarmed by the situation, communicated with Chamberlain and announced that France was in no position to fight, imploring the British Prime Minister to leave no stone unturned to find a way out. Thirty-six hours later, Chamberlain made his first trip to Berchtesgaden. You can find a subdued reference to the conversation in M. Daladier's statement to the French Chamber on October 4th, in which he said he got in touch with Mr Chamberlain on the night of September 13th–14th, and told him 'how useful it would be if diplomatic démarches were superseded by personal contact between responsible men'.

My friend told me that Sir Robert Vansittart, in his role of Chief Diplomatic Adviser to the Government, had been urging the British Cabinet (as had Winston Churchill) to declare open support of Czechoslovakia. Whether or not he might have succeeded will never be known, for when Daladier and Bonnet flatly announced that France wouldn't fight, the ground had been cut from under his feet and from then on the cause was a lost one.

Vansittart was not only staggered by the blow to French and British security (he told me a day or two later that he believed England and France would be at war with Germany within a year), but he was also staggered that France had perpetrated such a monstrous betrayal. He loved France deeply and the humiliation he felt was almost that of a father whose son turns out to be a cheat at cards.

The story of the French debacle was never published for fear of rupturing the Franco–British alliance, and the international press continued to attribute the entire responsibility to British 'pressure'.

In England there was a flood of angry and humiliated reaction against the Government. But most of it was the reaction of people who still believed Hitler was bluffing and could have been defeated (diplomatically) if England and France had stood firm. At the end of the week, however, Mr Chamberlain made a second trip to Germany, only to find that the Führer (with a technique now familiar) had greatly increased his demands, and added an ultimatum stating that the territory must be handed over in a week's time, starting October 1st.

The demands were so unreasonable that it seemed unlikely that even Chamberlain and Daladier could have the face to ask the Czechs to accept them. For the first time people began to wonder if Hitler was as opposed to war as they had thought. Mad though it seemed, perhaps the man was actually willing to take on Czechoslovakia, France and Great Britain! This was not exactly what the opposition had bargained for. Suddenly, everybody began to ask: how could the French get to Czechoslovakia? How could the Russians get to Czechoslovakia? How could the English get to Czechoslovakia? Would anyone get to Czechoslovakia, and how big was the German Air Force? At last the fact was dawning that it was not *policy* that prevented aggression but *armaments*.

The same day that Chamberlain talked to Hitler at Godesberg, the Czechs mobilised and once again the crisis was in full swing. I dined that night with Roger Chetwode, his wife Patricia (one of the prettiest girls in England), and Seymour Berry. In spite of attempts to make light-hearted conversation, it was a grim evening. We went to Quaglino's, where Roger ragged the Italian waiters and told them they had better hop it for Italy before it got too late. Mr Quaglino insisted firmly there wouldn't be a war. 'Of course, with a man like Hitler there is bound to be a little uncertainty. Now, if he were *normal*, like Mussolini . . .'

Seymour Berry, who had been running the *Daily Telegraph* in his father's absence, argued bellicosely and said he would rather fight a war now than watch England die in her sleep. Roger laughed and said it was odd to think peace had become so lugubrious a thought; in the forceful phraseology of *The Week*, Chamberlain had turned 'all four cheeks' to Hitler.

On Saturday, workmen were feverishly digging shelters; on Sunday, trucks with loudspeakers careened through the streets shouting to people to be fitted with gas-masks; on Monday, Hitler made a speech in Berlin announcing that Czechoslovakia would either hand over the territory by October 1st or else Germany would take it, and the Nazi press ran banner headlines: 'War or Peace. Let Benesch choose now'.

Even Mrs Sullivan was alarmed. She brought my breakfast, her hat perched indignantly over one eye, and said: 'What do those dictators think they're up to, causing decent people all this worry? My old man says the trouble is, they're common. He says they're no better born than me!'

War seemed a certainty. Roosevelt sent an eleventh-hour peace message; Chamberlain communicated with Mussolini; and Horace Wilson, Great Britain's Chief Economic Adviser, flew off to Berlin with a letter imploring Hitler to have patience. But it didn't look as though Hitler would. I rang up the Air Service and booked a ticket for Prague. The Dutch Service was the only one flying and I left Croydon at eight o'clock the following morning.

The airline bus swept down the embankment and we passed the Houses of Parliament, half pink in the early morning light. I had a queer feeling in my stomach as I wondered whether I would find them still standing when I got back. Most of the passengers in the plane were bound for Holland and the others for Budapest. We stopped at Amsterdam and I went into the waiting room to get a cup of coffee. The waiter, a small Dutchman with a shock of blond hair, commented on the situation and asked me where I was going. When I told him Prague, he threw his hands in the air. But he came back with a cup of coffee and a ham sandwich in a more reassuring mood. 'Don't worry,' he said, 'there won't be a war. Hitler's already got what he wants. He may be crazy, but he can't be *that* crazy.'

'Perhaps he wants the whole of Czechoslovakia,' I suggested. 'Perhaps,' he said meditatively. Then, with sudden fierceness, 'My God, what a terrible curse these Germans are. Europe will never be happy until she gets rid of them. But who will do the job? That is the trouble. No one wants to take it on.' He brought me an extra cup of coffee, explained it was 'on the house' and wished me the best of luck.

From Amsterdam the flight took about two hours. In the cabin of the plane, with the passengers casually reading their papers, and the stewardess hovering about like an anxious governess, the events on the earth below were strangely remote. It was only when we landed at the Prague aerodrome that the situation grew real again. The airport manager, a young Czech in his thirties (who had stamped my tickets and put me aboard the French plane for Paris the week before), came running out of the office, his face torn with dismay. 'Oh, mademoiselle,' he cried, 'why have you returned to all this misery? You must get back into the plane at once. At once! You must not remain here. It is madness.' He seemed genuinely distressed, but fortunately Major Lowell Riley, the American military attaché, had come to the aerodrome to meet me and succeeded in calming him down. He finally went away, still muttering, 'It is madness.'

If Lowell hadn't appeared I don't know how I would have got into town, for all cars had been requisitioned. As we drove along I saw a different Prague than I'd ever seen before. For weeks the Czechs had been faced with the grim choice of war or dismemberment, and now the answer was war. All the machinery of the twentieth century was tuning up in preparation for the awful event. The streets were thick with uniforms. Tanks and armoured cars rumbled through the city. Women were blacking out their houses, shopkeepers pasting their windows with strips of brown paper to keep the glass from shattering, and children walking along the pavements with gas-masks swinging from their shoulders. But it was the ordinary things that were the most surprising. As we drove up the Václavské Náměstí (the 'Piccadilly' of Prague), I saw two workmen standing inside one of the arcades, hanging a mirror on the wall. One stood back to tell the other when he'd got it at the right angle. With the hourly expectancy of German bombers this detail had a whimsical appeal. I wondered how long the mirror would remain intact.

Lowell left me at the Hotel Ambassador and this time the placid desk clerk looked surprised. 'You shouldn't have returned,' he said – almost as forbiddingly as the aerodrome manager. I was careful to get a room on the first floor, then went in search of John Whitaker and Knickerbocker. I found them in Knick's room, sitting in the middle of the floor with enormous maps stretched out in front of them.

'My God, how did you get here!' exclaimed Knick. I learned that all the French and English journalists had left the day before on what was presumably the last plane. The frontiers were closed, no trains were running, and even the telephone wires had been cut. Evidently, it was easier to get into Czechoslovakia than to get out. The only communication with the outside world was the telegraph, which was delayed as long as eighteen hours.

We all three sat on the floor and began to study the map, trying to work out (from our point of view) the most likely vantage places. 'I hope you've brought enough things to last a year,' said Knick gloomily. 'There's no way out. We'll be trapped in Central Europe for the duration.'

'Yes,' agreed John, looking disdainfully at my shoes, 'and I hope you've got something with flatter heels than those, because we're going to have a hell of a lot of running to do!'

That was, of course, if the war came off. There was always that 'if'. In spite of the grim preparations around us, we wondered. The Anglo–French proposals had presented Hitler with Central Europe; what was there to fight about? If the British and French Governments had succeeded in persuading the Czechs to give in so far, why not a little further? Chamberlain was making a broadcast that night and we tried to tune in, but there was so much static we heard only a garbled report. We got the part about 'how horrible, fantastic, incredible it is that we should be digging trenches and trying on gas-masks here because of a quarrel in a far-away country between people of whom we know nothing'; and we got the bit at the end which said: 'As long as war has not begun, there is always hope that it may be prevented, and you know that I am going to work for peace until the last moment.'

'Yes,' said John, 'we know. But what we don't know is whether Hitler is going to work for peace, and that's what matters.'

The hotel was so depressing that night, we wandered through the Old Town trying to find a place to dine. All the street lamps had been painted a dull blue against air attacks, and in the weird light the people we passed looked like corpses fished out of the water. We tried half a dozen restaurants but found them all closed, and finally came back to the small nightclub connected with the hotel. No one was there except two dance hostesses with dyed hair and low-cut evening dresses, who sat in the corner getting drunk. But the band played bravely. All the old tunes: 'If You Were the Only Girl in the World' and 'On a Night Like This'. For a while we forgot the war, but I had a nasty jolt when I got upstairs and found a huge gas-mask reclining on the pillow of my bed. Lowell Riley's card was attached and a note that said: 'With the compliments of the American Embassy'.

The next morning John Whitaker banged on my door at ten o'clock and told me to hurry and get dressed – a rumour was circulating that the Germans were going to bomb the capital at two that afternoon. (Hitler had set 2 p.m. as the expiration of his final ultimatum.) John and Knick went to the War Office to get papers accrediting us to the Czech Army, and I managed, with the help of Lowell Riley, to find a car and chauffeur, and what was more important, some petrol. We all met at lunch and congratulated ourselves that nothing had been overlooked. 'Except your shoes,' said John fiercely. 'For God's sake, go out and buy yourself a pair of flat-heeled shoes.' I obeyed meekly, but discovered that all the shops were closed – it was King Wenceslas Day!

Two o'clock came, three o'clock and four o'clock, and still nothing happened. We went to Knick's room, turned on the radio and tried to get a London station. The dial swung across the yellow board, through Paris, Berlin, Moscow and Bucharest, giving international reports in a dozen languages until finally, through a wave of static, came the sound of an English voice. The air attack was off; Mr Chamberlain was going to Munich.

We knew then the grim comedy was ended. The result of the conference, which finished at two-thirty in the morning, didn't appear in the Prague papers and wasn't communicated to the Czech people until the following afternoon, when Benesch broadcast to the nation. The huge square in front of the hotel (the Václavské Náměstí) was strung with loudspeakers and soon after lunch people began to assemble. Most of the foreign journalists gathered in Knick's room, overlooking the square, and Maurice Hindus brought a Czech girl to translate the speech as it went along.

The broadcast was a short one, telling the nation of the final decision to partition the country. Then the pathetic words: 'Our state will not be the smallest. There are smaller states than we shall be.' The Czech stenographer put down her pencil, buried her head in her hands and wept. As the President's last words died away, the solemn music of the Czech National Anthem rolled over the square. The people below stood stiffly at attention as though they hadn't grasped the full significance of the words. Then the crowd broke and swept down the avenue, thousands of people shaking their fists and crying, 'No, no, no! Down with Benesch! Let Czechoslovakia live! Long live Czechoslovakia!' Hundreds of

Czech policemen surged into the square and swung a heavy cordon across the streets leading to Hradschin Palace where Benesch was staying, but the cries hung in the air like the cries of a wounded animal. They were terrible to hear.

* * *

An hour or so later, John, Knick and I were in a car headed for the Czech–Austrian frontier. Knick had heard that this was to be the Reichswehr's first zone of occupation, scheduled for any time after midnight. 'The second time in seven months,' he said unhappily, 'that I've had to watch the German Army invade a sovereign state without a shot being fired.'

It was a grim thought and an even grimmer drive. The countryside was still blacked out and our blue headlamps threw an eerie pattern against the ground. Our chauffeur (a White Russian émigré) had a difficult time as many of the bridges were mined and the roads blocked with farm wagons and machinery, hastily dragged out at the last moment. The wind had begun to rise and soon it started to rain, which made the going even harder. About forty miles from Prague we rounded a bend to see a long column of soldiers coming towards us – the Czech Army in retreat. They were marching in silence; the only noise was the sound of wind and rain, the roll of the gun-wheels and the slosh of boots in the mud. In that awful quiet you could feel the penetrating bitterness of the defeat.

In the villages it was the same. The squares were crowded with people standing forlornly in the rain as though they couldn't bear to go home for fear of being alone. And when we stopped for dinner at a town called Tabor, we found the restaurant filled with people sitting quietly at their tables drinking beer and cups of coffee, but not talking, just staring into space.

It was nearly eleven o'clock when we reached Budweiser, the last big Czech town before the Sudeten frontier. We went to the police station to try and find out the exact route of the German Army. It was an awkward question, but the Czech police inspector listened politely as though it were the most natural query in the world, pulled out a map from his desk, and began to study it. He was an unusual type for a police officer, with an intellectual brow and a delicate, sensitive face. He spoke English and told us that he had once been to America. 'A country for which I have great admiration.'

'Not more than we have for your country,' replied John. He made no comment, but said 'Thank you' in a quiet voice.

After a good deal of consideration, he advised us to go to a town called Oberplan, about seven or eight miles from the Austrian frontier. 'But you'll never find it at night. The roads are difficult and half of them are blocked. I'll send an officer with you.'

We begged him not to go to such trouble, but he insisted, and called a young policeman into the room. The boy couldn't have been over twenty, with blond hair and babyish pink cheeks. The inspector spoke to him in Czech and the boy pointed to his uniform. Then he disappeared and came back a moment later in a long black coat. He laughed and said something we couldn't understand and the inspector explained he thought it better not to cross into Sudeten territory without concealing his uniform.

Once again we started off and a few miles outside Budweiser came to a Czech patrol of thirty or forty men standing by the side of the road. It was ten minutes past twelve and we learned they had withdrawn from Sudeten territory on the dot of midnight – and for the last time. Our chauffeur and the policeman talked to them in Czech while they inspected our papers, then they handed them back, saluted, and a few moments later we crossed the new boundaries of the Third Reich.

We hadn't driven far before we discovered that the Sudeten peasants, heavily armed with rifles and shotguns, had taken over the Czech patrols. The atmosphere was electric and hostile; twice men jumped out of the bushes swinging lanterns and shouting to us to stop. They were gruff and sullen, but after inspecting our papers finally let us go.

Near Oberplan, however, we weren't so lucky. This time a dozen men sprang from the roadside, surrounded the car and thrust their rifles through the windows. They were evidently in a high state of excitement, for they shouted for help, as though we were a group of desperadoes, and more men came running down the road. One of them fired his rifle in the air (a signal of danger) and soon a crowd of over fifty had gathered. They were a group of the toughest, meanest-looking peasants I have ever seen. Most of them wore large swastika armbands and had home-made Nazi badges pinned on their coats. One of them, a man in a leather jacket, boots and breeches (obviously the local Führer) ordered us to produce identification papers. He snatched them out of our hands and walked up to the front of the car to inspect them under the headlamps. But they failed to interest him for long, for he suddenly caught sight of our registration plates. He strode back, thrust his head through the window, and said triumphantly: '*Ach so! Sie kommen aus Prag!*' ('So! You have come from Prague!')

Knick tried to explain that we were newspaper reporters on our way to watch the German Army cross the frontier, but it made no impression. He just stood glaring at us, repeating over and over: '*Ach so! Sie kommen aus Prag! Aus Prag!*'

In an ugly voice he announced that we would have to come to the village courthouse to be searched. Several men jumped on the running-board, their rifles still pointing into the car, and ordered the chauffeur to drive slowly. The others walked along on either side. It was an uncomfortable drive, for the Germans were keyed up to such a pitch of excitement that a false move by any of us might have led to a nasty accident.

When we reached the village square, about a mile and a half away, we found it thronged with men, women, children, all dressed up in their best clothes; some were shouting and waving swastikas, others were drinking beer, laughing and dancing. It was an extraordinary spectacle at one o'clock in the morning; they were waiting to be among the first to greet the German Army.

When our car stopped, the local Führer shouted at the crowd to make a passageway and we were led through the mob, with people staring stupidly at us, to the courthouse on the other side of the square. We were taken upstairs to a small room with a table and half a dozen chairs – probably the town council's meeting place – and with three or four henchmen still pointing their rifles at us. The local Führer began to search us for firearms. He carefully went through my bag and emptied the contents of John and Knick's pockets on the table, but when he got to the chauffeur's identification papers, he was stumped, for he stared hard, then asked what nationality he was. 'Russian,' the man replied. 'He's a Bolshevik!' exclaimed one of the henchmen excitedly. After a long explanation, the chauffeur finally established the fact that he was a White Russian and the excitement died. Then the leader turned to the Czech, who was still bundled up in his long coat, and ordered him to take it off. It was an awful moment but there was nothing for him to do but obey, and a moment later he stood there in full policeman's regalia. There was an amazed silence. Then the Führer shouted, 'A Czech! We've caught a Czech!'

He walked up to him swinging a rubber truncheon and cracked it down on the table. 'Do you know you are now in the Third Reich? That we no longer tolerate Czechs prowling around our villages?'

He plunged his hand into the policeman's pocket, yanked out a pair of gloves, a keyring and a wallet, and threw them on the table. Then he put his hand in the other pocket and pulled out a revolver and – of all things – a swastika armband!

The Czech had probably taken it from a Henleinist during one of the recent riots, and the mixture of triumph, hatred and revenge on the German's face was frightening to watch. 'So you have brought a revolver, to shoot down innocent German men and women. That is bad enough. But a swastika! A Czech with a swastika!' ('*Ein Tscheche mit Hakenkreuz!*') His voice trembled with rage. He walked around the room, every now and then punctuating his sentences by cracking the truncheon down on the table. '*Ein Tscheche mit Hakenkreuz!*' Then he turned to his men. 'Take him outside. We'll show him the way we deal with Czechs.'

The boy's face turned white. The Germans grabbed his arms and dragged him out of the room. I was very nearly ill. 'The dirty swine!' muttered John under his breath. 'They'll probably beat him to death.'

'It won't be the first time,' said Knick grimly.

I was still wondering whether I was going to be sick. 'But can't we do something!' I gasped. 'We can't just sit here.'

It was a foolish remark, for sit there was exactly what we had to do. The local Führer had worked himself into such a fit of anger that he shouted for a man with a sub-machine gun and told him to keep us under guard. 'If they move,' he said, 'shoot them.' Then he told us we would have to stay there until the Gestapo agent arrived from the Reich, strolled out and locked the door.

Our guard was a stupid-looking peasant who had never held a machine-gun before. He clung to it grimly, his eyes fixed on us as though at any moment we were going to make a dash for liberty.

We were so afraid that a move would upset him, we scarcely dared to turn our heads. Outside, we could hear the noise of the crowd: every now and then the voices rose to a wild cry, '*Sie kommen gleich!*' ('They're coming!'), but it was always a false alarm.

We wondered how long it would be before the Gestapo agent arrived, and what would happen when he did. Knickerbocker had been expelled from Germany and was the object of frequent attacks by the Nazi press. 'Don't worry,' I said. 'They'll be afraid of Americans.'

'Oh yeah?' replied Knick. 'Just the way they're afraid of England and France.'

However, we were lucky. The agent arrived at five o'clock in the morning – a typical SS man in black uniform: severe, unsmiling, overcorrect. When he came in the room, he bowed, clicked his heels and told us he would examine our papers immediately. Knickerbocker was evidently not on his blacklist and the words 'foreign journalists' seemed to make a deep impression. A few minutes later he came back, apologising for the inconvenience we had been put to, and ordered our release. But when we asked him about the Czech policeman, his mouth tightened. 'That is a different matter. We will have to deal with his case separately.'

By this time we were so exhausted we went to the small inn across the square and slept until eight o'clock. The crowd had thinned out but there must have been over a hundred people (slightly bedraggled now) still waiting.

In the morning, when we were ready to start again for the frontier, our chauffeur announced we had run out of petrol. The garage wouldn't give him any without a special permit, so Knick and I went back to the courthouse. We found the SS man sitting at a desk, already hard at work, poring over the local administration books. Although he'd not been to bed, he was wasting no time in establishing the authority of Nazi Germany; when Knick remarked that he ought to get some sleep, he replied unsmilingly, 'Soldiers of the Reich only rest when their work is done' – exactly like a Hollywood film!

As we were leaving his office, a Sudeten farmer with a degenerate face pushed his way excitedly into the room. He said two Communists were hiding down the road and he wanted permission to arrest them and take them to jail. 'Are you sure they're Communists?' asked the SS man. 'Oh yes,' replied the farmer. 'I heard them speak against the Führer.' The SS man nodded and the Sudeten hurried off.

We got the authorisation for petrol, but in the end we never saw the German Army cross the frontier. We drove to the barrier posts near Hohenfurt and even there found village people, with flowers and wreaths, waiting to welcome the troops. We hung about for several hours, but at noon there was still no sign of the long grey columns. Knick and John had afternoon editions to catch and there were no communications with the outside world apart from those in the capital. We didn't dare cross into Germany for fear of not being allowed back again, and finally decided the only thing to do was return to Prague and write the story we already had.

We were still badly shaken by the fate of our Czech policeman and stopped at Budweiser to tell the inspector what had happened. He received the news with great distress. 'He will never return. I know those Germans. They will kill him.' We told him we would do everything in our power to get him out, and when we reached Prague made representations through the American Embassy as well as telegraphing to Berlin ourselves. Several weeks after we had left Czechoslovakia, we heard that, although badly beaten, he was still alive and had finally been released.

The drive back to Prague was long and uncomfortable. The rain had made the roads even worse than the day before, and as we jogged along we tried to write the 'leads' to our stories. I remember Knick's opening sentence, for it was only three words long: 'Evil has won.'

* * *

In Prague, the Munich anti-climax was tragic. The foreign embassies were deluged with people begging for passports to flee the country, and even the journalists had pathetic requests for help. John and I were sitting at the café in front of the hotel when an old man overheard us speaking English and came up to the table. He was a German writer who had spent two years in a concentration camp, and had only been released in 1936 when he had come to Prague. 'You must help me to get away,' he said. 'I couldn't stand it again. I'm too old.' There was nothing we could do and John tried to reassure him. 'But you're all right in Prague.' The man shook his head. 'They will be here soon. Everybody knows that.'

It was the awful sense of doom that wrung our hearts. When the Czechs had thought they were going to fight, their spirits were high, but now that they were pulling the strips of brown paper off their windows, lighting the street lamps and throwing away their gas-masks, hope was gone. The Czech professor (the one who had sighed over the cherry blossoms the May before and who is now in a concentration camp) came to the hotel to see me. Already he looked older and his voice was tired. 'I hear they are celebrating in London and Paris. I hear Mr Chamberlain has become a hero. We should celebrate too, for in Prague the time is short. In six months half of us will be in concentration camps.'

I was so upset by what I had seen, my one idea was to leave as quickly as possible, but I stayed long enough to hear Hitler's

speech in Carlsbad the following Tuesday. I made the trip with
Ralph Murray of the British Broadcasting Corporation. It was a
grey rainy day and when we arrived, about eleven o'clock in the
morning, we found the town already overflowing with German
troops and SS men. Hundreds of workmen were erecting triumphal arches across the streets – huge wreaths with flowers
entwined which spelt the words '*Wir danken unseren Führer*'
('We thank our Leader'). But the most feverish activity was on the
part of the Propaganda Section. Since early morning, armoured
cars carrying microphones, loudspeakers, cameras, recording
machines, banners, propaganda leaflets and swastikas had been
pouring into the town. The Schmuckplatz, the large square where
Hitler was scheduled to speak, was being strung with loudspeakers and every now and then orders were shouted to the crowd that
had begun to assemble. The Propaganda boys were stealing the
limelight, which is exactly as it should have been, for if this wasn't
Dr Goebbels' victory, what was?

I was wandering along the crowded streets when I ran into
Dr Boehmer, head of the German foreign press: he told me that
the correspondents from Berlin had a place on the corner of the
Schmuckplatz, and I went in search of them. After pushing my
way through a long line of SS men I finally caught sight of Euan
Butler and Ed Beattie. They were standing in the rain, waiting
for the great event, so depressed they could scarcely summon a
smile. They had been covering the story from the Berlin angle,
and had already accompanied the German Army on three zones
of occupation.

Major Hinzinger, a dapper figure in boots and breeches, was
in charge of the group and hovered about making gay remarks.
I remember my surprise when Ed Beattie looked at his watch,
turned to the Major, and said: 'How long is that pop-eyed bastard

going to keep us waiting?' But the Major accepted it as though it were all part of the comical way in which Americans expressed themselves. 'You mean the Führer?' he asked brightly. 'Oh, I don't think he'll keep us in suspense much longer.'

At a quarter to two the loudspeakers suddenly boomed: 'The Führer is in Carlsbad.' The crowd broke into a roar of cheering and kept it up until, fifteen minutes later, the great man entered the square, standing as usual in the front seat of a long black car with his hand outstretched in the Nazi salute. There was a wild frenzy of '*Sieg Heil*' when he appeared on the balcony of the Municipal Theatre.

He wore a long grey military coat that made him look smaller than usual. His speech was short, and had, I thought, an impatient ring; I remembered what Unity had said about his getting bored and wondered if now that the world was quieting down again he had suddenly lost interest. The only time his voice rose with conviction was when he hit the microphone and said: 'That I would be standing here one day, I knew.'

When it was over, Major Hinzinger came up, still smiling brightly, and I asked him how he felt after his victory over the Czechs. 'I suppose I shouldn't say it,' he replied, 'but, after all, I *am* a soldier. And I can't help feeling just a little disappointed that we weren't allowed to have a crack at them!'

Geoffrey Cox of the *Daily Express* drove back to Prague with Ralph and myself. Two miles outside Carlsbad a small group of Czech soldiers had drawn up alongside the road where the new frontier began. They stopped our car and one of them asked us, curiously, what the celebration was like. He listened quietly, then remarked in German: 'I suppose you'll be leaving Czechoslovakia soon. Are you going to France?' Geoffrey nodded and the soldier said: 'When you get there, you can tell them for us that one day they will look across that Maginot line of theirs and ask, "Where are those two million Czechs?" And we won't exist. They will fight alone.'

We drove the rest of the way to Prague in silence.

* * *

Sidelight for America: a few days after the Munich agreement, Jan Masaryk, the Czech minister in London and son of Thomas Masaryk, the founder of Czechoslovakia, was walking through Hyde Park when Joseph Kennedy, the American Ambassador, drove past him. The car stopped and Kennedy called out:

'Hi there, Jan! Want a lift?'

Jan got into the car and Kennedy slapped him on the back. 'Oh, boy! Isn't it wonderful!'

'What is?' asked Jan.

'Munich, of course. Now I can get to Palm Beach, after all!'

5

Neville Chamberlain

I watched the girl in the scarlet taffeta dress and the young man in tails whirl round the Ritz ballroom so fast they looked like a red and black top. I was at a dinner party, sitting next to Alfred Duff Cooper, who, two weeks before, had resigned from the British Cabinet. Earlier in the evening he had said to me: 'It was "peace with honour" that I couldn't stomach. If he'd come back from Munich saying, "peace with terrible, unmitigated, unparalleled dishonour", perhaps I would have stayed. But peace with *honour!*'

The girl in the scarlet taffeta dress wasn't bothering herself about honour or dishonour, and neither were the other couples on the dance floor, from the look of them. Peace was the important thing. Once more the music was playing and Mr Chamberlain was the hero of the day. Business firms advertised their gratitude in the newspapers; shops displayed Chamberlain dolls and sugar umbrellas; and in Scandinavia there was a movement to present the British leader with a trout stream. Only a few people like Duff Cooper shook sad and sceptical heads over 'peace in our time' and stared gloomily into the future. When the girl in the scarlet taffeta dress spun past us, Duff said: 'I wonder where *that* couple will be a year from today!'

But sceptical people, like Duff, were soon written off as jitter-bugs and praise for Neville Chamberlain continued unabated. It was during this period of adulation – in fact, a few nights after the evening at the Ritz – that I was invited to dinner to meet him.

The dinner was given by his sister-in-law, Lady Chamberlain, widow of the late Sir Austen Chamberlain, former Foreign

Minister and half-brother of Neville. I can see the dining room now with its yellow curtains and its huge bowls of yellow flowers. There were only ten people at the table: the Prime Minister and Mrs Chamberlain, Lady Birkenhead, Prince and Princess Ruspoli from Rome, the Duke of Alba (Franco's representative), Lady Chamberlain's daughter and son-in-law, Mr and Mrs Terence Maxwell, and myself.

The Prime Minister had a more vigorous appearance than his photographs indicated, and I was surprised (as I had been by Hitler) to find that he was an animated conversationalist with a quick sense of humour. I sat several places away from him at dinner, but when we went into the drawing room Lady Chamberlain told him that I had just returned from Czechoslovakia and led us to a sofa in the corner. I shall never forget Chamberlain's opening remark: 'Tell me,' he said, smiling. 'Did you find that the Czechs had any bitter feeling towards the English?'

I was so astonished for a moment I couldn't reply. Then I described some of the things I had seen and heard and he listened with grave attention. 'From what I saw, the Czechs behaved with extraordinary self-control,' I added. 'All the stories of Czechs "persecuting" Germans were completely unfounded – manufactured by German propaganda.'

Mr Chamberlain nodded sympathetically. 'I know. No accusation was too wild for them. Even while we were in conference at Godesberg, Ribbentrop kept coming into the room with announcements of Czech atrocities, reading them out in a sensational manner. Of course, it was ridiculous. We knew they were inventions. We had only to check up with our own people in Prague to learn the truth. But that's the trouble with the Germans. They have no sensibilities. They never realise the impression they are making.'

'What did you think of Ribbentrop?' I asked.

'A terrible fellow.'

'And Hitler?'

'Not very pleasant, either. I thought he had an extraordinary face – almost sinister. And a temper that's quite unmanageable. Several times at Godesberg he got so excited I was able to carry on a conversation only with extreme difficulty. In fact, several times I had to tell Herr Schmidt (the interpreter) to say that we would get nowhere by such a demonstration, and ask him to keep to the subject. A most difficult fellow. It's hard to understand the fascination he has for the German people. But I think he's beginning to lose his power.'

'Hitler?' I said, surprised.

'Yes. When I arrived in Germany I noticed there was a good deal more cheering for Goering than for Hitler. I think Goering may become the real power in the country.'

I told Mr Chamberlain the lack of boisterousness didn't strike me as odd; Goering was the Balbo of the country – the popular flesh-and-blood idol who used filthy words and drew good-natured shouts from the crowds of 'Good old Hermann'; but Hitler was almost sacred. People didn't shout as they did for Goering; often they wept.

'Perhaps,' replied Mr Chamberlain. 'But I'm not sure. I don't think the German people liked being led to the brink of war. I was astonished by the reception I got and already I've had hundreds of letters from Germany thanking me for the part I played. When I arrived at Munich, even the SS men cheered me! They were the last people I should have expected to welcome peace.'

'I can understand the Germans cheering better than I can the French,' I replied. 'After all, the Germans got peace and everything they wanted as well. But in France they got peace only at the price of an appalling surrender. What *they* found to cheer about I can't imagine. The French position seems to me the worst of all.'

I made the remark as a deliberate challenge, and was completely taken aback by Chamberlain's reply. He nodded his head in agreement and said, 'Unless the French find some new and vigorous leaders *at once*, they are finished as a first-class power.'

He then went on to relate the same story that the Foreign Office official had told me: how the French had communicated with the British Government at the last moment and flatly renounced their pledges. 'If we had known this several months before we might have been able to help the Czechs get a far more reasonable settlement,' said Mr Chamberlain, 'but the French assured us, both privately and publicly, that they were determined to honour their treaty obligations – until the eleventh hour. I prophesy that unless the French pull themselves together at once they will not survive as a democracy much longer. If the Czechs are bitter at anyone, they should be bitter at the French.'

'Everyone knows,' I said inelegantly, 'that Mr Bonnet is the biggest crook in Europe.'

Mr Chamberlain laughed. 'He doesn't inspire much confidence.'

'Do you think Hitler is contemptuous of the French?'

'I don't know, but I think he suspects them of great weakness.' Then he said suddenly, 'What a curious man he is! In judging him, one must revise all one's ordinary ideas and try to remember what a strange life he has led, for he's quite different from anyone else. What I found so difficult – apart from his fits of temper and his habit of wandering off the subject – was the fact that he was so irrational. For example, at Godesberg he told me in one breath that the Czech problem was so vital it couldn't wait a day; and in another breath, suggested my taking a trip to Berchtesgaden in order to see his mountain retreat. I told him if the problem was so vital I didn't see how he could afford to waste time taking me sight-seeing, but he didn't seem to think it odd!' Mr Chamberlain laughed, and added: 'Someone reported to me that Hitler was shocked when he was told I enjoyed shooting and remarked that it was a cruel sport. Now, fancy anyone with Hitler's record objecting to shooting birds!'

Mr Chamberlain looked amused. Then his smile disappeared and he asked curiously: 'What was it like in Prague when you heard the result of Munich?'

I told him about the crowds sweeping down the main square, and the drive through the black and rain-swept villages; and, finally, of the hours we had spent under the supervision of the German with the machine-gun. I told him how we had hung over the radio until three o'clock on the night of the Munich Conference, waiting for the final report, and asked him why it had taken so long.

'German inefficiency,' he replied with a smile. 'I had always been led to believe that the Germans were a thoroughly efficient people, but when we arrived at Munich we found that nothing was prepared. There were no interpreters, no stenographers, no pencils, not even any paper. It took hours to get the thing arranged. But the climax came at two-thirty in the morning, when the document was finally ready for signature, and Hitler jumped up from the table, walked over to the desk, plunged his pen in the inkwell to find there wasn't even any ink! Now even in London we would have had ink!'

At this point the conversation came to a close, for Mrs Chamberlain came up and told the Prime Minister it was time for him to go to bed. It was the only conversation I ever had with Chamberlain; when I went home I wrote it down as I have given it here.

Chamberlain had surprised me by his outspokenness and impressed me as a man of sincerity. The bitter criticisms levelled at him, depicting him as a villain, and accusing him of totalitarian sympathies, were grossly unfair. He believed in democracy and the British Empire with the same fervour as Winston Churchill; but what he didn't believe in with the same fervour as Winston Churchill was the wickedness of Germany.

Although he neither approved of the Nazis nor liked Hitler, there is little doubt that he was deeply impressed by the German people's desire for peace. The fact that 'even the SS men' cheered him had left a deep mark. He didn't seem to grasp the fact that in totalitarian states public opinion is manufactured and fashioned overnight to suit the purpose of the moment. His remark about Hitler's declining power indicated to me a dangerous lack of understanding.

But on looking back, even more curious were his comments on France. His prophecy has been borne out, but what is difficult to understand is why (and how I wish I had asked this question), if he believed France's position to be so precarious, he was not more alarmed for the future of her ally, Great Britain.

I think myself the answer was that Chamberlain was so strongly convinced that another war would mean the end of civilisation (a phrase you heard repeatedly was: 'In war there are no winners'), he couldn't believe that even Hitler, 'if treated justly', would plunge Europe into such a catastrophic maelstrom. He seemed to regard Hitler as a curious, rather unbalanced sort of creature who could be managed by 'clever handling'. This led him to underestimate the driving force and ambition he was up against, for he was a man who lacked the human understanding of Churchill; he couldn't visualise the world as 'a tired horse', always flogged 'a bit further down the road' by some ambitious new master.

There is no doubt that he sincerely believed the promises Hitler gave him: 'I have no more territorial demands in Europe'; and that he meant the words he himself had spoken on September 27th when he said '. . . if I were convinced that any nation had made up its mind to dominate the world by fear of its force, I should feel that it must be resisted'. The tragedy lay in the fact that he couldn't be convinced. He will go down in history as a man who was deceived, but whether or not he had a right to be deceived in the face of the overwhelming evidence with which he was confronted, is a matter for argument. At any rate, the mass of people in Europe shared his complacency. Although the British Government ordered an increase of armaments (just in case . . .), everybody drifted back to normalcy; it was exactly like the cartoon printed in *Punch* of John Bull settling down comfortably in a chair while 'WAR SCARE' flew out of the window with the caption: 'Thank God, that's gone'.

Tom Mitford, Unity's brother, came back from Germany, where he had spent a day with Hitler, and told me that the latter had referred to Chamberlain as a 'dear old man'. Hitler appeared to have taken a liking to him and remarked to Tom that he was upset because 'the old man' had to make three such long trips! He said on the second occasion he (Hitler) had planned to go to London instead, and even ordered his plane, but his advisers had told him it was out of the question as the trip would have come under the category of a 'State visit', and meant a three-day stay. 'Anyway,' Hitler added, 'it's probably just as well. I know the English. They would have met me at Croydon with a dozen bishops!'

Tom said that although he and Unity had been the only people in the room, when Hitler talked about the Czechs, his voice rose to a shout as though he were addressing an enormous audience. Then his mood changed and he was calm again. 'I can't understand any Englishman being willing to shed his blood for a single Czech. But if England *had* gone to war with us, of one thing I am certain: not a single British plane would have succeeded in fly-ing over Germany!' (Tom never gathered what he meant by this remark and thought perhaps he was referring to a 'secret weapon'; if so, it hasn't been a great success!)

Hitler asked why the English had dug trenches all over Hyde Park, and when Tom replied they were air-raid shelters, he threw back his head and laughed loudly. 'So that's what they were! Here in Germany we couldn't imagine! We thought the English were under the impression we were going to land troops, and were actually digging front-line trenches.' (I remember remarking to Tom: 'What an idea! He must be crazy to think English people are such fools!')

Tom shared his sister's conviction that Hitler, in spite of his ambitions on the continent, sincerely desired friendship with England and was eager to reorganise the world on an Anglo–German basis. This was not an uncommon view in London, though on what evidence it was based was difficult to understand. Hitler soon changed his mind about Mr Chamberlain being 'a dear old man', for scarcely three weeks after Munich the German press began to attack the British increase of armaments and to label the peacemaker of Munich the warmonger of Europe.

When I went to Berlin at Christmas-time (on my way to Russia), I found a cold, unsmiling city almost as belligerent as when I had last seen it in the summer. In August the army had been mobil-ising and the avenues resounded to the roar of motorcycles and the rumble of armoured cars; now the capital was buried beneath a blanket of deep snow and had a silent, almost melancholy air; there was scarcely any traffic on the icy streets and the great build-ing projects dotted all over the capital and left unfinished through a scarcity of labour lay under the snow like giant corpses respect-fully covered with sheets.

But the atmosphere was as bellicose as last August. The first person I saw when I arrived was Dr Karl Silex, whom I ran into in the Adlon Bar. I scarcely had a chance to say hello before he began, 'So you've come from London. Well, we've changed our opinion about Mr Chamberlain, here in Germany. Instead of making peace he seems to be making arms. If the hypocrisy goes on our patience will come to an end.'

Then with a reasoning of which only Germans (in spite of their reputation for logic) are capable, he went on to prophesy that 1939 would see further changes in the European map. 'You can be sure of one thing,' he said defiantly, 'Germany's frontiers are not yet permanently drawn in either Eastern or South-Eastern Europe.'

I wrote this in an article for the *Sunday Times*, adding that the only change I had noticed in the aggressive spirit of Nazi Germany was in the man in the street. In August the average German had expressed a staunch faith in the leadership of the country and repeated with almost childish faith that the Führer would not lead the nation to war. Now they realised that peace had been kept only by the surrender of Chamberlain. The knowledge that Hitler had been willing to risk a war seemed to have made a deep impression, and on all sides one heard grave doubt as to the future. My waiter in the Adlon told me that the hotel was having a boom, for people felt the future so insecure that they no longer tried to save their money; on another occasion a taxi driver asked me how long I thought the peace would last, adding with a sigh, 'If only the country could have a little quiet.' And when Jimmy Holburn's wife, Margaret, went into a shop, the salesgirl rattled the box of the Winter Relief Fund and explained in a cynical, rather tired voice: 'For guns.'

But this anxiety and weariness meant nothing, for ordinary people didn't count. The propaganda machine was churning up fresh hatred against the democracies and Nazi Party leaders were already well converted. We had an example of the strange mixture of friendliness and hostility towards England running through the capital. Robert Byron had come to Berlin to spend a few days with his sister Lucy, who was married to Euan Butler, the *Times* correspondent, and on Christmas night we dined together and later in the evening went to a nightclub called '*Der Goldener Hufeisen*' ('The Golden Horseshoe').

It was the most extraordinary nightclub I have ever been to. The room was packed with people sitting at small tables drinking beer, and in the centre of the room was a dance floor, around which was a dirt circus ring with three live ponies, which guests could ride for a mark. The band struck up, the riding-master cracked his whip, and the audience shrieked with delight as brave but inexperienced riders jogged painfully around the circle. The women riders cut the most comical figures, for their hats rolled off and their skirts went up above their knees. One of them had on a pair of bright pink knickers that made the onlookers howl with laughter.

Robert Byron and his sister Lucy were expert riders, and as the evening wore on the temptation grew too strong for them to resist. Robert was wearing a dinner jacket and Lucy a trailing blue satin dress, so their offer to do a turn created a mild sensation. Lucy rode side-saddle, and when the riding-master cracked his whip and the horses went round the ring at a wild gallop, she made a spectacular picture with her blonde hair shining in the light and her satin dress billowing into the air like a blue cloud. The riding-master was so delighted with the exhibition that he presented both of them with an elaborate diploma. Then the band stood up, raised their beer glasses, and toasted 'The English Visitors'; the audience joined in with a burst of whistling and cheering. That is, everybody except for two Storm Troopers at the next table. They were young men in their twenties, and one of them, with a swarthy complexion and dark, angry eyes, leaned over to Euan and said in an ugly voice: 'So you come from England. We don't like the English. All English people are hypocrites.'

'And we don't like being interrupted!' retorted Euan.

This had little effect, for the man went on: 'We read that your Mr Chamberlain isn't so peaceful as he tried to make us think. He's busy making arms to use against Germany. Well, if he wants it, we will give him his war!'

'You may not like it, when you get it.'

The man laughed derisively. 'Oh, the democracies always talk big, but perhaps they won't talk so big when they come up against the Luftwaffe.'

'Perhaps,' replied Euan. 'But I'd rather wait and see than take your word for it.'

Here, the younger of the two interrupted heatedly. His cheeks were red and he spoke with passionate intensity. 'England must realise Germany is not a country to be trampled on any longer. Your "old men" are not so clever as they think. Our Führer isn't deceived by your false friendship; he won't allow Germany's enemies to escape unpunished. We don't want a war, but if he tells us to march, we will follow him to the end!'

'Yes,' replied Euan acidly. 'And perhaps it will be the *end*.'

This last remark was lost, for just then four friends joined the Storm Troopers and there was a round of hand-shakings and introductions. But when we left, the dark, swarthy one broke off from his conversation, and in a contemptuous voice flung a 'Heil Hitler' after us.

On that same day, people in England were opening Christmas cards from Mr Chamberlain, showing the picture of an aeroplane with the simple inscription: 'Munich'. People in Germany were

stopping in the streets to look at the New Year's posters showing the picture of a soldier in a steel helmet with a fixed bayonet.
These, too, bore a simple inscription: '1939'.

Part V

SOVIET RUSSIA

1

Introduction to Russia

The Russian frontier guards, with the snow clinging to their boots and the red stars gleaming from their peaked caps, had already boarded the train. We had left Stolpce, the last Polish frontier station, twenty minutes before, and in another few minutes would reach the Soviet customs house at Negoreloye.

The train moved through the darkness slowly. The windows were covered with frost and it was impossible to see out. I left my compartment and went into the corridor. I was surprised to find how quiet it was. I walked through the carriage and discovered there were only three passengers besides myself: two couriers with the diplomatic mail – an Englishman and a Pole – and an English businessman. It reminded me of a ghost train; the stillness, the blank white windows, and the groaning of the wheels as they moved through the darkness.

The English courier (officially known as the King's Messenger) and the English businessman sat in their compartments reading magazines and eating chocolates, obviously bored (in the best British manner) by their surroundings. But the Polish courier was nervous. He was a small, dark man who paced up and down, every now and then rubbing the window-pane and trying to see out. As I walked past him he spoke to me in French, his voice almost a whisper. 'I don't like it. It's a bad business.'

'What is?' I asked in surprise.

'Going into this country. When you cross the frontier you never know if you will ever return to the world again.'

His remark took me aback. For me, the trip to Russia was almost a holiday. On the continent hatreds were flaring up more brightly than ever; Hitler was denouncing Chamberlain as a hypocrite and Mussolini was shouting, 'Savoy, Corsica, Tunis.' All over Europe governments were divided against each other and life had become even more restless than in the days before Munich.

When the *Sunday Times* suggested I make a six-week trip to Moscow to write a series of articles on current conditions, I welcomed the chance to escape from the gloom of London. Somehow Russia seemed another world. As a country it had always fired my imagination, and as a political force, the subject of so much heated controversy, it aroused my curiosity. I had no bias either for or against the Soviets; I wanted to see for myself. In fact, I had wanted to see for myself for some time, but my application for a Russian visa two years before had been refused with no explanation. This time, Randolph Churchill had taken me to lunch with Mr Maisky, the Soviet Ambassador in London, and Sir Robert Vansittart had unofficially recommended me to him. When I arrived in Warsaw the visa was waiting. I sent a wire to a friend in Moscow, Fitzroy Maclean, the Second Secretary of the British Embassy, and told him he could make good his promises of introducing me to Russian hospitality; I also hoped to see General Gal, the Russian soldier who had tried to convert me to Communism in Spain. Altogether, I was determined to enjoy myself.

My holiday spirit was a little dampened by the Polish courier's depressing comment, but a few minutes later we rolled into Negoreloye, and anything more of a contrast to the sinister atmosphere he had suggested would be difficult to imagine. The station was a large white concrete building blazing with lights. The walls were decorated with photographs of Stalin, Lenin and Marx, and inscribed with huge letters: 'Workers Of The World Unite'. Unsmiling porters with burlap aprons boarded the train to take off our luggage, and we walked into a room swarming with husky-looking frontier guards.

I had been warned that the Soviet customs inspection was laborious and had been careful to clear my bag of letters and documents. I had even selected my reading matter carefully: Shaw's *The Intelligent Woman's Guide To Socialism*, which I had bought in Warsaw expressly for the trip. I was pleased with my forethought, and when I saw the customs inspector frowning upon the English businessman's Agatha Christie detective story, I was even more complacent. But, alas, Mr Shaw's spirited plea for socialism also failed to impress him: one suspicious flip through the pages and he confiscated it. After a long examination my suitcases were returned to me intact, but the Polish courier did not fare so easily. He had a bag of lemons which aroused deep distrust. Each lemon was taken out and inspected under a magnifying glass. But this was not enough: another official appeared with a knife and one by one the lemons were cut open to make sure they contained no secret codes. The Polish courier watched the process unhappily, for by the time the inspectors had completed the job the lemons were of little use to anyone.

Once again the train crawled and creaked over the broad-gauge rails. It was getting late and the porter lumbered down the corridor to tell us dinner was ready. I discovered that I was the only one who hadn't brought food from Warsaw. The two couriers were not allowed to leave their diplomatic bags even to go into the dining-car (the Polish courier said he had instructions to stay awake all night) and the businessman was already munching sandwiches and drinking beer.

No one seemed to mind being deprived of the benefits of the dining-car and I soon understood why. It was a small room with three or four tables, separated from the kitchen by a wall with an opening through which the dishes were passed. The window was open and I could see the cook, a woman with untidy grey hair streaming about her face and a pair of dirty hands with a bandage on one of her fingers. This was enough to put me off, but the prices settled the matter. The official exchange was twenty-five roubles to the pound: an omelette was twenty-three roubles. I finally had some tea and a caviar sandwich (the least expensive thing on the menu), which came to eighteen roubles. The sandwich was meagre and I went back to my carriage almost as hungry as when I had left; the King's Messenger gave me a cookie and some cake and the Polish courier a glass of lemonade, which he had made himself, angrily determined that his mutilated lemons should not be wasted.

The next morning I was up early, eager not to miss any of the Russian landscape. It was bleak and dreary; miles of snowbound plains, dark clumps of trees, and every now and then a cluster of small wooden houses. Occasionally you saw people trudging along the roads; they looked so infinitesimal against the great sweep of snow that I could already feel the morbid despair reflected in so many Russian stories.

About noon the train drew in at the Alexandrovsky station in Moscow. Although Fitzroy Maclean had come to meet me, he looked astonished when I stepped off the train. 'What a surprise!' he exclaimed. 'I got your wire but I didn't actually think you'd turn up. People have a way of saying they're coming to Moscow, but they don't always make it.' Fitzroy was a strange sight bundled up in a huge coat with a wild-looking fur hat pulled down over his ears. He was the sort of man you could never mistake for anything but an Englishman – and an English diplomat at that. Tall and thin, he had a lackadaisical appearance that belied the fact he had 'bummed his way' from Moscow to China and India, across the dangerous tribal lands of Central Asia, had been captured by bandits en route, escaped, and finally reached Delhi two months later – one of the few foreigners to succeed in making the trip. Fitzroy spoke Russian fluently and was considered not only one of the most enterprising but one of the ablest young men in the diplomatic service.

As we drove through the streets, I craned my neck to get a glimpse of the city. I was surprised by the tall, modern buildings and the broad thoroughfares; but I was even more surprised when we reached the Embassy, a large stone residence on the Sofiyskaya Naberezhnaya, and Fitzroy glanced through the back window and said, casually: 'We haven't lost the rest of the party. We're all safely home again.'

A green car with two men in the front seat had pulled up a few yards behind us – the GPU (the secret police) car. Fitzroy explained it usually followed the Ambassador, but as he was away on leave, the honour fell to the lesser members of the staff. I was astonished. My conception of 'secret police' was of a mysterious force that flourished in the shadows. 'But what's the point of following people about openly?' I protested.

'Oh, I don't know. But it's a great convenience to have them tagging on behind,' said Fitzroy. 'You grow dependent on them. When your car gets stuck in a snow-drift, or you run out of matches, you just whistle, and they give you a hand!'

* * *

Everyone who goes to Russia has a very definite first impression. Mine was a feminine one. At lunch I met a French journalist (I can't remember his name) who offered to take me sight-seeing; I asked him to drive me to the shopping centre because I wanted to buy some woollen stockings.

His jaw dropped. 'You don't mean you've come to Russia without any woollen stockings?'

'Why not? I thought I'd buy them here.'

'Good heavens! Do you *really* think you can buy woollen stockings here? Where do you think you are?'

'In one of the coldest countries in the world. Why shouldn't I buy woollen stockings in Moscow?'

'Don't ask me. Ask Mr Molotov.'

Already the broad streets and the tall buildings seemed less impressive. Our car drew up before the Mostorg, a large co-operative store on the main street, glittering with lights and swarming with human beings. It was one of the noisiest stores I have ever been in. Three gramophones were playing, all blaring American jazz tunes and all different ones. Crowds shoved their way past the counters but nobody seemed to be buying anything. The people were rough-looking peasants: women with broad red hands and kerchiefs tied round their heads, men with leathery faces and short, square bodies. Everyone seemed warmly dressed but their clothes were oddly assorted. Some had pieces of flannel wrapped around their legs and bits of rags inside their coats. They looked as though they had preserved every bit of cloth since childhood and wrapped the whole lot around them; and they smelled as though they had.

The counters on the ground floor were stocked with an amazing array of cheap perfume, artificial flowers, banjos, gramophone records and children's toys. But when you got upstairs and looked for shoes, gloves, stockings, coats – in fact, any form of wearing apparel – you found the counters empty. In one corner of the store a long queue twisted through the shop like a serpent's tail; news had spread that a supply of ribbon had arrived.

The shop was as unreal as a stage set. Everything looked real until you got close. I could understand why no one was buying anything and my friend explained that most of the people came in chiefly to get warm.

As we were walking down the street on our way home, we passed a dingy window showing a silver fox fur, priced at a thousand roubles. 'No woollen stockings but a silver fox fur,' I protested. 'And, anyway, what good is it? Who can afford to buy it?'

'Oh, some commissar's wife. I can see you've got a lot to learn,' said the journalist.

2

Shadow over the Kremlin

Stockingless Moscow with its silver fox furs made a deep impression on me. But I soon discovered that this was only one of many paradoxes. The modern buildings and the broad streets shielded a world of dingy shops, dark overcrowded flats and empty markets. The queues – waiting for anything from milk to shoes – were even more numerous than they had been in Madrid after a year of siege.

Everywhere you looked you found incongruous contradictions. The Moscow drinking water was chlorinated, and the gas unreliable, yet the streets were dotted with the latest type of snow-sweeper imported from America; the buses broke down, and the street cars stalled, yet three magnificent new bridges spanned the Moscow river; the dwelling-houses were insanitary and the rooms overcrowded, yet construction had already begun on the 'Palace of the Soviets', which officials proclaimed would be 'bigger than the Empire State Building' with a statue of Lenin on top 'bigger than the Statue of Liberty'.

The emphasis on glamorous subway stations, modern cinemas and American jazz in a capital where the postage stamps wouldn't stick, the water-taps broke down, and the doorbells were invariably out of order, caused a French diplomat to shrug his shoulders and say despairingly: '*Mais, c'est une façade!*'

Certainly Soviet life was a strange travesty on Western civilisation. For a nation that sent its disciples abroad to convert the 'pluto-democracies' to the leadership of Moscow, it seemed to have little to offer from a practical point of view, other than squalor and poverty. But far more disconcerting than the wretched conditions was the tyranny that gripped the capital. It was estimated that the purge, which had swept the country during the past two years, had sent over six million people to concentration camps. The GPU were interwoven throughout the life of the nation; you couldn't be in Moscow long without feeling its influence. Foreigners were avoided like lepers as many 'purge' victims had been accused of connivance with capitalist powers, and Soviet citizens no longer dared run the risk of being seen in bourgeois company. I soon relinquished any hope of seeing General Gal; during the month I was in Moscow not a single Russian visitor crossed the threshold of any of the embassies.

The only contact foreigners had with Russian life was through their servants, or with officials who received them at their offices. But limited though one's associations were, dread tales of the secret police were constantly brought to one's attention. The Russian secretary of Harold Denny, the *New York Times* correspondent, was 'taken' in the middle of the night and not heard of again; a Russian chauffeur's fourteen-year-old son was imprisoned in the Lubyanka as a protest against one of the despatches his employer, a journalist, had sent; and at one of the embassies one of the footmen was sent off to Siberia because he studied French at night, giving one of his colleagues the opportunity of denouncing him as a Trotskyist. Magnify these things a million times and you can get some idea of what Russia was like.

When I think of Moscow now, I always think of the stately yellow buildings of the Kremlin in the late afternoon. When it snowed the Oriental cathedral domes gleamed against the darkening winter sky like pearls. One evening I looked out of the window at the silent white scene and saw the sky grow black with carrion crows. They swept over the Kremlin in a mighty wave, then dropped down on the roof ledges, with a quick, falling movement, as though their spirit had suddenly died. To me that dark cloud seemed symbolic of the terrible shadow that hung over Russia.

Certainly the shadow was as strong as a prison bar, for it had shut the frontiers, and now the nation was as insulated as a hermetically sealed laboratory. Indeed, the state of isolation in which Russia existed seemed scarcely possible in a world so closely knitted together by transport and wireless. Tourist trade was almost non-existent; ninety per cent of the foreign correspondents had been expelled; and of the hundreds of foreign engineers who had swarmed over the country several years before, only forty or fifty Americans had been allowed to remain. It was no longer a mystery to me why there were only three people on the train going into Russia, and I understood Fitzroy's surprise at seeing me. The more I thought of it the more surprised I was myself. Why had I been granted a visa? Both Sir Robert Vansittart and Randolph Churchill (who had put in a word for me with Mr Maisky) were 'anti-appeasers'; I could only come to the conclusion that the Russians imagined I had been sent to write in praise of the Soviet Union – in an attempt to counteract a point of view, current in England, favouring the exclusion of Russia from European politics.

Whatever was in their minds, I was received at the Foreign Office by Mr Schmidt, the foreign press chief, with marked cordiality. Four of Mr Schmidt's predecessors had been liquidated, but his manner gave no indication that he regarded his job as a precarious one. He was an affable, smiling man who sat in front of a large window, overlooking the grey confines of the Lubyanka prison. He rubbed his hands and said: 'Well, now, tell me your first impression of Moscow.'

The woollen stockings were still uppermost in my mind, but I decided they were better left unmentioned and murmured the dull, non-committal phrase I was to murmur a hundred times before I left: 'Oh, very interesting.' He asked me what I wanted to do in Moscow, and when I told him I would like to see as much of the everyday life as possible, he drew up a long list ranging from factories and collective farms to schools and museums.

From then on my education began. Every morning punctually at eleven, a Soviet car (American make), with a middle-aged Russian woman as interpreter, appeared to take me around the city. Not being an economic expert, the figures and statistics showered upon me made little mark, but I was left with vivid impressions – unconnected vignettes that don't fit in anywhere: the two peasant women crossing themselves fearfully before riding down the escalator of the Moscow subway; the factory radios blaring propaganda eight hours a day; the number of women bending over heavy machines; the doctor at the Railway Workers' Hospital hurrying me past the squalid rooms to show me the magnificent electric baths built by Soviet engineers; the matron in the candy factory leading me across an alleyway, where garbage had been dumped and left to rot, into the packing room where she called attention to the fact that the workers wore hygienic aprons; the wretched group of peasants waiting in the cold to see the director of a collective farm who was busy compiling statistics for me on the record production of hot-house vegetables.

I saw nothing new. The factories, club-houses and schools I was shown were third-rate imitations of Western progress. All this I had expected; but what I hadn't expected was that I should be asked to marvel at the most commonplace conveniences, as though I had come from a jungle, where even the tick of a clock was an unknown miracle. For instance, when I visited the Railway Workers' Hospital I was shown a committee room where the doctors met. It was a room with grey and green wallpaper and a long, polished, wooden table, with eight or nine chairs around it. There was nothing to distinguish it from an ordinary committee room anywhere. But the doctor who was conducting me round, pushed open the door and gazed in rapturously. 'Isn't it marvellous!' he exclaimed. 'It was decorated entirely by Soviet architects.'

It wasn't the enthusiasm for Soviet achievements that surprised me, but the fact that these achievements were presented as unique. I found the misinformation and ignorance of conditions in the outside world grotesque. When I went to the Kaganovich Ball-Bearing Works, I was shown a shabby canteen where workers could buy snack lunches. One of the women foremen, a twenty-five-year-old Stakhanovite, exclaimed over it and gave me a short lecture.

'I suppose you have never seen anything like this before. You see, here in Russia we believe in the *happiness* of our workers. First of all, they must be well fed, so we have organised this wonderful canteen. Of course, I know people in capitalist countries laugh at such ideas. But one day they will advance to our way of thinking.'

On another occasion, I visited the Modern Art Museums in Moscow. The corridors were swarming with people: groups of soldiers, factory workers, and schoolchildren who were being lectured on the paintings – (carefully interpreted in terms of the 'economic conditions' that flourished at the time). My guide, a young woman in her late twenties, commented proudly on the visitors.

'Here in the Soviet Union the museums are open to the workers.'

I remarked that in America we, too, had museums and libraries open to the public.

'But just for the bourgeois classes.'

'Oh no. They are open to the public. That means everyone.'

'Perhaps you're not sure of your facts,' she said gently. 'We have studied the problem closely and the Soviet Union is the only country which allows its working people the advantages of culture.'

I said no more and a few minutes later she asked me how long I was staying in Moscow. When I replied only a week or so, she gave me a pitying look. 'It must be sad for you.'

'In what way?'

'Oh, I always feel sorry for people who have to return to a bourgeois world. After seeing the comradeship of Russia, it must be difficult to adjust oneself to the greed of capitalist life again. Everything here is an *inspiration*.'

During all these trips I wondered what went through the mind of my interpreter. She was an educated woman who had travelled abroad before the revolution, and much of what we saw and heard must have seemed as naïve to her as it did to me. However, I never had any indication of her reactions. She was Madame X – not because she was fascinating in any way – she was just an ordinary, plain, middle-aged woman – but because of the mystery behind her drab life. She shivered in the cold in a cloth coat and a pair of patched gloves. When she appeared in the morning, I always wondered what sort of house she had left, and what kind of life she had led before the revolution. But aside from the fact that she spoke English with an American accent, and told me she had once spent a year or two in Chicago, I never learned anything further about her. She made no attempt to sound out my impressions nor to give me propaganda lectures. In fact, she registered nothing: neither surprise, disapproval nor enthusiasm. She talked in a flat, mechanical voice that never varied and to the bitter end remained an enigma.

Only once did she show any interest. That was when I decided to send a telegram to Stalin. For a brief moment, astonishment crossed her face, then she recovered herself and told the chauffeur to drive to the telegraph station. (When I had asked Mr Schmidt to make my request through the Press Bureau he had laughed self-consciously and suggested I make the application direct.)

I wrote out my telegram in English and asked Madame X to put it into Russian, but she drew back alarmed, and said it would be better to send it in English. The telegram said:

> Joseph Stalin The Kremlin I wish to call your attention to the fact that you have never been interviewed by a woman journalist stop since the Soviet Union professes equality between the sexes I should be grateful if I might have the honour to correct the illogical precedent you comma no doubt inadvertently comma have set stop.

When I handed the telegram to the girl behind the counter there was a moment of awful silence. She got up and went into consultation with her colleagues. Whispered conferences went on for some time; at last, the manager appeared at the window. 'Your telegram,' he said stiffly, 'will be delivered at the Kremlin in twenty-two-and-a-half minutes.'

Why twenty-two-and-a-half I never discovered. And whether twenty-two-and-a-half or just twenty-two, it didn't matter – for I never got an answer.

* * *

At night the red stars in the Kremlin spires gleamed through the heavy fall of snow like gigantic fireflies. The Red Square was deserted and lonely and the sentries by the Kremlin gates stood as stiff as snowmen. One evening, Fitzroy and I were walking past the Embassy when the silence was suddenly broken by a large green Lincoln motor-car that came hurtling towards us. You knew a 'big shot' was inside by the bullet-proof windshield and the tightly drawn curtains. It may have been Stalin. Whoever it was, as the car swept through the Kremlin gates to a click of arms and disappeared in the darkness, my imagination was stirred; the authority of the Czars suddenly seemed pale compared with the power of the ruler of all the Soviet Socialist Republics.

This, like everything else in Russia, was paradoxical. Indeed, paradoxes were more the rule than the exception. I was becoming used to lines queued up for milk under the shadow of billboards that said brightly: 'Drink Soviet Champagne'. To the fact that although you couldn't buy a yard of cloth to make a dress, the shop counters were decorated with pictures of the latest French fashions; that although the salary of the average working man was 240 roubles a month, ballet dancers earned as much as 100,000 roubles a year; that although Soviet Russia claimed to be a dicta-torship of the proletariat, under the label of the 'Intelligentsia' you found a class of privilege and power.

The Intelligentsia was not confined to the arts. Officially defined in 1938, it included technicians, police officials and bureaucrats – in fact, the white-collar class of the Soviet Union. You saw them dining at the leading hotels; driving through the streets in their state-owned cars; flowing through the lobbies of the movie houses; sitting in the best seats at the opera and the ballet.

On the night before a 'free day' they thronged the restaurant of the Metropole Hotel. I went there one evening with Walter Duranty, Harold Denny and his wife Jean. The air was blue with smoke, and the large marble floor, with an old-fashioned fountain in the centre, was packed with dancers doing the latest American steps. Most of the women had hennaed hair and were dressed in blouses and skirts and white berets; the men wore uniforms ranging from the khaki of the army to the dark blue breeches and tunic of the ordinary citizen. Vodka and champagne flowed freely; Walter told me the wooden railing round the fountain had been put up because so many people fell in. Never have I been to a more noisy party. Hundreds of balloons were distributed through-out the room and the guests amused themselves by wrapping the strings with paper, lighting them, and watching them drift up to the ceiling. They exploded midway and the noise sounded like an artillery barrage. The orchestra grew louder in an effort to be heard and conversation became impossible.

The Intelligentsia set the nation's standard of elegance. With the rise of this new class, many ideas and customs, formerly classed as 'bourgeois', were being accepted. The severe post-revolutionary buildings were gradually giving way to more elaborate structures; Christmas trees, formerly frowned upon, had reappeared under the title of Father Frost trees; and although Soviet citizens didn't wear evening clothes, except at official functions, you saw the con-ductor of the opera in tails and a white tie.

The energies of the Intelligentsia were bent on the acquisition of 'culture'. This determination was reflected in every branch of Soviet life. The main amusement park in Moscow was called 'The Park of Rest and Culture', while the chief organisation that dealt with foreign tourists was labelled 'The Society for Cultural Relations'. The word 'culture', however, was elastic. It applied as easily to a restaurant with clean tablecloths as to a man of learning. When Alfred Cholerton, the *Daily Telegraph* correspondent, refused to buy a gas range from a Soviet salesman, saying that he considered a coal stove more reliable, the latter protested with the argument: 'But gas is so *cultured*.'

The height of modern culture was symbolised by jazz – spelled 'djaz'. Most of the cinemas were equipped with jazz orchestras and the salaries of the band leaders ran as high as 1,500 roubles a month. One evening Fitzroy and I went into a movie house to find the lobby packed with people listening to a jazz concert. The music was awful. The saxophones tore the air and the trumpets caterwauled in melancholy discord, but the audience sat in their chairs listening as intently as though they were hearing a symphony conducted by Sir Thomas Beecham.

We saw a film called *The Oppenheim Family*. Like most Soviet pictures it was a propaganda film. But it was an odd one. Although it dealt with the Nazi persecution of the Jews, the producer's aesthetic sense had evidently got the better of him, for the young Jewish hero was portrayed by a tall blonde Nordic, while the Nazi persecutors were the most odious types of Jews. Several scenes showing concentration camps met with an uncomfortable silence, suggesting that the director had skirted too close to reality.

Soviet 'culture' had little to recommend it. However, the brilliance of the Moscow theatre and ballet, run in the old bourgeois manner, more than made up for the dreariness of the new art. The Soviet State spent thousands of roubles on the ballet, and the magnificence of costumes and sets, the quality of the dancing, were unsurpassed. The Opera House was crowded nightly, and tickets had to be booked well in advance. The stalls were filled with important Soviet officials, but the galleries were often turned over to groups of factory workers. The shabbiness of the audience seemed curiously out of place when the lights dimmed and the great curtains swept apart on a glittering pre-revolutionary setting. Princesses and noblemen moved about against a background of luxury which was difficult to reconcile with the Soviet conception of life. The first ballet I saw was *The Prisoner of the Caucasus*, in which Simyonova, the star of Russia, danced. She was small, dainty and unbelievably graceful. The audience cheered her to the rafters.

Incidental was the fact that her husband, Mr Karakhan, a former Ambassador to Turkey, had been one of the victims of the 1937 purge.

3

Water, Water, Everywhere

How often I blessed my miraculous passport. Moscow seemed to me the dreariest city on earth, and the depression penetrated my bones like a damp fog. I never walked out on the streets without clutching my bag to feel if my passport was really there, and counting the days before I was to leave.

Perhaps the fact that it was new to me made it seem all the more appalling. Most foreigners who had lived in the country for some while seemed to take the conditions around them for granted, ignoring them, and leading their own lives as best they could. I didn't stay long enough to grow indifferent to the squalor. But it wasn't only this that depressed me. It was the stagnant mentality that hung in the air like stale tobacco-smoke, undisturbed by a single original current of thought.

The chief distinction between man and animal is the critical faculty of the human mind. In the Soviet Union – just as in Germany – the critical faculty was carefully exterminated, so that the mass might sweat out their existence as uncomplainingly as oxen, obedient to the tyranny of the day. Truth was a lost word. Minds were doped with distorted information until they became so sluggish they had not even the power to protest against their miserable conditions. The *Pravda* never tired of revealing to its readers the iniquities of the outside world, always pointing the same moral: how blessed were the people of the Soviet Union.

To me, the contempt for intellectual and moral values and the ruthless disregard of the individual was not only depressing: it was evil. I felt the same way as I had in Spain and Germany: that if I didn't get a breath of fresh air I would stifle. The physical appearance of Moscow helped to accentuate this feeling. The streets were as drab as the mentality of the people. It was a world of grey, black and white unrelieved by a single splash of colour; not a single gay headdress, a bright shopfront, or even a happy smile. The only wall decorations were photographs of Marx, Lenin and Stalin. It became my own particular theory that the reason crowds filed into the mausoleum to see Lenin lying in state, white and waxy, was that the softly lighted marble death-chamber was a pleasant escape from reality.

One of the few interesting features of Moscow life was that foreigners, isolated as they were from contact with Russians, were completely dependent on one another; you found that the political enmities of the continent were forgotten, and Germans, French, British and Italians were bosom friends. On the second day of my arrival Fitzroy took me to lunch at the German Embassy. It was a strange contrast to step off the dim Moscow streets and sit down for lunch in a large dining room with five footmen hovering about. The food was imported from the Baltic States and we fared well on six courses and four wines. I was told this Embassy was given a larger allowance than any other German embassy in an effort to 'impress' the Russians.

Lunch was presided over by Count von der Schulenburg (the Ambassador who six months later engineered the Russo–German pact and who was leaving the next day for Berlin 'on business'). It was an odd experience to hear his staff murmuring about the iniquities of the concentration camps and the ruthlessness of the Stalin regime.

* * *

One of the most popular 'foreign' meeting places was the American *datcha* – a cottage about twelve miles from Moscow belonging to Charles and Avis Bohlen of the American Embassy. On Sundays dozens of people gathered there for skiing. The road you drove along from Moscow was a state road, near which one of Stalin's villas was situated. All you could see was a large green fence and some trees, heavily guarded. Although the road was wide enough for three cars, traffic was kept in single file lest the Great Man should choose to come by in a hurry. Once a foreign diplomat was driving along when one of the Kremlin cars, with blinds tightly drawn, passed him at sixty miles an hour. He swung out and followed it, but a minute or two later was stopped by an angry policeman.

'Don't you know the speed limit is thirty miles an hour?'

'But that man ahead was going sixty and you didn't stop *him*.'

'That has nothing to do with it!'

The diplomat's tone was shocked. 'Do you mean in Russia some people have privileges and others have not? I was told this was a socialist country. Are you trying to deny it?'

The policeman evidently wasn't, for his manner changed and he waved the embarrassing foreigner nervously on.

The *datcha* was always crowded with people: military attachés who had never seen a Soviet army manoeuvre; naval attachés who had never seen a Soviet battleship; journalists who had never interviewed a Soviet statesman; ambassadors who had never met the Soviet ruler. All of them living in Russia, yet carefully excluded from Russian life; water, water, everywhere and not a drop to drink.

One afternoon I remember the Italian Ambassador, Signor Rosso, coming in shaking the snow off his boots and protesting indignantly that his GPU men had taken it upon themselves even to follow him skiing. His wife told him he mustn't get so upset.

'But how can I help it?' cried the Ambassador excitedly. 'I go down a hill and they go down a hill. I go over a jump and they go over a jump. And who falls down? *I* do!'

I heard George, the Russian servant, murmuring in his flat, metallic voice: 'There, there.'

* * *

I soon sympathised with the Ambassador's irritation, for a few days later I went to Leningrad for the weekend with 'Chip' and Avis Bohlen, and found out for myself what it was like to be under the supervision of the GPU.

There was great excitement amongst the maids in the Bohlen household on the night we left. At first I thought they were impressed by our trip, but Avis explained that a shipment of cloth had arrived at the Co-operative store and now that we were leaving they were planning to spend the night in the queue in order to be the first to get in when the doors opened in the morning.

Our train was the 'Red Arrow' – the crack Soviet express. (It averaged thirty-two miles an hour and arrived in Leningrad an hour late.) I shared a compartment with a middle-aged Russian woman, who was already in bed when I walked in; I was surprised to find she spoke English.

'Tell me,' she said, 'how do you say "Switch off the lights"?'

'Oh. Do you want me to put them off?'

'No, no. But do you say switch *off* the lights or switch *out* the lights?'

I became nearly as puzzled as she and murmured that either one would do.

'Oh! you say *eye*ther – not *ee*ther.'

She explained that she taught English in a school in Moscow. But as she had learned the language by herself and never had the opportunity of talking with anyone whose native tongue it was, there were a good many problems she was unable to solve.

'For instance,' she said. 'What do you say when you want to *switch* off the *switch*?'

She had me there, and as soon as I climbed into my berth, I pretended I was asleep. But the next morning I awoke to find her hovering over me.

'Excuse me. One more thing. Do you say look *out* the window, or look out *of* the window?'

Fortunately, the ticket-collector intervened and I never had to give an answer.

* * *

We had come to Leningrad for two days of quiet sight-seeing, but the moment we stepped off the train we found ourselves surrounded by porters from the Astoria Hotel, by Intourist guides and representatives from the Society of Cultural Relations. A schedule was already planned: a cigarette factory, a crèche, an inspection of the Peter Paul fortress where some of the Old Bolsheviks had once been incarcerated. We added we would also like to visit the Hermitage and the palaces of Catherine the Great and the late Czar Nicholas the Second.

Our sight-seeing was supervised by three members of the 'secret' police – small men with caps pulled down over their faces – who trailed us everywhere we went. They became almost an obsession to us; we found ourselves hurrying around corners and darting in and out of doors in an effort to lose them; sometimes we thought we had succeeded, but a few minutes later they always turned up.

We first became aware of them on our way to Pushkin, a town not far from Leningrad where the palace of Catherine the Great was situated. The country roads were deserted and there was no

mistaking the police car behind us. It was an extraordinary performance, for although the GPU followed us openly and blatantly,
when we reached Pushkin, the men climbed out and took pains
to put on an elaborate act (gesticulating and pointing) to pretend
they had come to look at the scenery.

The Russian guide who had accompanied us never referred to
them. In spite of their paralysing effect, we persevered with our
sight-seeing and tried to appear as oblivious as she. We spent
hours in the palaces, walking through rooms so cold we had to
jump up and down to keep warm. The Czar's palace was simple
in comparison with the grandeur of Catherine's. It was about
the size of a large English country house. It was filled with over-
stuffed Victorian furniture and cluttered with knick-knacks and
photographs, fashionable at the period. I was surprised by the
modesty with which the Czar had lived, but our Communist guide
evidently preferred Catherine's splendour, for she remarked con-
temptuously: 'You can see for yourself the decadence to which the
royal house had fallen.'

I wondered what she thought of Leningrad with its beautiful copper-domed and golden-spired buildings crumbling and
neglected, with its streets uncared for and its fine parks going to
seed. It had the sad, melancholy air of a person who has lost his
mind and lives solely in the past.

Only in the Hotel Astoria was the atmosphere different. Here
the restaurant was crowded with Soviet 'Intelligentsia', who
seemed to have plenty of roubles to spend and gulped down their
vodka with relish.

The word *culturi* was on everybody's lips, and if we heard it
once, we heard it a dozen times. The manager asked us if we had
slept well, explaining: 'I have given you our most cultured beds.'
And in the restaurant, when we hesitated over a choice between

cutlets and boiled chicken, the waiter intervened: 'I think you will
find the chicken more cultured.'

But the time we found the word most surprisingly employed
was in the cigarette factory. In one of the packing rooms we
noticed a group of sailors nailing down the crates. When we asked
why they were there the director replied there was a shortage of
labour and they had come to help. 'They're friends of the factory
workers,' he explained earnestly. 'You see, we have a club where
our girls maintain cultural relations with the navy.'

We went back to Moscow on the 'Red Arrow'. We walked
through the train to see if the GPU men were still with us, but
saw no one. We thought we had lost them, but when we got off
next morning we looked around to find the three little figures with
their caps pulled down over their faces only a few yards behind us.
As we climbed into our car I turned around and waved goodbye.
Two looked embarrassed and turned their backs, but the third
grinned, showing a flash of gold teeth.

* * *

When the Bohlens got home they learned that their servants had
stood in the queue from midnight until noon the next day. But
there were so many others ahead of them, the cloth had run out,
and they had been turned away empty-handed.

4

The Leopard Changes Its Spots

One afternoon I drove back from the American *datcha* with the wife of an official in the German Embassy. She told me she believed a European war inevitable, owing to the fact that the German economic system was designed for one thing and one thing alone: expansion.

'Of course, if we could get an agreement with Russia, perhaps it would serve as an outlet for us. Many people in the German Foreign Office favour it, but Hitler is so anti-Bolshevik, he won't give his consent.'

'But what about the Soviets?' I said in surprise. 'Surely they wouldn't consider it?'

'Oh yes. The Russians are willing. They are afraid of coming up against Germany.'

That was February 1939, six months before Russia signed her non-aggression pact with Germany. At the time I didn't take the rumour seriously; too much bitterness seemed to block the way. But observers were already noting significant changes in Russia's policy. It was swinging, pendulum-like, from an aggressive policy of world revolution to a negative policy of self-defence. That February, the army discarded its oath to the world proletariat and, for the first time, bound its allegiance solely to the Soviet Fatherland. It was also noted that when Hitler attacked Czechoslovakia in his pre-Munich Nuremberg speech, the Soviet press dismissed the occasion with only four lines. What was happening? Was Russia forsaking Communism and going Fascist herself?

The answer to Russia's policy, both internal and external, both then and now, lay in one thing: those empty shops, those queues and those dark, overcrowded dwelling-houses.

The struggle in which the Soviet Union was involved that winter, on the eve of its swing-over to Germany, was the same struggle upon which the country embarked in 1928 when it announced its five-year plan: namely, the struggle to industrialise a vast backward agricultural country with a mixture of dozens of nationalities and a largely primitive people.

But in 1939 the problem had become more acute than ever. Heavy industry was showing little increase, a fact which foreign engineers attributed to the workers' inability to handle highly complicated machinery; to wastage, bureaucracy and a general lack of co-ordination – difficulties which were a result of an attempt to superimpose twentieth-century industrialisation from above rather than let it develop gradually from below.

The Soviet Union was discovering gradually and painfully that Marxism was not a philosophy designed for an agricultural country; it was a philosophy of *distribution* rather than of *production*. The expert engineer was proving far more important to Soviet industrialisation than the zealous party man; and for this reason the power of the Communist Party was steadily declining. Although Communism was still the philosophy of the nation, in 1939 the party resembled nothing so much as a vast publicity organisation to sell the Stalin regime to the worker.

These salesmen were invaluable in bolstering up the sagging morale of the people; impressing on them the iniquities of the capitalist system and assuring them they were better off than the workers of other countries. But the Communist theory 'from each according to his ability, to each according to his needs' had been discarded for the more workable, but un-Communistic, slogan 'from each according to his ability, to each according to his *worth*'.

This meant that the majority of Soviet workers and peasants were paid not regular salaries but by piece-work and labour days. The average worker's wage was estimated at 240 roubles a month, but the minimum wage was sometimes as low as 130 roubles. The purchasing power of the rouble was roughly estimated at three-pence. (The official exchange was 25 roubles to the pound.) Food prices were so out of proportion that if meat had been available every day (which it was not) it would have cost the average working man a quarter of his weekly salary.

The majority of workers and peasants lived on bread, which was kept at a low fixed price, on cabbage, soup and porridge. Although rents were cheap, in Moscow it was impossible for a worker to rent more than a few feet of floor-space. Sometimes three or four families shared the same room. When a Russian girl (who worked at one of the embassies), known to be unhappily married, was asked why she didn't divorce her husband, she replied that since the law forbade her to turn him out of their living quarters she was afraid he might get married again and add an extra person to an already crowded room.

The important Soviet police official or bureaucrat had none of these inconveniences. He was rewarded not only by a far larger salary than an ordinary worker, but in his ability to get a room or a flat to himself; to get vegetables and meat without standing in a queue; to have a car and chauffeur at his disposal rather than waiting endlessly for overcrowded buses. When manufactured goods appeared on the market, he had the first and usually the last choice. Since positions of power in the Soviet Union carried with them privileges which in other countries would be considered everyday necessities of life, the struggle that went on for bureaucratic jobs was fierce and ruthless.

Although the Communist Party performed an indispensable job as Stalin's 'super-salesmen', they had little power in running the country. Stalin ruled and he ruled by means of the secret police. GPU agents were interwoven in the fabric of every dwelling-house, of every factory and village. Any rebellion or dissatisfaction with the regime was conveniently bracketed as 'anti-Communist'. Although the constitution of the Soviet Government proclaimed freedom of speech, a volume issued that winter, entitled *A History of the Communist Party of the Soviet Union*, carefully explained that disagreement equalled diversion; that diversion equalled dissension; and that dissension equalled sabotage. Thus, when it was considered advantageous to liquidate a rival it could always be done on an orthodox basis.

In view of the difficult conditions, and the fact that the Soviet Union was abandoning many Socialist principles in practice, there is little doubt that some of the old Bolsheviks came into disagreement with Stalin on methods of procedure. There even may have been plans to take the control of the Government in their own hands. Since it would have been impossible for Stalin to eliminate Lenin's 'old guard' on grounds of disagreement, it became necessary to fabricate stories of treason and connivance with foreign powers. It is interesting to notice that Mr Ivanov, one of the defendants in a trial in 1938, was accused of 'wrecking' by means of putting ground glass and nails in the butter. This evidence was received with immense satisfaction, as it seemed to explain the great scarcity of butter throughout the country.

The purge not only swept through Soviet political and army life, but continued like a mighty avalanche through the industrial life into the most humble home. The Russian imagination had been fired, and with ambition and envy playing a prominent part in the 'denouncing' of rivals, the purge continued until it grew out of all proportion. In the winter of 1938, Yezhov was replaced by Beriya as the head of the GPU, and there was an effort to bring it to a halt. But it was too late. Russia was weak and exhausted. The question as to whether the Soviet Union was abandoning Communism could be answered in a single phrase: the Soviet Union was struggling to keep alive.

* * *

One of the articles I had been sent to Moscow to write was a review of the Red Army. How had this internal upheaval affected the Soviet striking force? The Red Army was numbered at over two million, with an estimate that, in the event of a general mobilisation, twelve million men could be placed in the field. Many people, overwhelmed by these figures, regarded the Soviet Union as one of the most powerful forces in Europe.

As Soviet garrisons and armaments factories were closely guarded secrets, there was no opportunity to get first-hand information; one could only draw deductions. But the breakdown of agricultural machinery, the lack of repair shops, the irregularity of fuel supplies, and the fact that a Soviet-manufactured car could not be relied upon beyond seven thousand miles led one to doubtful conclusions. Most of the railways had been left in the same condition as when they had been taken over by the Bolsheviks. The total mileage of paved roads in the whole of the Soviet Union was equal to the paved mileage in Rhode Island – the smallest of America's forty-eight states.

Judging from these things alone, in an article which was published in the *New York Times*, I wrote:

The striking power of a nation does not depend solely on the strength of its armaments but on the co-ordination and sustaining power of its industries. The tremendous difficulties with which the Soviet Union is faced in its efforts to superimpose twentieth-century civilisation upon a backward and primitive country are not likely to be realised in the near future; and until the nation's industries are more competently organised and its people supplied with adequate wants, the Soviet Union can in no way be regarded as a first-class military power.

Apart from the economic conditions there was also the purge to reckon with. The purge had cut a deeper swathe through the army than through any other branch of Soviet life. That winter, military experts calculated that seventy-five per cent of the officers of the rank of colonel and above had been liquidated in the two previous years. The extent of this sweep became significant when, out of the eight officers who court-martialled Tukachevsky and his seven colleagues, six were themselves later executed; that when the Red Army paraded past Stalin in November 1937, officers were not allowed to carry guns in their holsters.

Stalin's accusations of treason rang a false note throughout the world and there seemed to be no logical explanation for the motives compelling him to disrupt the very forces upon which the security of the nation rested. Upon examining the gradual change in the structure of the army during the past twenty years, however, one found a thread of consistency running through the Soviet upheaval.

In 1937 the officer class of the Red Army represented a privileged and powerful clique. This was a far cry from the early twenties, when, under the guidance of Trotsky, little distinction was made between officers and men. In those days officers received the same pay as their subordinates: they wore no badge or rank, they cleaned their own boots, shared the mess rooms, and took an oath which bound them to the International World Proletariat.

The change in the structure of the Red Army was largely due to the influence of German militarism. Until Hitler came into power in 1933, the Soviet Union worked in close collaboration with Germany. As early as 1923 German aeroplane factories were constructed in Russia, while from the date of the Rapallo Treaty onwards hundreds of German military experts conducted training schools in the Soviet Union. Beneath the methodical German influence, fraternising between officers and men ceased and the officers gradually became segregated into a class of their own.

Although military collaboration between Russia and Germany ended with the advent of the Nazi Party, the Soviet Union continued to build on the established foundations. Ideas once considered bourgeois gradually crept back: officers' pay was increased, medals were reintroduced, and many of the old uniforms revived.

In 1937 Stalin was suddenly confronted by an army clique with a visibly swelling power. Although it is extremely doubtful that members of this group were conniving abroad, there may have been dissension among them as to the methods which Stalin was employing in his ruthless and whirlwind efforts to industrialise the country. It is apparent that Stalin foresaw a force which might eventually threaten his own position; and waging the same preventive war with which he stripped the Communist Party of its leaders and, later, rid industrial forces and police organisations of their chiefs, he struck a blow at the army.

Indeed, there was evidence that for some time Stalin had been concerned in transforming the army into a thoroughly passive instrument. In 1925, eighty-five per cent of the army was composed of peasants, and the remainder of industrial workers, which was more or less in proportion to the nation's division of labour.

Since the famines of 1932–33, however – a direct result of the Government's ruthless collectivisation of the land – the loyalty of the peasant population was evidently considered of a dubious character, for now nearly fifty per cent of the army was recruited directly from the ranks of industrial workers. Also significant was the fact that the number of Communists had increased from nineteen per cent in 1925 to over fifty per cent in 1939; in fact, most of the motorised troops were recruited exclusively from among the latter.

Although the Soviet Government argued that the purge had strengthened the army by the elimination of dissenting elements, it was obvious it could scarcely have increased its technical efficiency. The promotion of junior officers to fill the gaps in the higher commands created such a dearth in the lower ranks that Voroshilov was forced to order ten thousand cadets, who had not completed their courses at the military schools, to be enrolled as lieutenants.

The reintroduction of political commissars was also a factor of significance. The functions of the commissars were more or less obsolete until they were revived by a decree in May 1937. From that date on, they had equal authority with the commanding officers. They countersigned all orders and in extreme cases could even veto plans for an attack. An indication of their power was revealed by the fact that Red Army soldiers took an oath binding their allegiance to 'Commanding Officers, Commissars and Superiors'.

The efficiency of an army operating under such dual control was obviously questionable. In 1918 when the commissars were first installed to prevent the desertion of White officers who were forced to serve in the Bolshevik ranks, the difficulties arising from the dual relationship were revealed in a letter written by Trotsky:

Re the participation of officers in White Guard revolts, I note that quarrels between commissars and military leaders have lately been increasing. From the evidence at my disposal it is apparent that commissars often take a directly wrong line of action, either by usurping operative and leadership functions, or by poisoning the relations between officer and commissar by a policy of petty quibbling carried out in a spirit of undignified rivalry.

There was no reason to suppose that in twenty years the human element has altered to such an extent that difficulties such as these would not arise again. But it wasn't until I went to Finland the following winter that I had a chance to judge the Red Army from experience rather than hypothetical reasoning.

Notes on the Ukraine

At night, the lights of Kiev flashed from the high bluffs above the River Dnieper like jewels in a coronet, while the ice-bound river far below shone in the moonlight like a white satin train. But with the daylight the beauty passed like a strange dream, and you found an atmosphere of desolation all the more accentuated by the bleakness of the winter sky. The paint was chipping off the buildings, the shop windows were cracked and dirty, and every few blocks there were queues. The poverty was oppressive. It was irreconcilable with the fact that Kiev was the capital city of the Soviet Ukraine – an area almost as large as France – with the most fertile farm lands in Europe.

In that winter of 1938–39 many people believed that these farm lands were Germany's ultimate aim. Not many months before, Hitler had declared that if 'the unending cornfields of the Ukraine lay within Germany, under National Socialist leadership, the country (Germany) would swim in plenty'.

The Russians had taken note of this. Although the Ukrainian newspapers carried no hint of a threat from abroad, the city flowed with troops. The villages were honeycombed with GPU agents and at night the factories were illuminated and guarded by watchmen to prevent any attempts at sabotage. Finally, all foreign consulates, with the exception of the Polish, had been abolished, and the region unofficially closed to tourists. Indeed, foreigners had become such a rarity that when Frank Hayne, the American assistant military attaché, and I wandered around the streets, we were regarded as a curiosity. In the shops, crowds collected around us to feel our clothes and ask us where we had bought our boots.

I was on my way out of Russia and had been given permission to leave via the Romanian frontier, travelling through Kiev and Odessa en route. Frank, with a diplomatic passport, was able to travel where he liked and had come with me to take a look round. Six years ago, when the Soviet Government had adopted drastic methods in an attempt to collectivise the land, over six million people had died of starvation in the Ukraine. Now most of the *kolkhozes* were established, and Frank and I were interested in learning something of present conditions in order to get an indication of what resistance the Ukraine could offer against a German attack.

But the Soviet authorities seemed to have another view on the matter. From the moment our train pulled into Kiev we were surrounded by GPU men and it looked as though we would have little opportunity of seeing anything. We were trailed by the police day and night, even when we inspected the mummies of the priests buried in the catacombs of an ancient monastery. This annoyed Frank more than anything else. He was a delightful, easy-going southerner from New Orleans, but he had a temper that could flare up forcefully and unexpectedly.

'Ah suppose they think we're goin' to start a Trotsky conspiracy among the mummies,' he said indignantly. 'If those fellows tag on behind me much longer ah'm goin' to take a crack at them. Ah don't mind being followed, but ah object to having them step on mah heels!'

When we asked the authorities for permission to visit a collective farm we were refused with a series of polite excuses. First, the director was out of town for the day; then the farm machinery was under repair; and last, the roads were too bad to travel over. As there were no taxis or public cars, we were helpless. But the more our path was baulked, the more determined we became to have our way.

In the end we visited a collective farm, but not with official consent. We finally called on the Polish Consul, a charming man by the name of Matuszyński, and when he heard our plight, he placed his car and chauffeur at our disposal. We arranged for the chauffeur to pick us up at ten the next morning, and drive us to a farm about twenty miles from Kiev.

Our trip had certain dramatic features. First of all, we succeeded in eluding our GPU men. We were wandering along near the hotel looking into the shop windows when the Polish car came by, and we hailed it in the middle of the street. When we got out on a deserted country road we looked back to find two police cars following us – but the chauffeurs were alone. We had left so quickly that our GPU men, who had been hanging about in the hotel lobby (thinking we must make our arrangements through the porter), had missed the bus.

It was good to get into the country; the landscape, with its white plains and its bright blue cottages glistening in the sunshine, looked like a painting from another century. Peasant women with thick shawls wrapped around their heads trudged along the road pulling crude, home-made sledges stacked with wood and straw; once a horse-drawn sleigh came dashing past us, the driver's face half smothered in an enormous fur cap. But soon we came upon a column of soldiers dragging some field guns, and the slosh of their boots in the snow and the roll of the artillery wheels jerked us back to the grim reality of 1939. According to Frank, the soldiers were members of the 44th Ukrainian Division – a division I was to see more of in Finland. They were husky, clean-shaven men and their high boots and long, thick coats offered a striking contrast to the shabby appearance of the peasants.

As we drove along, the countryside became more and more deserted, but we jounced through snow and mud, across incredible roads; over one particularly nasty bit we looked back to see both our police cars stuck in a snowdrift. We whooped with delight at this piece of luck, and a mile or so further on reached our collective farm – unescorted.

A more desolate sight would be hard to imagine. It was a small village of perhaps two-dozen cottages on either side of a narrow lane; and the lane was a sea of mud. The fences in front of the cottages were sagging, the walls dilapidated and the roofs in a bad state of repair. There was not a soul to be seen.

'Now that we're here, what do we do?' asked Frank.

'We're going in to talk to the people. And you must do the interpreting!'

'But we can't just burst into people's houses!'

'Why not? We'll never be lucky enough to escape from the GPU again.'

'Good Lord!' said Frank. 'Before we're through with this trip, I'll be the journalist and you'll be the military attaché.'

We walked through mud that oozed up over our boots, pushed our way through a rickety gate and walked round to the back of the cottage. We banged on the door and a few minutes later a frightened-looking woman opened it. She might have been any age. She had wispy, blondish-grey hair that hung in strands about her face, red hands and a dirty smock. She stared at us in bewilderment. Frank explained we were Americans who were making a trip through Russia, but the words seemed to make no impression, for she just stood there gazing at us dumbly. We asked her if we could come in and she moved aside and opened the door. The cottage consisted of two rooms: the floors and walls were bare and the only furniture was three stools, a cupboard and a table. In one corner of the room was a large porcelain stove; two babies, bundled up in cloth, were sleeping on top of it.

Conversation was difficult as the woman didn't talk, but just kept staring at us. We asked her what conditions were like and if she had plenty of food.

Her face brightened at this. 'Oh yes,' she replied. 'We have bread.' She hurried over to the table, lifted a cloth, and showed us a plate of black bread. As far as we could see there was no other food in the house. We left with her still staring after us and walked down the road to another cottage.

This was a more lively affair, for inside we found a family of eleven people, ranging from a grandmother to a child of four. The grandmother was a very old woman. She had a yellow, withered face, but a pair of incredibly bright eyes; it soon became apparent that she was still very much the matriarch of the household. She was tremendously excited at our arrival, dragged two stools from the corner, and, chuckling and bowing, told us to sit down.

'What have you got in your hat?' she said, pointing at me. Frank said it was a veil.

'But what's it for?'

The difficulty of an explanation was avoided, for her attention suddenly shifted to my silk stockings. She knelt down and felt them. 'Aren't you cold?'

We asked her about conditions in the village and she nodded her head in satisfaction and gave us the same answer we had heard in the first cottage: there was bread. Then she chuckled and added there was vodka as well.

The cottage was as bare of furniture as the first one. When we asked where everybody slept, she pushed open the back door and pointed to a loft filled with hay. Near the door there were two ikons hanging on the wall. Frank commented on them.

'I didn't think you kept those any more.'

The old woman laughed. 'The younger people don't have them, but I like them. They're so bright.'

In the meanwhile, the rest of the family clustered round, the children staring at us with their fingers in their mouths. One of the boys suddenly darted into the next room and came back with a battered accordion. He squatted on the floor and began to play, while two of the girls clasped hands and did a little dance. The grandmother said something: one of them broke off, ran over to the cupboard and pulled out a dress. It was made of homespun cloth, painstakingly embroidered with flowers. She slipped into it, her sister did the buttons up, and then resumed the dance.

When we were ready to leave, the grandmother called our attention to a small faded snapshot tacked on the wall. She said it was a picture of herself taken many years ago, then pointed to Frank's camera and remarked how wonderful it would be to have a new one. We suggested a family group and at this the cottage went into an uproar. The boys knelt down to clean their shoes, the girls began to smooth their hair, and the mother wiped her children's faces. Finally, they lined up outside the cottage, their expressions tense and nervous. When the camera clicked, a sigh of relief swept through the group. They surged forward while we wrote down their address, then one by one shook hands and said goodbye.

When we reached the car again we discovered that news of our arrival had spread through the village. All along the lane neighbours were hanging over their fences discussing the event. Our Polish chauffeur told us the police cars had just arrived, and the drivers were reporting us to the farm director. He advised us to pay our respects immediately.

The director's headquarters were in a large cottage, a few yards back from the lane, known as an 'agitation point'. We walked in to find him in conversation with a uniformed militia man. Both of them gave us hostile looks and demanded our papers. But Frank's diplomatic passport evidently made an impression, for after questioning us for ten or fifteen minutes, they finally let us go.

On the way home we looked back and saw the police cars following us; this time they each contained three GPU men. Where they all came from still remains a Soviet mystery.

* * *

Before we left Kiev we said goodbye to Mr Matuszyński, the Polish Consul, who had been so kind to us. Six months later, when the Russians marched into Poland, he was called out of his bed at midnight, and taken to police headquarters for questioning. What sort of a third degree he was put through no one knows, for he was never seen again. When the Soviet authorities were questioned about this brutal act, they disclaimed any knowledge of his whereabouts and suggested that perhaps he had met with an 'accident'. They offered, ironically, to make a search for the body.

* * *

In Odessa, Frank and I met two British sailors who had come into port on a cargo ship carrying oranges from Valencia. They were an amusing pair. The first mate was a tall, lumbering Lancashire man and the engineer a wiry little Cockney. We invited them to have supper with us, but when the bill came they drew large wads of roubles out of their pockets and insisted on paying. With the exchange at twenty-five roubles to the pound, Frank and I were astonished, but the engineer explained that the moment they stepped ashore Russians had begun bartering for their clothes.

'A thousand roubles for my pants, five hundred for my coat and a hundred for my socks. If I hadn't thought I'd be arrested for indecency I'd have stripped in the middle of the street. Instead, I went back to the ship and dug up all the old shirts and sweaters I could find, and now we're living like a couple of millionaires.'

'Yes. And you wouldn't believe how far these things will go.' The first mate dug deeply into his pockets and drew out three oranges. 'In this country they're as good as diamond bracelets,' he chortled. 'You've no idea how fast you can get acquainted. Perhaps I shouldn't boast, but I've already had two proposals of marriage – one from the girl at the restaurant and the other from the cook at the club.'

The engineer interrupted to explain that the girls were so anxious to get away from Russia, any foreigners would do.

'Well, personal appearances count a little,' insisted the first mate, slightly ruffled.

The pair had had many hazardous experiences running the Spanish blockade; once their ship had been bombed and sunk in Barcelona harbour, but they had promptly signed up with the crew of another. There was little danger of their being converted to Communism, for although they had travelled to many out-of-the-way places, they seemed to regard Russia as the strangest of them all.

'On the whole,' said the first mate, 'foreigners are a pretty loony lot. There's no stability about them, if you know what I mean. But as for this Russian system where you can win a girl with an orange, it's definitely *queer.*'

'At least we're saving a lot of money,' interrupted the engineer. 'When we get back to Marseilles we can stock up on sweets for the kids in Barcelona.'

The Spanish War came to an end three months later, and I often wondered what happened to the pair. The first mate said when it was over he was going to buy a cottage in England and settle down; but I suppose both of them are still on the high seas – this time running the blockade of the German U-boats.

* * *

Odessa was as desolate as Kiev, but it was warmer. The streets ran with mud, for the snow was melting, but in the country you could see the first signs of spring. The Intourist guides were more accommodating than they had been in Kiev and arranged to take us to several factories and farms, but, unfortunately, our programme was upset by a final encounter with the GPU.

When foreigners travel in Russia they must arrange their itinerary in advance and get special permits which are marked with the exact number of hours they wish to remain in each town. Although my visa for the Soviet Union didn't expire for another week, my pass for Odessa was stamped one day. Mr Schmidt had told me if I wished to change my plans in any way, to notify the local police and they would make the proper readjustments. But when I applied for a forty-eight hours' extension for Odessa the authorities sent back my card with the reply that since Moscow had stamped it for one day, one day it must remain. The telephone lines were government-controlled, so we were unable to ring up the Foreign Office ourselves, but sent back a message asking the police to get in touch with Mr Schmidt, who, we assured them, would straighten out the matter. But the police, smothered by the red tape of bureaucracy, had no intention of using any initiative. Back came the irritating comment that one day was one day. As Frank was travelling on a diplomatic pass, he was all right, but I was ordered to leave not later than eight in the morning.

Frank telegraphed to Mr Schmidt and Chip Bohlen – although we had little chance of getting a reply in less than twenty-four hours – and sent the police a second message saying that I flatly refused to leave. 'That will show them they can't push us around as though we were Russians,' he said angrily.

That night we went to the local ballet and when we got back to the hotel the porter told us the police were waiting to see us. We went into the manager's room and found a strapping GPU man in uniform. Frank painstakingly re-explained the situation, but the officer sat there shaking his head and stubbornly repeating: 'One day is one day.'

'Now, look here,' said Frank, 'I've had about enough of the Soviet police force. If you want to straighten out the matter all you have to do is to lift the telephone and ring Moscow, but it's a waste of time ordering us about. If the lady doesn't want to leave she's not going to leave. Do you understand? Now, we'll ask her. You don't want to leave, do you?'

'No,' I said weakly.

'There! You heard her yourself. She doesn't want to leave. What are you going to do about it?'

'She refuses to leave?'

'Absolutely.'

'That's final?'

'Absolutely.'

'Then she must be prepared for the consequences.'

The GPU man gave me a menacing look and left the room.

'You don't mind, do you?' said Frank. 'We must keep the Stars and Stripes flying.'

'Yes,' I agreed. 'But not from the inside of a concentration camp.'

I don't suppose anyone had ever talked to the GPU like that before. In the hall we saw the manager whispering to one of the porters, evidently telling him about the episode; both were grinning from ear to ear.

The next forty-eight hours in Odessa were slightly disconcerting, for although we had a telegram from Chip Bohlen saying he would do his best, we heard nothing from Mr Schmidt. No further messages came from the police, but each time we went out of the hotel I expected to arrive back to find a posse waiting for us. The day finally came for Frank to leave for Moscow and for me to leave for Romania. The trip to the frontier town of Tiraspol was a three-hour journey, and, although Frank assured me I would be all right, I feared I might be intercepted on the way.

On the train I noticed a plain-clothes man obviously following me. This was not out of the ordinary, but my heart sank when I reached Tiraspol and found the GPU man that Frank had quarrelled with waiting for me in the customs house. He gave me a look that seemed filled with meaning, told me to leave my bags and identification papers and to wait in the restaurant while he examined them.

I sat down at a table and ordered some tea and a bun. Suddenly I looked up to see the plain-clothes man standing over me, a smile on his face.

'I speak English,' he said.

I thought this was the prelude to an arrest, but he pulled up a chair and I discovered he was only seeking an opportunity to practise his English. In Russia, languages are evidently taught with an eye on propaganda, for although he spoke only pidgin-English, his vocabulary was sufficient to express the party line. This is the conversation we had.

'Russia good country. You English?'

'No. American.'

'Unemployment in America?'

'Yes. Some.' (Not wishing to let the home team down.)

'Bourgeois government.' (Pause.) 'Unemployment in England, too?'

'Yes. Some.'

'Bourgeois government.' (Pause.) 'Bourgeois government, always unemployment. In Russia, workers' government, no unemployment.'

I asked him if he considered Germany's government a bourgeois one, and he said that he did.

'Well, they haven't any unemployment. How do you explain that?'

He lifted his hands in consternation. 'Oh, mustn't talk about Germany. Germany very bad country. Many concentration camps.' He shook his head gloomily, got up, bowed, and left.

My worries were needless, for after an hour I was called back to the customs office and my papers and bags were politely handed back. Evidently Mr Schmidt had intervened. Most surprising of all was the GPU man, who shook my hand and bade me return to the Soviet Union again!

I left on a musical comedy train. It was painted bright green with chintz curtains and flower-pots in the windows. It was used only to run back and forth across the frontier, and especially designed to impress the Romanians. I was the only passenger on the train, and when we reached the frontier the guards got off and only the engineer and an assistant remained – the Soviet Union trusted few of its people on foreign soil.

Under ordinary circumstances, Tighina would probably seem a drab little town, but on that particular afternoon it had a glamour all its own. Everything was so bright: the bowls of fruit in the restaurant; the waitress's green earrings; the red ribbon round the cat's neck; the gaudy photograph of King Carol on the wall; the blue and white check tablecloth. The windows were shining, the floors were clean, and everybody looked plump and cheerful. The Kremlin was a long way off.

* * *

On the way back to England I travelled across Romania, Poland, Germany, Belgium and France. During that long trip I thought a good deal about the misery and inhumanity I had seen under totalitarian regimes. I had seen the extremists on both sides of the war in Spain; I had seen Nazism in Germany, Communism in Russia. And I knew more than ever that I believed in democracy.

In America I had believed in democracy because I had been taught to, but now I believed in it because I had learned what it meant. It meant the right of the majority to rule and *the right of the minority to exist*. This last seemed to me the most important of all, for wherever the minority has the right to exist, men can think and speak according to their conscience.

I had heard people argue that 'freedom of speech' was a misused privilege; that on the whole it was a small deprivation to be forbidden to criticise the government. But 'the government' was not an abstract term. The government was the clothes you wore; the cigarettes you smoked; the food you ate; the schools you went to; the books you read; the streets you walked along. It conditioned your thoughts and fashioned your ambitions. When you surrendered your right to oppose the government, you surrendered your right to live as a human being.

I had also heard it argued that the mass of people were not fit to guide their own destiny and it was therefore proper for the state to be unobstructed in directing the lives of their people for the common good. Those words 'the state' were always misleading. The state was a group of men. And I knew I didn't believe any group of men infallible enough to be awarded powers that could not be checked. The totalitarian regimes boasted of the swiftness of their administration; when they plunged into war, I thought, that would be swift, too.

War seemed a certainty, and I knew the forces gathering to oppose each other were not merely the forces of Imperialism. It was man versus the ant-heap. As an American, I might be neutral; but as a human being, it was already my fight.

* * *

It didn't take long to become re-acclimated to the electric atmosphere of the continent. I spent only twelve hours in Berlin, dined with Charlie Post, an American businessman, and took the night express to London. About midnight I was awakened by the shuffle of footsteps and the sound of voices. The door of my compartment was flung open and three Nazi Storm Troopers walked in. One of them addressed me in English and said he would have to search my bags. But first he asked me the name of the man who had taken me to the station. I told him and he shook his head.

'He was not an American. He was a Russian. You were speaking Russian to him on the station platform.'

I told him I couldn't speak a word of Russian, but he smiled unbelievingly, and proceeded to rip my suitcases to pieces.

I don't know yet what they were searching for. The porter told me later they had also questioned him, asking if he had overheard me speaking Russian. They said they had been ordered to make the search by their headquarters in Berlin. It was four weeks before the Germans marched into Prague, and I can only imagine that, with the move impending, there were instructions to watch all foreigners closely; the fact that I had been travelling through the Ukraine, Romania and Poland – territory regarded as 'German spheres of interest' – might have led them to suspect me of being a spy.

Whatever the explanation, they pulled everything out of my suitcases until the compartment looked as though a tornado had hit it. They pounced on the Marxist literature I had. 'Ach so! You are a member of the Communist Party?'

They wrote down the titles of the books but to my surprise returned them, and told me that at the next stop a woman would board the train to search the bed. The leader of the group evidently had orders to remain in the compartment lest I hide anything, for he leaned against the wall and lighted a cigarette. He was a good-looking young man, not more than twenty-five years old, but with the arrogant manner and swagger his uniform suggested. His voice rang through the quiet sleeping-car.

'So you are on your way to England. Well, you tell Mr Chamberlain from us that if he tries to block our way in Europe any longer' [Mr Chamberlain was at this time predicting a golden era of peace] 'he'll have a war on his hands. We don't want a war but we'll fight. We aren't going to sit back taking orders from any-body. Germany is too big to be strangled.'

'Where do you want to go?'

'Oh, I don't know. But somewhere. We need more room.'

'What about the Ukraine?'

'What's it like there?'

I described it and he suddenly grinned. 'I don't think you're a Communist, after all. It would be a fine country for Germany, wouldn't it? It would give us all the things we need. But, person-ally, I would like to have a farm in Africa.' His tone became almost confiding. 'I'm tired of my job here. I would like to take my wife to Africa, where it's nice and warm, and have a cottage with some chickens. The English don't pay any attention to their colonies, but we would take trouble over them. And we deserve them. We're a nation of eighty million people.'

He elaborated this theme for some time. The more he talked the more genial he became. When the customs woman came aboard he evidently told her to cut the search short, for she only half pulled back the bedclothes, looked beneath the pillow, then bowed apologetically and left.

The Storm Trooper came back into the compartment, said perhaps he would run into me on the train again one day, heiled Hitler, and departed.

I drew a sigh of relief and took out my passport. Eagles look the same the world over, but the one stamped on the cover was a tough old bird. Tougher, I thought, than the German eagle. At least, so far.

Part VI

WORLD WAR SECOND

1

England Awakes

On March 15th, 1939, Hitler's troops marched into Prague. That date will go down in history as the date when England woke up. Sugar umbrellas disappeared from shop windows and Mr Chamberlain asked angrily: 'Is this an attempt to dominate the world by force?'

But it was the fact that Hitler had violated his solemn declaration of only six months before, in which he had asserted that the Czech State would hold no interest for him after the Sudeten German problem was settled, that shocked English people the most. The village pubs resounded with the single damning phrase: 'Hitler's broke his word.' And that was the end of English tolerance. From then on the nation prepared for war. Soon armoured trucks began rumbling through the countryside, housewives turned on the radio to hear the latest news bulletin, National Service placards began to appear and large yellow posters said: 'Join the Balloon Barrage'. The British Government slapped down guarantees on Poland, Greece and Romania and introduced conscription. Even Mrs Sullivan became politically minded and summed up the psychology of the country with the remark: 'My old man says now as we can't trust 'Itler any more there's no use arguing with him; now we've got to give 'im a licking.'

Many foreign observers did not understand the change that had swept the country. Some had associated the policy of appeasement with a 'ruling class' of England, which, they claimed, had grown so effete that it was willing to drive a bargain with Nazi Germany to preserve peace (and property) at any cost. Others accused

Chamberlain of Fascist tendencies, claiming that his supporters were pro-German. Nothing could have been further from the truth. Englishmen are first and foremost 'pro' their own country. Many people had been genuinely taken in by Germany's well-publicised grievances; they had sympathised with the German occupation of the Rhineland, with the Austrian *Anschluss*, and even with the claim for Sudetenland on the grounds that the German population had shown an overwhelming desire to become incorporated in the Reich. There was a case to be argued for all three of these developments. But there was no case to be argued for a man who demanded the principle of self-determination and, six months later, violated that very same principle by the brutal destruction of the Czech State.

From that date England's unanimous verdict was Guilty. From that date the policy of appeasement was dead.

* * *

I had been very happy in London. Not only because I was interested in the political life, but because I had grown to have a deep admiration for many of the people I'd come to know. Most of them were members of the much-criticised 'ruling class'. The better I knew them the more I was impressed by their regard for justice, and their granite-like quality of loyalty and integrity. Many could be accused of stupidity, but none of dishonesty.

England is a puzzling nation. As John Gunther has pointed out, it is at one and the same time, 'the world's strongest oligarchy and freest democracy'. This oligarchy is one of the phenomena of the civilised world. The old school tie has been the butt of many jokes, but in history you will find that the tradition it embodies has led England during her most enlightened periods and fortified her in months of peril.

To explain the tradition one must examine the structure of the oligarchy or 'ruling class'. Drawn from the public schools (private schools in the American sense) which educate the sons of the aristocracy and the upper middle-class families, it supplies the country with the bulk of its statesmen, civil servants, diplomats, army and navy officers and county squires; in other words, the leaders of the nation.

But the interesting feature of the oligarchy is its elasticity. It is by no means a rigid caste. The British aristocracy, unlike any other aristocracy in the world, is constantly refurbished by new blood. Every year men who have distinguished themselves in business, science, medicine, politics, in the arts or in the fighting services, are elevated to the peerage. Thus the best brains of the country are lassoed into the service of the nation. Unlike America, where the public life of successful businessmen is confined for the most part to lending their names to philanthropic institutions, in England they are given an opportunity to take a responsible part in the life of the nation. (A notable example is Rufus Isaacs – later Lord Reading – who went to India the first time as cabin boy, the second time as Viceroy.) As members of the House of Lords, they can make their views known and bring an influence to bear on the events of the day; they are eligible for membership in the Cabinet. Present-day illustrations are Lord Beaverbrook and Lord Woolton.

Admission to the ruling class is achieved not only by way of the peerage. The Tory Party keeps a wary look-out for new ability which might reinforce the ranks of the Opposition; let any really able champion of the Left arise, and the doors of the oligarchy swing open. (For example: Ramsay MacDonald.) But all those who enter the ranks, whether by way of the public school or by outstanding merit, are bound together by the old school tie tradition.

This tradition is not, as many Americans imagine, preserved by a snobbish group which takes delight in singing sentimental songs about their lost youth and has sworn to 'stick together' at any cost. Eton, for example, which supplies England with seventy-five per cent of its ruling class, offers no tangible evidence of a 'fraternity'. It is a curious but important paradox that Old Etonians seldom wear Old Etonian ties, never have reunion dinners, and rarely refer to their school except in anecdotes directed either at the sanitary arrangements or the stupidity of their masters. This extraordinary freemasonry which admits no symbols, tolerates no passwords, and ignores the usual paraphernalia of the exclusive society, is bound together by an intangible code of ethics – a code unwritten, unmentioned, but understood and accepted by all.

This code is the fibre of England. Public-school boys are educated to be the future leaders of the Empire and from an early age are taught to assume responsibility. But more important, they are impressed with a sense of *noblesse oblige*. They must set the standard for the nation; in peace-time, their honour must be unassailable; and in war-time, their courage unquestionable.

In America and France the men of the highest ability and education go into business, for the most part, and leave politics to the professional men; as a result, self-interest often comes before public interest; graft is accepted as the rule rather than the exception and politics are generally regarded as a 'dirty' trade. But in England, since the cream of the country *serves* the country, the standard is the highest and government departments are incorruptible. As an American I had become so accustomed to the fact that one always regarded politicians sceptically, that I was astonished on my first trip through England to hear the confidence with which the ordinary people referred to the Government. When I drove through the North with Martha Gellhorn, we were assured over and over again that whatever the outcome, the Government was 'doing its best' – and that the Government was 'the best Government in the world'. Now this is the last sort of remark you would hear either in America or France.

The governing class in England has not maintained its position without justification. On the whole, its policies have been enlightened and far-sighted. In 1906 it passed a vast programme of reforms, initiated by Lloyd George, ranging from Old Age Pensions and Workmen's Compensation to Town Planning and Unemployment and Health Insurance, which were not introduced in America until nearly thirty years later by Roosevelt's New Deal – and even then were considered 'radical' by many Americans.

And in 1911 the King himself became the champion of democracy by compelling the House of Lords to pass the Lloyd George Budget (stripping the Lords of monetary powers) by threatening to create a *bloc* of peers to form the necessary majority. Throughout English history you find violent social changes taking place, but always with the equilibrium of the nation being maintained, like a see-saw that rights itself, largely through the moral force of the 'old school tie'.

But the most outstanding virtue of this class, in my opinion, is its incorruptibility. Because this quality is known and accepted, the English people have a deep-rooted faith in their leaders and support them with, at times, almost surprising loyalty. When, on March 15th, Chamberlain's policy of appeasement was shattered into a thousand pieces, the country did not turn against him but commended him for having done his best. 'If Mr Chamberlain can't keep us out of war, no one can,' was the verdict.

This English quality of loyalty (which can exist only in a country where the people have respect for their leaders and the leaders have respect for each other) was further illustrated when Winston

Churchill became Prime Minister the following year. He allowed
Chamberlain and Halifax to remain in office; and some months
later appointed David Margesson (who, as Chief Whip, was the
man most responsible for having kept him in the wilderness) to the
War Ministry – on the grounds that if Margesson had been efficient
enough to keep him out of the Cabinet he must be a very efficient
man indeed. No wonder England is difficult to understand.

Of one thing I am sure: you will never understand it unless
you accept idealism as a force in the shaping of British policy. A
diplomat once made the remark: 'England is the most dangerous
country in the world because it is the only one capable of going to
war on behalf of another country.'

Now British self-interest happens to coincide neatly with British
idealism; the absence of tyranny on the continent and the freedom and independence of small states. But that does not mean the
idealism is artificial. You can attribute wide and varying motives
to any single act or policy; but on the whole you will come closer
to understanding England if you make a practice of giving her
the benefit of the doubt. If you don't, and you try to interpret her
policies solely in the light of self-interest, you will go badly astray.

March 15th was an illustration of this. Cynics were bewildered
by the sudden swing-over. When Chamberlain signed the Munich
agreement they took it to mean that Great Britain had washed
her hands of Europe and surrendered her long overlordship. They
failed to understand that the Chamberlain Government was not
compromising from fear, but from a genuine belief in Germany's
capacity to prove herself a good neighbour.

Look at Germany's position in the five and a half months
between Munich and the occupation of Prague. Hitler's prestige
was enormous and National Socialism was gathering more and
more adherents every day among people discouraged by what

they called 'the cumbersome and old-fashioned methods' of democracy. British and French statesmen were only too eager to open conversations with Hitler and find a new design for Europe, to take the place of the League of Nations. In fact, only a few days before March 15th, Sir Nevile Henderson, the British Ambassador, asked Hitler to submit for negotiation any problems which still stood between him and complete understanding with Great Britain. And Oliver Stanley, the Minister of the Board of Trade, was scheduled to go to Berlin on March 16th to discuss plans for a new trade agreement.

Without war, Hitler had become the most dominant figure in Europe. If he had chosen to exercise his great position in the interests of peace there might indeed have been a golden era. So much lay within his grasp that many of the most hard-boiled foreign observers couldn't believe he would deliberately choose to fashion the future with the sword. On every side one heard the gloomy prophecy that France and Great Britain were already dwindling away under the great new force; that Hitler no longer needed a war to get the mastery he wanted.

Logically, they were right. Hitler didn't need to employ violence; but he took a short cut, failing to heed the moral issue. With Munich, Czechoslovakia had become his vassal. The physical occupation of Prague in no way detracted from Great Britain's position; what it did do was to shatter the Chamberlain Government's belief in Germany. Forty-five million people in England were shocked by the crime. That was the cause of the awakening.

* * *

That spring I went to America for several weeks to see my family. New York was lively and refreshing, but the problems uppermost in people's minds (mostly New Deal versus Republicanism) seemed so far removed from the tide of world events that it was almost with a feeling of relief that I came back to England again. It was July now and the London season was in full swing. The hotels were overflowing with tourists, and there was a fever of entertaining – parties, balls, country houses with the doors wide open. Everyone seemed determined to squeeze in the last ounce of fun before the war started. Politics were discussed less than at any time during the last two years. The die was cast. If Germany attacked Poland, England would fight; there was nothing left to argue about. Everyone made plans for the summer holidays casually, as though there were no crisis at all. In August I went off to Rome to see if I could get an interview with Mussolini.

Before I left, Randolph took me down to Chartwell for tea. It was beautiful there, with the wind blowing through the grass and the sun streaming down on the flowers – and this time the pond actually had some goldfish in it. Once again I found Mr Churchill in his torn coat and battered hat peering into the water, fascinated. After tea, he took me upstairs and showed me the high, oak-beamed study where he did all his writing. He was working on a three-volume history of the English-speaking peoples and over half of it was already completed. 'But I'll never be able to finish it before the war begins,' he remarked gloomily.

When it came, he said, he was going to close the big house and move into the cottage.

'You won't be living there,' said Randolph indignantly. 'You'll be at No. 10 Downing Street.'

'I'm afraid I haven't got the same fanciful ideas that you have.'

'Well, at any rate, you'll be in the Cabinet.'

'Things will have to get pretty bad before that happens.'

They did. The next time I saw him he was the First Lord of the Admiralty.

2

Roman Holiday

It was hot in Rome that August – the sort of heat that hangs in the air, gradually stifling energy until people move about more and more slowly like toys that are running down. The Piazza Colonna, usually one of the capital's busiest squares, lay beneath the full glare of the sun and on this particular day was almost deserted. Occasionally a horse and carriage clattered over the cobblestones, the driver mopping his brow, too hot even to crack his whip, but that was all.

I crossed the square and went into a café to read the day-old *Times* which had just arrived. The German press attack on Poland had begun and the news from Berlin was exactly the same as the year before, only this time you substituted the word Poland for Czechoslovakia. The Italian waiter knew English and made several attempts to read over my shoulder. Then he came out into the open, apologetically: 'Is there any news? Here in Rome it's sometimes difficult to know what's going on.'

I told him the German press attack on Poland was increasing.

'Oh, we know all about *that*. But real news,' he said anxiously. 'Is there going to be a war?'

I replied that if the Germans invaded Poland I was certain England and France would fight – and asked him what he thought the Italians would do.

'Heaven knows. We don't want a war – least of all fighting with the Germans. I was wounded in the last war fighting *against* the Germans. I can't forget that. At heart, most of us are for the English and French.'

I was surprised by his outspokenness. I don't know whether or not he reflected the general opinion of the moment, but his remarks certainly showed a change of heart from the Rome I had known another August four years before.

August is always Rome's dead season, but in 1935 the ghost of war was walking and the air was tense with apprehension. Then, the cafés on the Piazza Colonna were crowded. Heads were bent over newspapers and every now and then you overheard excited snatches of conversation on potential British air-raids, key positions in the Mediterranean, Italian land defence. I remembered the bookshops along the Piazza plastered with photographs of Abyssinia; the soldiers ready to embark for Africa, strolling through the streets with boots laced halfway up their legs and strange-looking brown caps that pulled down over their faces as protection against the desert sands; the cinemas that advertised films on the horrors of Ethiopia. The films always ended with pictures of the Italian Army – flashes of marching feet, tanks, aeroplanes, warships, then Mussolini, strong and dynamic, addressing his people. I remembered the excited applause he got.

On October 3rd the Abyssinian invasion began, and on October 6th the League of Nations declared sanctions against Italy. The following week I interviewed Mussolini.

It was the first interview I had ever had with an important statesman. The capital was overflowing with experienced journalists trying to see the Duce, and it never occurred to me that I had any chance at all. Certainly I was unqualified for it. I had come to Rome to write a few descriptive stories for the Hearst papers, but my knowledge of foreign affairs was negligible. One night at dinner, however, I happened to meet Dino Alfieri, the Minister of Propaganda, who told me that he, and he alone, had the authority to control the interviews Mussolini gave to the foreign press.

I begged him to arrange for me to have one, but never expected he would. When he rang up the next morning and said Mussolini would see me at six o'clock in the evening, I was appalled. He added that I could have no written questions and the conversation must be 'off the record'.

I hadn't the faintest idea how one went about an interview and had a ghastly premonition I would find myself tongue-tied. I was so nervous I couldn't eat any lunch and all afternoon racked my brain for the proper questions to ask. As the hour approached, I grew more and more unhappy. It was dark and rainy, and as I drove to the Piazza Venezia the automobile lights flashing on the wet pavement and the sound of the wind seemed to lend an eerie emphasis to the occasion. The fact that I was to talk with the Napoleon of the day, at a moment when he challenged the peace of the entire world, seemed to me stupendous.

I walked into the Palazzo, past two Blackshirt guards with rifles, and presented my card of admission to the attendant. He led the way up a long, curving marble staircase, through an iron framework door, and down the length of two rooms – rooms decorated with early Renaissance paintings and furniture; rooms not only alive with the forces of Fascism, but rooms that breathed the air of 1455, when the palace was built by a handsome young cardinal from the Venetian Republic who wanted a residence from which he could watch the horse-races on the Corso.

I was shown into a small reception alcove and told to wait. The silence of the vast, empty rooms around me was broken now and then by the echoing whispers of attendants, the soft mysterious sound of bells. Every now and then uniformed men passed by and gave me the Fascist greeting. After a wait that seemed interminable, an attendant in a black swallow-tail coat announced the Duce was ready to see me. He led me into a huge room with a high, lofty ceiling. At the end, far, far away, was a desk with a man behind it. I walked towards him, my heels clicking loudly on the marble floor. Not until I had gone three-quarters of the way did he look up. Then he rose from his seat.

Never shall I forget my first impression. Instead of the solemn black-uniformed dictator, a small, stocky man in a light grey suit and a pair of brown and white sports shoes bounced forward to meet me. A word unassociated with the strong man of the masses flashed through my mind: dapper. He gripped my hand, flashed a mechanical smile and went back to his seat behind the desk. He walked with a peculiar strutting step – his head back and his chest thrown out – as though half his body was too large for the rest of him.

I soon realised that my worries lest the conversation should lag had been needless. He fixed his eyes on me menacingly, leaned across the desk and pointed a pencil at me, angrily.

'Do you think I'm a despot?' he rasped.

'Oh no,' I said weakly.

'Do you think my people admire me?'

'Oh yes.'

'Do you think I have led them to war against their will?'

'Oh no.'

'Do you think they believe in their cause?'

'Oh yes.'

'Well, then, go home and tell the people of America that. Go home and tell them I'm not the tyrant their papers make out. Go home and tell them that the Italian nation has a right to a place in the sun. That England and all her hypocritical statesmen can't bluff Italy out of her just demands. That Italy is a great power and as a great power she fears no one!'

Here he banged the table. Then for the next ten minutes I was subjected to an angry tirade (in fluent but ungrammatical English) on the strength of Fascist Italy, the treachery of England, and the supreme idiocy of the League of Nations. I had the impression that his intimidating manner was all part of an act – the way he kept his huge eyes riveted on me, the way he waved his pencil and struck the table to illustrate his points. Instead of wondering what to say I began to fear the interview would be over before I'd had an opportunity to ask a single question. I finally decided to chance an interruption.

'Could I ask Your Excellency a question? If you dislike the League of Nations, why do you remain a member?'

Mussolini had been regarding me fiercely, but suddenly his manner changed.

'Because I'm a very clever man,' he replied almost coyly. 'Politics is a difficult game and the way I'm playing it is my best chance to win. It's not easy. I'm at war with fifty-two nations.'

He stumbled over the words 'fifty-two', and to make sure that I hadn't misunderstood, jotted the figures down on a scrap of paper and held them up. '*Cinquantadue*,' he repeated.

'Do you think you can beat fifty-two nations?'

'I don't know,' he smiled, still almost coyly. 'But I'll try. If the English have a right to an African Empire, *we* have a right to an African Empire. The Mediterranean is more our sea than theirs. My people understand and they are with me. You have seen the reception they give me?'

I told him that I had seen the crowds in the Piazza Venezia a few weeks before when he had given the signal that had started the war in Abyssinia.

'Good. Very, very good.'

I never knew whether he was referring to his speech or the fact that I had heard it, for he suddenly jumped up and I saw that the interview had come to an end. He walked down the length of the room with me, shook hands and the door closed.

I had not been impressed. Mussolini's personality was too aggressive and flamboyant for my taste, and his arguments against England and the League so exaggerated they had failed to be convincing. But most of all I resented being told what to do. My reactions to his command to go home and tell the American people this, that and the other thing, was: 'You can tell the Italians what to do, but, thank God, you can't tell me!'

Although many people supported Mussolini's case, there was very little logic about it. He was trying to justify Italy's attack on Abyssinia on the grounds that the latter was not fit for League membership; yet it was Italy, and Italy alone, who had urged Abyssinia's inclusion in the League of Nations – against Great Britain's repeated advice. Mussolini had been hailed as a great man for having raised the standard of living in Italy (you still hear him praised for this), but conveniently ignored was the fact he had achieved it by such artificial means that from now on the nation must expand or burst. That is the great thing to remember about Fascism. It always lives above its income, relying on the scheme that when its capital is exhausted it can steal someone else's money to keep the account square.

When I described Mussolini in an article, published in the Hearst papers, I said that if he had been born in a past era his fierce patriotism and intolerant ambitions undoubtedly would have carved him a great Empire. 'These qualities,' I wrote, 'were virtues yesterday, but are they today? Mussolini rides a high wave. I wonder whether its thunder will echo victory or catastrophe.'

Well, I needn't wonder any longer.

* * *

Italo Balbo, the Air Marshal of Italy, was a very different type from Mussolini. On October 6th, the day the League of Nations voted sanctions against Italy, I flew to Libya and spent a few days in Tripoli. Needless to say, the situation was strained. The British Fleet was concentrated in the Mediterranean and when we reached Sicily our pilot announced we wouldn't make the usual stop at Malta. Instead, when we neared Malta, the plane swooped down and cruised around for half an hour, while the wireless operator picked up the numbers on several British ships and radioed them back to Rome.

Tripoli was thronged with troops; there was the khaki of the colonial troops, the red sashes and fezzes of the Arab soldiers and the grey-green of the Italian regiments. Along the main streets hundreds of Italian flags waved their red and green colours against tropical buildings, so white in the dazzling sunshine they almost hurt your eyes.

I had known one of Balbo's secretaries in Paris, and the night I arrived was invited to dinner at His Excellency's house – an exotic Moorish villa overlooking the sea. There were several army generals at dinner and in spite of the tense situation everyone appeared to be in high spirits. Balbo was a man with a rough, easy-going charm, a quick sense of humour, and was obviously adored by his followers. I remember noticing that, unlike most Fascist leaders, Balbo had no picture of Mussolini in the house. There were only pictures of the King and Queen, the Crown Prince and Princess. When I asked Balbo how he liked Libya he replied with a shrug of his shoulders: '*Il faut l'aimer. Je suis un prisonnier ici.*' I don't know whether or not this was wholly true. Balbo's life was agreeable and his job important; I suspect he rather liked to dramatise himself.

After dinner, the guests went out in the courtyard while Balbo gave an exhibition of night shooting, his favourite sport. With a

rifle pointed towards the dark sky, he took pot shots at stray birds
that fluttered overhead, half distinguishable in the moonlight. The
performance struck a comic note, for although he failed to hit
anything, his generals and officers stood behind him praising him
and telling him what a wonderful shot he was. And behind them
stood two huge black servants, one with a towel and one with a
basin of water, for him to wash his hands when he had finished.
These trusted servants were both Abyssinians.

One afternoon Balbo took me flying. I had always imagined
that flying with the Air Marshal of Italy, the man who had led
a squadron of Italian planes across the Atlantic and back again,
would be a memorable experience. It was, but not exactly as I'd
imagined. He took me up in a two-seater Berda, which was so
old it could scarcely get off the ground. Once in the air the engine
shook so violently I was sure the wings would fall off. The wind
whistled through the cockpit, the machine bumped up and down
uncertainly, and Balbo kept shouting, '*Magnifique, n'est ce pas?*'

The only thing that was magnificent was the view. As we rose in
the air the Arab mosques turned into tennis balls and the village
looked like an assortment of square white candy boxes. On one
side there was the majestic sweep of the Mediterranean, and on
the other the long white stretch of desert; in the west the sky was
pink with a fading sun, and in the east a red moon had begun
to show its shadow. Balbo suggested doing a few stunts for my
benefit, but I managed to restrain him by inventing a weak heart.
When I felt my feet on terra firma again I drew a breath of relief.

On looking back, those few days were an extraordinary interlude.
Although the Italian 'crisis' was holding the world breathless, Balbo
and his generals didn't seem in the least alarmed by the possibility of
war. They didn't even appear to have much to do. In fact, Balbo suggested that I take a couple of days' holiday and fly down to Gadames

with him – a fascinating Arab village several hundred miles from the coast. Nothing would have induced me to get into the same plane with the Air Marshal again, and I told him I was sorry but I had to return to Rome. He argued for some time, then shook his head sadly: 'I know. The trouble is, you don't like my beard.'

There the matter rested.

* * *

It was so hot in the Colonna café, in spite of the heavy striped awnings and the electric fans, I went back to the hotel. Before I left, the Italian waiter said: 'If we were to take our own papers seriously, it would mean war tomorrow. But I don't believe it. Mussolini has a good head on his shoulders. I think he'll keep us out of it.'

Many other people in Rome seemed to have the same faith. Although over a million and a half men had been called to arms and the newspaper headlines screamed startling developments, the capital showed little sign of alarm. You found the usual peaceful life: carriages moving slowly through the streets, people taking their afternoon siestas along the banks of the Tiber, café life as leisurely as ever. There was not even a rush for newspapers.

Italians in every walk of life went out of their way to demonstrate their friendship to English and American visitors, and for the first time I heard the Fascist regime criticised openly. A favourite joke that summer was the man who went up to the cab-driver and said: 'Are you free?' 'Of course not,' came the reply. 'I'm an Italian.'

But more curious than the general unconcern was the lack of military preparation. In spite of the mobilisation, no precautions were being taken against air attacks; the only marked activity was the energetic wave of building for the 1942 World Fair.

I had struck Rome at a bad week – even the officials I wanted to see were away – so I went down to Capri to spend a few days with

Mona and Harrison Williams. It was heavenly there, swimming and lying in the sun all day, but I hadn't been away long before the crisis took a new turn. Ciano had gone to Berchtesgaden to confer with Hitler and there were already rumours that the date for the war had been fixed. I returned to Rome on the same morning that Ciano returned from Germany, and the following day had lunch with him at Ostia.

It was so hot in Rome no one worked in the middle of the day. At one o'clock everyone who could drove to the seaside, a few miles from Rome, and went swimming, returning to work about four o'clock. Prince and Princess del Drago invited me to go with them and we joined Ciano for lunch on the beach.

Ciano was good-looking, spoke perfect English, and was an animated and amusing conversationalist. But he had an air of unbelievable arrogance; you felt all the time that he was trying to imitate his father-in-law, even to the way he threw out his chest and strutted when he walked. Although I was longing to find out what had taken place at Berchtesgaden (the conversation was still a matter of the greatest secrecy), I didn't raise the subject hoping that Italian indiscretion would give me an inkling of what had happened. Ciano guessed what was in my mind, for after lunch he took me for a motorboat ride – one of the most uncomfortable rides I have ever had – and when we got about a mile from the shore, dived off the boat and went swimming. Suddenly he bobbed up from under the water, his hair dripping over his eyes, and said: 'I bet you'd like to know what I talked to Hitler about.'

'Yes, I would. But perhaps because I have a shrewd opinion *he* did most of the talking.'

'Well, don't be too sure,' replied Ciano, irritated. 'He is not the only one. I can make history too. When I think how many lives depend on my thoughts, it's a relief to come out here for a few hours and get away from it all.' (You may not believe it, but that's what he said.)

That night Ciano, the del Dragos and I dined together at the Hotel Ambassador. Ciano was treated like royalty. When he walked into the room everybody stared at him; the waiters bowed low, and acquaintances made exaggerated efforts to draw an acknowledgment from him. He was not oblivious to the effect he created; when he asked me where I'd like to go after dinner and I suggested a place with music, he replied that the crowds made such a fuss about him he had to be careful where he went; his father had just died and he didn't want to make himself conspicuous.

He finally decided on a small restaurant a few miles outside Rome. When we climbed into his car he proudly called my attention to the bullet-proof glass: 'If anything should happen to me, history might alter.' Although we arrived at the restaurant, we didn't go in, for Ciano sent for the manager and asked if his favourite guitar-player was still there. 'No, Eccellenza,' (and here the manager's voice took on an almost accusing note) 'è mobilizzato.' ('No, Excellency, he has been called up in the mobilisation.') Ciano looked slightly taken aback, and we returned to Rome.

Ciano was careful to keep off all political subjects and had given me no indication of what was happening. The following day, however, I again lunched with the del Dragos, Ciano and Alfieri (the Propaganda Minister, who had arranged my interview with Mussolini), and an incident took place that told me what I wanted to know. Lunch with Ciano was always rather a comic affair, for a steady stream of waiters panted up and down the beach with huge dishes of spaghetti and buckets of red wine. As we were lying on the sand, under the shade of umbrellas, an elderly man and his daughter, both in bathing-suits, came down the broad walk. Ciano and Alfieri sprang up and went forward to greet them, but

del Drago wandered off in the opposite direction. I was surprised
to see Ciano making such a fuss over anyone, and when del Drago
came back I asked him who the man was.

'General Długoszowski, the Polish Ambassador,' he answered. 'I
would have liked to have clasped his hand and told him we would
save his country for him. But, alas, it's too late. We can't.'

So that was what had happened at Berchtesgaden. The Germans
had fixed the date for war and decided to go ahead at any cost. No
wonder Ciano found swimming a happy relaxation.

Although many people believed that Ciano and Mussolini
held varying views on foreign affairs, I thought Ciano much too
much of a lightweight to cross his father-in-law in a serious way.
Mussolini still held the reins and from what I could learn was not
a man to be influenced by anyone in making a decision.

I didn't think Italy would come into the war at that time and
wrote to that effect in an article in the *Sunday Times*. But I never
doubted that the Fascist Party was eager for a German victory
and would facilitate one in every way it could. Dino Alfieri was
one of the prime movers in this group. Before I left Rome I went
to lunch with him and he told me whatever happened he didn't
believe England and France would fight. 'But if they do,' he added,
'it might as well come now as at some later date. Every now and
then there comes a time in history when the lands of the earth
must be re-divided.'

Italian foreign policy seemed to me even more contemptible
than the German. It ignored the great civilisation that had been its
heritage, and contained not even a shellacking of principle; it was
out-and-out piracy.

I learned there was no chance of interviewing Mussolini again
and at the end of the week left for the south of France to spend
a few days' holiday with Freda and Bobby Casa Maury. On the

day that I flew from Rome to Genoa, news of the German–Soviet pact burst upon an astonished world. There it was, the overture to World War No. 2. For the first time, the war odds were in Germany's favour; Hitler was free to smash Poland, then turn his back on Russia and hurl his full striking force at the West in a final bid for European domination. Now nothing would stay his hand.

3

Last Hours in Berlin

My holiday went *caput*. Twenty-four hours later I was in a car with Marc Lauer, a friend of Bobby Casa Maury, headed for Paris. A good many other people were headed for Paris too, for the news of the German Pact was like the proverbial wind before the storm. One minute summer visitors were going evenly about their lives; the next they were scattering pell-mell in a hundred directions, trying to get home before the lightning struck. The French Government had already begun calling up its reservists; the roads were crowded with trucks and motorcycles, and you could almost hear the moan of the gale.

French people are never unhappy in a dim way: they become sullen and angry. All along the way we were greeted by dark looks and irritable comments. When we stopped for lunch at Valence the waiter vented his feelings by rattling the dishes, and banging the door as though we were personally responsible for what was happening. Later on, when we went into a café at Lyons and asked the proprietress if there had been any news on the radio, she replied sharply: 'I am too busy to listen.' Then added: 'Besides, there is nothing I want to hear.' Never, I thought, was a country going to war with so little stomach for it.

The roads were so crowded we didn't reach Paris until four o'clock in the morning. We came in by way of Fontainebleau. It had grown cold, and the great forests on either side of us had an eerie silence. The mist was thick on the ground and strange white shapes rose up in front of our headlights; ghosts, I thought, of twenty years ago coming to life again.

Paris was as beautiful as ever, but it had a troubled look, like a lovely woman who has lost her usual composure. Everything seemed to move faster: people, taxis, cyclists – even the water that sprayed up from the fountains at the Rond Point.

The hotels were filled with frightened American tourists badgering the porters and offering large sums of money for tickets to get them away before the trouble started. I went to see the Baroness, and found her alone in the flat. Her two maids, Yvonne and Germaine, had already left to join a hospital staff somewhere in the north.

The Baroness was a slender woman with a small scar on her nose from a piece of shrapnel that had fallen when she was standing on her balcony in the last war. No one hated the Germans more than she. Once one of her friends had brought an Austrian girl to call; later Madame had upbraided her indignantly for bringing a Boche into the house. The friend had argued that she was Austrian, but Madame fiercely insisted they were all the same.

Madame cried a little when she saw me and asked if I really thought there was going to be a war this time, but it was only a conversational question for she already knew the answer. She had worked in a Paris hospital during the last war and told me she had arranged to work there again. I said goodbye to her unhappily.

Before I left, I went to see the concierge, the woman who always argued so fiercely with the baker. The year before, when I had come back from Prague and asked her what she thought of Munich, she had shrugged her shoulders and replied with a single sentence: '*Ce n'est pas chic, ça.*' This time she again commented with a single sentence. '*Il faut en finir.*'

* * *

I was lucky to get back to England, for the trains and boats were overflowing with holiday travellers and tickets were at a premium;

there were so many delays the trip took nearly twelve hours. When at last we arrived at Dover we were confronted by a press poster, saying: 'Hitler's Patience at an End'.

But Hitler's 'patience' lasted five more days, and one lived keyed up on hourly radio bulletins and news flashes: 'A Thousand Tanks on the Polish Frontier'; 'Midnight Talks In Whitehall'; 'Children Leave Paris'; 'Two Million Under Arms In Poland'; 'Roosevelt Sends Message to Italy'; 'Henderson Flies Home'; 'Hitler Receives British Note'; 'Hitler Replies'.

You knew that none of it made any difference – whether Henderson flew home or stayed in Berlin, whether Hitler replied or didn't. The end was going to be the same. When you walked through Hyde Park with the sun streaming down on the flowers, it seemed unreal: I remember thinking it was almost indecent of nature not to behave more lugubriously.

But the unreality of the weather was no stranger than the people around one. English people react to a crisis unlike any other people I know. The more tense the situation the calmer they become. In fact, no one referred to the impending war at all. Taxi-cab drivers, waiters and porters went about their work as though they were oblivious to the fact that soon they would be caught up in one of the greatest storms the world had ever known. The most you could get out of anyone was a short comment such as: 'Things aren't too bright, are they?' and you suddenly felt guilty of bad taste for having referred to it.

I had let my flat when I left London, and spent the crisis with Maureen and Oliver Stanley at their house in Romney Street. The telephone rang continuously and Oliver went to endless Cabinet meetings, but the household revolved in such an ordinary way it might have been any week – except the one it was. Yet underneath, everyone knew what was in store for them. Oliver had fought in the last war at the age of eighteen. Now his son was eighteen and would soon fight in this one. Millions of people's happiness was at stake, yet they were powerless to prevent the future from exacting a terrible repetition of the past.

In his pamphlet *Black Record: Germans Past and Present*, Sir Robert Vansittart writes:

> In 1907 I was crossing the Black Sea in a German ship. It was
> spring, and the rigging was full of bright-coloured birds.
> I noticed one among them in particular, strongly marked,
> heavier-beaked. And every now and then it would spring
> upon one of the smaller, unsuspecting birds and kill it. It was
> a shrike or butcher-bird; and it was steadily destroying all its
> fellows . . . That butcher-bird on that German ship behaved
> exactly like Germany behaves. I was twenty-six at the time,
> and life looked pretty good, or should have looked, for there
> were four hundred million happinesses of a sort in Europe.
> But already I could feel the shadow on them, for I had spent
> long enough in Germany to know that she would bring on her
> fourth war as soon as she thought the going good.

In the spring of 1939 the going was again good.

* * *

At a quarter to one, exactly seventeen hours before German troops began their attack on Poland, Jane Leslie and I landed at the Tempelhof aerodrome in Berlin. From the moment we saw the grim rows of fighter planes lined up in the field – planes painted black with white swastikas – we felt the full drama of the awful moment. The capital was an armed camp. All private cars had been requisitioned and the only traffic in the streets was a stream of military lorries, armoured trucks and gun carriages that rumbled and clattered over the stone surfaces, terrible harbingers of the things to come. The hotels were crowded with the black uniforms of the Nazi Storm Troopers, and that night, for the first time, men were silhouetted against the sky, manning the anti-aircraft guns on the roof-tops along the Unter den Linden.

Everywhere you felt the sinister force of the German nation on the eve of launching its fifth war on Europe within the space of seventy-five years. You felt it even in the wind that blew through the capital exactly as it had the previous August; it caught up bits of paper and rubbish and sent them scraping along the pavement with a queer noise that sounded like a death rattle.

You knew the machine was ready. This was the moment that Nazi Germany had worked for for six years. Now the planes and tanks were waiting and the guns were in position. Everything had been completed down to the polish on the last button of the last uniform. All that remained was for the lever to be pulled.

I had come to Berlin for only forty-eight hours to write a Sunday story. Jane was a friend from New York who had been spending the summer in Europe. Although I warned her we would probably be caught in Germany at the outbreak of war and it might take weeks to get back to England, she decided to come with me. She had never been to Berlin before and the atmosphere struck her even more forcibly than me. All the way to the hotel she peered out of the cab window, and when we walked into the Adlon lobby, past a group of unsmiling Blackshirts, she stared at them as though they were slightly unreal – characters that had stepped out of a Hollywood film.

We went into the Grill and found Pete Huss of the International News Service and Dr Boehmer, the German press chief. Dr Boehmer had lost his usual air of confidence and looked haggard and ill. He told us gloomily that nothing could save the situation now and prophesied the whole world would soon be involved.

I have never seen a man more depressed. Pete Huss told me that at the morning press conference he had broken down and cried. I had become so accustomed to Nazi self-assurance that the dejection surprised me, but I realised that up till now I had seen German officialdom only when the cards were being played their way. At an afternoon conference in the Foreign Office the official spokesman was almost as melancholy as Boehmer. A dozen journalists sat around the table hurling questions at him, but he kept shaking his head and replying in a low, strained voice: '*Ich weiss nicht*' ('I don't know'). Pete Huss, who was sitting next to me, whispered: '"I don't know" is the only thing anyone *does* know in Berlin.'

The agency correspondents were sending bulletins every few minutes and the diplomats looked harassed and tired. We found Sir George Ogilvie-Forbes, the British Counsellor, working in his shirtsleeves; Alexander Kirk, the American Chargé d'Affaires, had moved a camp-bed into his office and for the last forty-eight hours had been on duty night and day.

The long hours that stretched out that afternoon and evening were like a death-bed vigil: the anxiety, the confusion, the solemnity, the hushed tones, even the false note of cheerfulness. The diplomats adopted a while-there's-life-there's-hope attitude, but all the while went ahead making preparations for the funeral; Sir Nevile Henderson left to have a final talk with Goering, but the first floor of the British Embassy was cluttered with luggage ready to be sent out on the diplomatic train when the signal came. Poor Peace! Nothing could bring the colour back into her cheeks, or warm her cold hands now.

Only twenty years before, ten million men had died in the most savage conflict the world had ever known. They had died violently:

burnt, suffocated, gassed, drowned, bayoneted and blown to atoms. Now once again the German nation was going to unloose the same, and even greater, horrors. Any hour now, one man would give the signal. A small crowd waited on the Wilhelmstrasse, outside the Chancellery. The special insignia showing that Hitler was in residence was flying from the roof. When I walked past, I suddenly felt ill.

The occasion was so immense that the things you took in with your eyes didn't seem to have any connection with what was happening. When Jane and I dined at Horscher's that night it was completely unreal: the dim lights, the excellent food, the attentive waiters, the laughing people, came from another world. I realised with a start that aside from a handful of officials, few people in Berlin were aware of the drama they were living through. They had lived through crises before. Their armies had been mobilised, and their men sent to the front – and each time they had found a bloodless victory in their hands. This crisis probably seemed no more serious to them than the one the year before. Most of them would go to bed that night trusting confidently in the divine inspiration of the Führer. In fact, a German acquaintance joined Jane and myself and told us she had heard a report that Poland was going to accept the German ultimatum – she felt confident there would be a last-minute peace. When we drove past the Chancellery on the way home, at midnight, the lights were still burning.

The next morning we were awakened by the tramp of marching feet – the steps of the funeral cortège. Our rooms overlooked the Unter den Linden and we hurried out on to the balcony to see Storm Troopers lining the avenue. We telephoned downstairs and learned that Hitler was addressing the Reichstag at ten o'clock. Owing to the fact that the speech had been arranged at the last moment, there had been no time to organise crowds of enthusiastic spectators. Only a handful of people saw Hitler drive past, wearing, for the first time, the field-grey uniform of the German Army. For his most epoch-making declaration, he rode through empty streets.

The speech was short: he enumerated the 'atrocities' the Poles had committed and announced that since five-forty-five that morning the Germans had been 'returning' Polish fire. Jane and I listened from the office of Colonel Black, the American military attaché. Its windows likewise overlooked the Unter den Linden. Although the avenue was strung with loudspeakers and the words rang through the capital with vehemence, we were struck by the unenthusiastic response they drew. Even the Storm Troopers showed little enthusiasm.

When it was over we walked down to the Chancellery and instead of the large crowd that usually gathers, found only fifty or sixty people. They shouted for Hitler to come out on the balcony, and, as we stood there, I reflected on the career of the man who had risen from house-painter to generalissimo.

Hitler didn't appear, but it is perhaps worth recording that two windows away, in a section of the building being redecorated, three painters in white caps and overalls leaned out of the window and stared stupidly at the crowd.

* * *

Jane and I lunched with Ogilvie-Forbes and Colonel Daly (the British military attaché) in the Adlon garden. They told us no news had been received regarding the British declaration of war, but it was expected any time. A group of German officials at a nearby table stared at the Englishmen curiously, but from Ogilvie-Forbes's smiling and impervious expression they could have learned little. I thought they seemed perplexed.

Even though the war had begun in the cold-blooded and calcu-lated way everyone had expected, I felt slightly dazed. I wondered what was going through the minds of the Germans. I finally went up to one of the desk-clerks and asked him bluntly how he felt about a world war. I shall never forget my surprise at his reply.

He looked at Jane and me in amazement. 'What do you mean, a world war? Poland is Germany's affair. What's it got to do with anyone else?'

A few minutes later we saw the clerk in a small group with two or three other people. He was evidently repeating what we had said, for he pointed towards us and the others laughed and made a gesture of disbelief.

'Look at them,' said Jane excitedly. 'They don't believe us. They're probably saying – "Oh, those two girls – they're crazy!"'

I was astonished. I hadn't realised up till now that the ordinary people were so ignorant as to the true state of affairs. But I suppose it shouldn't have seemed so surprising. The morning papers had carried no news of the British and French ultimatum. German propaganda had been concentrated solely against Poland and even in Hitler's Reichstag speech there had been only a slim reference to England and France to the effect that he could 'only regret the declarations of foreign statesmen that this (the attack on Poland) affected their interests'. Germany, he had added, had no interest in the West; had no aims of any kind there for the future.

When the waiter brought us tea we sounded him out and got the same reaction the clerk had given us.

'The Poles provoked Germany too far. Now they can pay the price.'

'But how do you feel about fighting Great Britain and France?'

'Who says we are going to fight Great Britain and France? Poland is no one's concern but Germany's. We couldn't sit back and let

Poles shoot down German women and children. Why should any-one else interfere?' He gave us an angry look and stamped away.

It was only when we talked to one of the porters – an older man – that we had a glimpse of alarm. When we told him England and France were going to war with Germany, he looked at us in despair, and said: '*Mein Gott*, I hope not. I had four years in the last one and that was enough.'

German complacency was slightly jarred about five o'clock when air-raid sirens suddenly moaned through the capital. Our first thought was: the British Air Force. We hurried on to the bal-cony. Below, cars were stopping beside the road and people were running in every direction. A truck pulled up so fast it went over the kerb. We went downstairs and saw people pouring into the lobby from the street. The manager appeared, raised his arms for attention, and told the crowd to follow him to the shelter. He led us through the kitchen into the back garden. The only ceiling was the sky – that was the Adlon shelter.

The crowd looked upwards apprehensively and an elderly German standing next to me asked if I had ever been in an air-raid before. I told him I'd been bombed several times by German planes in Spain and he relapsed into silence. Twenty minutes later the all-clear blew and we heard later it was only a rehearsal.

All this took place on a Friday. I had to file my story to the *Sunday Times* on Saturday, and as the communications between England and Germany were liable to snap at any moment we decided to leave for Holland that night. The train services were already dislocated. We were told we could get tickets only as far as Cologne and would have to make further arrangements from there.

That night, for the first time, the trains travelled through a silent and darkened Germany. The lights were dimmed and the blinds

tightly drawn. There were no sleeping-cars and we had to sit up all
night in a compartment with six other people. There were three
middle-aged *Hausfrauen* loaded down with parcels and bags; a
portly gentleman with cropped hair, who might have posed for
a caricature of a German; a fifteen-year-old boy; and a dark wiry
little man who spoke English, and told us he was a musician on
his way to Düsseldorf. The three women were evidently friends.
They kept up a stream of conversation and seemed to regard the
blackout as an hilarious adventure. They were in such high spirits
we realised they must be as oblivious to the situation as the people
in Berlin. We couldn't resist raising the subject, and this time Jane
started. She turned to the musician. 'Has there been any news
about the British and French declaration of war?'

'War? We're not at war with England and France. Just Poland.'

'I think war's already been declared,' Jane continued stubbornly.

The women wanted to know what she was saying and the musician translated her remark. They gasped, and the caricature spoke
up.

'I don't believe it. Germany is only taking police action in
Poland. No one will go to war for that.'

The musician agreed. 'You mustn't believe rumours. They're
always wrong.' Then he grinned: 'After we cut Poland's throat' (and
here he drew his finger suggestively across his throat) 'we'll settle
down to peace again.'

Everyone laughed. The women looked reassured and resumed
their spirited conversation. What a story, I thought. Germany on
the eve of a world war and no one willing to believe it; everyone
confident that Hitler would pull it off again – always the palm
without the dust.

We arrived at Cologne in the morning and caught a train for
Rotterdam. We were in a fever to know what was happening in

England and France, but the German papers omitted such details and carried only glowing accounts of the advance into Poland. When we reached Kalden, the German frontier station, it was like scaling the last wall of a terrible prison. A group of SS men boarded the train and began searching the compartments. In one of them they even ripped up the cushions. What they were looking for we never discovered, but they took three or four people off – all weeping and protesting.

In our compartment there was an old Jewish couple who told us they were going to America where a professorship was awaiting the old man. When the customs officials came to inspect their visas their hands trembled so much they could hardly show them, and we suffered for their anguish lest something upset their plans. But finally it was all over and the train was heading for Vlissengen, the Dutch station. The professor reached out for his wife's hand and held it tightly.

But the incident ended in a heart-breaking fashion. When the Dutch customs officials came aboard they asked the couple to show their boat tickets to America, and the old gentleman replied the tickets were awaiting them at Amsterdam. The authorities shook their heads and said there was a rigid law that no Germans could travel through Holland unless they could prove they were going on to another destination. They would have to return to Germany.

The old lady began to cry and the professor argued pathetically. Jane and I became infuriated with the authorities, but, since we couldn't speak a word of Dutch, were able to be of little help. However, a Dutchman in the next compartment interfered and tried to persuade the customs men to let them stay at Vlissengen until they could arrange for someone to bring the tickets to them. But when our train left, the officials were still shaking their heads. Our last glimpse was of the old couple sitting on the platform bench, their bags piled up beside them. We never learned how the story ended.

The rest of the way to Rotterdam Jane and I hung out of the window at every stop and asked for news. Had England and France declared war? Some nodded their heads, some shook them; some said an ultimatum had been sent, some said it hadn't. No one seemed to know. But one thing was certain: the sympathy of the Dutch for the Poles. People clutched hopefully at any bit of news detrimental to Germany. One of the Dutch papers carried a headline (which a man on the train translated for us): 'Poles Shoot Down Six Planes' – and it was selling like hot cakes.

Jane and I had a stroke of luck, for we reached Rotterdam just twenty minutes before a Dutch steamer left for England. Jane spent the afternoon sleeping and I wrote my story. The trip took five or six hours and we didn't reach England until nine o'clock that evening.

For the first time the English island was darkened. It was a strange experience pulling up stealthily to the dock and only knowing you were there when the steamer bumped against the pier; hearing the shouts of the dock hands, the noise of the ropes swinging over the side of the ship, the splash of the water, and seeing nothing.

At last the gangway was lowered. When we stepped ashore we asked one of the dockers – a large shadowy bulk – whether war had been declared.

'Not yet. But I hope it won't be long now. This waiting around is making us all nervous.'

I just had time to put in a telephone call and file my story before the train left. On the way to London we had a nasty start. We hadn't been going very long before we heard the sound of far-away explosions. We leaned out and saw the sky lighting up with sharp, spasmodic flashes – obviously bursts from anti-aircraft fire. We hung out of the window for some time. But when we got within ten miles of London we felt the rain coming down and realised it was only a thunderstorm.

* * *

The next morning at eleven o'clock Neville Chamberlain broadcast to the world that the British Empire was at war with Germany. While he was speaking, air-raid sirens pierced the air. That, like the warning in Berlin, was a false alarm. But this wasn't a rehearsal. I learned later that the assistant French military attaché in London, Captain de Brantes, had not expected the British declaration of war until later in the day. He was in Paris when he heard the news and hired a private plane to fly him back to England. He was mistaken for a German.

At any rate, he provided everybody with a good deal of excitement. Before it became known the alarm was a false one, I talked on the telephone with a journalist who solemnly assured me he had heard the explosions and that his building had even rocked – ever so slightly. When I saw him the next day he didn't refer to the matter.

4

Polish Tragedy – Second-Hand

As I wandered through the lobby of the drab little hotel on the main street of Cernăuți – a Romanian town two miles from the Polish frontier – I thought how many terrible stories could be written about the people in that one room alone.

For three days Polish refugees had come streaming across the frontier before the massacre of the German tanks and planes. Some had come on foot with knapsacks over their backs; some in carts and wagons; some in battered motor-cars with the few possessions they had been able to save piled on top. The narrow Romanian streets ran with mud and the police, detailed to avoid congestion, spent most of their time cursing at the donkey-carts of the local inhabitants, invariably stuck in the middle of the road. The Romanian peasants seemed bewildered by the war thunder-bolt that had suddenly transformed their quiet town; groups of them collected around the battered Polish cars, peering at the registration plates with morbid curiosity.

The small hotel on the main street had become a tragic 'Grand Hotel'. It was so crowded people were sleeping on the floor of the lobby – not only were there refugees, but foreign journalists, diplomats and military attachés, who had crossed the frontiers a few hours before. But it wasn't hard to pick out the Poles. You could tell them by their mud-stained clothes and the dazed looks in their faces. In one corner of the lobby a Polish woman, with a fine head and long slender hands, sat alone, crying. She didn't make any sound but sat quite motionless, hour after hour, the tears streaming down her face.

All around you, you felt the tragedy of smashed lives. Every now and then an incident caught your eye, like a fragment of a broken picture, and your imagination flared up as you wondered what story lay behind the scene. I remember the two neatly dressed little Polish boys who came into the lobby clutching tin aeroplanes and explaining to the desk clerk, proudly: '*Mon père est un pilote*' – and the look on their mother's face as though she had been struck when they spoke the words; the man who had been wandering listlessly round the lobby, staring at a girl who came through the door as though he had seen a ghost, then running up and flinging his arms about her and both of them laughing hysterically; the three children sitting on suitcases propped up in the corner of the hall waiting for the parents they had become separated from, and the desk clerk telling us he didn't know how to explain to them the frontier had been closed for several hours and now there was little chance of their coming.

That was Tuesday, September 19th, exactly two weeks and four days after the German attack had begun. The Russian Army had crossed the frontier forty-eight hours before and Poland's two powerful neighbours were squeezing in on her like a giant nutcracker. The last border – the Romanian – had slammed shut, and now the country was sealed up, isolated, and awaiting its doom.

I had never imagined that Poland could be destroyed so quickly there wouldn't even be time to get to it. The day after Great Britain and France declared war I had decided to go to Warsaw. The only route open was London to Bergen (Norway) by boat; Bergen to Oslo (Norway) by train; Oslo to Stockholm (Sweden) by train; Stockholm to Helsinki (Finland) by aeroplane; Helsinki to Riga (Latvia) by aeroplane; Riga to Kovno (Lithuania) by train; Kovno to Warsaw by train.

It took me five days to get the proper visas. When at last I had them, Mr Rogers of Cook's Travel Bureau rang up to say the frontier between Lithuania and Poland had been closed and now my only chance was via Romania, which meant travelling through France, Switzerland, Italy and Yugoslavia. The new visas took another five days, and by the time I was ready to leave, the German onslaught had moved so fast it was already doubtful whether even the Romanian frontier would stay open.

That trip across a darkened Europe, at war for the second time in twenty-one years, was a strange experience. It stands out in my mind now as a series of impressions: crossing the Channel at night on a boat that took a fourteen-hour zig-zag course to escape a German U-boat; the nine-hour train trip to Paris with its interminable stops and the stage porter who kept shrugging his shoulders and repeating the old cliché, 'C'est la guerre'; the deserted, unfamiliar look of Paris with its shopfronts boarded up and its men at the front; the Simplon Express from Paris to Rome with its shaded lights, obsequious waiters and luxurious dining-car – the only train in France with sleepers and a restaurant as all the others had been requisitioned as hospital trains; the rigid inspection of the Swiss frontier officials by order of a government determined not to have the country turned into the same spy centre it was in the last war; and the hysterical scene created by three Italians, unfamiliar with the new visa regulations, who were put off, bag and baggage, in the middle of the night; and, finally, Rome with the street lights blazing and the peaceful clatter of carriages along the cobblestones.

I discovered that lights were one of the few luxuries the capital could boast, for Italy, neutral though she was, was already undergoing more hardships than the belligerent countries. There was no petrol and no coffee. This last, to a nation that spends half its days in the cafés, wasn't a deprivation to be taken lightly. I arrived in Rome late at night and left by plane for Bucharest early the next morning, so I didn't have a chance to see any friends; but at the Hotel Excelsior the porters and waiters pressed me with questions about France and England, expressing eloquent sympathy for the Poles and a firm resolve to keep their end of the Axis out of the war.

The moment I arrived in Bucharest I felt myself jerked back into an atmosphere of crisis. With Soviet troops massing on the Romanian frontier and rumours that Germany was concentrating her forces in Hungary, tension was at a fever pitch. In the crowded restaurants, when loudspeakers began broadcasting the news bulletins, people put down their knives and forks and conversation stopped; everyone listened with painful intensity.

I didn't know that the Polish frontier had been closed, and as soon as I reached the hotel looked up the trains for Cernăuți. There was one leaving that night, but the porter told me there was so much delay no one could guarantee how long the trip would take. But I went to see a friend at the British Legation and had the good luck to run into Lord Forbes, a young man I had met in London, who had just been appointed air attaché. He was flying to Cernăuți in the morning in his own plane and offered to take me with him.

When we arrived at the Bucharest aerodrome in the morning we were greeted by a strange scene. Twenty-four hours earlier the Polish High Command had ordered its aviators to fly into Romania to prevent their planes from falling into German hands. Nearly three hundred planes – forty twin-engined bombers and over two hundred fighters – had arrived at the aerodrome. Over a hundred pilots, exhausted and unshaven, were sleeping on the floor of the waiting room; their uniforms were torn and dirty and many of them had bandaged hands and faces.

One of the officers had brought a plane in with sixteen bullet-holes in it after a fight with the Russians. He was a tall, slender man, with a medal on his ragged brown jacket on which were the words: '*Virtuti Militari*'. He told us he had won it in 1921, when the Poles had succeeded in driving the Bolsheviks from Warsaw. 'This time,' he said bitterly, 'they have succeeded.'

Although he had not eaten for more than twenty-four hours and seemed close to exhaustion, he refused to accept any money from us. He drew himself up proudly, shaking his head, and saying over and over again, '*Non, merci*, I am an officer, a colonel in the Polish Army.'

This same indomitable pride existed among all the officers with whom we talked. There was no plea for pity, no request for help of any kind; only a passionate determination to escape from Romania, to join up in the French Air Force. One of the pilots came from a town in the Polish corridor. His family had been killed in the bombardment, and his two brothers, both aviators, shot down in air battles a few days before. 'What are they going to do with us?' he kept asking Lord Forbes over and over again. 'They can't shut us up. We must *go on*.'

We took him into the restaurant and gave him some tea (the only drink there was), and although he had only a few coins in his pockets, he tried determinedly to pay the bill. Fortunately, the manager came up and saved the situation by insisting that we were all guests of the airport.

The aeroplane trip to Cernăuţi took about two hours and we arrived just as it was getting dark. Some of the Polish planes had landed here as well as Bucharest; one of them had nose-dived into the ground and the tail stood up, silhouetted against the fading light of the sky, like a huge black cross.

The first person I ran into at the hotel was Ed Beattie, the United

Press correspondent, whom I hadn't seen since that grim, rainy day in Carlsbad just a year ago. Ed had come from Warsaw and he told me that within the first forty-eight hours the German Air Force had succeeded in smashing the telephone and telegraph centres, the bridgeheads, railway junctions – in fact, all the important lines of communication throughout the country. From then on the front didn't exist – only scattered, isolated groups unable to reach each other, or even relay orders.

This total warfare, which depends on disrupting the civil life of the community, and claims as military objectives towns and villages as far as one hundred and fifty miles behind the front line – on the grounds that they are either food bases or communication centres – had been experimented with in Spain. In Poland it was brought to its full flower of perfection. Ed told me he had seen a German map on which all the important junctions, factories and bridgeheads were marked with exactly the weight of bombs required to destroy them.

And here in Poland, the large-scale Fifth Column activities, which have since become recognised as an integral part of German strategy, were used for the first time. Agents with short-wave wireless transmitters were dispersed throughout the country to relay whatever information they could get. Anthony Biddle, the American Ambassador, told me the spy ring was so effective that the moves of the Polish Government were broadcast from German stations an hour or so after the most secret decisions had been made. On several occasions he had heard the news of his own proposed movements (even when he was going from one remote village to another) broadcast before he had started on the journey.

The strategy of the Soviet Army was more subtle than that of the Germans. Major Colbern, the American military attaché in Warsaw, who crossed into Romania just before the frontier closed, told me that he was driving along a Polish country road near the Russian frontier on Sunday morning when he suddenly saw a tank regiment and a column of troops coming over the brow of a hill. He had never seen tanks of this type in Poland before and drove towards the column greatly puzzled. It was only when he was a few yards away that he suddenly saw the Soviet red star on the commander's cap. Near the rear of the column Polish troops had joined in with the Russians and were fraternising happily. The Soviet officer approached the military attaché smiling, inspected his papers, then saluted him and said that he might pass. When he asked the Russian officer where he was going, the latter replied cheerfully that they were on their way to fight the Germans. With this he ordered the column to move to one side of the road so that the attaché's car might pass, and courteously saluted goodbye.

At first it was thought that many of the Soviet officers actually believed they were entering Poland to fight the Germans, but it later became apparent they had merely been given orders to tell the Poles this. Thus, instead of offering resistance, the Poles greeted them as brothers, allowing the Soviet columns to sweep through village after village without firing a shot.

The first Soviet wave made no attempt to disarm the Poles, and it was not until the vanguard had made a sufficiently long advance that the rearguard was given orders to deprive the Poles of their guns and ammunition. This gave the Soviet Government the opportunity to announce that the Poles greeted their Russian comrades with open arms.

* * *

I went back to England badly shaken by even the second-hand glimpse I'd had of the Polish massacre. I flew from Bucharest to Milan and caught the express to Paris. We reached the French frontier about five in the morning and I was awakened by the sound of excited French voices. An American woman had overlooked the necessity of getting a visa to enter France. The authorities told her indignantly she must leave the train at once and I heard her voice rise shrill and insistent above the hubbub. 'But I only want to buy a dress at Schiaparelli's.'

She was deposited on the platform, expostulating angrily, but I have a nasty feeling she got there in the end. If the dress is still in fashion, she's probably wearing it now at cocktail parties in New York.

5

The 'Bore' War

Once you got used to tin hats, gas-masks, siren suits and sand-bags, London looked surprisingly the same. Hitler, hitherto quick to strike at those who defied him, appeared to have ignored Mr Chamberlain's momentous declaration of war. Air-raid wardens and fire-fighters manned their posts, and the public peered sky-wards anxiously, but nothing happened. The hospital wards, ready to receive thirty thousand casualties a day, remained empty and people began to wonder, sheepishly, if the war was going to be as savage as they had thought.

Certainly war had lost its old-time glamour. Missing was the enthusiasm of 1914; missing were the bands, the flags, the columns of marching men, the pretty girls raffling kisses for war funds. This time there were no trimmings or decorations, not even any slo-gans. Just a dignified billboard over Marble Arch, saying: 'Lend to Defend the Right to be Free'.

In fact, there was so little war atmosphere it was only at night that you felt the dread significance of the moments you were liv-ing through. I had been in Madrid and Prague when the lights had gone out, but somehow in London the great curtain of blackness seemed an entirely new experience. Those first nights stand out in my mind as a series of impressions: buildings jutting up so darkly the sky looked almost white; cab-drivers hurtling through the blackness faster than they'd ever driven before; air-raid wardens shouting 'Put out that light'; cigarettes gleaming like glow-worms; buses lurching down Piccadilly with shadowy blue lights; people stumbling and cursing along the streets. John

Gunther broadcast to America that a porter in his hotel (I think it was the Dorchester), a VC in the last war, had already become a casualty in this one by tripping over some sandbags in the black-out. He was not the only one. British casualties for the first two months of the war were: Army – none; Air Force – 79; Navy – 596; Blackout – 1,130.

That period of inactivity seemed interminable. The official conception of the war was, briefly, that Great Britain would blockade Germany until the latter was forced to attack across the Maginot line, which as everyone knew was impregnable; when the Reichswehr had battered itself to pieces and the German people were hungry and subjugated, the conflict would end. But the British public had an uneasy feeling it wouldn't be as simple as that. People switched off their radios, fretting over the laconic French war communiqués, and the undramatic British pamphlet raids. Pamphlet raids became so irksome to the public that a joke went round that a pilot had been reprimanded by his superior officer for not untying one of his bundles before he dropped it out of the plane. 'What are you trying to do?' he was upbraided. 'Kill someone?'

Wits promptly dubbed World War No. 2 'The Bore War', and Lord Haw-Haw's spirited broadcasts became the nation's chief amusement. But although the outside world was alarmed by democracy's lame start to the grim business in front of them, England, in spite of her placid appearance, had already under-gone a gigantic upheaval. Overnight everyone's life had changed. Houses were shut up, families separated, careers abandoned, and new jobs begun. The great economic engine had come to a halt, creaking and groaning; the brakeman had thrown the switch and now the machine was diverted to a new track: war production.

The first taste of the struggle was not death but readjustment. Besides the hundreds of thousands of men swept into the fighting services, thousands more were summoned to munition factories, aerodromes and dockyards. Women were called to work on the land and children evacuated from their homes. Veterans of the last war rejoined their old regiments as subalterns, and volunteers flooded the ARP Services. Taxes went sky-rocketing and everybody's future became the same question mark. Money was already such an uncertain commodity that those who had any spent it more freely than ever; restaurants and cabarets were packed, and debutantes and their boyfriends sat up all night at a hilarious new bottle club called 'The Nut House'. Underneath, most people knew the period of waiting was only the first round; before the fight was over blood would flow more freely than ever before.

* * *

As soon as I got back from Romania I gave up my flat in Eaton Mews and went to live with Freda Casa Maury. The owner moved back again, so Mrs Sullivan and Pickles were not at loose ends. Mrs Sullivan's 'old man' had been called up in the Naval Reserve and at Christmas she sent me a pencil with my name on it 'to help me in my work' and a card saying that she was doing part-time work for the ARP. Somehow, the picture of Mrs Sullivan's portentous frame clearing the streets when the sirens blew threatened to be almost more frightening than the raids themselves.

Freda was an Englishwoman married to a Spaniard, Bobby Casa Maury, who had served in the British Air Force in the last war and had now gone back to serve in it again. Like so many others, she was appalled by a second war in a lifetime, but readjusted her life with determination. The first move was pasting the mirrors with strips of brown paper. The house seemed to be entirely made of glass and it took Vernon, the butler, nearly a month to do the job. When it was finished it looked like an exotic trellis-work stage set. 'If this house is ever hit,' remarked Vernon morosely, 'there'll be bad luck all the way back to the Stone Ages again.'

I was writing a series of articles on various war organisations, and Freda worked all day at the Feathers clubs – clubs which she had organised in the poor sections of London. In spite of the war, there was little gloom here. Once a week the members had a party. They provided their own band, and, judging from the shrieks of laughter, the singing and shouting, it was always a wild success. Most of them came to Freda with their problems. She got a good many started on war work, but conspicuous among her failures was the sixteen-year-old girl whom she sounded out as to what sort of things she was best at. 'Laughing and love,' came the prompt reply. I never learned where her talents led her.

Highly intelligent, Freda was alarmed by the easy-going optimism of the winter. Unlike the Hyde Park pavement artist who exhibited a poster: 'Latest Rumours – Hitler Sends For Two Aspirins', she had a healthy regard for Germany's strength. 'The trouble with us,' she complained, 'is that we're too complacent.' She did her best to offset it, however, for whenever people asked her brightly how long she thought the war would last, she replied firmly: 'Ten years at least. Possibly more.'

Most of the young men I knew were scattered around England at the various training stations. Englishmen have such a natural aversion to militarism that the first time they appeared in London in their uniforms they looked self-conscious and embarrassed. When I walked down the street with Tom Mitford and a group of soldiers saluted him, he blushed scarlet.

For many of them – particularly those in their thirties – giving up jobs and careers and starting a wholly new life was a severe wrench, but I never heard any of them complain. They all joined up as regimental soldiers, and took delight in jokes at their own and each other's expense. When I went down to see Roger Chetwode and Seymour Berry, officers in an anti-aircraft regiment, they complained they had had the opportunity to go into action only once. That was when two bombers were sighted. Fortunately they missed them, for both were British.

A few months later the monotony was broken when a German bomber – a mine-laying plane – actually did appear. It crashed, late at night, in the middle of Clacton-on-Sea, where they had gone for a few weeks. They ran out, helped the wardens evacuate the damaged area, roped off the streets, and generally took charge of the situation. They were interested by the curious fact that the blast had blown a kitchen boiler into the middle of the road. Seymour sat down on it and lighted a cigarette. Soon after a group of naval experts arrived and advised him to move, as he was sitting on a magnetic mine.

Another time I went down to see Aidan Crawley, who rejoined the 601 Squadron when war broke out. The 601 was an auxiliary air squadron that had been started about fifteen years before by boys, most of whom had enough money to have their own planes. It was a current joke that the men gave their girls the squadron emblem, the flying sword, in rubies and diamonds, and that the village where the squadron was stationed was crowded with Rolls-Royces. When the 601 went into action the following spring it proved itself a crack fighter force; its Squadron Leader, Max Aitken (Lord Beaverbrook's son), was awarded the DFC for shooting down ten planes in his first three months of combat.

Before the war Aidan had been nursing a constituency as a Socialist candidate. Although he appeared that day in his blue uniform with the wings embroidered on the front, he had a huge book of economics under his arm which he said he was reading in his 'spare' time. Somehow fighter planes that travelled at four hundred miles an hour and economic theories seemed an odd combination.

Another weekend I went to Oxfordshire to spend a few days with Sheila and Freddie Birkenhead. In peace-time, Freddie, the son of the brilliant 'F. E.', one-time Lord Chancellor of England, had been Lord Halifax's parliamentary private secretary; now he was a lieutenant in an anti-tank regiment. He asked me to talk to his troops on Germany, and although I had never made a speech before, I agreed, thinking it was only to a small group. When I arrived at the barracks I was astonished to find several hundred men assembled. But it was Freddie's reassurance that nearly undid me. 'Don't worry,' he hissed in my ear, 'they won't dare boo. If they misbehave they know they'll be sent to the guard room.' To him this was the great feature about the army; you could always have an audience and no one dared answer back. His remark cut both ways, for when the men applauded at the end I had an uneasy feeling they had been threatened with a fatigue unless they showed appreciation.

Freddie was a clever and charming person who, at the age of thirty-one, had already published two biographies – one on his father and one on the Earl of Strafford – and was considered one of the most promising young men in England. No one could have been less military-minded, but he accepted his new life with a good deal of ironical amusement. One day an expert lectured his regiment on anti-tank weapons and told them bluntly that their chances of survival were limited. Soon after, Freddie went to lunch with Winston Churchill and the latter's son, Randolph. He told them what the expert had said and Winston expostulated indignantly: 'What a monstrous thing to say. On the contrary, you'll be sitting there, picking off the tanks one by one.'

'Well, what about me?' interrupted Randolph. Mr Churchill had overlooked the fact that his son was in a tank corps. He scratched his head and dropped the subject.

* * *

Most of the big houses in London were shut, and there was little entertaining that winter. One of the few exceptions was 58 Romney Street, where Maureen and Oliver Stanley lived. You walked through a red door and were confronted by a notice on the hall table warning the butler to be careful about taking in parcels that 'might explode'. Oliver was then in the Government and the notice had been sent round to all Cabinet ministers in view of recent IRA activities.

Romney Street was in Westminster, only a few blocks from the Houses of Parliament, and every afternoon from six o'clock on, it was crowded with Cabinet Ministers, MPs, Foreign Office officials and Service chiefs. Oliver had entered the Cabinet at the age of thirty-eight and was considered one of the most able men in the Government; when he was appointed War Minister in January, he was the fourth generation of the Derby family to hold the same office.

Maureen had also inherited a political sense. Her grandmother, the Lady Londonderry of the day, had been a great political hostess in the early part of the century. A staunch Tory, she refused even to nod to a Whig, and, when Winston Churchill joined the Liberal Party, fiercely upbraided Lady Birkenhead for allowing 'F. E.' to associate with him. A woman of great charm, she was also one of decided opinions which at times proved trying to her household. Once her maid got so angry when she was helping her dress that she plaited her hair into the back of the chair and left the room.

Maureen's mother, the next Lady Londonderry, also wielded great influence. Ramsay MacDonald was enchanted with her, and her balls at Londonderry House were supposed to have played a large part in diverting his nationalisation of the mines to his less drastic nationalisation of the Cabinet.

Maureen, one of the most popular women in London, kept up the family tradition in a more informal but no less effective way. Her gatherings usually included a mixture of people that ranged from British Cabinet Ministers to Romanian diplomats; French staff officers to Swedish businessmen; American journalists to Italian officials. Maureen had an easy-going manner that made everyone feel at ease and she never appeared disconcerted no matter how many stayed for dinner at the last moment.

One day, about three months after the declaration of war, I went to Romney Street for lunch and sat next to Winston Churchill. He was then First Lord of the Admiralty, and on this occasion was in particularly buoyant spirits. I remember his telling us the story of a destroyer that had dropped a depth charge, but instead of finding a submarine, bits of an old wreckage had come to the surface. 'And would you believe it?' he added with relish, 'there was a door bobbing around with my initials on it!' He had recorded this incident in one of his speeches but Neville Chamberlain cut it out.

I also saw Mr Churchill at Maureen's New Year's party. The house was overflowing with people and an accordion-player went around the room playing all the popular tunes. I remember Mr Churchill singing 'Run, Rabbit, Run' with great verve. But when the clock struck twelve a solemnity fell over the group. Mr Churchill took Freda Casa Maury and me on either side of him; we all joined hands in a circle and sang 'Auld Lang Syne'. In everybody's mind was the question of what 1940 would bring. When Mr Churchill sang out the old year he seemed deeply moved, as though he had a premonition that a few months later he would be asked to guide the British Empire through the most critical days it had ever faced.

* * *

That night also had a special significance for me. The war in Finland had started about three weeks before. When the headlines announced that Helsinki had been bombed I thought it would be another Poland – that the country would be obliterated so quickly there would be little chance of getting there before it was over. Then the papers began recording the amazing feats of the Finns; incredible though it seemed, the Russian 'steam-roller' was being held in check.

I made my arrangements to go to Helsinki and left a few days after the New Year's party. Maureen had a fortune-teller that night, and when he read my hand he said: 'You are going on a long trip.' I was impressed until he added: 'You will be surrounded by lights, gaiety and laughter.'

I found none of those things.

Part VII

DAVID AND GOLIATH

1

The Sky That Tumbled Down

It was a strange feeling flying from one war to another. The transition was a gradual one. When you took off from the aerodrome 'somewhere in England' and flew over the North Sea in a plane with the windows frosted over so you couldn't see out, it was very much World War No. 2. It was still World War No. 2 at Amsterdam and Copenhagen; but at Malmo, a port in southern Sweden, the issue began to get shaky. When you asked for the latest war news, the answer was: 'Which?' And by the time you reached Stockholm there was no longer any doubt: 'The war' meant Molotov cocktails and Soviet bombers.

Stockholm was in a state of tension. The papers carried advertisements calling for volunteers, the restaurants were filled with women canvassing for funds, and the hotels decorated with posters saying: 'Defend Sweden by Helping Finland Now'. The war on the Western Front was as remote as China. I stayed there only twenty-four hours; besides a general impression of excitement and confusion I chiefly remember how cold I was. I was wearing a thick suit, fur-lined boots and a sheepskin coat, but the biting wind penetrated my bones. I had a suitcase filled with sweaters, woollen underwear, woollen socks, a ski suit and a windbreaker. I put on everything except the ski suit, and tried not to think what it would be like when I got to the Arctic Circle.

Every day a Finnish aeroplane flew from Stockholm to Turku, a town in the south of Finland. The plane left 'some time'. The hour was never certain, for Turku was often bombed and the pilot had to await an all-clear signal before he took off. On the day I left, I arrived at the aerodrome at three o'clock, but we didn't leave till nearly six. There were only half a dozen passengers: four Finns – two army officers and two women – a Swedish journalist and a German-Jewish photographer. The photographer told me he had left for Turku the afternoon before, but when the plane was halfway there the pilot received a warning of bombers and had to return to Stockholm.

It was dark when our plane took off from the hard, snow-packed field. It seemed odd to me to fly to a war. One moment you were walking peacefully along brightly lit streets, and an hour or so later you were groping your way in the dark, your ears strained for the sound of planes. When I used to fly from France to Barcelona and Valencia, the transition was so quick it was almost incongruous. Here it was the same. First, the lights of Stockholm fading away, then the sheen of the ice on the Gulf of Bothnia, then the Finnish forests like ink-stains against miles of frozen fields and lakes. After about an hour and a half, the pilot dropped a flare which made a pink streak through the darkness. Suddenly, far below, a circle of lights went on like candles round a huge birthday cake. A notice flashed in front of the plane: 'Landing – Fasten your Belts', and a few minutes later our wheels were running along the icy field.

We were led to a small wooden shack where our baggage was examined. Two elderly women journalists were waiting to interview the passengers; one of them cornered me and asked in an impressed voice whether I had come all the way from America to cover the war in Finland. When I replied no, only London, she said: 'Oh.' I could tell by her expression I was no longer front-page copy.

When the baggage was inspected a bus drove us to the station. Ordinarily the train trip to Helsinki took about three hours, but as the railroad was often bombed we were told the length of the journey was uncertain. At any rate, the train was a pleasant surprise. I had prepared to freeze to death, but now found myself sweltering on a centrally heated train. It was so hot I peeled off three sweaters. The next surprise was the dining-car. I had expected to go hungry, too, but instead I had an enormous dinner: soup, meat, vegetables, and all the bread and butter I could eat.

Besides the German photographer, there were two Finnish soldiers and a Swedish woman in our compartment. The latter kept asking the conductor nervously what time we were due to arrive. The conductor was a large man with a melancholy voice. His reply was always the same, but despatched with an air of profound wisdom: 'One can never tell.'

I soon found out what he meant, for shortly after midnight there was a screeching of brakes, the train came to a jarring stop, and the conductor shouted to everyone to clear off the train and take cover in the woods. We climbed down the embankment in snow several feet deep, only to have him shout a few minutes later that it was all a mistake, the planes were not coming after all, and now we could climb back again. We arrived in Helsinki at two in the morning without further excitement. There were no porters or taxi-cabs, so we had to walk to the hotel, about a mile away; the German photographer carried my bag and I thought what a fine thing it was to be the female of the species.

* * *

Twenty-four hours later, I took a trip along the coast to Hanko. Here I saw for the first time what continuous and relentless bombing was like. The deep quiet of the snow-bound countryside was broken by the wail of sirens five or six times a day as wave after wave of Soviet bombers – sometimes totalling as many as five hundred – came across the Gulf of Finland from their bases in Estonia, only twenty minutes away. All along the coast I passed through villages and towns which had been bombed and machine-gunned; in Hanko, the Finnish port which the Soviets demanded in their ultimatum, twenty buildings had been hit, and when I arrived, ten were still burning.

It is difficult to describe indiscriminate aerial warfare against a civilian population in a country with a temperature thirty degrees Fahrenheit below zero. But if you can visualise farm girls stumbling through snow for the uncertain safety of their cellars; bombs falling on frozen villages unprotected by a single anti-aircraft gun; men standing helplessly in front of blazing buildings with no apparatus with which to fight the fires, and others desperately trying to salvage their belongings from burning wreckage – if you can visualise these things and picture even the children in remote hamlets wearing white covers over their coats as camouflage against low-flying Russian machine-gunners – you can get some idea of what this war was like.

I left Helsinki early in the morning with two Swedish journalists. We travelled in a white camouflaged press car, driven by a six-foot-two police officer in a huge reindeer cap with two revolvers strapped to his belt. He drove forty miles an hour along the hard, shining white road, but ice formed so thickly against the car he had to stop every few minutes to pour glycerine over the windscreen. We passed miles of frozen lakes, desolate white fields and endless forests. Although we were smothered in sheepskin coats and fur rugs, the cold was so intense we stopped at village restaurants every half-hour for coffee.

As we neared Ekenäs, a small town not far from Hanko, two sentries sprang into the middle of the road and waved at us to stop. They shouted that the Russian planes were coming, and told us to run for shelter. When we got out we heard the whine of engines and, straining our eyes against the sky, counted nearly twenty silver specks. We ran across a field and into the cellar of a farmhouse; there were already a dozen people there, several women, the rest farm labourers. The brick ceiling was so low, most of them were sitting on the floor between sacks of potatoes, jars of preserved fruit and huge pails of milk. There was no trace of alarm, only a quiet weariness. An elderly farmer, evidently the head of the household, told us that the day before they had spent six hours in the shelter; more than two hundred planes had flown over the village and dropped nearly one hundred and fifty bombs. Most of the bombs had landed in the fields and lakes and only three houses had been hit. Fortunately, they were empty and no one had been hurt. He spoke dispassionately as though the ordeal had been an act of nature, as unavoidable as an earthquake.

The planes soon disappeared and although the all-clear had not sounded, our chauffeur said he would go on if we wished to take the risk. Ten minutes later, we once again heard the drone of engines. We left the car on the roadside and scrambled for the protection of a field until nine bombers, flying very low, passed overhead.

We arrived in Hanko to find that great billows of smoke were still rising in the air. The roads were littered with mattresses, chairs and household articles which the soldiers had salvaged from the fire. The charred framework of the houses stood out blackly against the snow, but there were no curious pedestrians to inspect the damage, for icy winds from the sea swept through the streets. I have never felt such cold. A twenty-year-old army lieutenant detailed to show us through the town forgot to pull down one of his ear tabs, and a few minutes later his ear went dead white. One of the Swedish journalists shouted at him, and he quickly rubbed it with snow. Half frozen, we finally stumbled into a corner café.

The proprietor brought us hot meat sandwiches and coffee. While he was serving us he informed us cheerfully that the top floor of the house was on fire. It had been struck by an incendiary bomb two hours before. His sons were fighting it, and he was confident everything would soon be under control. Somehow it was an odd experience to be sipping coffee in a burning building; also somewhat of a contradiction trying to get warm in a house that was on fire.

The young Finnish lieutenant had spent considerable time in America and spoke English fluently. He was an engineer in ordinary life, and now his job was to detonate unexploded bombs. He told us he had heard only that morning that his house, some distance away, had been bombed and completely destroyed. Fortunately, he had sent his wife and children away the previous week. Apart from a few reserved remarks he did not discuss the war. It was only when we left and wished him good luck that he said, 'It will take a miracle to save us, but perhaps a miracle will happen.' Then, almost beneath his breath, 'It *must* happen.' This boy was typical of many Finns with whom we talked. Although they were aware they couldn't hold out indefinitely in such an unequal struggle, they clung to a stubborn faith that some event, unforeseen though it was, would save them from final destruction.

We drove back to Ekenäs, where we had taken shelter earlier in the afternoon, and had dinner in the local inn. The porch was sprayed with machine-gun bullets, but the joviality of the atmosphere suggested a mining town in a boom period rather than war. The room was crowded with soldiers, police officials and strapping men in fur caps and huge reindeer boots. There was no shortage of food; plates of *hors d'oeuvres*, meat, potatoes and large bowls of butter. On the wall was a picture of General

Mannerheim, still decorated with holly left over from Christmas. One of the soldiers tried to play the gramophone, but the waitress said it was forbidden; with the music going, it was impossible to hear the sirens.

Our chauffeur, who was the chief police inspector for the district, found it impossible to leave for Helsinki before midnight, so we spent the evening drinking schnapps with the burgomaster and six village officials. The strain of the last few days had been so great, the burgomaster said, that now they only wanted to laugh, and the conversation was subsequently maintained at a high pitch of hilarity. Members of the party took turns in relating amusing incidents that had occurred during the raids. Someone passed a bag of sugar around the table, and everyone laughed very much because the shop printed on the cover had been blown up that very morning.

We left for Helsinki at one o'clock and the climax of the trip was yet to come. The temperature had now dropped to thirty-six degrees Fahrenheit below zero. The night was brilliantly clear, and the sky glittered with a thousand stars. With only dim blue headlights on the car and the ice forming thickly on the windscreen, the driver had difficulty in distinguishing where the road ended and the white fields began. We had driven for nearly two hours and I was half asleep when suddenly there was a deafening crash and our car skidded across the road and landed, still upright, against a tree. We had hit an empty white truck which had been left standing by the roadside with no lights.

Our car was badly wrecked – the windows broken, the radiator and headlights smashed – but fortunately no one was hurt. We climbed out, to find ourselves confronted with endless miles of desolate forests and frozen fields. It was four o'clock in the morning and there was little prospect of anyone passing for many hours.

It was so cold, the chauffeur said it was best to keep moving, and we started walking along the road.

We were lucky, for after a mile or so we caught sight of a dim glow far across the fields. We walked across country in snow several feet deep, and finally, numb and exhausted, reached a large barn. We pushed the door open to find lights blazing and over a hundred sleek brown cows being milked by a bevy of farm girls. One of the milkmaids led us up to the big house and ran to awaken her mistress. A few minutes later the lady of the house appeared, a middle-aged woman, immaculately groomed, with a string of pearls around her neck, and apparently unperturbed by the fact that it was five in the morning. She spoke English fluently, sympathised over our plight, brought us dozens of blankets, and soon a log fire was roaring and a tea-kettle humming on the stove.

She said the weather had not been so cold for many years, but added it was to the advantage of the Finnish Army; she said it had been the same in the terrible winter campaign in the days of Charles XII of Sweden, when the Finns had succeeded in repelling the Russian onslaught. She told us she had forty evacuees, mostly children, staying in the house, and that scarcely a day passed that the Soviet bombers had not flown over the house, but it was so isolated she was not afraid of bombs. She had told the children, however, to run indoors when they heard the sound of engines, for she feared the planes might fly low and machine-gun the roads.

When a car arrived at seven to take us to Helsinki and we wished her good luck, she said quietly: 'I believe God will not let us perish beneath so terrible a foe; in the end all will be well.'

An hour after we reached Helsinki the sirens were moaning again. I was so tired I crawled into bed and went to sleep.

* * *

If you happened to be lunching at the Hotel Torni in Helsinki when the air-raid sirens sounded, you could climb up on the roof and watch the city crawl into its shell. Between the jumble of ice-covered roofs you saw the people running for cover, the snow trucks pulling up by the roadside, and the police officers taking their positions on the street corners. Soon there was a silence so ominous that you could hear a door bang many blocks away.

Occasionally you saw the grey flash of bombers against the sky, but usually the planes flew so high you could hear only the drone of the engines. You could count the dull thud of bombs falling as far away as ten or fifteen miles; when the air was suddenly shattered by a *mélange* of machine-guns, pom-pom guns and coastal batteries all firing at once, you knew the planes were passing over the city. Although they flew backwards and forwards several times a day, Helsinki had been bombed only once. This was when the Russians, aiming for the docks, had smashed several blocks of houses near the waterfront. On the whole, the damage was not great.

Helsinki was not a beautiful city. The long domination of first Sweden and then Russia had left little imprint, and most of the buildings were modern, square and ugly. Whoever had dubbed it 'The White City of the North' had a truly romantic soul, for the ice-bound streets, rather than adding glamour, seemed to accentuate a bleak and dismal atmosphere. Granted, the war didn't help: the normal population of three hundred thousand had dwindled to thirty thousand; cars had been requisitioned to save petrol and most of the shops were boarded up. There were only a few people in the streets. They hurried along, bundled up in thick coats and fur caps, walking with their heads down against the terrible cold.

The Hotel Kämp was the capital's war-time centre. When I arrived late at night it was deserted. But when I went downstairs

the following morning I found it overflowing with a noisy conglomeration of people; there were Finnish soldiers, women
volunteers, politicians, and foreign journalists and photographers
of a dozen different nationalities. They came stamping in from
outside, shaking the snow off their boots, their faces beet-red from
the cold. Some wore ski suits; some sheepskin coats; some leather
jackets and windbreakers. Most extraordinary were the Swedish
women journalists. Every paper in Sweden seemed to have sent
a 'special correspondent' and there were dozens of them. They all
had blonde hair, big blue eyes, and wore dainty white fur coats and
little white hats that tied under their chins. They looked like the
front row of a Cochran chorus.

Out of the general confusion I managed to find Webb Miller of
the United Press and had lunch with him. He had just returned
from the Mannerheim Line and was filled with admiration for the
Finnish soldiers. 'They're the damnedest fighters I've ever seen.
They don't seem to be afraid of anything. And talk about impro-
visation – they invent their weapons as they go along. They've got
a new trick which is to tie a mine to the end of a string, then hide
in a ditch until one of the Russian tanks comes along and jerk it
across the road. I talked with a soldier who'd accounted for three
thirty-ton tanks this way!'

I pressed Webb with questions about the war and he told me
the only way to understand what was happening was to keep in
mind that two wars were taking place. The first war was the regular trench warfare, based on Western Front methods, being fought
behind the Mannerheim defences on the Karelian Isthmus; the
second war was the guerrilla fighting waged through the forests
on all the other fronts in Finland. In the trench war, the Russian
attack on the Mannerheim Line had been repulsed; and in the
guerrilla war, not only had the Russian thrusts been halted, but the

Finns, by brilliant strategy and ferocious courage, had succeeded in wiping out entire divisions.

It was the second week in January and fighting on the Isthmus had come to a temporary halt; I therefore decided to travel to the north and try to see something of the forest patrols. However, when I filed an application at the Finnish Press Bureau I had a nasty shock. On a trip to Viipuri the day before, a Swedish woman journalist had reported that one of the Finnish press officers had made advances towards her. The authorities, exasperated, had promptly slapped down the rule that no more women could visit the front. My heart sank and I wondered if I had come all the way from England merely to sit in Helsinki. Fortunately, my apprenticeship in Spain helped me; after a series of telegrams to the Finnish Minister in London, I finally received permission to travel to Rovaniemi, the capital of Lapland, where the press headquarters for the northern section was established.

I left with Harold Denny, the *New York Times* correspondent, whom I had known in Moscow. The trip took twenty-four hours; overnight we found ourselves in a world of white forests and glassy lakes. When we reached Rovaniemi we were a mile and a half from the Arctic Circle.

2

Dead Man's Land

What the Finns thought of the six foreign journalists laden down with sleeping-bags, knapsacks and typewriters, who jumped off the train at every stop and bolted into the station restaurants to gulp down cups of hot coffee, I never discovered. We all knew the Finnish word for coffee – *kahvi*, that was easy; and we could all count up to four because it sounded like: 'Ooxie, coxie, call me, nellie.' Beyond that we had to rely on gestures or go behind the counter and help ourselves.

When at last we reached a rather primitive hotel in the small town of Kajaani, the proprietress looked at us in bewilderment, as though we were part of a travelling circus. Soon, I think she decided a lunatic asylum was more likely, for during the next forty-eight hours her telephone rang with calls from New York, Amsterdam and Copenhagen, and everybody sat up all night typing out endless stories. Besides Harold Denny and myself, there was Walter Kerr of the *Herald Tribune*, Edward Ward of the BBC, Desmond Tighe of Reuter's, and Ebbe Munck, a Danish journalist.

Kajaani served as GHQ for the Central Command. There in the slender waistline of Finland, some of the fiercest battles of the war were taking place. During the previous seven weeks, over a hundred thousand Russian troops had crossed the frontier, in repeated attempts to cut Finland in two. But the Finns had repulsed the onslaughts with some of the most spectacular fighting in history; they had annihilated entire divisions and hurled back others thirty and forty miles to the border from where they started.

To understand how they did it, you must picture a country of thick-snow-covered forests and ice-bound roads. You must visualise heavily armed ski patrols sliding like ghosts through the woods; creeping behind the enemy lines and cutting their communications until entire battalions were isolated, then falling on them in furious surprise attacks. In this part of Finland skis outmanoeuvred tanks, sleds competed with lorries, and knives even challenged rifles.

The evening we arrived in Kajaani we dined with General Tuompo, the brilliant fifty-year-old ex-journalist general, who had only begun his military career ten or twelve years previously and who, before the Finnish war was over, took a toll of nearly eighty-five thousand Russian lives. He arranged for us to visit a front-line position on the Russian–Finnish frontier, where we saw the patrols at work and had our first taste of Soviet artillery fire. We started off with the idea of, perhaps, accompanying one of the Finnish border patrols on a quick jaunt into Russia and back. Not that any of us imagined the frozen Russian landscape would prove interesting, but we all thought it would be fun to step into the Soviet Union without the formality of getting a visa.

Accompanied by a Finnish army lieutenant, we left at four o'clock in the morning, hoping to arrive at the front before dawn. But the roads were so slippery our car skidded into the ditch three times, delaying us considerably; it gave us a small idea of what the mechanised Russian units were up against. We approached the village of Suomussalmi just as dawn was breaking, and here I witnessed the most ghastly spectacle I have ever seen.

It was in this sector that the Finns, a few weeks previously, had annihilated two Russian divisions of approximately thirty thousand men. The road along which we drove was still littered with frozen Russian corpses, and the forests on either side had become known as 'Dead Man's Land'. Perhaps it was the beauty of the morning that made the terrible Russian debacle all the more ghastly when we came upon it. The rising sun had drenched the snow-covered forests, their trees like lace valentines, with a strange pink light that seemed to glow for miles. The landscape was marred only by the charred framework of a house; then an overturned truck and two battered tanks. Then we turned a bend in the road and came upon the full horror of the scene. For four miles the road and forests were strewn with the bodies of men and horses; with wrecked tanks, field kitchens, trucks, gun carriages, maps, books and articles of clothing. The corpses were frozen as hard as petrified wood and the colour of the skin was mahogany. Some of the bodies were piled on top of each other like a heap of rubbish, covered only by a merciful blanket of snow; others were sprawled against the trees in grotesque attitudes.

All were frozen in the positions in which they had died. I saw one with his hands clasped to a wound in his stomach; another struggling to open the collar of his coat; and a third pathetically clasping a cheap landscape drawing, done in bright, childish colours, which had probably been a prized possession that he had tried to save when he fled into the woods. They were everywhere, hundreds and hundreds of grotesque wooden corpses; in the ditches, under the trees, and even in dugouts beneath the snow where they had tried to escape from the fury of the attack. I learned, with a shock, that they had been members of the 44th Division – the same division that just a year ago I had seen swinging along the country roads in the Ukraine.

What these troops must have suffered in the cold was not difficult to imagine. They were wearing only ordinary knitted hoods with steel helmets over them, and none of them had gloves on. This was accounted for by the fact that the Russians didn't wear 'trigger finger' mittens as the Finns did; they wore only ordinary mittens which they had to take off to fire their rifles. And how they must have suffered from hunger; the horses had even eaten the bark off the trees.

I was staggered by the amount of equipment they had brought with them. Although the Finns had hauled away all the usable stuff, the ditches were still full of battered lorries, machine-guns, bayonets, helmets – even an amphibian tank which seemed pretty useless in a country of frozen lakes. Our Finnish officer told us that for at least a week after the battle it was impossible to drive down the road at all. As it was, our chauffeur had to thread his way along the four-mile stretch slowly. Near the end of it, we passed a group of Finnish boys playing in the roadside, curiously prodding the corpses. They had taken one of the bodies and stuck it head down in the snow; all we could see was two brown stems with boots at the end. I was very nearly ill.

About an hour later we reached our destination. A sentry in a white cloak stepped out of the forest into the roadway and motioned us to stop. The car was backed into a clearing between the trees, and as we followed our guide through the twisting paths, the woods suddenly became alive with stalwart Finnish soldiers, only their black rifles visible against the snow, moving noiselessly in and out among the trees.

The Major's hut was built of logs, half underground, and covered with snow. The camouflage was so clever the only way we knew we had arrived was by the skis stacked up against the trees. We crawled in the shelter, which had two beds in it, a long desk covered with maps, and a small stove that kept the temperature at thirty degrees. The Major, a strapping man with a red face, greeted us in halting English and told us breakfast was ready; he motioned us to a table laden with coffee, bread and butter, reindeer meat, cheese and pickled fish. A few minutes later we were interrupted by the whine of an engine, which broke into a loud roar as a plane passed only a few hundred feet above our heads. The Major said the Russian planes patrolled the forests for several hours each day and often did a considerable amount of machine-gunning. 'That's what *we* want – planes.' Then he asked us if we thought the outside world would send any to Finland and searched our faces eagerly for our replies. 'If only,' he murmured, 'those kind old ladies in America who send us comforts could knit us some aeroplanes and crochet us some anti-tank guns.'

When we asked him if there was any possibility of our sneaking across the frontier into Russia, he smiled and said he would send us up to the observation-post, where we could have a look at the situation, and if we still wanted to go it was ours for the asking. He then detailed a captain to look after us.

The Captain's hut was some distance away; it was made of beaverboard built around the trunk of a tree so that the smoke from the stove would be diffused by the thick branches. The Captain was a gay fellow who showed us with great relish the huge Russian samovar he had captured in the Suomussalmi battle. He also had a pair of field-glasses he had taken from a Russian officer, but his most prized possession was a machine-gun from a Russian tank. He said every time a plane went by he took a pot-shot at it; adding that it wasn't exactly his business, but with the gun so handy it was difficult to resist.

The Captain led us through the woods to the observation-post. It was some distance away and we were accompanied by a ski patrol of eight men equipped with rifles and wicked-looking machine pistols. They slipped in and out through the trees like wraiths, managing their skis with astonishing agility. One moment they slipped behind the trees and we thought they were lost; a few seconds later they were on the path in front of us.

The observation-post was just a shallow pit dug in the snow; in it there was an observer with a pair of field-glasses and a telephone. But we did not need glasses to see the Soviet Union. Only three hundred yards away across an icebound lake lay the frozen landscape of Russia.

We had been in the pit only a few minutes when Finnish artillery in our rear opened fire. The shells rushed past only a few yards over our heads; they landed in the lake in front of us and a fountain of ice and snow shot up. The observation officer corrected the range on the telephone and soon they were disappearing neatly into the trees on the other side. The Russians were not slow to reply, and a few minutes later the air resounded to the nasty whistle of incoming shells, and the pine trees sang with the low moan of grenades and the thud of mortars. Twice tree branches, chipped by grenades, fell on top of us, and when two shells landed only twenty yards away, wounding two Finnish soldiers, the Captain decided we had better go back to the hut. He told us to leave in pairs, so the Russians wouldn't spot us; my heart pounded as we made our way through the woods with the shells exploding on either side of the path. I thought: Russian guns may have lost their prestige, but they can still frighten me.

Before we left, the Captain gave us a cup of tea. While we were drinking it a husky Finnish soldier crawled into the shelter. His cheeks were red with the cold, but his blue eyes shone with excitement. He had just come in from a five-hour patrol behind the Russian lines, and had penetrated as far back as three miles. He took out a map and explained to the Captain the various changes in the enemy positions. We learned that the boy was a farmer in ordinary life, and had distinguished himself as one of the bravest men in the patrol. The Captain said that during the Suomussalmi battle he had destroyed a tank by jumping on top of it, forcing the lid open with a crowbar, and throwing a grenade inside. A few minutes later another soldier came into the hut to say that a Russian patrol of two hundred men were heading towards the Finnish lines. The Captain ordered him to start out with a detachment and meet them on the way.

We could see that things were going to be pretty busy soon, so we decided it was best to leave. Outside, a group of soldiers were already strapping on their rifles and adjusting their skis. When we shook hands with the Captain, he said: 'Well, what about Russia? If you want to join the patrol just starting out, you have my permission.'

We thanked him very much, but I, for one, said I was quite happy where I was.

* * *

How had the Finnish Army, with a force of scarcely more than three hundred thousand men, been able so far to stem the sweep of the Russian tide? I think it was due first to a free people fighting, with a courage never surpassed, against an Asiatic despotism for their homes, their liberties and their lives; second, to the brilliant strategy of the Finnish military leaders; third, to the natural obstacles of the terrain which was broken by seventy thousand lakes and three-quarters covered with forests; fourth, to Soviet blunders.

From a military point of view, the Russian onslaught will be studied as one of the most fantastic campaigns in history. All through the north the Russian High Command ignored the elementary necessity of keeping open its lines of communication. Thousands of Russian soldiers were sent into the wilds of Finland to be isolated from their bases and swallowed up by the forests. This extraordinary stupidity was hard to understand. The only explanation was that Russia had reckoned on a blitzkrieg lasting only a few days and had organised the campaign accordingly. The first divisions had been equipped with an enormous amount of propaganda, banners and pennants, which they had expected to distribute among a vanquished people; and in the north, a division entered with a brass band, actually expecting to be welcomed by the people it had been sent to 'liberate'. The reason the Kremlin was so grossly misinformed as to the political stamina of Finland may have been due to the fact that Soviet observers were afraid to reveal the true state of affairs for fear of being shot as saboteurs.

For days I was haunted by the scene of those frozen, twisted bodies of the 44th Division. But the story of this division (one of those, incidentally, which invaded Poland in September) was typical of the whole blundering strategy for which the dictatorship of the proletariat now paid freely with the lives of the proletariat. It had crossed into Finland on December 30th to relieve the 163rd Division, which was cut off, without supplies, near the small village of Suomussalmi. It marched twenty miles along a hard, snow-packed road cut through the heart of the forest, but was unable to join forces with the other, six miles away, across a roadless country. The Finns succeeded in first routing the 163rd, then turned their attention to the 44th; they cut off its supplies, and five days later attacked and annihilated the entire division.

Before we left Kajaani, one of the Finnish press officers took us to an internment camp at Pelso, where we heard a version of the battle from a high-ranking officer of the 44th Division, who had been captured by the Finns. The officer was a clean-shaven man of middle age who had served with the Red Army for twenty-two years. The Finnish warden requested that we withhold his name and rank, and informed the prisoner he was not obliged to answer any questions unless he wished.

The officer, however, gave an account of the battle which dove-tailed completely with the Finnish version. He said the division was cut off on January 2nd and was without food until the final debacle on the 7th. The only supplies they received were six bags of hard tack dropped by plane. He told us that on January 2nd several of the officers begged the Commanding General, Vinogradov, to retreat, but the latter replied it was impossible without an order from the Kremlin. And the order came too late.

The officer made three points of interest: he declared that the army had been misinformed as to Finnish resistance, many of the leaders actually believing they were entering to liberate Finnish people, that the army was badly organised for a severe campaign, and that the Russian troops, superstitious by nature, were particularly unsuited to the Finnish terrain as they were mortally afraid of the dark forests.

When I questioned him regarding the commissar system, he replied evasively that the commissars were necessary to infuse the soldiers with the proper spirit. I asked what he thought the final outcome of the war would be, and he hesitated; it was only when the warden bade him give an honest opinion that he replied he felt the Soviet Union, with its preponderance of men and material, was bound to conquer in the end.

Out of the 44th Division of eighteen thousand men there were only a few hundred survivors. We went through the jail and talked with them, accompanied by the warden and a Russian interpreter. In the first room there was a group of thirty or forty dressed in their brown tunic uniforms and high felt boots. Many had frozen hands and feet, wrapped in bandages; but compared to their comrades, lying in heaps along the roadside, they were lucky. They stood up when we entered the room, but there was no sullenness or reticence about them; their eyes lighted up with friendly interest and they seemed pleased to have visitors. As a group of soldiers of a crack division, however, they were a pathetic lot. Most of them were small of stature, with low foreheads and ugly features. Their intelligence was so elementary I was torn between pity and revulsion for the civilisation their Government was so eager to extend. Some of the prisoners stared at us dumbly with melancholy brown eyes; others interrupted each other in a rush of conversation.

When I questioned them about the war they replied that they had been mobilised to repel a Finnish invasion of Russia. Some of them said they now realised they had been grossly misinformed, but I was astounded to find that many of them were still unaware of the fact that they had been captured on Finnish territory; they thought the battle of Suomussalmi had been fought 'somewhere in the North of Russia'.

When we questioned them about general conditions in Russia, a small, wiry little man with a black beard became the self-appointed spokesman of the group by silencing his comrades with menacing looks. With typical Slav cunning, he answered the questions in a manner which he thought best likely to please. He denounced the Soviet Union with such an exaggerated emphasis and paid the Finns compliments of so lavish a nature that his replies were obviously worthless.

The second room into which I was taken was filled with Russian lorry drivers who had been in the Army Service Corps attached to the 44th Division. Most of them, I discovered, had never had military training of any kind; they were merely truck drivers picked up off the streets of Kiev. They spoke bitterly of the fact that they had been mobilised and, pointing to one of the group, said, 'And look at Feodor. He is over forty years of age with a wife and many children.' Feodor seemed pleased to have the spotlight turned on him and nodded his head emphatically, declaring that, indeed, he was forty-two years old and had never heard the sound of a gun until he found himself driving a supply truck on the Suomussalmi front.

The most amazing story of all, however, was from the Russian nurse with whom I talked. This twenty-three-year-old girl, the only woman prisoner in Finland, was captured when the Finns routed the 163rd Division. She was a girl of medium size, with broad Slavic features and eyes which were filled with sadness. She wore a wool dress provided for her by the Finns; her only other clothes were the man's army uniform she had been wearing when captured.

A few months before, she had been living quietly in Leningrad with her husband and small child; then she received a mobil-isation order. Thinking it was only for the autumn manoeuvres, she was not particularly worried. In November, however, she was attached to the 163rd Division and a month later forced to cross into Finland. Although miserable and frightened, she was sent, with two other nurses, to a front-line first-aid post. The other nurses were wounded and removed to a field hospital behind the lines; when the retreat came, the girl was unable to get back to the base and for twenty-four hours wandered through the woods with a Russian doctor. The pair were finally picked up by a Finnish patrol on the shores of a lake.

The bodies of the other two nurses were later found by the Finns in the field hospital – an old farmhouse – alongside the corpses of hundreds of soldiers. Ebbe Munck, who had visited this hospital four days after the retreat, told me it was a ghastly sight. The yard at the back of the house was piled with naked bodies; when patients had died, the Russian doctors had simply thrown the corpses out of the window to make way for newcomers. Inside, hundreds of wounded men had died in their beds; when the order to retreat came, they had been abandoned. Ebbe said a man had even been left, half cut open, on the operating table.

When the Finnish warden heard this story, he remarked bitterly: 'And that's the civilisation they want to bring to Finland.'

3

The Best Arctic Circles

Due to the daylight raids, the hours before dawn were usually the safest travelling. When Harold Denny, Desmond Tighe and I started out from Rovaniemi on a two-hundred-mile drive through the Arctic, we left at two o'clock in the morning. The temperature was thirty-two degrees below zero, which was considered a moderate day. I wore a skiing suit, a windbreaker, a sheepskin coat, eight sweaters, four pairs of socks, three mufflers, two pairs of gloves, and somehow survived. A mile and a half outside Rovaniemi we passed a large white sign tacked to a tree. We flashed a light on it and saw, written in English, German, Swedish and Finnish: 'Arctic Circle'.

When the Soviets slid over the world's roof-top from the Petsamo port on the Arctic Ocean, they began the coldest war in history. Never before had war been waged so far north. Soon the icebound forests, scarcely inhabited save for herds of reindeer, rang with the sound of rifle bullets and the crackle of machine-gun fire. The Russians advanced sixty miles down the 'Great Arctic Highway', but in spite of repeated attempts to penetrate further along the road – which swept down through Lapland to the centre of Finland – they were checked by Finnish patrols working in the deep forests through which the Highway was cut.

The Finnish front line was a series of patrol tents and machine-gun posts scattered through the woods. Every time the Russian mechanised columns tried to advance along the road, the Finns crept through the forests and cut their lines; sometimes blocking the icy road by knocking out a tank, sometimes laying mines and cutting off their supplies in the rear.

When the three of us started out from Rovaniemi to visit this front, accompanied by Hugo Mäkinen – a Finnish press officer – fellow journalists who had already made the trip told us we wouldn't get much 'copy'; the fighting had more or less come to a stalemate. Not to discourage us, they added that the scenery was well worth observing and assured us we could all write very nice little pieces on Old Mother Nature. As it turned out, the trip was one of the most uncomfortable any of us had made. The Russians chose this particular moment to open up an intensive bombing attack on the Arctic Highway, to prevent Finnish reinforcements from reaching the front.

At first, things were quiet. We drove all night through desolate white forests, the Northern Lights making eerie patterns against the sky; for five hours we didn't pass a single car or see any sign of life except for an occasional reindeer that ran across the roads, startled by our headlights. As dawn was breaking we stopped at a farmhouse for breakfast.

The family consisted of a farmer and his wife, a little girl of ten, and two boys about fourteen. They lighted a fire, brought us coffee and rolls, then gave us an account of the bombings of the last few days. In the midst of the conversation the telephone rang, and one of the boys came back with the news that the morning raids had begun and three planes were now headed in our direction. (There were no sirens in the district and it was up to the operator to warn everyone.) There was a scramble for coats and the little girl, who seemed to regard it as a great joke, led us out of the house through the woods to a large pine tree. Underneath the branches was a small tent with four rugs inside.

A few minutes later we heard the sound of engines and three bombers appeared, flying fairly low. When the planes were over the house, one of them swooped down with a loud roar; there was a burst of explosives that sounded like a bunch of giant fire-crackers, followed by the staccato noise of machine-gun bullets. When the planes passed we ran back to the house to see what damage had been done and found that the bombs had landed in a field twenty or thirty yards away. A few seconds later a boy came skiing breathlessly up the road.

We discovered it was he and not the farmhouse that had been the target. He had forgotten his white coat and the Russians evidently had spotted him moving against the snow. They had dropped eight-een small bombs, then tried to machine-gun him. It seemed an extravagant gesture to say the least. Desmond commented dryly: 'If that's any indication of the lines along which Soviet economy is run, no wonder there are hungry people in Moscow.'

Although there was a large and comfortable inn at Ivalo some fifty or sixty miles away, 'Mak', our press officer, refused to travel along the road until dark. As brave as lions on the battlefield, the Finns were almost foolishly overcautious on the home front. When the air-raid sirens sounded, whether you liked it or not, you were pushed into a shelter. In Helsinki, the journalists wore spe-cial badges allowing them to move about, but on a trip you were at the mercy of your press officer. It seemed to us our chances were just as good one place as another, but we were unable to persuade 'Mak' of this, and didn't continue our journey until late afternoon.

It was the most uncomfortable day I have ever spent, for the farmer was convinced the planes were after his house and would soon return to bomb it. Every time the telephone rang with a warning he insisted we take cover under the pine tree in the yard. We pleaded and argued, but it was of no avail – each time we were pushed out into the bitter cold. A good five hours crouched under a tree in the snow gave us a small idea of what life had become in Finland.

We finally reached Ivalo in time for dinner. It was a small road-junction village that had the distinction of being the most bombed spot in Finland; nearly four thousand bombs had been dropped on it, but most of them had landed in the fields and lakes and surprisingly few houses had been destroyed. The village was almost entirely evacuated, but the local store was still doing business; you could buy chocolates and raisins.

The inn where we dined was run for road-workers who were patrolling and repairing the highway. The atmosphere was like a huge lumber camp; half a dozen girls bent over large cauldrons helping with the cooking, while streams of men came stamping in from the cold, rubbing their hands and shaking the snow from their boots. Everyone ate in the kitchen because it was warmer nearer the stove, and we all sat down at table together for a dinner of reindeer steak, boiled potatoes and milk.

Just as we were ready to leave there was an air-raid alarm. Harold, Desmond and I looked at each other and groaned. We urged Hugo to let us go on, anyway, but he shook his head stubbornly. A gong resounded through the inn, the girls put on their coats, picked up their blankets and led the way to the shelter. The shelter was made of logs buried deep beneath the snow. The temperature must have been forty degrees below zero, but Harold, Desmond and I seemed to be the only ones who minded, for the girls kept up a spirited flow of conversation as though they were out on a party. We sat there for over two hours, while we counted the thud of twenty-five bombs.

When the all-clear finally sounded, Hugo telephoned to army headquarters and asked what the situation was. He came back with a grave face and told us the Russians were bombing the road all the way up to the front. We didn't know it then, but the Russians were preparing a new offensive; the Arctic Highway was the only road over which supplies could be sent to the Finnish soldiers, and this was the beginning of a desperate attempt to cut them off. 'Mak' wanted to turn back, but we begged him to go on. Not that any of us were particularly brave, but, after driving a hundred and fifty miles and suffering hours of boredom and cold, to return to Rovaniemi without a story seemed unthinkable.

We finally got our way, and the drive was not a pleasant one. To begin with, although 'Mak' was more than particular where air-raid shelters were concerned, he allowed the chauffeur to drive with his headlights full on. As ours appeared to be the only lights in the entire Arctic forest, it seemed likely they would be noticed. With the engine running and the windows closed, it was impossible to hear the sound of aeroplanes, so we had to stop every few miles, get out of the car, and listen. We passed through an isolated stretch of woods, and as we neared a farmhouse a group of men stepped into the path of our lights and waved at us frantically to stop. One of them told us another alarm had sounded and the bombers were near. We decided to take cover in a field as soon as we heard the engines, and began walking up the road to keep warm.

It was a strange night, with the stillness of the forest broken only by the low sound of men's voices, with the snow-covered pine trees taking queer shapes in the darkness, and the Northern Lights playing across the sky like gigantic searchlights. I was looking at the sky when suddenly I noticed the largest star I had ever seen. I thought it was a peculiarity of the Arctic until a second one appeared. One of the men ran up and told us the Russians were dropping parachute flares to illuminate the countryside. Nowadays, when London is bombed, there are dozens of flares in the sky, but these were the first any of us had seen; moving slowly earthwards, with a terrible beauty that lighted the way for destruction, they seemed almost uncanny. The farmhouse telephone rang, warning us the planes were headed in our direction. There was no shelter, so a sentry led us across the road to a small bridge two feet above the frozen lake and told us to crawl under. First I went, then Desmond, then Harold, then half a dozen Finns.

Desmond's last assignment had been in Egypt. 'If anyone had prophesied two months ago I'd soon be lying on the ice in the middle of the Arctic Circle,' he gasped, 'I would have told them to have their heads examined.' All Harold could say: 'My God, and we're paid to have brains!' Fortunately, we didn't have to stay there long, for the roar of motors grew loud, then soft again, as the planes headed eastwards. We crawled out and saw one of them, fully lighted, moving across the sky – a bitter testimony to Finland's lack of anti-aircraft guns.

We didn't arrive at the front-line sector until the early hours of the morning. A sentry was waiting for us in the road. We parked the car and walked to a shack some way in the woods. Inside were half a dozen officers sitting round a table. They were all over six foot tall, rangers who'd spent most of their lives in the forest. The Major apologised for the delays we'd had in arriving and 'Mak' translated his remark: 'When we get some anti-aircraft guns we'll promise to keep the Highway clear.'

The shack was warm and comfortable, but the doors and walls were drilled with bullet-holes where the Russian planes had machine-gunned it. As we were warming ourselves by the fire a woman suddenly appeared from the next room with a pot of coffee and some rolls. She was a middle-aged woman, a placid, motherly type. Ordinarily she worked in a shop in Helsinki, but when the war broke out had joined up with the Lotta Svärd volunteering for service in Petsamo. She had the distinction of being the only woman serving at the northernmost post. We asked if she didn't get frightened when the planes machine-gunned the house, and the men laughed and said she was the calmest of the lot. Then the Major told us in an off-hand voice he would be unable to take us any further up the line as the Russians had attacked with two companies at eight o'clock and the battle was still going on about a mile away.

'Where are they headed?' I asked nervously.

'This way. But don't worry, they won't get through.'

Thank God, I thought, I'm covering this war from the Finnish side. I strained my ears for the sound of rifle fire, but could hear nothing. I pictured the Finns slipping in and out of the trees, then the sudden flash of knives, and wondered how many grotesque corpses the morning light would find. The dark, lonely forest seemed terrifying enough from the inside of a shack, and I pitied the poor creatures at the mercy of the stealthy huntsmen.

We learned that only eight hundred Finns had stemmed the whole Russian Army in this neighbourhood. The Major told us that aeroplanes provided the greatest problem, but added that he had an expert machine-gunner who had already shot down three. He showed us a briefcase belonging to a Russian pilot. Inside was a copy of *Pravda*, a few charts and a card with an elementary multiplication printed on it.

Harold asked if the Russians had learned to ski yet and the Major hesitated. 'Well. When they're really in a hurry they take off their skis and run.' Everyone laughed, for there was nothing the Finns enjoyed more than jokes at the Russians' expense.

It seemed strange to be sitting sipping coffee while a life-and-death struggle was going on only a mile away. Before we left, the telephone rang with a message to say it was over and the Russians had been driven back. The Major put on his coat, strapped on a rifle and disappeared into the night. On our way down the road a large white ambulance came racing past us and we wondered what the casualties had been.

We spent the next day at a lumber camp a few miles behind the front, which 'Mak' declared was the safest spot in Finland due to the deep shelters. One of the lumbermen's wives offered to give us coffee, but the alerts sounded so continuously from dawn till noon she never had the time to prepare it. We protested to the camp manager, asking him if it were necessary to take cover at every warning, and he replied: 'Indeed it is. The place is packed with dynamite. If a single bomb drops, the whole camp is likely to go up.' 'Mak' looked startled, but made no comment.

We left for Rovaniemi at dusk and the trip was uneventful save for a final incident. Some miles from Ivalo we heard a wild rumour the Russians had dropped a parachute squad in the vicinity and were warned to be on the look-out for them. At that time no one took the idea of parachute troops seriously; nevertheless, driving through a particularly deserted stretch of forest, it was difficult to dismiss it completely. Suddenly we turned a bend in the road and saw a man standing in the path of our lights. He was wearing a white suit and a white helmet. He waved us to stop and the chauffeur drew his pistol, got out of the car, and advanced cautiously.

I needn't say it was a relief to find he was only a Swedish volunteer with a motorcycle that had run out of petrol – if you can imagine running out of petrol in the middle of the Arctic.

We siphoned some off into a bottle and waved goodbye.

* * *

Rovaniemi had been badly bombed in our absence. The main street was a mass of charred timber where the wooden houses had burned to the ground, but the principal objective, the bridge across the Kemi river, was still intact.

The proprietor of the Hotel Pohjanhovi, where the journalists were staying, was badly shaken by the experience. As the Russian bombers had a habit of coming back to the same spot for several days running, he refused to allow anyone to remain in the hotel during the daylight hours. In spite of a good many protests, we were pushed out at eight-thirty in the morning and instructed not to come back until three. In peace-time Rovaniemi was a winter sports centre and a few miles from the hotel there was a very good ski-run and a large pavilion where we could get coffee and sandwiches. There was also a shooting range, and once we held a competition.

As we represented half a dozen different nationalities, we paired off in teams and made it a small Olympic Games: England, France, Finland, Sweden, America, Germany. The Finns won, and I am ashamed to say I let Walter Kerr down so badly America got the booby prize. Herbert Uexküll, a Baltic German, who worked for the United Press, turned to Eddie Ward and said in a melancholy voice:

'I suppose you and I really ought to be shooting each other.'

'Good God, why?'

'The war.'

'The war? Oh, you mean the *other* war! Come to think of it, I suppose we should. Extraordinary how one forgets.'

Extraordinary, I thought, what a mad world it is: that was the only time I heard 'the other war' mentioned. In fact, it was difficult enough to think about the one at hand when you went down the ski-run with the sky above you a warm thick blue and the sun sparkling on the snow. The only thing to remind you of it was the odd experience of weaving in and out of the machine-gun emplacements scattered through the woods.

I use the word 'weave' fancifully, for if I did a quarter of the run on my feet I was lucky – or, in fact, if I got to my feet at all. Once down, I usually stayed down until someone came to my rescue. A young Finnish army lieutenant took pity on me and made a practice of following me down the run to lend a helping hand. Each time I floundered in the snow he pulled me up, saying: 'There, there, I'm sure you'll do better next time.'

I never did, and on the occasion I needed him the most he wasn't there. One day Herbert Uexküll, Eddie Ward and I were skiing across the frozen Kemi river on our way back to the hotel. The river was pitted with bomb-holes where the Russians had missed their aim at the bridge, and as we were in the middle of it the air-raid sirens sounded. We hurried for cover. I tried to kick off my skis, but could only unfasten one. I heard the roar of engines; Eddie and Herbert shouted at me from the top of the bank, but I promptly fell down and got so tangled up I couldn't move at all.

'For God's sake,' shouted Eddie, 'can't you cut out the acrobatics?' He came running down the bank, unfastened my ski and pulled me up. The sound of the planes was louder and the three of us crawled into a flimsy bathing-hut waiting for a shower of bombs. Three planes came roaring overhead only five hundred feet from the ground, but to our astonishment we saw they were Finnish fighters – British Gloster Gladiators flown by Swedish pilots. They were the only fighters I saw the whole time I was in Finland; soon the all-clear was resounding triumphantly through the town.

* * *

The Russians with their relentless and continuous air attacks were evidently trying to copy the methods the Germans had used against the Poles. When the Germans attacked Poland they had every objective in the country mapped out; the objectives included railroad junctions, roads, bridges, telegraph communications, radio stations, telephone buildings and power plants.

After forty-eight hours of accurate and intensive bombing they had broken the communications from one end of the country to the other and paralysed the operations of the enemy.

In Finland the Russians scored no such great success; after two months of bombing, the trains were still running, the roads were still intact, and although I drove many miles about the country, I never saw a bridge that had received a direct hit. This did not mean that the Russians always missed their objectives. They hit many roads and railroad tracks, but the Finns, in spite of the need for every able-bodied man in the army, realised the importance of keeping their communications open. Fast-working road patrols were organised to repair damage as soon as it had taken place. The thick layers of ice on the roads prevented bombs from doing any great damage, and the small craters could be quickly filled in with snow. As for the railroads, most tracks are built in sections, and it was estimated that a hundred men could repair thirty miles of track a day. Although train journeys took from four to five times the normal time, all through the war you could travel to any point in Finland by train – and well-heated ones at that. This meant that the distribution of food was possible and even out-of-the-way villages were well stocked with meat, potatoes, bread, butter and milk.

In spite of the heavy raids few lives were lost. Day after day there were anywhere from five to eight hundred planes over the country, yet the casualty lists each night numbered no more than thirty or forty people. This was due first to the fact that three-quarters of Finland was composed of forests and lakes and the houses were widely scattered; and, secondly, that people obeyed the warnings and always took refuge in shelters.

The damage done to property, however, was far greater than I had seen after two years of war in Spain. Most of the Finnish houses were wooden houses that burned to the ground when they were hit by incendiary bombs. The Russians claimed they were bombing only military objectives, but the words stretched a long way. Military objectives were no longer limited to munition factories, airfields and troop concentrations, but appeared to include the entire communications of the country. Scarcely a town or village could consider itself immune. For example, the Russians didn't confine themselves to railroad junctions, but claimed that even the railroad lines running through the country villages were legitimate objectives. When a village was wiped out by bombs wide of their mark, it still came under the heading of military operations.

So many hospitals were hit that the red crosses were removed from the roofs. A story went round (I never learned whether or not it was true) that when one of the Russian pilots was questioned as to why he had bombed a hospital, he replied that his commanding officer had instructed him to go to a certain town and had marked the objective on his map with a red cross. He had taken it literally.

4

The Twilight

We were the only civilians on a troop train. The corridors were so jammed with kits, rifles and greatcoats, it was almost impossible to move along them. The soldiers had been home on leave and were now returning to the front. They were husky, broad-shouldered men in high spirits; a few of them slept, a few of them stared silently out the window, but most of them sat laughing and talking, every now and then breaking loudly into the chorus of marching songs. We were sorry we couldn't open a conversation in Finnish, for they eyed us curiously and offered us some dried apricots, bread and sausages. Ed Hartrich dug in his pocket and brought out a package of cigarettes; all Ed Beattie could contribute was a bar of chocolate, which he found in the bottom of his knapsack, left over from the siege of Warsaw.

It was hot on the train and the air got so close we climbed off whenever we could and walked up and down the platform. Once we all surged into a restaurant for coffee and sandwiches. The windows had been shattered by a bomb explosion and were covered over with cardboard. A dim light burned inside and in the semi-darkness half a dozen waitresses behind a counter poured out cups of coffee, serving the whole lot of us in twenty minutes.

The troops were evidently on their way to the Isthmus. It was February 20th, and three weeks previously the Russians had opened up their second big attack against the Mannerheim Line. They had prepared an artillery barrage more ferocious than any since the World War in a final desperate effort to break through the Finnish defences. They had been advancing slowly, and the

Finns, with their tiny army, were throwing in every available man to stem the terrible onslaught. I looked at the faces around me and wondered how many would return.

The Russians had also tried to force the back door to the Isthmus. They had sent several divisions north of Lake Ladoga in an outflanking movement to bottle up the Mannerheim Line from the rear. But in this sector the Finns had been able to use guerrilla tactics. They had attacked and destroyed one division and chopped another into small remnants, surrounded and iso-lated from their bases. Ed Beattie, Ed Hartrich and I were now on our way to the GHQ of the Lake Ladoga front, near the town of Sortavala, to see the spoils of the victory.

Normally the trip from Helsinki to Sortavala was only a six- or seven-hour run, but the railroads had been disrupted by bomb-ing and the journey took nearly two days. Some of the time we read and some of the time just stared out of the window. The great sweep of snow was not monotonous; there was an awesome grandeur about it, and every now and then you caught a picture which stamped itself vividly on your memory. I remember the hospital trains moving slowly across the white panorama, the blinds pulled down and the red crosses painted on the sides frozen over with ice; the freight trains panting into the stations, some of them with cars riddled with machine-gun bullets or smashed where bombs had hit them. I remember the cavalry train headed for the front; the doors of the box-cars were open and we caught a glimpse of the soldiers and horses. Some of them stood in the openings – huge men with brilliant red cheeks, dressed in fur caps and ankle-length coats – a race of giants going to war.

In the daylight, with the brilliant blue sky and the sparkling snow, it was difficult to feel the drama of the struggle going on, but at night a grim curtain fell. We arrived at the town of

Pieksämäki as it was getting dark, and from there to Elisenvaara, about a hundred miles away, we travelled in the wake of terrible destruction. Russian planes had been bombing all afternoon, and we were the first train to pass through the area since the attack had taken place. Often we stopped for several hours at a time while workmen tested the rails. We passed through countless villages with only the framework of houses silhouetted against the snow; others had collapsed in a crazy fashion, and still others were blackened by fire and blast. At one of the stations we had such a long wait we made our way across the platform and asked the stationmaster for the hotel. He was a huge man bundled up in a white coat and hood. He couldn't speak English very well; he could only shake his head, point to the sky, and say, 'Molotov.' But we knew what he meant.

We pulled into Elisenvaara to find the station burning. It was a terrible spectacle, for an icy wind had whipped the flames into a roaring inferno. They licked the dark sky savagely, turning the snow pink for miles around. Men with buckets and hoses were trying to get them under control, but it looked a hopeless task. The soldiers surged off the train to make another connection, and our last glimpse of them was standing on the platform, silhouetted against the red night.

We arrived at Sortavala the following morning. Normally the town had a population of thirteen thousand inhabitants, but now it was almost deserted. In spite of its gaily painted pink and white houses, it presented a desolate appearance. We passed through street after street entirely razed to the ground, with only a forlorn row of chimneys and a heap of bricks to mark the spot where houses had stood. Although there was little left to bomb, a Finnish press officer who met us at the local hotel told us the bombers still came over several times a day.

Unlike most Finns, generally reserved and rather dour, our press officer, known to all as 'Larry', was a gay young man. He told us he had learned English by going to see Al Jolson in *The Singing Fool* eighteen times. He drove us out to a country villa, about fifteen miles outside the town, which was being used as press headquarters. Here we slept for the next two nights. It was a charming villa on the shores of the lake, and in the summer must have been a delightful place to live. But in the winter it was a different matter. The wind whistled through the thin walls and it was impossible to light any of the fires for fear the smoke would attract the enemy's attention. 'None of the houses around here light fires,' 'Larry' explained. 'If the Russians thought people were living in these villas they'd be sure to bomb them.' When we went outside we were cautioned to keep to the path so that we wouldn't leave footprints in the snow. In spite of all these precautions the villa was bombed a few days after we left and 'Larry' informed me cheerfully that one of the bombs had gone straight through my room.

'Larry' made arrangements for us to visit the front the day we arrived. As the roads were continuously swept by enemy planes it was impossible to travel in the daylight and we didn't set out until late afternoon. We stopped at GHQ and picked up a Finnish Army officer – a captain who had taken part in the battle. We drove through miles of countryside, deserted save for an occasional farmhouse, but as we neared the front we heard the rumble of trucks and the jingle of sleighs. We passed a long line of lorries hauling back captured field guns, then a column of white-hooded soldiers in small horse-drawn sleds, stacked high with ammunition. For the next five miles the road and the woods were alive with Finnish soldiers hauling back their war booty. It was getting dark and we could only half distinguish the objects that passed us.

The scene at the front was even more terrible than the 'dead man's land' of Suomussalmi. The night accentuated the gruesomeness; a full moon shone uncertainly through dark-moving clouds and the rising wind moaned through the pine trees, blowing sudden gusts of snow across the roadway like the fitful passage of evil spirits. Before us lay the dreadful wreckage of the battle. The road was strewn with the hulks of tanks turned half over like giant beetles, with field-kitchens, battered lorries and heavy guns. And on either side of the road, scattered through the woods, lay hundreds of frozen bodies of the dead, shapeless mounds beneath a blanket of freshly fallen snow.

It was only when you saw the carnage of the battles that you realised how deadly and dramatic these forest wars had been. You could visualise the Russian columns moving down the roads, every now and then the heavy tanks and tractors floundering into the snowbanks, blocking the advance for hours; you could picture the Russian soldiers, with their deep superstitious fear of the forests, clinging in bewilderment to the roadside, and the invisible, white-coated Finns creeping up from behind the trees to launch their attack. I remember one of the Russian prisoners in the internment camp summing it up naïvely: 'The trouble was, we could never *see* the Finns!'

We walked for two miles along the road until we turned a bend and came within sight of the Russian lines, a dark rolling hill about half a mile away. As we trudged along we heard the sharp crack of bullets singing through the forests, and every now and then the low rumble of artillery. Several times the sky lighted up with a sudden flash as the Finnish guns opened up behind us. In the woods on either side of the road were hundreds of pits dug under the snow and walled by logs, where the Russians had lived. Near one of the dug-outs, among a litter of books and cartridge-cases, we found an odd object: a woman's shoe. We discovered it was a Finnish shoe which had probably been looted by one of the soldiers to give as a present upon his return to Russia.

The suffering which the Russian troops must have undergone living week after week in the bitterly cold forests wasn't difficult to imagine. Their food had given out some time before and for the last ten days they had lived on bits of horseflesh and occasional meagre supplies dropped by planes. 'But even when we had them completely surrounded and their position was hopeless,' said the Finnish captain, 'they refused to surrender.'

This was partly due to the propaganda leaflets dropped by aeroplanes promising them aid would soon arrive; and partly to the fact that Russian soldiers were systematically told that Finns shot their prisoners. Carl Meidner, a photographer who was taking pictures for *Life*, told me that when the Finns had brought in a Russian prisoner at Salla, he had asked the guard to bring the man into a barn so he could photograph him. The Russian walked into the shed and when the light of the camera flashed he crumpled to the ground in a heap. A few seconds later he rose slowly, rubbing himself, with a bewildered expression on his face. He thought he had been taken into the barn to be shot; when he was convinced he was still intact, he ran up to Carl, clasped his hands and thanked him over and over again.

The Finnish captain led us off the road, a few yards into the woods. He said when the attack came many of the Russians huddled together like sheep; at one point, five hundred of them, refusing to surrender, had been mowed down in a single heap. But the most ghastly sight was the dead gun-crew. In the moonlight they looked like badly executed waxworks: one of them had fallen over the gun carriage, his hands still on the lanyard, two of them sprawled against the wheels, and a fourth lay half propped up against the tree as though he were still giving orders.

'Poor devils!' said the Captain with sudden compassion. 'I suppose they didn't even know what they were fighting about.'

Curiously enough, although the Finnish soldiers were waging one of the most desperate struggles in history, most of them had little hatred for the Russian soldiers. Their feelings were more akin to pity. I heard many of them express horror at the fact that the enemy was made to advance like cattle on completely hopeless attacks. 'We don't mind shooting them with rifles,' continued the Captain, 'but what's so horrible is when they won't surrender and we have to mow the whole lot of them down with machine-guns!' I remembered the officer at Suomussalmi who told me on a similar occasion that one of his machine-gunners had gone mad and came back to the dug-out with tears streaming down his face.

We walked up the road for two miles. I learned that the Finns had used only a few thousand men against two Russian divisions numbering about thirty thousand. But the Captain seemed much more worried about the Russian advance on the Isthmus than in his own victory. 'We can hold them up in the forests,' he said, 'but on the Isthmus it's a different matter.' Then he asked with an almost touching anxiety: 'Do you think the outside world will be disappointed in the Finnish Army?'

In spite of their fantastic victories, the Finns, a quiet, reserved people, made no show of bravado. The only thing which they were openly gleeful about was the capture of Russian war material. At almost every front the officers delightedly showed you their captured guns and field-glasses. As we were walking along, the Captain found a Russian pistol half buried in the snow, and the chauffeur was lucky enough to ferret out a rifle. All the way back they discussed the relative merits of their newly acquired weapons, as pleased as a couple of children.

We started back for our villa at Sortavala about midnight. We dropped the Captain off at headquarters. Before he shook hands with me, he pulled a red star out of his pocket – a star embossed with the hammer and sickle, worn by Russian officers on their caps.

The first time I'd seen one of these stars was on a train coming down from the north. At one of the stops two wounded Finnish soldiers climbed on. They had evidently just come from the front, for they were still wearing their white capes. One of them had a bandage round his head, the other a leg in splints. They sat down across from me and nodded politely. Then the second one pointed to his leg and said, 'Molotov.' He didn't leave me in doubt as to what had happened to the Russians unlucky enough to have taken a shot at him, for he then produced a wallet from his uniform pocket and proudly showed me three red stars. He evidently collected them with the same fervour that cowboys used to notch their guns.

The Captain handed me the star, bowed solemnly, and said: 'With the compliments of a Russian major.' I wore it on my bracelet for a few days, but every time it caught my eye I wondered to whom it had belonged. I finally took it off and put it away.

* * *

We returned to Helsinki to learn that the attack on the Isthmus was increasing in fury. On the ten-mile Summa section the Russians fired three hundred thousand shells in twenty-four hours – nearly three times the number of shells used by the British Army during any one day of the Great War. The Russians had thrown nearly four hundred thousand men into the attack – a hundred thousand more men than the total of the Finnish Army fighting on four fronts. Although the Finnish communiqué revealed little, by studying the map you could see the Russians were slowly battering their way through the Mannerheim zone of fortifications. But you could only guess at what was happening, for no journalists were allowed to cover the attack.

We had been permitted to visit front-line positions before a battle began; to talk to Russian prisoners; to inspect captured war material; to be bombed as often as we liked – or didn't like. We had been allowed to visit forest patrols, and some of us had been lucky enough to be at headquarters when minor skirmishes had taken place. But no journalist was allowed at any front while a major battle was taking place. For news we had to rely on the laconic official communiqué which was handed out in Helsinki each evening; on land operations it usually averaged no more than a hundred and fifty words.

The reason the Finns observed these restrictions was that success depended on the secrecy of their movements, the surprise of their outflanking attacks, and the cunning of their strategy. They couldn't take the chance of correspondents, with first-hand knowledge of their tactics, leaving the country and inadvertently giving information to the enemy. It was also forbidden by the censorship to criticise the Russian tactics for fear the enemy might profit by his mistakes and correct them; and, needless to say, the number of Finnish troop concentrations and casualties were never revealed.

The journalists, therefore, could work only on conjecture. The press room of the Hotel Kämp overflowed with correspondents from a dozen different capitals, arguing, doubting, grumbling, questioning. The telephone rang continuously. From one end of the hotel to the other you could hear journalists shouting their stories across Europe – to Stockholm, Copenhagen, Amsterdam, Paris and London, and even across the Atlantic to New York. Much to everyone's annoyance, New York was the only connection so distinct you could hear as well as though you were sitting in the next room. I usually telegraphed my stories to London, but they were often delayed for five or six hours, and occasionally I was forced to telephone. The line was so bad I had to repeat every word three or four times, and I hate to think what the charges must have been. Some of the delay, however, was due to the fact that the *Sunday Times* telegrapher couldn't understand my American accent; once, in desperation, I handed the telephone to Eddie Ward.

'I say, is that really Mr Ward speaking? Why, I heard you over the radio only an hour ago. And am I really talking to *Helsinki*? By Jove! What's it like there? Pretty cold, eh?'

The communiqué was issued every evening about eight o'clock and there was always a mad scramble among the big agencies as to who got the news over the wires first. All of them put in telephone calls to Amsterdam, Stockholm and Copenhagen – blitz calls at nine times the normal rate. Once the Associated Press hung on to the telephone for twenty-five minutes waiting for the communiqué to be issued. Five minutes after hanging up in despair a call came through for the United Press, and at the same moment a boy walked into the room with the communiqué. Black looks were exchanged. As a matter of fact, all calls that came through seemed to be for the United Press, and I learned later this was due to a very handsome arrangement with the Hotel Kämp telephone operator.

The daily routine was constantly interrupted by the air-raid sirens. Although Helsinki was bombed only twice during the war – and not badly at that – when the warnings sounded everything ceased automatically. Unlike Spain, everyone was forced to take cover. Customers were cleared from shops and restaurants, people evicted from their offices and pedestrians shooed from the streets. The city became so quiet you could almost hear a pin drop.

As the sirens sounded five or six times a day the boredom was immense. The policemen on the street corners occasionally tried to break the monotony by starting snowball fights. Guests in the Kämp dining room shook their heads angrily, picked up their plates, and carried them across the street to the shelters in the park. You heard the telephone operators cutting off the calls with the outside world in voices of irritation: 'Sorry, Copenhagen, we're having another warning.'

Journalists had special permission to stay above ground, but even so it was impossible to go on working. Besides the operators knocking off, the Finnish press officers surged downstairs, and even the censors stopped censoring. The censors, by the way, were mysterious people who lived behind barred doors. No one ever saw them. A boy took your copy to them and when it came back red-pencilled you might as well complain to God for all the good it did. We used to watch the people filing into the shelter and try to guess which were the censors. There was one very old gentleman who always carried a black satchel. We were sure he was one of them and took great pains to smile at him until we discovered he was the local veterinary.

Owing to the inconveniences of the alarms, many foreign diplomats and attachés moved out to Grankulla, a town about fifteen miles from Helsinki, where they could carry on their work undisturbed. Here I found Frank Hayne, the assistant American military attaché to Moscow with whom I had made the trip through the Ukraine the year before. He had been transferred to Finland for the war and greeted me jovially. 'I thought you'd turn up sooner or later. I saw your friend Martha Gellhorn a few weeks ago and we were wondering where you were.'

Martha had come to Finland in December to write an article for *Collier's* and had left a few days after the war broke out. Frank had never met her before, but on the night that the Russians presented the Finns with an ultimatum threatening to bomb Helsinki off the map unless their demands were accepted, he saw a beautiful, demure-looking blonde sitting in the corner of the Kämp restaurant. He thought she was an American and much in need of protection. He went up, introduced himself, told her about the ultimatum and asked her if she wanted to be evacuated.

'Christ, yes.'

Frank, somewhat taken aback, told her to go upstairs and get her things. 'And five minutes later,' he said, 'she came downstairs with a pair of pyjamas and a bottle of whisky. I knew at once *that* girl had been evacuated before.'

Frank's activities were even more curtailed than those of the journalists. The Finnish authorities were unwilling to allow the German and Italian military attachés at the front, and, being unable to discriminate against them separately, made it a set rule that no attachés could visit the front. Frank pored over the maps and studied the positions on the Mannerheim Line, but with only scanty information it was difficult for him to determine the true state of affairs. One day, Frank's Finnish chauffeur received a letter from his brother, who was an officer on the Isthmus. Frank had the letter translated into English, and one day when Ed Beattie and I had lunch with him, he showed it to us. This was the letter:

Dugout Cat,
February 10, 1940. 6.35 a.m.

Dear Brother,
Now I know what an artillery barrage is like. Friend 'Klim' Voroshilov certainly has done his best to appease the 'father of nations' and to slake his thirst for blood. He has tried and tried again and is continuing to try to break our resistance, but with

bloody heads the Russians have been thrown back time and time again.

Thousands of them lie bleeding in silent, immobile shapes on these sparkling February snowfields. They share the fate of the other thousands who in former times have invited the carrion birds and wolves of our forests to a feast.

If there had not been that frightful, tearing artillery fire with its rending explosions, one would almost have felt pity for the grey Russian masses who in their long overcoats waded up to their thighs in soft snow against the death-spitting mouths of our machine-guns. Obediently and silently, they came, trying to make use of armoured shields, but in vain. Everything was futile. Murderous fire swept the field time after time leaving only twisting heaps of bodies, which soon became immobile.

The tanks advancing ahead of the infantry were destroyed by our anti-tank weapons and by skilfully thrown bundles of hand grenades tied together. One would have felt sorry for these grey hordes marching to the slaughter, but the incessant artillery fire aroused merciless hate in us who were subjected to it.

I am not ashamed to confess that artillery fire to me, as well as to most of the others, is simply revolting. I have not yet suffered from 'artillery sickness', although I feel like pressing my hands against my ears and crying out in pain. The explosion of six-inch shells on an average of every fourth second during nine consecutive hours, the incessant detonations, screaming splinters and blinding bursts of flame create in our bodies unspeakable terror, which can be overcome only by exercising one's entire psychic courage. It is killing to try to be an example to one's men; to joke, suck calmly on one's pipe, feeling at the same time that every nerve is taut as a violin string.

To know that if one should for one second give up one's
self-control the hands would begin to shake, the head to nod
and the eyes to flinch, which has happened to several of my
men. It is terrible to try to make such a man carry on his duty
by encouragement and threats, but so far I have succeeded
and every time prompt action has been required the men have
been ready.

If the Russians had been subjected to a fraction of the
drum-fire that has been poured over us in the last twenty-
four hours, the entire seventh army of the USSR would
have been in wild, panicky flight towards their steppes. The
superiority of material and masses is so overwhelming that it
is inconceivable how we can withstand it, but we do.

Up to now I have been afraid that we either stand or fall,
but now there is no longer an alternative – we will stand.
The whole battalion has lost only one man dead (he died
in a field hospital) and we have had on the average one
wounded man every second day. Usually the wounds have not
been dangerous. I have not lost any of my men, not even as
wounded, although our quarters are far from being safe.

A couple of men have gone off their heads, and a couple
of others are on the way, but it is because of our heavy guard
and patrol duty and the consequent lack of sleep, not because
of anxiety. We are tired, and we need beside pursuit-planes,
guns and anti-tank instruments, men – plenty of men who
would at least do manual labour and stand guard duty so that
we could get some rest once in a while. I know that we are
going to be replaced soon and taken to the rear to rest, and
then I hope to get a few days' leave. But at the same time my
mind is burdened with anxiety for those who remain here. Not
because of any fear of defeat, but because, while the Russians

change their men four times, we can change ours but once, and we always have fresh forces against us. My dear brother, what is Sweden doing for us? And will England and America help? Write soon and tell me. I am starved for news.

Yours,
Lassie.

Flags at Half-Mast

A group of Finns, patrolling across the bay of Viipuri, came upon a Russian soldier who was lost and had been wandering about the ice for hours. He was a miserable spectacle, half frozen, with a shaggy beard and clothes in rags. When he saw the Finns, his arms shot into the air in surrender. 'Don't shoot! I am a Russian capitalist.'

I never discovered whether or not this story was true; it was published in all the Finnish papers and provided people with one of the few laughs they had those last grim days. At the beginning of March the Finnish communiqué announced that the Russians were fighting on the outskirts of Viipuri – which meant they had broken through the Mannerheim defences. The Finnish press staff came in looking white and strained. Miss Helsinkius, the girl who usually arranged our trips, was in tears. What the Finnish losses were, none of us knew. Whether or not the Finns could continue the war once Viipuri fell was, therefore, a matter of speculation.

It was an extraordinary situation. On all the other fronts the Russian advances had been halted by some of the most spectacular fighting in history; on the Waistline front, Russian attempts to drive through to the Gulf of Bothnia, cutting Finland in two, had met with smashing defeats and a loss of nearly eight-five thousand lives; on the Arctic front the Russian sweep down the Great Arctic Highway to the centre of Finland was stopped after a penetration of only seventy miles; and on the front north of Lake Ladoga the Russian thrust designed to outflank the Mannerheim Line had been broken.

But on the Isthmus the story was a different one. Although the Finns had succeeded in out-manoeuvring and out-fighting the Russians on every occasion where strategy and tactics had come into play, on the Isthmus front – the only sector in Finland where actual trench warfare was taking place – only two things counted: men and guns. Wave after wave of Russians had fallen before the Finnish fire, but there were always more to take their place. The Finns, with a total army of only three hundred thousand – no more than half of which could be used on the Isthmus – had not been able to risk their men in large-scale counter-attacks; and the Russians, through tremendous superiority, had succeeded in smashing their way forward.

But apart from the army chiefs, the politicians, and a handful of people in the Press Bureau, the majority of Finns had little conception of the true situation. The Finnish papers were filled with the victories in the north, and the official communiqués on the Isthmus battle were so brief it was impossible to draw conclusions from them. The Finns knew they could not hold out indefinitely against overwhelming odds, but most of them clung to a deep and stubborn faith that some unforeseen event would save them from final destruction. Morale was high and fierce and on all sides you heard the dictum: 'The Russians will only conquer when every Finn is dead.'

Much of this passionate determination was due to inbred contempt for Russians. The proud and capable Finns regarded them as an uncivilised horde. One night I rode around Helsinki in a sleigh driven by a huge Finn with a drooping moustache. He had a large medal pinned on his coat which he had won against the Russians in 1918. He took me past the old Greek Orthodox church with its onion domes glittering in the moonlight like diamonds; then through the bombarded section, where the charred remains of houses lying beneath a sheet of ice presented a gruesome contrast. The windows of the abandoned Russian Legation had been shattered by a bomb and the white curtains blew out into the night air, beckoning like hundreds of ghostly arms. 'What animal,' asked the driver, 'most resembles a human being?' The answer was so obvious he did not give me a chance to reply. 'The Russian,' he roared, and went into a fit of laughter that echoed all the way down the street.

With this common sentiment in mind the Finns were determined to fight to the end; when the following paragraph was published, without comment, on March 8th, the public dismissed it with a laugh:

> According to information in possession of the Finnish Government, the Soviet Union is believed to have planned the presentation of demands to Finland of a more far-reaching character than those presented last Autumn. Details, however, of these demands are so far lacking.

A few people were puzzled, then drew the optimistic conclusion that the Russians' enormous losses were beginning to tell; that they were trying to open conversations in an effort to make a peace that would save their face.

But in the press room the tune was a different one. The telephone rang continuously as queries poured in from all over Europe. 'Is it true the Finns have lost a third of their army? Have peace negotiations started? What terms are they discussing? Can you verify whether Sweden is acting as mediator?'

We couldn't verify anything. Bottled up as we were in Helsinki, we were at a loss to know what was happening ourselves. Every journalist had a theory of his own. Some claimed the capture of Viipuri was not of strategic importance and the Russians still had a long way to go; others that the Finns were beaten; still others that they would fight to the bitter end. Ed Beattie was pessimistic. He had a long and sorry list of wars behind him: Abyssinia, China and Poland. 'The Finns were doing all right until I got here,' he remarked gloomily. 'Now the jig's up.'

There was so little information in Helsinki I decided to go to Stockholm to see if I could get a story there. Eddie Ward was also leaving, so we travelled to Vaasa together by train, and then flew across the Gulf. Negotiations or no negotiations, the Russian bombers were as active as ever. The journey took nearly thirty-six hours; again those burning towns; those interminable waits; those short blasts by the engine whistle that sent everyone stumbling through the snow to take cover in the woods.

There was a Frenchman on the train, a rather timid creature, who mislaid his tickets, lost his baggage and asked the porter a dozen times in a harassed and nervous voice when we were due to arrive. He seemed so hopelessly out of his depth that we were sorry for him. It was only when we climbed aboard the aeroplane at Vaasa that we learned he was Colonel de la Roque, the dynamic French *Croix de Feu* (Fascist) leader.

We arrived in Stockholm on March 11th. On the same day the Finns issued a communiqué admitting that peace discussions were being held in Moscow and that Sweden was acting as mediator. That was all. There were no details, and the lobby of the Grand Hotel was filled with journalists trying to get a 'line' on the conversations. That night Gordon Young of Reuter's invited Eddie and me to dine with himself and Mr Erkko, the Finnish Minister to Sweden. Erkko was non-committal, but genial; he gave us champagne and confided nothing. We told him we might return to Helsinki in a day or so, and, as it was impossible to secure seats on the plane without reserving them several days in advance, he offered to get them for us at an hour's notice.

The following day there were more peace rumours. I ran into a Danish journalist – I don't know his name – who told me he was positive an agreement had been reached in Moscow, but was unable to get official confirmation of it. He said that Sweden, intimidated by Germany, had refused to allow the transit of troops from England and France, and had forced the Finns to throw their hand in. Eddie and I had decided to return to Helsinki that night and rang up Mr Erkko to arrange for the aeroplane seats. Not expecting a reply, but just as a parting shot, Eddie said to him: 'Is it true that an agreement has been reached in Moscow?' To our astonishment, Erkko replied that it was. (Why he admitted it to Eddie, I never discovered, for he spent the rest of the evening emphatically denying it.)

This gave Eddie a world-wide scoop. He sent a telegram to London which was read over the BBC on the six o'clock news – the first semi-official report that the Finnish–Russian War had come to an end. We arrived at the Stockholm aerodrome about seven o'clock – an hour later – and heard the people in the waiting room discussing it. One of the passengers, a Finnish colonel, commented on it angrily. He turned to Eddie and said: 'Did you hear the report the BBC is putting out? That fellow – Ward Price, I think his name is – must be crazy. Peace! We'll make peace when the Russians withdraw every last soldier from Finland. And not before!' Eddie agreed and quickly moved away.

When we took off from the aerodrome the lights of Stockholm sparkled like diamonds against the snow and we wondered what price Sweden had paid to keep them blazing. It was a sad trip. Eddie and I were apparently the only passengers who knew what we were returning to, and somehow it seemed to make it worse. I looked at the faces around me, strong, confident faces, and dared not think what the following day would bring. The pilot was the same man who had flown me to Turku two months before. He took the usual precautions of wiring ahead to find if the way was clear, of circling the aerodrome and dropping his flares. In fact, everything was the same except that the trip was slightly more dangerous, for six or seven seats had been ripped out of the plane and the floor packed with boxes marked: 'Explosives – Second Class'.

We arrived at Turku about midnight and drove to Helsinki the following morning in a bus. Although it was March 12th, the day the peace terms were announced, people were still unaware of what was in store for them. The Turku morning paper carried headlines of the number of Russian planes shot down the previous day. The only item referring to the negotiations was a small box in the corner of the front page announcing that foreign radio stations were reporting a solution had been reached in Moscow. And this was encircled by a large question mark.

It didn't seem to attract much attention. The bus was packed with farm girls and road-workers with white capes over their clothes, who read the papers casually; they appeared to find nothing unusual in them. We stopped at one of the villages for coffee and the driver told us if the air-raid alarm sounded to climb in the bus as fast as possible so that we could get under way once more before the police stopped us and forced us into a shelter.

We drove up in front of the Hotel Kämp at eleven o'clock, just as the radio was blaring out the announcement that peace had been made. But it was not until an hour later when the Foreign Minister, Mr Tanner, spoke, that the people of Finland realised they had been defeated.

The shock was staggering. None of them imagined they were even approaching capitulation; and many actually thought it was the Russians who had been forced to come to terms. The people on the streets seemed completely dazed. The Finnish women in the press room broke down and wept and the men turned their faces away. None of the journalists knew what to do. Commiseration seemed hopelessly inadequate. I was so miserable I went downstairs and sat in a corner of the half-empty restaurant. A group of officers came in and took the table next to me. They had the latest edition of the morning paper in which the peace terms were published. They read it silently, then one of them crumpled it up angrily and threw it on the floor. No one spoke. They just sat there staring into space. I went out and walked down the street. The flags of Finland were flying at half-mast.

That same afternoon workmen began replacing the bulbs in the street lamps and ripping down the wooden protections from the shop windows. Otherwise, there was little change in Helsinki. You expect a national crisis to mark itself on the face of a city, but somehow it never does. War or peace, peace or war, life manages to drag on in a more or less routine fashion. People filled the shops, the restaurants, the cinemas, as they always did. The only real contrast was in the press room. A few days previously it was a scene of wild confusion; now it was almost deserted. The slate which used to announce the time the communiqué would be released was wiped clean, but tacked above it was a slip of paper:

'BOMBING NEWS WILL BE GIVEN OUT AT TWENTY-THREE O'CLOCK.'

No one bothered to take it down.

* * *

Twenty-four hours later, with the flags still flying at half-mast, miles of country roads resounded to the rumble of lorries and the jingle of sleighs as the evacuation of four hundred thousand people began.

The port town of Hanko, about eighty miles from Helsinki, was the first territory to fall beneath the sickle and hammer. I drove there with Frank Hayne and Eddie Ward. The streets were thronged with a medley of firemen, farmers, gunners, shopkeepers and policemen, who had volunteered to help with the evacuation; everywhere there were army trucks and sledges, groaning under furniture and household goods.

We spent several hours wandering about in a temperature of fifteen degrees below zero. The spectacle was a grim one, for Hanko had been badly bombed and we passed block after block with only gaping caverns to mark the places where houses had stood. When I had last visited Hanko, two months before, ten buildings along the main street, hit by incendiary bombs, were burning. Today there were no fires or air-raid alarms; only the wind sweeping desolately through houses with no window-panes; only shops with caved-in roofs and charred ruins thickly buried under layers of ice and snow.

In the midst of these grim ruins the evacuation was going on. From one house with a bomb crater only ten feet away and a front blackened by blast, two soldiers were carrying tables and chairs piled high on their backs; from another, three small children were bringing kitchen utensils and packing them carefully onto a small sled; from a third, an old man was carrying a mattress stacked with lamps and crockery. The sidewalks in front of the houses were covered with dressers, sewing-machines, bicycles, pictures and stoves waiting to be put on the lorries.

We talked to many of the people and found that grief had already given way to bitter resentment. Why had Finland made peace? According to General Mannerheim, the Finns had lost only fifteen thousand dead, and 'after sixteen weeks of bloody battle with no rest by day or by night our army still stands unconquered'.

What had happened? Why had Finland not continued the fight? In his last Order of the Day, General Mannerheim had said:

We were not prepared for war with a Great Power. While our brave soldiers were defending our frontiers we had, by insuperable efforts, to procure what we lacked. We had to construct lines of defence where there were none. We had to try to obtain help, which failed to come. We had to find arms and equipment at a time when all nations were feverishly arming against the storm which sweeps over the world. Your heroic deeds have aroused the admiration of the world, but after three and a half months of war we are still almost alone. We have not obtained more foreign help than two reinforced battalions equipped with artillery and aircraft for our fronts, where our own men, fighting day and night without the possibility of being relieved, have had to meet the attacks of ever fresh enemy forces, straining their physical and moral powers beyond all limits. . . . Unfortunately, the valuable promises of assistance which the Western Powers had given us, *could not be realised when our neighbours* (*Sweden and Norway*), *concerned for their own security, refused the right of transit for troops.* (Italics, my own.)

There it was – the fine hand of Germany. But why, people asked, had Finland plunged into a hopeless war to begin with if only to capitulate, still unbeaten, to even more drastic terms than had been submitted in the first place? Not only in Hanko, but from the Finns in Helsinki, you heard many bitter remarks. 'Our politicians have betrayed us. There is no life this way. Far better to have fought to the end . . .'

The people who were being evacuated felt it even more strongly. Eddie and I talked to a soldier wheeling a bicycle through the snow, and Frank's Finnish-American chauffeur translated his remarks. He told us he was a garage mechanic who had lived all his life in Hanko. He said when he heard of the peace he refused to believe it. Even now it was a bad dream. 'If it was necessary to make concessions in other directions, very well. But the Russians should have been made to *fight* for Hanko – every inch of the way.'

Near the police station we talked to a woman and daughter who ran a small *pension*. They had just registered their names for a lorry to evacuate their belongings.

'When it comes I don't know where we'll go. We've got no relatives and no other prospects of making a living.'

The mother shook her head sadly. 'Perhaps it's wrong to say it, but it would almost make me happy to hear the sirens again.'

But we found that what people seemed to resent the most was turning over their houses to Russians, who, they feared, would take little care of them. Three nurses, standing at the street corner, told us it wouldn't be so bad if any other nation were occupying Hanko, but try as she would, it was impossible to think of the Russians as human beings. The second one agreed. 'At least, they won't find anything in my house but four walls and a roof. I've even taken the brass water-taps away.'

'Yes,' said the third. 'But what a pity it is we have to leave our water tower for them.' She pointed to the old brick tower, an ancient landmark in the middle of the town.

'Oh, don't worry about that. After a day or so they're sure to have it out of commission.'

An old man, a factory worker, joined the group just before we left. 'We've had a lot of bombs fall on Hanko since November thirtieth,' he said, 'but the worst bomb of all has been this peace.'

Everyone nodded.

* * *

Richard Busvine of the Chicago *Times*, Eddie and I left Helsinki a few days later. Once again we had the strange experience of passing from one war atmosphere to another. We took a plane to Stockholm, a train to Malmo, another plane to London. At Malmo, the aerodrome waiting room was overflowing with people. Suddenly a man shouted in a loud voice: 'Please form two lines. Berlin passengers to the left. London passengers to the right.' Everyone surged apart and stood glaring angrily at each other. Then they filed through the door and climbed aboard their respective planes. The engines roared. First one disappeared into the grey haze, then the other.

'Who said "never the twain shall meet"?' asked Richard.

'Bit awkward, that,' said Eddie. 'I wish those people would stay in their own b—— country.'

'You and a hundred million others,' said Richard sourly.

Part VIII

THE FALL OF FRANCE

1

Spring-Time Is Hitler-Time

London was a pleasant place to be that last week in March and that first week in April. The sun streamed down on the first spring flowers and the air was warm and sweet. I walked through St James's Park thinking how good it was to see green grass again. I drank in the scene around me: the fat, pink-cheeked children with their nannies; the two old ladies sitting on a bench with high button boots and top-heavy hats like a George Belcher drawing; the man in the pin-striped suit, grey hat, spats and tightly rolled umbrella striding briskly in the direction of Whitehall. Ahead of me two very old gentlemen were in earnest conversation. As I passed them I heard one remonstrating indignantly about the number of old houses being torn down to make way for modern ones.

I smiled. With the world on the threshold of a titanic struggle, with hundreds of thousands of houses soon to crash to the ground, these gentle protests seemed almost comical. It was the sort of conversation you expected to hear from two very old gentlemen strolling through St James's Park. When I first came to London that curious detachment known as 'English insularity' used to bewilder and alarm me. Now I found something strangely comforting in the placid, unruffled atmosphere. You felt that no matter what happened, London would always stand. Everything about it was so slow, methodical and deliberate. The routine of life seemed as determined as the regulated moves of nature. Even the ponderous houses and the heavy buses had an air of stability about them. I remembered Martha's remark: 'If the world ever comes to an end and if there is only one person left, it's bound to be an Englishman.' I had a feeling she was right.

Underneath this air of serenity, everyone knew the great test was coming soon. But most people were determined not to let it worry them till it happened; shops and restaurants were crowded and the debutantes still sat up all night at the Nut House.

Freda had closed her house and I went to live with Anne O'Neill at Montagu Square. As Anne's husband, Shane, was serving with a regiment in the north of Ireland and her two children were in the country, half the house was shut up; but the atmosphere was far from gloomy. Gay and pretty, Anne refused to allow the problems of war-time housekeeping to disturb her, and every afternoon dozens of people drifted in for tea. One day her Irish maid, Lily, who had been with her for a good many years, grumbled about the irregularity of the household, complaining that none of the servants was doing any work. 'The trouble is, they're taking advantage of the situation. They all know how young and foolish your Ladyship is.'

Young but far from foolish, Anne went on her way unperturbed, and 35 Montagu Square ran as joyfully and haphazardly as ever. Finland seemed a long way off. I stayed in bed till noon and spent the rest of the day shopping. It was a peaceful life, that last week of the 'bore' war. Even the newspaper headlines were unalarming: April 1st, 'Allies Tighten Blockade'; April 2nd, 'Toll of War Strain on German Workers'; April 3rd, 'Nazis Accuse Norway Neutrality Violation'; April 4th, 'Reynaud says: No "Phoney" Peace'; April 5th, 'Chamberlain says: Hitler Misses the Bus'; April 6th, 'Halifax Sends Notes to Norway and Sweden – "Don't be Afraid of Nazi Bullies"'; April 7th, 'British Envoys Plan Tighten Trade Grip Germany'.

During the week I went over to collect some books which I had left with Mrs Sullivan and was surprised to find her apprehensive. Impending disaster usually left her unperturbed. Her fat face beamed when she saw me.

'My goodness, you must have been cold in Finland. It made me shiver to read about it. When Sullivan came home on leave I said to him: "Poor Miss Cowles, the way she used to shiver in this flat without any central heating. I don't expect we'll ever see her again. That's the trouble with Americans," I said, "living in those overheated houses of theirs and never eating anything so they're all skin and bones." Old Sullivan said, "Now, if it 'ad been me I wouldn't 'ave felt the cold at all." Cheeky, isn't he? I say, miss, what sort of people are the Finns? What colour are they?'

Her face fell when I told her they were just ordinary people like herself.

'I had an idea they were red like Eskimos. Well, it's a good thing they did away with all those Russians. There was a Russian woman living in the neighbourhood – I don't know what's happened to her now but I never took to her much. She had those foreign ways. You know, never taking a bath. She cheated me out of three bob once. After that I always thought I'd like Russians better dead than alive.'

Mrs Sullivan went upstairs to collect the books. She brought them down in a cardboard box.

'And didn't my old man enjoy reading them,' she said. 'He particularly liked that book of Mr Lloyd George's – *World Crisis*, isn't it? Do you remember those apples, miss? Pity you can't go down and call on him again. Maybe he'd give us some more. But, Henry, over at the pub, says they'd better get him back in the Government quick or something awful will happen. He said he didn't like that remark of Mr Chamberlain's yesterday – 'Itler's missed the bus. He says buses run every ten minutes, never forget that.'

No one forgot it for long. Four days later when Hitler struck, I thought of Mrs Sullivan's words. That night I wrote in my war diary for the first and only time. A day or so after the declaration of war, Anne and I had walked down to Smythson's in Bond Street and bought ourselves large leather notebooks with gilt-edged pages, determined to keep a day-by-day record. Except for April 9th, mine is still virginal. This is what it says:

Today the Germans invaded Denmark and Norway. I suppose I ought to be used to these awful moments by now, but a chill still goes up my spine. At ten o'clock Esmond Harmsworth rang Anne up with the news Oslo had been bombed; at 11 o'clock Seymour sent us a basket of plover's eggs; at 12 o'clock Poppy Thursby and Bridget Parsons dropped in and ate them.

We turned on the radio and heard a report that the Germans had already made a good many landings at various points along the Norwegian coast. Poppy was belligerent. 'What's happened to our navy, that's what I want to know? Anne, can't you telephone Esmond and find out?'

'Darling, you know how gloomy he is. He'll tell me it's at the bottom of the ocean.'

'But if we haven't got a navy,' insisted Poppy, 'what *have* we got?'

'Mr Chamberlain,' said Bridget.

'Do be serious,' said Poppy. 'You know our army's ridiculous. Still drilling with broomsticks and all that. But the navy's a different matter. If Hitler, with his tuppeny-ha'penny boats can cruise around wherever he pleases, where are we?'

'Dished!' said Anne cheerfully.

Poppy insisted that I ring up someone and try to get some news. I telephoned Webb Miller, but he told me all communications with Scandinavia had been severed and nothing was coming through.

Anne and I lunched with Maureen and Oliver Stanley. I gathered that, Norway or no Norway, an invasion of Holland

was believed to be imminent. The Dutch Minister telephoned
Maureen during lunch and said the country was in a state of
tension and that every precaution had been taken; but so far
no new developments.

In the afternoon, Eddie Ward and Richard Busvine dropped
in for cocktails. They had just come from the Swedish
Consulate where they had tried to get visas for Sweden, but as
Richard said, it was all a lot of wishful thinking, for how the
hell d'you get to Sweden? I advised against. From the point of
view of news it seems more sensible to wait for the invasion
of Holland or Romania than rushing off and getting yourself
bottled up in Sweden for the duration – or for that matter in a
German internment camp.

I had dinner with Tommy Thompson, who spoke
indignantly about the neutrals, always trying to have it both
ways, always refusing to ally themselves with Great Britain
until it was too late. The Government begged the Norwegians
to immobilise some of their ports and aerodromes a few hours
before the German attack, but they didn't do it. And today, of
course, they're all in German hands. He says the Americans
learned a long time ago: 'United we stand, divided we fall.'
Why can't they learn it in Europe? Why? (Instead, they seem
to look the poor old gift-horse straight in the mouth. Before
dinner I telephoned Freda, who's got a Norwegian cook; she
said her kitchen was full of moaning Norwegians, wringing
their hands and crying: 'The trouble with the Bree-tish is, they
are always too late.')

The head-waiter came up to our table – we dined at Scott's –
saying he'd just heard that British troops had already embarked
for Norway. I wonder if it's true. He also told us that the
manager of Scott's – a Dane, with a family in Copenhagen –

had broken down and cried when he heard of the invasion. 'He's not the sort of man to cry,' said the waiter. 'These are terrible days.' Yes, I thought, and worse to come.

Here my diary ended, but I need no notes to remind me of the next few weeks. The war had really started. For six months the Allied powers had blockaded Germany with the object of forcing her to strike out against defences which they believed to be impenetrable.

But Norway came as a surprise. The British Intelligence Service was aware that Germany had been practising large-scale embarkation manoeuvres; but the exercises had begun during the Finnish war and were believed to have achieved their purpose when Scandinavia heeded the Nazi warning and refused to allow the right of transit to Allied troops.

The Government's first reaction was one of optimism. Mr Chamberlain referred to the German move as 'a rash deed'; Mr Churchill said: 'It is as great a strategical blunder and political error as that which was committed by Napoleon in invading Spain.'

But this was a new kind of war. This was the first total 'Fifth Column' war of history. Treachery presented the Germans with seventy per cent of their victory; forged documents and faked orders forbade Norwegians to fire on German ships. Indeed, so cleverly organised were Norway's Quislings that many towns and ports fell into the enemy's hands during the first few hours. By the time British troops landed, their positions were already strategically impossible to defend. On May 2nd, Chamberlain had the sorry task of announcing to the House of Commons that Norway was lost and Great Britain's withdrawal had begun.

The Norwegian campaign had tremendous repercussions. First, it made people Quisling-conscious, impressing them with the revolutionary aspect of Nazism; second, it awakened Britons to the fact that islands were not unconquerable; third, it displaced the Chamberlain Government and brought in Winston Churchill.

Now Mr Churchill had been right on most of the issues where Mr Chamberlain had been wrong. It is curious that on the particular occasion that brought him into power his judgment had been as much at fault as anyone else's. In the House of Commons debate he assumed as First Lord of the Admiralty his full blame for the fiasco. But Mr Lloyd George in a devastating attack on the Government ('The whole world knows that we are in the worst strategic position this country has ever been placed in') replied sharply to Mr Churchill's acceptance of full responsibility, saying that he hoped the First Lord would 'not allow himself to be converted into an air-raid shelter to keep the splinters from hitting his colleagues'.

The blast blew Mr Chamberlain out of office. The country had steadily been losing confidence in the Prime Minister ever since the fateful day of the German occupation of Prague; now, his unfortunate phrase, 'Hitler's missed the bus', was on everyone's lips. When the Opposition called a division and the House voted, Tory MPs ignored the crack of Margesson's whip (for the first time) and the scoreboard showed the figures:

For adjournment	281
Against adjournment	200

The Government majority of only eighty-one was too small for the Prime Minister to carry on. He invited the Opposition to join the Cabinet, but was refused. On March 10th, the day Germany invaded Holland and Belgium, Chamberlain resigned and Winston Churchill became Prime Minister.

I was not in London at the time. On May 2nd, the day the Government announced the withdrawal from Norway, I flew to

Rome. Just before I left I saw Mr Churchill at Maureen Stanley's house. In spite of the disheartening news of the time, he was in vigorous spirits. When I told him I was going to Rome and asked whether or not he thought the Italians were coming into the war, he shook his head.

'I don't know. I certainly hope not. I'm very fond of the Italian people. But if they do,' and here his eyes twinkled, 'of one thing I'm certain – it won't be necessary to go to Pompeii to see the ruins.'

2

Roman Candles Burning at Both Ends

I hadn't seen John Whitaker since the night we had spent under the muzzle of the Sudeten German machine-gun on the Austrian–Czech frontier, nearly a year and a half before. We sat now at a pavement café at the top of the Via Veneto eating a strawberry ice. The sun streamed down and the wind blew gently through the trees and we both thought what a nice place the world ought to be. 'But it isn't,' said John emphatically. 'Why the hell did the British muck up Norway? It's had a disastrous effect here. Particularly in the face of all the initial optimism that came flowing out of London. It's cut the ground right out from under the feet of the anti-German crowd here. People who were getting pretty sore at the Duce for tying them up with the Nazis are beginning to say perhaps the old boy was right after all. No Italian wants to be on the losing side. I don't think they're coming into the war right now, but Mussolini's got the bit between his teeth and anything may happen. In the last few days the temperature's gone up fifty degrees.'

That was May 4th, five weeks before Italy entered the war. You could already feel the tension. Gone was the lazy indifference of the previous August; now everyone pored over the newspapers, clung to the radio, talked, gesticulated, remonstrated, argued and moaned.

You could feel the Nazi grip tightening. Germans were everywhere: the Embassy staff had swollen to over eighty; there were Nazi officials, military experts, all manner of technicians, and an endless flow of tourists. You saw them dancing in the hotel restaurants by night, wandering about the streets, Baedekers in hand, by day. The Italian tourist bureau displayed large posters advertising cut-price trips to Germany; the newspapers carried vitriolic despatches signed by the Deutsches Nachrichtenbüro; the cafés were well stocked with copies of the *Völkischer Beobachter* and the *Berliner Tageblatt*. I was surprised to find that many of the maids, porters and hairdressers in the leading hotels had been replaced by Germans. Everywhere you heard whispers that the Nazi Gestapo was already operating on its own.

Superimposed on the apprehensive atmosphere was an artificial gaiety. It was the big season in Rome; there was a round of feverish entertaining that reminded me of the hectic days in London the summer before the war. I found to my surprise that the idle gentlemen and the elegant ladies of Roman society, usually dismissed as decadent, were standing up fiercely (if inconsequentially) to the pro-German current. They refused to have anything to do with the Germans. It was their proudest boast that not a single German had ever crossed the threshold of the ultra-smart golf club. They went out of their way to entertain members of the British and French Embassies and professed anti-Nazi views with dangerous frankness. Even the beautiful Princess Bismarck, wife of the German Counsellor, was ignored. Rumour had it that the Nazis had sent her to Rome to thaw out some of the chilliest aristocrats – and not to overlook Count Ciano in the rush. (As far as the latter was concerned, however, the French Government had been a jump ahead by exporting a very pretty nineteen-year-old movie actress who was already monopolising his attention.)

I had a good many friends in Rome and each one took me aside and asked me anxiously if I thought America was coming into the war. Many of them were despairing. 'We're already German vassals. Whatever happens, we're doomed. We're caught between the frying-pan and the fire.' One man seriously suggested that I try to get an interview with Mussolini, then shoot him. 'You will have the thanks of the entire Italian Nation,' he said. 'Yes,' I agreed. 'And a harp thrown in.'

In spite of the general pessimism, some of the French and British diplomats believed Ciano to be pro-Ally at heart and clung to the hope that he might prevent Mussolini from throwing in his entire hand with the Germans. I was always doubtful of this. I had heard too often from reliable sources that Ciano was the only man Mussolini trusted. This never sounded to me as if there were any grave differences of opinion. Besides, Ciano seemed too much of a lightweight to maintain an independent line of his own; I felt he was playing a part only, and obeying instructions in maintaining friendly relations with the British and French diplomats so that Mussolini could bargain better with the Germans. However, on this particular occasion, I had little opportunity to judge from personal experience. The first day I went to the golf club I saw Ciano and Alfieri lunching together. They took one look at me, then carefully gazed in the opposite direction. Afterwards I asked Benedetto Cappo Mazzo, the foreign press chief (whom I'd known in the Italian Embassy in Washington), what the trouble was.

'They didn't like the last article you wrote,' he said. 'You said the Italian people weren't with the Duce and that they didn't want to fight.'

'Well, they don't, do they?'

'The point is, you *said* it. Besides that, they think you're dangerous. You're too pro-Ally.'

During the next week I must have encountered Ciano half a dozen times at the golf club, but on each occasion he went to such painful lengths to ignore me I began to feel like Mata Hari.

I did talk, however, with his chief assistant, Signor Anfuso, a dark, wiry little Foreign Office expert. But it was by mistake. I was placed next to him at a lunch-party. He gave me one uneasy look, then plunged into a violent pro-German harangue. I asked him if he'd ever read what Claudius, Emperor of Rome, had written about the Germans, and he replied coldly: 'The modern world has nothing to do with the old one. That's what the democracies can't seem to realise. Their feeble statesmen like to imagine that we Italians are secretly hostile to the Germans. I can assure you of the contrary. We have the same ideas, the same philosophy, the same purpose. In fact, we are perfect complements to one another. What we have, they lack; and what they have, we lack.' (And how, I thought.) 'Make no mistake about it,' he continued. 'The Germans are our allies. We're as good as in the war right now.'

I asked him what he thought Italy's position would be if Germany won, and he replied: 'There's plenty of room for two great powers in Europe.'

I nodded. 'It's just a question of which two.'

With this he turned to his other partner and the conversation ended. I saw only one other Italian official during my ten-day stay and that was Air Marshal Balbo. He came to Rome for twenty-four hours to confer with Mussolini. There were a good many rumours that he was opposed to the Axis Alliance, which I believe were substantiated. I heard from a friend that he warned Mussolini not to judge Allied resistance solely by the Norwegian fiasco; he believed that England and France, with the aid of America, were bound to conquer in the end through a preponderance of reserves and war material. My friend said that although Balbo was himself disturbed by the Norwegian campaign, he had been greatly impressed by the House of Commons debate which had taken place the day before (May 8th). 'You've got to hand it to them,' he exclaimed. 'When they're wrong they stand up and admit it. That's what I admire about the English!'

I ran into Balbo in the lobby of the Hotel Excelsior, just as he was leaving to catch a plane to take him back to Africa. He was as lively and gusty as ever. 'Why don't you come to Libya with me? Right now. P'raps we could squeeze in that little flight across the desert! Or are you still afraid of my beard? One day I'll shave it off, but then you wouldn't recognise me. You'd say, who's that funny-looking man? But p'raps you say that anyway.' He roared with laughter at his joke. Just then several friends interrupted him and urged him to hurry. He asked where I was going after Rome, and when I told him England he winked slightly and whispered: '*Bonne chance. Bonne chance!*' That was the last I saw of him.

I spent most of my time in Rome talking with economic experts, and naval and military attachés, trying to assess Italy's potential war strength. Rumours were growing more lively each day. When Prince Philipp of Hesse suddenly arrived in Rome, speculation reached a new pitch. Prince Philipp was a German Prince, married to Princess Mafalda, a daughter of the King of Italy. He was a fanatical Nazi, entrusted by Hitler to act as intermediary between himself and Mussolini.

I had met Prince Philipp the summer before when I was staying with Mona Williams at Capri. He was a stolid, middle-aged German with an agreeable manner and a passionate devotion to Hitler. A nephew of the ex-Kaiser, he was the only member of the large Hesse clan who had embraced Nazism, and was, I gathered, regarded as the black sheep of the family. He had joined the party before Hitler came into power, and in 1933 was rewarded with the appointment of Governor of the Prussian Province of Hesse-Nassau.

Every morning he used to appear at Mona's to go swimming. He was an amiable, simple sort of man who took great pleasure in looking through the powerful telescope on the terrace at the small boats moving across the harbour; summer visitors liked to row round the island and he often caught couples in amorous embraces which caused him immense amusement.

Only once did he discuss Germany with me. When he spoke of Hitler his eyes lighted up and he launched into an eloquent adulation of the Führer's extraordinary personality, his gaiety, his friendliness, his gentleness and humour! He told me that Hitler and Mussolini were undoubtedly the two greatest men the world had ever seen. When Mussolini went to Germany for the signing of the Munich Agreement, Prince Philipp travelled to the frontier to meet him. He said the moment Hitler boarded the train the two dictators put their heads together, and five minutes later the entire Czech problem was solved. 'That's what I like,' commented Prince Philipp enthusiastically. 'Men who know their minds.'

He went on to add that although the dictators shared many dynamic qualities, temperamentally they were complete opposites. Whereas Hitler was sociable, Mussolini was a recluse; whereas Hitler liked entertaining at his house, Mussolini rarely received people except at his office; whereas Hitler trusted everyone, Mussolini trusted no one.

'Of course,' said Prince Philipp, 'neither one would do in the other's country. Imagine trusting anyone in Italy. You'd be out of office in a week!'

Now, this anxious spring, Prince Philipp was evidently once more on the job. I read of his arrival with interest, but since I was decidedly *persona non grata*, I didn't expect to see him. One day, however, I returned to the hotel to find a message asking me to go to the palace at six o'clock for cocktails. I assumed he was having a cocktail party, but when I arrived I found myself the only guest. He was waiting for me in the drive and greeted me warmly; then he led me into the drawing room and mixed a cocktail.

'I hear you spent the winter in Finland,' he said. (I wondered why it was that Germans always seemed to know everything.) 'Do tell me about it. I have a great admiration for the Finns.' For the next ten minutes he plied me with questions, interrupting every now and then to praise Mannerheim's gallant resistance. In the middle of the conversation his wife, Princess Mafalda, entered the room.

'I was just talking about Finland,' he explained. 'I was telling Virginia how sorry we were in Berlin we couldn't help the Finns. But, naturally, our pact with Russia prevented us from interfering.'

'But, darling,' said Princess Mafalda, 'you told me you *did* interfere. You told me you persuaded the Finns to sign the peace treaty by promising to put things right for them later on.'

Prince Philipp flushed. 'Certainly not. You're completely mistaken. It was quite impossible for us to interfere. We had nothing at all to do with it.'

'But, darling, you said . . .'

Prince Philipp gave her a stern look; she lapsed into silence, and a few minutes later left the room.

We sipped our cocktails and exchanged pleasantries. It seemed odd that I should be the only guest and I wondered curiously what was at the back of Prince Philipp's mind. Suddenly he swung on to the subject of the war. His eyes shone with relish.

'I told you last summer what a genius Hitler was. Well, now I think he's even more of a genius. Do you know he planned both the Polish and Norwegian campaigns himself? I think he's the greatest man that's ever lived. No other man has taken two capitals in a single day. Oslo and Copenhagen all within twelve hours! It must have been quite a surprise for the British, wasn't it?'

I replied that it had been. Then he said: 'Of course, the real war hasn't started yet. When it does, there will be destruction on an unprecedented scale. Half Europe will be destroyed. What's so sad is that it's quite unnecessary. It could be prevented if only Great Britain would see reason. Naturally, it would involve a little loss of prestige, but she must get rid of her old-fashioned ideas and realise the world is changing. I'm very fond of the English. After all, I have English blood in my veins – my grandmother was Queen Victoria – but I know how stubborn they can be. It seems frightful they should bring all this misery on the world. I can assure you Hitler is deeply distressed by it. I drove into Warsaw with him and when he saw the devastation his face turned white – literally white. I shall never forget it. He turned to me, and said: "How wicked of these people to have resisted us and *forced* us to take such measures!"' (Even Dr Goebbels, I thought, couldn't have invented a better one.) Prince Philipp continued: 'I haven't much hope of England coming to her senses of her own accord, but, of course, America could force her to.'

(So this was what our cocktail party was about.) 'How?' I asked, fascinated.

'Very simple. All America has to do is to tell England and France plainly and simply that she isn't going to give them any help; if she takes a firm enough stand, they will be forced to come to terms. You American writers should use your influence to this effect. It's tragic to think of all the beautiful things in Europe being smashed to pieces.'

'But who's done the smashing? Certainly not the Poles, the Danes or the Norwegians.'

'But, don't you understand? On all these occasions England had forced our hand.'

'In that case, do you really think Hitler would be willing to make peace? I should have thought by this time his hatred was too bitter.'

'Not at all. I'm sure he would. Hitler is both shrewd and practical. In fact, he's the most practical man I've ever known. He would never allow pique or anger to influence his judgment.'

'The world certainly doesn't view him in that light. If anyone has created a picture of temperament and instability, he has.'

Prince Philipp smiled. 'Oh, that's only the German manner. We Germans like a certain amount of drama. It's characteristic of us, just as it's characteristic of the English to be over-reserved.'

In the months that followed I often thought of this extraordinary conversation. After the destruction of France, Hitler announced that the 'war in the west' was over. I am sure he believed he could persuade England to make peace: the snag was, of course, that 'little loss of prestige'.

* * *

On the morning of May 10th the German Army launched its long-awaited attack on the West. I had sat up the night before until two in the morning, writing my article for the *Sunday Times*, which I had arranged to telephone to London the following afternoon. I had laboured long and hard over it. With all the varying currents in Rome, with all the contingencies each one dependent on the other, with the likelihood of an attack both in the Balkans and on the Western Front, it was difficult to predict the next Italian move. I finally began this way:

> The Spring of 1940 will undoubtedly see the German, French and British armies locked in a struggle so decisive that its outcome will affect many generations to come. What role Italy will play is still unpredictable. But judging from Italian vulnerability, there is every reason to believe Mussolini will not renounce his present state of belligerent neutrality unless

the Germans gain an important victory on the Western Front. Italy is not prepared to aid Germany at a costly expense; she cannot afford to take an active part in the war until she calculates a German victory is within three months of realisation.

At eight o'clock the next morning the telephone rang and John Whitaker said: 'Tear up your article, honey. No one wants to read about the Wops now. Hitler's invaded Holland and Belgium.'

I arranged to meet John for dinner and decided to leave for Paris the following day. I got up and began to dress. While I was combing my hair the maid brought in my shoes. She was a fat, middle-aged woman, and I was surprised to see she looked as though she'd been crying. She closed the door, gazed cautiously around the room, unhooked the telephone (in case of a dicta-phone) and said in a low voice: 'You've heard the news?'

Now, I couldn't speak Italian and she couldn't speak English, so we didn't have much conversation. But I understood what she meant when she said: '*È terribile. Il povero Belgio. Terribile. Odio i Tedeschi. È sempre lo stesso. È terribile.*' Her poor fat face was twisted with distress.

She was not the only one. All over Rome that morning you saw people reading their papers unhappily. For months everyone had prepared for this, yet it still came as a shock. Somehow it seemed to bring back the terrible days of 1914 with a fresh violence, and the awfulness of the repetition made it even worse. Many Italians remembered the last time only too well and were stirred with a deep pang of sympathy for their former allies. When I went into a shop on the Piazza di Spagna to cancel an order I'd given, tears came into the eyes of the proprietress. 'If you go to Paris, Mademoiselle, tell the French people *all* of us are not their enemies.' And later on when I went to have some passport pictures taken the photographer shook his head in disgust: 'Those Germans . . .'

I spent most of the afternoon trying to get necessary visas. It was a lovely day and I rode over to the French Consulate in a carriage. As we wound our way in and out of the twisting streets, through the Campo di Fiori blazing with spring flowers, it was hard to realise that at that very moment guns were shuddering and blood was flowing. But when I reached the Consulate it came closer. The rooms were crowded with people looking tired and anxious, all trying to get back to France. How often, I thought, have I seen those strained faces; soon no one in Europe will know how to smile.

That night John and I dined with 'Taffy' Rodd, the assistant British naval attaché, and George Labouchère, the Second Secretary of the British Embassy, in the latter's flat off the Via Nomentana, overlooking the Alban Hills. We hadn't had any news all afternoon and about nine o'clock turned on the radio and tried to get London. Every language seemed to flow into the room except English, then suddenly we heard a voice saying: 'Hitler has chosen a moment when, perhaps, it seemed to him that this country was entangled in the throes of a political crisis. He has counted on our internal differences to help him. He has miscalculated the mind of this people.'

It was Mr Chamberlain. He went on to say that after the parliamentary debate of May 7th and 8th (the debate on Norway), he had no doubt

that some new and drastic action must be taken if confidence was to be restored to the House of Commons, and the war carried on with the vigour and energy essential to victory. It was apparent that the essential unity could be secured under another Prime Minister. In those circumstances, my duty was

plain. I sought an audience with the King this evening and
tendered my resignation.

The King has now entrusted to my friend and colleague
(here there was a slight pause and John whispered: 'Lord
Halifax?'), my friend and colleague, Mr Winston Churchill,
the task of forming a new Administration . . .

We whooped with delight. John cried: 'Oh, boy, oh, boy, now
everyone will start going places!'

We were so delighted, after dinner we decided to celebrate.
'Taffy' Rodd, who knew Italy well, took us to a café in a fascinating little piazza in an out-of-the-way part of Rome. There was
an accordion player and a violinist who gave us all our favourite
tunes; we drank a jug of wine and sang to our hearts' content.

We didn't feel like going to bed, so when we got back into the
car we drove up to the Janiculum, the highest summit in the capital. It was a wonderful night. There were so many stars the sky
looked like a great and splendid chandelier. To the west we could
see the dark outline of the Vatican; to the east, a blaze of lights
flashing from the Seven Hills of Rome. Heaven and earth seemed
one and the same; the stars were lights and the lights were stars, all
glistening through a single sweep of darkness.

About midnight we started home. The streets were deserted and
the noise of the car penetrated through the stillness. We turned a
bend and saw a group of men standing on the corner. A few blocks
further on there was another group. Then still another.

'I wonder what's up,' said 'Taffy'.

John was leaning out of the window. 'They look like the *squadristi* – the old-time street fighters.'

'P'raps there's going to be a *coup d'état*,' I said hopefully. 'P'raps
we're seeing a second march on Rome.'

We swung into the Piazza Barberini, and drove up the Via Veneto to my hotel. We saw hundreds of large white posters pasted on the buildings. When we reached my hotel – the Regina – we found two on either side of the door. George translated the headings: 'England Has Missed the Bus!' Then followed a vitriolic attack, branding the British as everything from cowards to degenerates.

We read them indignantly: 'So that's what the *squadristi* have been up to,' said John.

George reached up and felt one. 'Yes. They're still wet.'

Just then the air was broken by wild cries: '*Inglesi! Inglesi!*' The gang of Fascist street fighters who had put up the posters were lying in wait around the corner. Thinking, evidently, we were trying to tear them down, they swept towards us, shaking their fists and shouting. There must have been fifty of them.

They fell on George, 'Taffy' and John, lashing out in every direction. The noise was appalling. The proprietor of the hotel came out on the pavement in his pyjamas and tried to restore order, but was immediately knocked down.

I stood near the door, not knowing what to do. George, his face bleeding, was hurled up against me, and the proprietor, who by this time had picked himself up, managed to pull both of us inside and bolt the doors.

'Whatever you do, don't open the door,' he said excitedly. 'I will telephone the police.'

I promptly disobeyed him. The commotion outside seemed to be growing louder, and I pictured John and 'Taffy' lying in a bloody pool on the pavement. I knew if I opened the door everyone would come pouring in, but I thought it might at least serve as a diversion. Being in no danger myself, as it was unlikely they would strike a woman, I told George to keep out of sight, walked up to the door and unscrewed the heavy bolts. I stepped back a good distance and a second later the mob surged in. At the same moment, the manager came running out of his office crying in a frenzy: 'What have you done?' He was promptly knocked down for the second time.

'Taffy' and John were swept in with the crowd; aside from a few cuts and bruises, they seemed to have held their own. But it was evidently George's blood the mob was after, for the air was filled with shouts for the '*altro Inglese*'. To my despair, George peered around the corner.

'There he is!'

It was an awful moment. 'Taffy' and George were reluctant to strike out at the gang for fear of creating an 'international incident' at so critical a time, and John had no wish to lose his job as permanent Rome correspondent of the *Chicago Daily News*. It seemed up to me. But, unable to speak Italian, there was little I could do. I decided to try being pathetic.

'*Messieurs – s'il vous plaît. Il est mon mari. Mon mari,*' I repeated, hoping the Italians had a word for 'husband' that began with an 'm'.

I took out a handkerchief and the leader of the group wavered. He replied in a stream of Italian I couldn't understand.

'*Mon mari . . .*'

He turned and muttered something to his followers, who all began talking at once. Suddenly, a newcomer pushed his way through the crowd. He was a dark, wiry little Italian in a black suit, with riding-boots and a whip. He spoke in an emphatic voice, pointing to George and shaking his whip. The leader looked uncertain and said something in a tone that sounded as though he were protesting.

'Tell her to get out, then,' snarled the newcomer. The others took up the cry and began shaking their fists. The leader looked uneasy.

'*S'il vous plaît, monsieur . . .*' I implored. '*Mon mari . . .*'

The man with the whip was getting indignant. 'Drag him out on the street, then.' Some of the group shouted, '*Si, si,*' and began pressing forward; the others – including the leader – shouted, '*No, no,*' and pushed them back. Before we knew what was happening the crowd had split into two groups and a minute later everyone was striking out wildly at each other. It was exactly like a Mack Sennett comedy; a crazy *mélange* of arms and legs, with bodies reeling up against the porter's desk and chairs and tables crashing to the floor.

'This is our chance,' said John. 'Come on. Let's beat it.'

The four of us made a dash for the lift, pressed the button and shot up to the fifth floor. The pandemonium echoed from one end of the hotel to the other, but gradually the commotion died away, which seemed to indicate that our side had won. The manager came upstairs with a large patch on his forehead and said they had left the hotel. George telephoned Sir Noel Charles, the British Minister, to report the incident, and half an hour later the latter arrived at the hotel to drive them home in his car.

I went to bed and didn't hear the end of the story until the next morning. When John and the three Englishmen went out in the street, the mob, who had been waiting for them around the corner, came running forward once again and encircled them. They heckled them for over an hour, jostling and pushing and refusing to let them leave. But they were evidently intimidated by the CD on Sir Noel's car, for no one dared strike. The police, conspicuous all this time by their absence, had obviously been told not to interfere. Two gendarmes came by and refused to help; some time later another passed, and, finally, in spite of much indignation, dispersed the crowd.

I left Rome for Paris the following day. I tried to cash a cheque in a bank on the Piazza Colonna, but was told English money was no longer acceptable. I walked back to the hotel, through the Via delle Muratte, past the Trevi Fountain. An old superstition invites travellers who are leaving Rome to throw a coin into the basin to ensure a speedy return. I walked past with my purse tightly shut.

3

God Is English

Twenty-four hours after I arrived in Paris I ran into Fruity Metcalfe, aide-de-camp to the Duke of Windsor.

'They've done it!' he said.

'Who's done what?'

'The Huns have crossed the Meuse in three places and broken into France at Sedan.'

'What does that mean?'

'Good God, anything! It *can* mean they'll be in Paris in a fortnight. Or even sooner.'

I stared at Fruity disbelievingly. For nine months England and France had prepared for this attack; for nine months they had blockaded Germany with the purpose of forcing her to destroy herself against the invincible steel and concrete of the Maginot Line. They had even extended a formal invitation to her: 'Come on, Hitler,' said General Ironside, Commander-in-Chief of the British Imperial General Staff, 'we're ready for you.' Indeed the invulnerability of the Belgian and French fortifications was so unquestioned you began to hear the fear expressed that Germany might *not* attack and that the 'bore' war would stretch on for years. When the onslaught finally came, brutal and savage as it was, people said with relief: 'At last the end of the war is in sight.'

'God knows the Meuse looked formidable enough,' Fruity continued. 'A great, broad, swirling river. Only a week ago I stood on the bank near Mézières and a French officer said: "This is an obstacle they won't ignore." And what happened? They just marched up to it, flung pontoons down, and went romping across as though it were a duck puddle. This isn't a war, it's a race. Blitz is too conservative a word. Why, you can't even tack a map up on the wall, much less put the pins in, before it's all over. Only four days ago the Duke spent two hours searching the shops for a map of Holland. When he pulled it down this morning, he said: "What country are we on now, Fruity?" I suppose tonight we'll take down Belgium and put up France.'

I thought Fruity was over-alarming and regarded his conversation sceptically; nevertheless, Sedan struck an ominous note. The last time the Germans had broken through at Sedan was in 1870 – the time they'd got to Paris. I thought of Chesterton's poem in which the old woman of Flanders says:

> Low and brown barns thatched and repatched and tattered
> Where I had seven sons until today –
> A little hill of hay your spur has scattered . . .
> This is not Paris. You have lost the way.
> You, staring at your sword to find it brittle,
> Surprised at the surprise that was your plan,
> Who, shaking and breaking barriers not a little,
> Find never more the death door of Sedan.

The death door. They had found it again. Did it still lead to Paris? On this wonderful spring day, it was impossible even to contemplate. Perhaps it was the unusual quiet, but Paris seemed so magnificently aloof, you couldn't imagine it being despoiled. Many people, afraid of air attacks, had already left and there was only a thin stream of traffic on the boulevards; shops and restaurants were half empty and even the Ritz had lost its diehard patronage of women in wild hats. In my hotel off the Place Vendôme, there was no one except the concierge, the cat and myself.

Somehow the deserted, early-on-Sunday-morning look gave the capital a fresh beauty; there was a new softness in the wind blowing through the trees, the graceful sweep of the long avenues, and the wonderful blue-grey of the houses along the Seine. Every now and then the sirens broke the quiet, but there were never any planes and no one bothered to take shelter; everyone did exactly what they were told not to do, poking their heads out of the windows and looking up at the sky.

But in spite of the tranquillity, underneath there was a current of apprehension. People seemed only too willing to believe tales of German invincibility. When the concierge brought me the morning paper, he added bits of information of his own: that the Germans were taking no prisoners, but shooting everyone indiscriminately, and that the whole of Holland was in ashes. He had wild stories about parachutists; how the skies were black with them, and how they came down machine-gunning and dropping bombs from the air.

He was not the only one. Parachute stories seemed to be on everybody's lips. You not only heard that nuns and priests were dropping from the heavens, but that whole choruses of ballet dancers were descending. When I went to see the Baroness on Tuesday afternoon, a friend came bursting into the flat with the news that one of them (I don't know which brand) had just landed on the Champs-Élysées. We hurried out on the balcony: all along the avenue groups of people were staring up at the sky. I never discovered the truth of the report, but Alexander Werth in *The Last Days of Paris* claims it was only a sausage balloon that settled in the Place de la Madeleine. The Baroness was most indignant. 'It is bad enough,' she said, 'having the Boches invade your country by land, but when they come floating down from the skies as sisters of mercy – of *mercy* – it is disgusting, the filthy pigs!'

After I left the Baroness, I walked down the Champs-Élysées, cut through the Faubourg St Honoré, and stopped at the British

Embassy to see Sir Charles Mendl. The BEF had a rule barring women correspondents from the front, and I asked Charles if he thought there was any possibility of getting round it. He seemed to think it would be difficult to manage in Paris and advised me to go to London and try and arrange it there.

Charles was none too happy about the situation. 'The German planes and guns are formidable enough,' he said. 'But even so, I don't think they're as dangerous as French morale. If that holds up, I'm confident everything will be all right, but if it doesn't . . .'

Now I'd known Charles Mendl for over four years. He was one of my first friends in Europe and I never went through Paris without going to see him. He was one of the wisest people I knew and his twenty-five years in France had given him a deep understanding of the people; on many occasions he had made predictions contrary to the strong beliefs of the moment which invariably had been borne out. I had doubted his judgment about France at the time of Munich and he had been right; but I hadn't learned my lesson and now I doubted him again. The French politicians might be defeatists, but surely not the French Army: everyone knew that Frenchmen fought like tigers on their own soil. It was one of the things you were taught as a child. I told him I thought his fears would be unconfirmed and he said: 'I hope so, but I don't think these are the same people that they were twenty years ago.'

I took Charles's advice and planned to leave for London the following day. On the way back to the hotel I ran into Euan Butler. I hadn't seen him since the night Robert and Lucy had ridden the horses in the Golden Horseshoe nightclub in Berlin. At the outbreak of war he had given up his job as *Times* correspondent and joined the army. Now he was attached to GHQ and had come up to Paris for a few hours on official business. He was returning to the front in the morning, so we decided to celebrate, and went to dinner at Le Bœuf Sur Le Toit. There were only a few people in the restaurant, all of whom stared curiously at Euan's Scottish plaid trousers (he was with the Cameronians), some of them smiling a little. Although the atmosphere was rather gloomy, we had a good dinner and Euan was in high spirits – the only really optimistic person I saw during my forty-eight-hour stay. When I asked him if the parachute stories were true, he said he believed a number of men had been dropped behind the French lines but certainly not dressed as nuns and bishops. He added someone had remarked facetiously that the French should advise the Germans that if they came down disguised as ballet dancers they must expect to be ravished by the troops. He said the morale was excellent at the French War Office and no one was in the least disturbed by the latest reports. The more the Germans extended themselves, the more likely they were to be cut off when the counter-attack came.

Of course! Why hadn't I thought of that myself? I went to bed immensely reassured and the next day left for London, my optimism fully restored. Even the French communiqué, which confirmed Fruity's report, laconically admitting that 'between Namur and Mézières German troops crossed the river at three points', didn't alarm me. As the bus rattled through the streets of Paris on its way to Le Bourget, I didn't imagine the next time I saw the capital would be four weeks later – exactly twenty-four hours before the German Army roared up the Champs-Élysées.

* * *

In London, everyone pinned their faith on the French counter-attack which never came. The French, people said, were wonderful improvisers. Although they had been surprised by the factors of the new mobile warfare, they were bound to rally, and when they struck it would be with terrible force. Day after day people picked up their morning papers expecting to read that the great offensive had begun; but the communiqué reported only fresh German advances. Then on May 28th King Leopold of the Belgians suddenly surrendered.

That same night I dined with a British staff officer who had just returned from the front. When I told him I was trying to get to France, he said: 'Find out why the French won't fight. Find out why they won't stick to their posts; why they won't engage the enemy; why they won't even counter-attack.'

When I asked him if the answer didn't lie in Germany's crushing superiority, he shook his head. In the last war, he said, the British and French Armies faced far more deadly fire than had been seen in this one. The tonnage of explosives from an artillery barrage was infinitely greater than that which the Germans could deliver by air. He also refuted the stories that the French anti-tank guns were too light to penetrate the heavy German tanks. (Experts claimed that the ordinary two-pound anti-tank gun, with which the French were well equipped, was powerful enough to disable tanks of the heaviest category.)

I asked him what he thought the chances of the BEF were, now that King Leopold had surrendered, and he replied bluntly: 'Absolutely nil. They haven't got a chance. The whole lot's gone. If we get ten thousand back, we're lucky.'

A few hours before, in the House of Commons, Mr Churchill had hinted at the same disaster. He had said:

> Meanwhile, the situation of the British and French Armies
> now engaged in a most severe battle and beset on three sides
> and from the air, is evidently extremely grave. The surrender
> of the Belgian Army in this manner adds appreciably to their
> grievous peril . . . I expect to make a statement to the House

on the general position when the result of the intense struggle
now going on can be known and measured. This will not,
perhaps, be until the beginning of next week. Meanwhile, the
House should prepare itself for hard and heavy tidings. I have
only to add that nothing which may happen in this battle can
in any way relieve us of our duty to defend the world cause
to which we have vowed ourselves; nor should it destroy
our confidence in our power to make our way, as on former
occasions in our history, through disaster and through grief to
the ultimate defeat of our enemies.

In spite of this warning the general public seemed unaware
of the gravity of the situation. Anne O'Neill's housekeeper, Mrs
Kinch, had two nephews with the BEF, but her only comment was:
'Things looked just as bad in the last war. In the end it will be all
right.'

For the people who knew, however, the following week was
a grim one. On Thursday May 30th, the attempt at evacuation
began. Two days later I went down to Mereworth with Anne to
spend the weekend with Esmond Harmsworth. The Germans
had reached the Channel ports and although the house was forty
miles from the coast, the ground reverberated every now and
then with the distant explosion of bombs. Loelia Westminster was
there, quiet and depressed; it wasn't until the weekend was nearly
over that she told us her brother was with the BEF. It must have
been an unpleasant experience for her, for all day long fighters
and bombers went over the house on their way to the battle. We
sat out on the terrace and watched them pass, their silver wings
almost indistinguishable against the sky. There always seemed to
be more going out than coming back and we began morbidly to
count the numbers.

Now the miracle of the evacuation has passed into history. Everyone knows how hundreds of small sailing vessels, trawlers, mine-sweepers and fishing smacks crossed the Channel and brought back over two hundred and seventy thousand men from the shores of Dunkirk. Anne and I drove down to Dover and saw some of the troops landing. Hundreds of them filed through the docks, dirty and tired. Some had equipment, some had none; some were in uniform and some in an odd assortment of sweaters and slacks. Most of them seemed in high spirits and waved at the crowd clustered against the railings to cheer them. The English soldiers grinned self-consciously and made jokes to each other; the French soldiers blew kisses to the girls. I went back to London by train and all along the way Union Jacks were flying.

Loelia Westminster's brother, Lord Sysonby, was among the last to return. A few days later I lunched at Loelia's and found him there. I was longing to get an account of the battle, but like most Englishmen, he revelled in understatement and it was difficult to fit the slender pieces into a composite picture. He said his regiment was fighting alongside a Belgian unit. When they heard the news of King Leopold's surrender, things became extremely awkward. They felt it would be in bad taste to raise the subject, but anxious to know what was going to happen, finally resorted to veiled hints. 'Is it likely – er – do you suppose – er – will you be shoving off soon?' The Belgians gave them angry looks and announced that King or no King, they were fighting to the end.

He went on to describe the refugees along the road; the thousands of tanks, lorries and field guns that had to be abandoned in the fields. He said a good many villages and towns were being cleared of civilians, but the strangest evacuation he saw was that of a French Trappist Monastery. As the Trappists were vowed to silence, the whole thing was carried out by frantic signs and gestures.

Although his own particular unit had been fighting one of the last rearguard actions, he minimised the part they had played. When I asked him if he'd come face to face with the Germans, he replied: 'Only once. A lot of them came over a hill and what an extraordinary sight they were. They were wearing the most peculiar uniforms. Sort of grey trousers and strange-looking ties. They looked like Eton boys.'

Basil Dufferin, also at lunch, made an ill attempt at humour. 'Could they run as fast?'

'Yes, thank God!'

Now if you hadn't taken into account that Lord Sysonby was an Englishman, you might have thought the whole retreat through Flanders to Dunkirk was one hilarious episode after another, and that his own particular role was one of a detached observer. But because he was an Englishman, you weren't surprised to read in *The Times* a few weeks later that he had been awarded the Distinguished Service Order.

* * *

Meanwhile, I was still trying to get to France. When the BEF collapsed I made an application to go into the French Army zone. The French Ministry of Information told me that although it was impossible to accredit me officially, they undoubtedly would be able to arrange a 'tour' of the front. The days passed, however, and I heard nothing further. Finally, on Monday morning June 10th, the Ministry rang up, suggesting that I should go to Paris and arrange the final details there. The French Consul stamped my visa: 'Good for one month'; that was four days before the Germans occupied the capital.

At the time it didn't seem extravagant, for the English papers were maintaining a persistent optimism. Although General Weygand had issued a desperate appeal in his Order of the Day, Sunday, twenty-four hours previously ('We have reached the last quarter of an hour. Stand firm'), the Monday headlines of the *Daily Telegraph* read: 'French Hold German Onslaught. Heaviest Defence in History. Nazi Prisoners tell of Serious Setback. Aisne Attacks Wholly Stemmed.'

Also on the front page was the following despatch:

From our Correspondent.
PARIS, *Sunday*.

Paris will never be Hitler's intact, according to a French Government spokesman today. When I asked whether, if the worst came to the worst, the French would declare Paris an 'open' city in an effort to spare the world's most beautiful city, the spokesman answered: 'Never. We're confident that Hitler's mechanised hordes will never get to Paris. But should they come so far, you may tell your countrymen we shall defend every stone, every clod of earth, every lamp-post, every building, for we would rather have our city razed to the ground than fall into the hands of the Germans.'

Faced with the decision of choosing between the fate of Warsaw and that of Rotterdam, the French – true to the finest traditions of a nation that has never yet asked for quarter – have decided that they would prefer their city, with its finest art treasures, to be destroyed to any sort of capitulation to invaders. If the army that has no face wants Paris, it will have to fight for it.

Incidentally, there is the fact that against a great city tanks are completely impotent. The German dead will be piled high in the suburbs before a single Nazi enters a great heap of ruins.

*

It looked as though Paris would stand for a while. My chances of getting there, however, seemed slim; for that night the Italians entered the war, the Germans crossed the Seine thirty miles southeast of Rouen, and Mr Rogers of Cook's Travel Bureau telephoned to say all planes had been suspended. That day, however, I lunched with Baba and Fruity Metcalfe. Lord Halifax was there and I took heart from his remark: 'I haven't any reason to be optimistic, but I have a feeling from now on things will take a turn for the better.'

Perhaps, I thought, I'll make it after all. Sure enough, the following morning Mr Rogers rang at nine-thirty and said a plane was leaving and could I be at the Imperial Airways Office in twenty minutes? I was still in bed. I rang every bell in the house, flung things haphazardly into a suitcase, pulled on a dress and bolted out of the door. I made it. Half an hour later I was in a bus, headed for Croydon.

It was only then that I had a chance to look at the papers. In the *Telegraph* I read:

> While the French Army is preparing to make a back-to-the-wall stand before the gates of Paris and the citizens of the French capital are pouring southwards, the enemy redoubled his efforts forty miles to the north and fierce fighting continued during the day.

A backs-to-the-wall stand before the gates of Paris. The siege might last for days.

4

The Last Twenty-Four Hours of Paris

There were about a dozen passengers on the plane, and none of us knew where we were landing – just 'somewhere in France'. We headed across the Channel, flew very low across Guernsey, and still lower when we reached the coast of France. At times it seemed as though we were barely missing the roof-tops of the farmhouses along the way.

The nose of our plane pointed first one way, then another, as we followed a zig-zag course. After about an hour and a half we began circling around a large aerodrome. The ground was gouged with bomb craters and two of the hangars were smashed. People came running out of the buildings gesticulating and pointing at us.

The field had been turned into a military aerodrome, and when we landed crowds of workers, in blue overalls, surged round the plane staring curiously at us as though we had dropped from Mars. I asked one of them where we were and he replied: 'Tours.' I couldn't imagine why everyone regarded us so strangely until I learned that ours was the first plane to arrive for forty-eight hours; the only reason we had come was that our pilot had argued with the company, finally persuading them at the last moment to let him risk the flight.

Certainly no one was expecting us. After a long wait at the aerodrome a bus arrived and drove us to a small yard at the back of the station. We were not allowed to leave the bus until the customs inspector arrived, and the customs inspector was nowhere to be found. We sat there for five hours while numerous French officials, all very excited, swarmed around criticising the situation.

We begged for permission to go to a restaurant, but the authorities were adamant: a fierce encounter took place between them and one of the passengers, an old man, determined to go to the gentlemen's room. He was finally taken off under guard.

Most of the passengers were English. Two were staying in Tours; three were trying to get to Marseilles to make a connection for North Africa; three to Bordeaux; and one, a young woman, to Switzerland to join her husband who was in the British Legation. Besides myself, the only other person headed for Paris was a fat, excitable little man with black hair greatly in need of cutting, and a yellow, greasy face. He spoke English with an accent, and I wondered what nationality he was. He seemed dreadfully agitated and kept asking what time the trains went to Paris. When one of the authorities shrugged his shoulders and said sharply: 'Paris is out of the question. No one is going to Paris any more,' he looked close to tears.

'I *must* go to Paris. Surely, there's some way . . .'

I promptly sided with him. 'I must go to Paris, too,' I said firmly.

'*Je crois que c'est impossible. C'est très dangereux.*'

'I don't care whether it's dangerous,' gasped the little man. 'Are the trains running? That's all I want to know.'

The official shrugged his shoulders and walked away.

'Don't worry,' I said. 'We'll get there some way. If the trains aren't running, perhaps we can hire a car.'

'Yes, yes,' he moaned. His fat face was more greasy than ever and he took out a handkerchief to mop his brow.

At five o'clock the customs inspector arrived and inspected our baggage. One of the Air France officials was with him and when we asked him about the trains he replied, as though it were the most natural thing in the world: 'Paris? *Certainement!* There is a train leaving in twenty minutes.'

The little man and I made a dash for the station.

It was an extraordinary sight. Overflowing with humanity, it looked like the sort of station you'd see in India, with people jostling, pushing, sleeping and even eating on the platform. Everyone had dozens of bags and bundles and hundreds of people sat around waiting for trains.

The little man pushed up to one of the ticket offices and made enquiries, but was told the train wasn't expected until eight o'clock. We bought our tickets and went to a café across the street to get something to eat.

It was the first time I had had a chance to take in the scene around me. Trucks and motor-cars piled high with possessions were rolling through Tours. Refugees were everywhere: wandering along the streets, and flowing into restaurants and cafés, just to get a place to sit down. The café proprietor refused to let us come in at first until we persuaded him we really wanted to *buy* something.

The little man (I never learned his name) told me that he was an Egyptian who had come to France for a few months' stay. He was an official in the Egyptian Government – an Under-Secretary of State for Public Works – and had gone to London on a few days' business. Owing to the suspension of aeroplane services he had been unable to get back to France until now. He had left his two small children in Paris and over a thousand pounds cash, which he had taken out of the bank and hidden in the house. 'I don't care about the money,' he kept saying. 'But my children. They've got a nurse looking after them, but she won't know what to do. Heaven knows what will happen to them if I don't get to Paris.'

I tried to calm him but he was so nervous he couldn't sit still. Every ten minutes he hurried across the square to enquire again what time the train was coming. He finally suggested that we wait in the station to be sure not to miss it; so, laden with bags and baggage, we pushed our way through the throng and sat on the draughty platform.

We sat there for exactly six hours, for the train, due at eight, didn't arrive until midnight. He was right to have insisted on our getting a place near the track, for when it came there was a wild scramble and hundreds of people surged on. We were packed in the compartment so tightly we could scarcely breathe. The congestion, however, lasted only a short while, for the train stopped at a station about twenty miles away, and everyone got off to make a connection for Bordeaux. The rest of the way there were only three of us as passengers: the Egyptian, myself and a middle-aged Frenchman who owned a shop in the Latin Quarter and was returning to look after it.

It was a strange trip with the empty train thundering over the tracks, the wind blowing through the windows, and the terrible stillness of the blackened countryside. The Frenchman was pessimistic and said he thought the situation was hopeless. 'We may arrive in Paris to find the Germans already there.'

'Nonsense!' I replied. 'They can't break through the city's defences overnight. If they have to fight for it street by street it won't be easy. Things always sound much worse than they are. We'll probably arrive to find everything more normal than Tours.'

I wasn't saying this to encourage the Egyptian; I believed it. I remembered the alarming reports I'd heard before I'd gone to Spain; I remembered how Franco's troops had marched up to the very gates of Madrid and how the capital had stood for over two years. The confusion in Tours hadn't been reassuring, but experience had taught me that often the closer you get to the front, the calmer it is. I hadn't yet realised I was seeing the beginning of the collapse of France.

Certainly I wasn't prepared for the scene that greeted us when we pulled into the Austerlitz Station in Paris. It was about five o'clock in the morning and dawn was just breaking. The station was almost deserted and there was no one to collect our tickets. In fact, there wasn't a sign of life: not a porter, not a taxi, not a newspaper-boy – nothing. But when we walked out to the street it was a different matter. The great iron gates in front of the station were bolted and in front of them was an enormous crowd of people, shouting and yelling. It was one vast sea of faces. Everybody was loaded with bags and bundles, even bird-cages and all kinds of pets. A squad of gendarmes had climbed up on the iron railings and were shouting at them to go away: 'No more trains are leaving Paris! The last train has left! Go home, I tell you, no more trains are leaving Paris.'

The crowd shouted back: 'Open the gates! Open the gates!' A man's voice rose above the tumult. 'If they won't run the trains for us, we'll run them ourselves!'

The policemen, tired and exasperated, kept replying it was hopeless, but it didn't seem to be doing any good. All the time more people were coming streaking across the square from every direction.

'Well,' said the French businessman acidly, 'what do you think of it? Is this what you expected? I don't think we've got a chance of getting a taxi.'

We pushed our way through the crowds and walked down the street. A taxi drew up and nine people spilled out. We went up to the driver, asked if he were free, and he nodded. I didn't realise at the time what a stroke of luck it was, but I later discovered we had what was apparently the only roving taxi in the whole of Paris.

The Frenchman said he lived only a block or so away and preferred to walk. The Egyptian and I climbed in and just as we were starting off, a French girl knocked on the window and asked if we would give her a lift. The Egyptian asked me to drop him on the way; when I left him I gave him my name and told him if I could do anything for him to let me know. I then asked the girl where she wanted me to take her. She was young and pretty and neatly dressed. She looked at me and smiled and said: 'Nowhere. I just thought I'd like to ride around.'

She certainly had a long ride, for we drove around Paris for nearly two hours. First, I went up and rang the Ritz doorbell. After five or ten minutes the concierge appeared, opened the door cautiously, and told me the hotel was closed. 'Everyone has left.' I begged him to let me have a room, but he just repeated: 'No, no, the hotel is closed. Everyone has left.' Then banged the door.

I next went to the Hotel Vendôme, a few blocks away; there I was told the same thing. Then began an endless trek over Paris. I must have tried fifteen hotels. Some of the porters slammed the door in my face, some shouted angrily, some refused to answer. When I asked if they knew of one that was open, they glared sullenly and shook their heads. All this while the girl sat in the taxi-cab, puffing a cigarette and watching the proceedings with interest.

'What's happened?' I asked. 'Has *everyone* left Paris?'

'Oh no, mademoiselle, it's curious, isn't it? There hasn't been any official evacuation. The only people who are leaving are the ones who are afraid of the bombs. They think Paris is going to be bombed.'

'What about you? Aren't you leaving?'

'Oh no, not unless the Germans get closer. I will leave before the Boches come. But that will be a long time from now.'

'D'you mean to say all these people are leaving just because they're frightened? Surely the Boches must be very close.'

'Oh no, mademoiselle, truly it is only on account of the bombs.

If there were any real danger, the Government would have told us to leave.'

'Have you got a family in Paris?'

'No, I'm all alone. But I've lived here all my life. I'm a Parisienne.'

'Do you work? Have you got a job?'

'No, mademoiselle.' (It suddenly dawned on me – she was obviously a *cocotte*.)

'But if it's only that people are frightened, why should all the hotels be shut?'

'The bombs, mademoiselle. Only the bombs.'

The taxi-driver nodded pleasantly, supporting her theory. It seemed extraordinary to me. In spite of all the reports about a 'backs-to-the-wall-stand before Paris', the capital certainly did not look like a city prepared to defend itself. Where were the barricades? Where were the troops? Where were the guns? In fact, where was anything or anyone? The only people I'd seen so far were a dozen concierges, three gendarmes, and a mob of panic-stricken civilians, trying to get away.

I finally gave up the hotels and decided to search for some of my friends. I told the driver to go to the Quai de Bethune where Knickerbocker lived. The big doors were shut, but after ringing the bell for ten minutes there was finally a buzzing noise and I pushed my way into the courtyard.

'*Qui est là?*' called the concierge through the window.

'Is Mr Knickerbocker in?'

'No, no. He left Paris three or four days ago.'

Now for the first time I began to get worried. If Knickerbocker had left, things must be bad. I drove up to the Place Madeleine where Eddie Ward was staying, but he, too, had gone. Then I drove up the Champs-Élysées to the Baroness's flat but found the doors locked and the house deserted.

I stood in the middle of the street and wondered what to do. The girl was still seated comfortably in the cab, puffing a cigarette; the driver, a middle-aged man with a large moustache, seemed to have settled down to a morning's work. I had only brought a hundred francs in French currency and had spent ninety of it on the ticket to Paris. I had only English money to pay him off with and wondered what was going to happen. Across the street was the Rue de Berri. From the back of my mind I vaguely remembered Walter Kerr remarking one day, in Finland, that some of the journalists used to gather there, at the Hotel Lancaster, for poker games. I decided to talk with the concierge and see if he could give me any news. 'Is Mr Kerr staying here?' I asked.

'*Oui, mademoiselle.*'

I was so astonished I couldn't believe my ears.

'I must speak to him immediately.'

The concierge argued that Walter was not yet awake, but I finally persuaded him to connect me on the house telephone.

'Who is it?' came a sleepy voice.

'This is Virginia Cowles. Will you lend me two hundred francs to pay off my cab? I haven't got any money.'

'What in heaven's name are you doing here? Have you come for the occupation?'

'Goodness, no! I've just come for a day or so.'

'Listen,' said Walter. 'Either you're not making much sense, or I'm not. I'll send this money down to you straight away and will meet you for breakfast in an hour. Will two hundred francs be enough?'

I gave the whole amount to the taxi-driver, told him to take the girl where she wanted to go and to come back at noon in case I wanted him. But he evidently got a better offer, for he went roaring down the Champs-Élysées and that was the last I saw of either one of them.

* * *

On Tuesday morning, June 11th, people in England and America opened their morning papers to read: 'Germans seventeen miles from Paris.' I wonder how many visualised what Paris was like. No one had ever seen a Paris like this before; only a handful of foreigners can tell the story of the gayest city in the world, silent and abandoned, with its boulevards empty, its cafés closed, its shutters drawn, its telegraph and telephone communications cut – the story of a Paris so quiet there was literally scarcely a cat stirring.

I was astonished. At five or six in the morning there was nothing unusual in the drawn shutters and the empty streets. But now it was ten o'clock. When Walter Kerr and I drove up the Champs-Élysées the sun streamed through the chestnut trees as it always does in May, but that was all to remind you of the Paris you knew. Gone were the noisy crowds, the rich smell of tobacco, the water splashing from the fountains. Today there was only an empty sweep. Ours was the only car on the whole avenue. It was so quiet the click of our tyres echoed loudly.

It was still a shock to me that Paris was not going to be defended. It must have been a shock to a great many other people as well, for it was only that morning that posters were pasted up on the buildings declaring the capital an 'open city' – the first warning the people of Paris were given. I thought of the little *cocotte* and wondered what she'd say when she read them. I couldn't understand why the Government had taken no pains to advise the civilians what to do, but Walter said they had behaved disgracefully all the way along. The officials had declared firmly they were remaining in Paris, then on Monday had fled overnight without a word. Apart from the fact that the police had taken over the shops and that men of military age, who had not been mobilised, had been advised to leave, the people had been told nothing.

We drove up the Champs-Élysées as far as the Arc de Triomphe. The eternal flame was still burning and three gendarmes were standing a lonely vigil. Then we drove down the Avenue Marceau, across the Pont d'Alma and past the Invalides where a fleet of five or six hundred cabs were lined up, evidently awaiting a last-minute evacuation of papers and documents. We passed the École Militaire. Here, too, men were carrying out cases of files and loading them on vans.

We cut through some of the side streets of the Latin quarter, and in the poorer sections found the streets crowded. Vendors with carts of fruit and vegetables were doing their usual business and housewives bargained as persistently as they always had. These were the people too poor to leave Paris. Back on the main boulevards once again the only signs of life were occasional groups laden with bags and bundles, starting out of the capital on foot; and every now and then an automobile that came hurtling out of a side street, careening under the weight of household possessions piled on the roof.

Walter shook his head grimly. 'This is a morning we'll never forget.'

'Yes. I suppose this is what people call seeing history in the making – or the unmaking. But I wish I'd missed this particular chapter.'

I didn't want to remember Paris like this. It was like watching someone you loved dying; like seeing a face unrecognisable through illness. With only twenty-four more hours to live, the heartbeat of the capital had already grown so faint you could scarcely hear it.

'You'll never get out of here before the Germans come,' said Walter. 'There's no way to get out. There isn't an automobile to be had for love or money in the whole city. I'd let you take mine, but I've got exactly one gallon of petrol and that wouldn't get you very far. Anyway, they may be in here any hour. God knows, there's nothing to stop them.'

'You mean there's no fighting going on?'

'Well, listen. D'you hear any guns? The Germans can't be more than twenty minutes away by car and d'you hear the sound of a single gun?'

All day long I kept my ears strained, but there was no gunfire: only a deathly quiet. When Walter and I drove down to the Place de la Concorde, we saw a group of soldiers – about half a dozen of them – plodding across the square. Their faces were grimy and their clothes caked with mud. Two of them were limping, a third had a bandage round his head, a fourth was walking in his stockinged feet, carrying his shoes. They were evidently stragglers who had got lost or deserted, and were making their way back to their homes. But there was no one to notice them. No one had time for soldiers now.

Walter was the permanent Paris correspondent of the *Herald-Tribune* and one of the half a dozen American journalists remaining in Paris for the German occupation. All the others had left three days previously. It looked as though I was going to see the occupation, too, whether I liked it or not, and I began trying to figure how eventually I would ever get back to England.

'With Italy in the war, your only hope will be travelling via Russia, the Orient and America. Or perhaps you could go by Norway and Sweden to Finland and get a boat from Petsamo across the North Sea.'

Neither particularly appealed to me. I pictured myself travelling for the rest of the war.

'But d'you mean to say you didn't *know* what you were getting yourself in for?' Walter persisted. 'Here in Paris the journalists have known since Tuesday the city wasn't going to be defended.'

I told him I hadn't seen a newspaper for twenty-four hours, but up till then there was no intimation in the English papers that Paris was to be an open city. On the contrary, they had printed despatches claiming it would be defended to the last ditch. I still had yesterday's *Daily Express* with me and showed him the British United Press story dated Paris, Tuesday:

> The Military authorities took over control of Paris today. All highways into the city have been barricaded, and preparations were being made to defend it street by street should this be necessary. Planes were heard throughout the night, and anti-aircraft at intervals. Heavier gunfire can be heard from time to time from the north.
>
> Meanwhile, the exodus of civilians goes on. Throughout the night, women, children and old people poured southwards and the trek continues today. But Paris refuses to panic. Shops open as usual; even jewellery is still on display in windows. The spirit of France is exemplified in *Le Matin* today. It says: 'Two thousand years ago the bridges were destroyed and the suburbs of the city set on fire for the purpose of holding the enemy. So there is nothing new under the sun. In the worst crises Paris remains unsubdued. Paris never submits.'

Walter admitted it didn't give much indication of things.

'But what do the people of Paris think?' I asked. 'Do they want to see their city handed over without a fight?'

'I don't know. Most of them are in such a panic it's hard to tell. They don't know what's going on, poor things. And if they did, there isn't much they could do about it. Right now, I can't bring myself to talk with any of them about it. For the last twenty-four hours I've avoided them like a plague and stuck with the journalists. It's too awful to talk about.'

I shared Walter's feelings. The last thing I wanted to do was raise the subject. In fact, the only conversation I had was with one of the men in a garage a few doors away from the Lancaster. While I was waiting for Walter, I decided to find out just how bad the automobile situation really was. I walked in and asked if there were any cars either for sale or for hire. The garage proprietor was a huge, bulky man and he glared at me angrily.

'Listen, if there was one car in Paris, *one* car, I would have it. In fact, if it were possible to steal a car, I would have it. I would even kill someone to get a car. Instead, I must stay here and watch the filthy Boches come into Paris.' He hissed the word 'Boches', then spat violently on the floor.

Walter and I decided the American Embassy was my only hope. The Ambassador, William Bullitt, and his staff were remaining for the occupation, and the Stars and Stripes still fluttered reassuringly from the flagpole. When we drew up in front of it, an elderly man who had been wandering around in the courtyard came running up to us and begged us to help him to get out of Paris. He spoke English with a thick accent and told us he was a German-Jew, the head of an anti-Nazi organisation. 'If they find me here, they will shoot me.' He was so agitated he could scarcely get the words out. We told him we had no way of leaving Paris ourselves and asked if the Embassy couldn't help him, but he shook his head and said he had tried everything. He went off, his shoulders bent in despair. Walter said the Embassy had been besieged by hundreds of these people and had helped all they could. 'But that poor devil hasn't got much of a chance. Anti-Nazi or not, no one's going to give a German a lift for fear he'll turn out to be a Fifth Columnist.'

Walter and I went into the Embassy and first called on Colonel Fuller, the American military attaché. He was none too cordial and I could scarcely blame him: stranded women journalists were a final straw. He said he would do his best, but offered little hope. Then we went to the Ambassador's secretary, who was more sympathetic but no more optimistic.

We walked down the white marble steps. 'There's no use bothering about it any more,' I said. 'Here I am and here I'll have to stay.'

Just then there was a voice, 'Hi, Walter.' It was Henry Cassidy of the Associated Press. They discussed the situation, then Walter told him of my predicament.

'Oh, I think I can give you a hand,' he said cheerfully. 'Tom Healy, the London *Daily Mirror* correspondent, has just arrived in Paris. He's like you, he didn't know what was going on either. He'd been cruising around the Italian–French frontier, hadn't had any news for a couple of days, and just drifted in by accident. He's got a Chrysler roadster and if he hasn't already promised to take someone else, I'm sure he'll be glad to give you a lift.'

The suspense of the next hour while Cassidy tried to get hold of Tom seemed endless. At one o'clock he finally sent a message to say the latter was leaving in the late afternoon and would take me with him.

'If the Germans aren't already here by then,' said Walter darkly.

I spent the next couple of hours typing out my story in the *Herald-Tribune* office. Walter wrote a despatch which I promised to send for him from Tours. A small bistro was open near the office and we tried to get something to eat, but all they had was coffee. There was plenty of food in Paris, they said, but no vans or trucks to distribute it. Walter had some biscuits which I was thankful for; except for a cup of tea the day before and coffee in the morning, I hadn't had anything to eat for nearly forty-eight hours.

I left Paris about five o'clock in the afternoon. When I went into the Hotel Lancaster to get my bag, the porter, who was sitting gloomily at the desk, said: 'You're leaving too?' His voice was almost reproachful and I had a sudden feeling of guilt, as though I had no right to go. 'Your country is our only hope now,' he added bitterly. 'Americans have always loved Paris. Perhaps now they will help us.'

What a hope, I thought. During the last nine months America had watched eight countries being overrun. The land of liberty sent plenty of sympathy but little else. 'How does it affect our interests?' That was what she asked, while Europe ran with blood. A feeling of anger surged up in me. What was the matter with my country that it could remain so indifferent to the obliteration of the civilised world – her world?

Tom Healy's car pointed southwards out of Paris. We drove along the banks of the Seine and saw the reflection of the wonderful blue-grey buildings shimmering in the water. Neither of us looked back.

5

The Beginning of the End

Try to think in terms of millions. Try to think of noise and confusion, of the thick smell of petrol, of the scraping of automobile gears, of shouts, wails, curses, tears. Try to think of a hot sun and underneath it an unbroken stream of humanity flowing southwards from Paris, and you have a picture of the gigantic civilian exodus that presaged the German advance.

I had seen refugees before. I had seen them wending their way along the roads of Spain and Czechoslovakia, straggling across the Polish–Romanian frontier, trudging down the icy paths of Finland. But I had never seen anything like this. This was the first *mechanised* evacuation in history. There were some people in carts, some on foot and some on bicycles. But for the most part everyone was in a car.

Those cars, lurching, groaning, backfiring, represented a Noah's Ark of vehicles. Anything that had four wheels and an engine was pressed into service, no matter what the state of decrepitude; there were taxi-cabs, ice-trucks, bakery vans, perfume wagons, sports roadsters and Paris buses, all of them packed with human beings. I even saw a hearse loaded with children. They crawled along the roads two and three abreast, sometimes cutting across the fields and straddling the ditches. Tom and I caught up with the stream a mile or so outside Paris on the Paris–Dourdan–Chartres road and in the next three hours covered only nine miles.

We saw terrible sights. All along the way cars that had run out of petrol or broken down were pushed into the fields. Old people, too tired or ill to walk any further, were lying on the ground under the merciless glare of the sun. We saw one old woman propped up in the ditch with the family clustered around trying to pour some wine down her throat. Often the stream of traffic was held up by cars that stalled and refused to move again. One car ran out of petrol halfway up a hill. It was a bakery van, driven by a woman. Everyone shouted and honked their horns, while she stood in the middle of the road with her four children around her begging someone to give her some petrol. No one had any to spare. Finally, three men climbed out of a truck and in spite of her agonised protests, shoved the car into the ditch. It fell with a crash. The rear axle broke and the household possessions piled on top sprawled across the field. She screamed out a frenzy of abuse, then flung herself on the ground and sobbed. Once again the procession moved on.

In that world of terror, panic and confusion, it was difficult to believe that these were the citizens of Paris, citizens whose forefathers had fought for their freedom like tigers and stormed the Bastille with their bare hands. For the first time, I began to understand what had happened to France. Morale was a question of faith; faith in your cause, faith in your goal, but above all else, faith in your leaders. How could these people have faith in leaders who had abandoned them? Leaders who had given them no directions, no information, no reassurances; who neither had arranged for their evacuation nor called on them to stay at their places and fight for Paris until the last? If this was an example of French leadership, no wonder France was doomed. Everywhere the machinery seemed to have broken down. The dam had begun to crumble and hysteria, a trickle at first, had grown into a torrent.

Even the military roads were overrun with panic-stricken civilians. Tom was an officially accredited war correspondent, so he swung off on to one of them. Although the entrance was patrolled by gendarmes, who demanded our credentials, there was no one to keep traffic from streaming in at the intersections and a mile or so further on we once again found civilian cars moving along two or three abreast. At one point an artillery unit on its way up to the new front south-east of Paris was blocked by a furniture truck stalled across the road. The driver, with perspiration pouring down his face, was trying to crank the car while the soldiers yelled and cursed at him. One of them paced angrily up and down, saying, 'Filthy civilians. Filthy, filthy civilians.' At last, the truck got started again and the unit moved past. Another time, a procession of ambulances, with gongs clanging frantically, were held up by congestion on the outskirts of a village for over an hour. The drivers swore loudly but it had little effect; I wondered what was happening to the poor devils inside.

The only military units that succeeded in getting a clear berth were the tanks. Once we looked back to see two powerful fifteen-ton monsters thundering up behind us. They were travelling about forty miles an hour and the effect was remarkable. People gave one look and pulled in to the ditches. They went rolling by, the great treads tearing up the earth and throwing pieces of dirt into the air like a fountain. After them came a number of fast-moving lorries and a string of soldiers on motorcycles with machine-guns attached to the side-cars. They all seemed in excellent spirits; one of the tanks was gaily marked in chalk '*La Petite Marie*', and the trucks and guns were draped with flowers. Two of the motorcyclists shouted at us, asking if we had any cigarettes. Tom told me to throw them a couple of packages. They were so pleased they signalled us to follow them, escorted us past the long string of civilian cars to the middle of the convoy and placed us firmly between the two tanks. For the next ten or fifteen minutes we roared along at forty miles an hour. Unfortunately, eight or nine miles down the road they turned off, the motorcyclists waved goodbye and blew us kisses, and once again we found ourselves caught up in the slow-moving procession of evacuees.

It was nearly nine o'clock now and we had covered little more than twenty miles. 'I wonder if we'll make it,' said Tom, looking at his watch. When we had left Paris at five o'clock there were already reports that the Germans were circling around on both sides of the capital to cut off the roads in the rear. Tom had a military map and we decided to try the cross-country lanes. Some of them were scarcely more than footpaths but we could at least average ten or twelve miles an hour, which was a great improvement. It was getting so dark it was difficult to see and twice we barely avoided running over people with no lights on their bicycles. Suddenly the sky lit up with a flash and we heard a far-away rumble. It was the first gunfire I had heard all day. 'Something's creeping up on us,' said Tom. 'Still, if we keep on like this, I think we'll be all right.'

We drove along the twisting lane for five or six miles. It was a relief to be in the open countryside away from the suffocating smell of petrol, but the road was so black the driving was a strain. Tom had some food in the back of the car and we decided to stop and have something to eat. He was in favour of finding a haystack to lean against, but the next few miles of country were barren and rocky. At last we saw a clump of trees outlined in the darkness. It seemed the best we could do, so we pulled over to the side of the road. The car gave a violent lurch and careened into a six-foot ditch. Only the right wheels were gripping the road. The left side was flat against the earth. We were suspended at such a sharp angle we had difficulty in forcing the upper door, but at last succeeded in climbing out.

The rumble of guns seemed to be louder and the flashes against the sky more frequent. 'Boches or no Boches,' said Tom, 'it looks as though we're going to linger here a while. Let's pick out a place to eat, then I'll see if I can find someone to give us a hand.'

But even here we were frustrated. The field was soaking wet. There was one miserable haystack in the middle of it, damp and soggy. We went back to the road and paced up and down for ten or fifteen minutes, wondering if anyone would pass. It was getting cold and I began to shiver. After having cursed the traffic for hours, it was slightly ironical to find ourselves longing for the sight of a human being.

Tom finally started back to the last village, several miles away, and I climbed back into the car (which was like going down a toboggan slide) to try and get warm. It was a beautiful night. The sky was clear and starry, and the only noise to break the quiet was the drone of crickets and the spasmodic thunder of guns. I wondered how far the Germans had got. Funny to think that people in America probably knew more than we did as to what was going on.

It was nearly midnight when Tom got back again. He had tried a dozen farmhouses but everyone was in bed. At last (with the help of a hundred-franc note) he had extracted a promise from one of the farmers to come at dawn with a team of horses and pull us out.

That was seven precious hours away, but it was the best he could do. As an American citizen, I was in no danger, but if Tom were captured, it meant an internment camp for the rest of the war. He appeared completely unruffled, however, and commented with characteristic English calmness: 'Well, there's nothing to be done about it. Now, let's eat. God, I'm hungry.'

We sat by the roadside, drinking wine and munching bread and cheese; then we got out all the coats and sweaters we could find, wrapped them round us, and climbed back into the car. The angle was so uncomfortable I slept only by fits and starts, expecting momentarily to be awakened by the noise of German tanks. Luckily, no such startling developments took place. The farmer kept his promise and shortly after five o'clock appeared with two large fat white horses who pulled the car out as easily as though it had been a perambulator. Once again we started on our way.

We stopped at the next village – I can't remember the name of it – to get some coffee. The first sight that greeted us was half a dozen British Tommies lined up on the crooked cobblestone street, the corporal standing in front of them, bawling them out for some misdemeanour. They were large, beefy-looking men who might have stepped out of a page from *Punch*. When the corporal dismissed them they grinned sheepishly and made a few jokes behind his back. Tom asked one of them where the officers were billeted, and I went into the café to try to get some of the grime off my clothes. In spite of the early hour there was a buzz of activity inside. Several people were sitting around, and a radio was blaring loudly. The announcer was saying something about the 'heroic resistance of our troops'. An old man made a gesture of disbelief and muttered something I couldn't hear. The woman with him replied angrily, her harsh voice echoing through the café: '*Ne dîtes pas ça. Il faut espérer.*'

I asked the waitress if there was any coffee, but she regarded me in mild surprise and replied that the refugees had gone through the village like a swarm of locusts. 'Everywhere,' she said, 'they have stripped the countryside bare.'

It took me some time to get clean again, and when I came out I found Tom waiting for me with two officers, wearing the insignia of the Royal Engineers. They offered to give us breakfast and led us down the street to the mess. They seemed to know little more than we did; they told us they had just received orders to move up to a new position. Most of them had been in France for the last five or six months and pressed us eagerly with questions about England. French morale may have been shaky, but there was nothing downhearted about this group. 'You don't think people at home will be discouraged by this setback, do you?' 'Setback!' That was a good one, I thought. When we climbed into the car again they all clustered around and one of them said: 'Well, so long. See you in Cologne next Christmas!'

We did the next hundred miles to Tours in about five hours. We had learned the trick now and kept entirely to the country lanes which, rough though they were, were fairly clear of refugees. It was only when we got within ten miles of Tours and were forced back on the main road again that the trickle once again became a mighty stream. Added to this, Tom's radiator began leaking. The water boiled up and clouds of steam began pouring out of the front. It took us nearly an hour to get into the city. The great bridge over the Loire looked like a long, thin breadcrust swarming with ants.

Finally, at one-thirty, with Tom's car gasping and heaving, we drew up before the Hotel de l'Univers. The first person I saw was Knickerbocker, just coming out of the door.

'My God! How did you get here?'

'You're always asking me that.'

'But where've you come from?'

'Paris.'

'Paris! But the Germans went into Paris hours ago. When did you leave?'

I told him.

'They were in the Bois de Boulogne last night. You must have rubbed shoulders with them on the way out. Probably you just didn't recognise them,' he added with a grin. 'All soldiers look grey in the dark.'

* * *

Tours was bedlam. The French High Command had announced that the River Loire was to be the next line of defence and all sorts of wild rumours were circulating: first, that the German Air Force had threatened to obliterate the town; and, second, that German motorcycle units had reached Le Mans only thirty miles away, and were likely to come thundering through the streets at any moment now. The Government had already left for Bordeaux and the refugees who had scrambled into Tours in a panic were now trying to scramble out again in still more of a panic. I ran into Eddie Ward of the BBC, who told me that Press Wireless, the only means of communication with the outside world (all cables to England were sent via America at eightpence a word), was still functioning, and that he and the Reuter staff were remaining another day. As it was my only chance to file a story, I decided to stay too. Eddie said Reuter's could probably provide me with a bed and he would give me a place in his car to Bordeaux in the morning.

There were a good many speculations about Winston Churchill's conversation with Reynaud and Weygand three days before; he was believed to have urged the French, if the worst came to the worst, to continue the war from North Africa. Although it had been announced in London that complete agreement had been reached, 'as to the measures to be taken to meet the developments in the war situation', most of the journalists were pessimistic about the prospects of France's continuation of the fight. French officials seemed in a state of moral collapse; even the censorship appeared to have broken down, but no one complained about that. Up till this time despatches had been censored so rigidly it was impossible to give any indication of the situation. Now, quite suddenly, everyone could say what they liked. I wrote a long piece about the panic and confusion along the road from Paris and not a word was cut. Gordon Waterfield sent a story suggesting that France was threatened with a defeat similar to that of 1870, and the next morning Harold King sent an even more pessimistic cable. Gordon told me later that when these despatches reached London the censors were so surprised they held them up for a considerable time while they found out from higher authorities whether it was really true that France was in such a bad way.

Eddie drove me over to Reuter's headquarters, a large, handsome edifice about a mile from the centre of the town. The house had been taken on a six-month lease to the tune of forty thousand francs and, as it turned out, was occupied exactly forty-eight hours. I spent the night there, which seemed an odd interlude. From a world of dirt and discomfort I suddenly found myself plunged into a Hollywood bedroom, decorated with mirrors and chintz, a thick white rug and a pale green telephone. That evening eight of us dined at a table with candles glowing and silver gleaming. We had turtle soup, tournedos with sauce *béarnaise*, fresh vegetables and a wonderful cherry pie. The world might be turning upside down, but it was difficult to realise it.

The house was run by a charming, middle-aged couple – a caretaker and his wife. The latter, plump and motherly, was also taut and defiant; she refused to let bad news alarm her and clung ferociously to the belief that France would rally in the end. 'If there were more people like her,' said Eddie, 'there wouldn't be an end. But, unfortunately, there aren't.'

I spent that afternoon writing my story for the *Sunday Times*. About seven o'clock the wail of sirens hooted through the town and a few minutes later I heard the drone of bombers. I tried to ignore it and went on typing. Suddenly I heard a shriek from the drawing room. I ran downstairs and found the eight- and nine-year-old children of the caretakers jumping up and down with joy. '*Nous avons vu les Boches!*' Then they both leaned far out of the window, pointing towards the sky. You could just make out a few small specks circling overhead. I wished I could get as enthusiastic over an air-raid; in spite of all the talk about sparing children the terrors of bombardment, they seemed to be the only ones who really enjoyed it.

I was surprised that their mother didn't order them into a shelter, but I learned later she was disdainful of people who took cover. The next morning when the German planes came over again, several bombs fell near us, shaking the house violently. Eddie and I went down to the kitchen. She gave us an enquiring look.

'You're not afraid of the Boches, are you?'

'Oh no,' said Eddie weakly. 'I thought perhaps you might have an extra cup of coffee.'

'Oh, certainly.' Her face brightened. 'I don't like to see people afraid of the Boches. They're all filthy bullies and cowards. My husband was in the last war and he said whenever they came up against equal numbers they turned and ran. They're all the same. There's nothing to be afraid of.'

'Nothing,' I agreed, my heart still pounding uncertainly. Eddie gave me a sour look.

We left shortly after lunch for Bordeaux. There were six of us: Gordon Waterfield, Harold King, Courtenay Young, Joan Slocombe (the pretty nineteen-year-old daughter of George Slocombe of the *Sunday Express*), Eddie and myself. Gordon had a Ford roadster and Eddie a Citroen, with an RAF number plate, which he had picked up somewhere between Brussels and Tours. They had been wise enough to do a good deal of shopping and it took over half an hour to load up the cars with blankets, sleeping-bags, cooking utensils and stores of food – not to mention typewriters, luggage, office files, a camping tent and a collapsible canoe.

Just before we started off, Courtenay Young and I hurried down to the Press Wireless office to send a final despatch. On the way back I heard someone call to me and looked around to see the little Egyptian with whom I had travelled to Paris. His hair was streaming round his face, his clothes were caked with mud, and he looked more agitated than ever. He had had a terrible time. He had found his house deserted, and his children gone; he hadn't yet discovered what had happened to them. He had left Paris only twenty-four hours before and had actually seen the Germans entering the city through the Aubervilliers Gate. Motorcycle units had passed as close as two hundred yards from where he was standing. He said the occupation had come as a shock to many of the people and the scenes of despair were unbelievable. Men and women wept openly in the street. 'Some of them went almost crazy,' he gasped. 'I saw one woman pull out a revolver and shoot her dog, then set fire to her house.'

The Egyptian was on his way to Bordeaux. He was in such a rush he couldn't stop to tell me more and I never learned the story of how he had managed to escape from Paris.

6

Sorry Separation at Bordeaux

Did you keep faith with me? When all was well
Yes; but I clave to you when all was not.
And, when temptation touched your citadel,
Your weakness won again, and you forgot –
Forgot your Self, and freedom and your friends,
Even interest; and now our vaunted glow
Becomes a blush, as the long story ends
In sorry separation at Bordeaux.

Robert Vansittart

Our trip to Bordeaux was off the beaten track. When I think of it now I think of stately châteaux, cool rivers, wooded glens, wine, sunshine and flowers. Although the main highways were choked with terror and misery, with the smell of petrol and the roll of gun-wheels, the country lanes belonged to another world. We found housewives gossiping on the crooked village streets and peasants working in the fields as peacefully as they always had. Their lives seemed so detached from the turmoil around them we began to wonder if they even knew a war was going on.

Certainly few seemed to know how critical things were. When we talked to them the majority shrugged their shoulders and said they had so little news it was impossible to judge the situation. Many had not even learned that the Germans had occupied Paris twenty-four hours before. (The French communiqué never announced the German entry – it merely stated that French troops had withdrawn to both sides of the capital 'according to the plans of the French

Command, aimed at sparing Paris the devastation which defence would have involved'. After that Paris was not referred to again.) The people in the country had either not heard the communiqué or not grasped what it meant. At any rate, they showed little alarm. The deepest doubt we heard expressed was from an old farmer who leaned over a fence, pitchfork in hand, to talk to Eddie and me. He said he didn't like the sound of things, scratched his head and asked gravely: 'Are we so sure we are going to win?'

We spent that night in a field near a brook on the outskirts of a tiny village. We pitched our tent and got out the blankets, our food and cooking apparatus. We dined on pâté de foie gras, chicken galantine, sardines, pickles, onions, bread, cheese and wine. We lay on the grass and talked for hours about France. Suddenly Harold King said: 'It's funny how already we discuss France in the past tense.'

'Well, there's no use fooling ourselves,' said Eddie. 'It *is* past. Past and finished. God, think of the Germans drinking this wine!'

The next morning we strolled down to the village, about half a mile away. It consisted of only a dozen houses, clustered around an old church; of a petrol pump, a café and an over-cluttered shop which was doing a thriving business selling everything from ribbons to wine.

At eleven o'clock the church bells started pealing for High Mass, and mothers and children, in their best Sunday clothes and neat, polished shoes, began assembling in the churchyard. We went into the café where half a dozen people were gathered. We asked for the *vin du pays* and a small boy brought us a jug of Vouvray. Certainly it was an odd and peaceful scene for a Sunday which will go down in history as the day when the Reynaud Government fell and the Republic of France entered the final phase of its collapse. The people around us were discussing the war; they were bewildered by what had happened to Paris, for they thought it was to be defended to the last. One said hopefully: 'Perhaps all this is a trick to trap the Germans.' Another, a woman with a broad face and rough red hands: 'Oh, well, Paris is not important. It is just another city.' As Paris was as dear to most French people as their own villages, this struck us as an extraordinary remark. We understood when we discovered she was a Belgian refugee from Liège. When we asked her opinion of King Leopold, she lifted her hands in anger and said: '*Cochon.*'

The most vivid character in the village was the café proprietress – an old woman of seventy-eight. She looked as though she had stepped out of a Flaubert novel; she was dressed in black with a voluminous skirt and a small white cap on her head. She had a brown, wrinkled face that lighted up with amusement. She was evidently the matriarch of the village, for people listened to her respectfully and whenever she wanted anything done everyone scurried about in half a dozen directions. She was so excited at our arrival she insisted on serving us herself. She kept hovering about, murmuring: 'The brave, brave English. Together we will drive the Boches back. Eh? Is it not so?' Each time she demanded an answer: when she got it, she nodded with immense satisfaction. She went on to say she was not depressed by the news of Paris. All her life she had been troubled by the Boches, but in the end things always came right. She could remember the war of 1870, for she was eight years old at the time. In the war of 1914 her sons had fought, and today her grandsons were at the front. 'This war is the hardest,' she sighed. 'But since it would be better to be dead than live under Hitler, we must never surrender. Eh? Is it not so?' We nodded. '*Bon!* Now you brave Englishmen will have some more wine, won't you?'

The brave Englishmen did. In fact the only thing that got us started for Bordeaux at all was that Gordon Waterfield's portable radio informed us the French Cabinet was meeting again that afternoon and would make an important announcement that night. Reluctantly we left. Although Marshal Pétain may have most of France in his pocket today, I'm willing to bet our little village is still die-hard anti-Hitler – and will stay that way as long as the old proprietress has a breath left in her body.

On the last lap of our journey to Bordeaux we passed a good many towns and villages inundated with refugees. Wherever we found refugees we found panic. Dr Goebbels couldn't have found a more effective method of spreading alarm and despondency; but it was not until that very day, June 16th, that the French Government took any measure to prevent it, for the first time requesting people to remain where they were.

Bordeaux was Tours all over again: cafés and hotels overflowing, cars careening under household possessions; people besieging the Spanish Consulate for visas; more rumours of threats from the German Air Force; more stories of the imminence of German tank and motorcycle units; more people angry, confused and dejected. We learned that the Cabinet was still discussing the question as to whether France should capitulate or carry on the war from North Africa. Reynaud, Mandel, Marin, Monnet and Delbos were said to be in favour of continuing the struggle, but the Pétain–Laval group were pressing strongly for surrender. Laval's dark, sinister face was very much in evidence at the Hotel Splendide restaurant; you saw him with a group of friends, head bent over the table, arguing and gesticulating vehemently. Knickerbocker went up to talk to him and in the course of the conversation said: 'Whatever you do, don't surrender. If you go on fighting, I'm sure America will put her full weight behind you and in the end you'll win. But if you give in now, you're finished.'

Laval smiled. 'Perhaps,' he said. 'But I'm not sure. You see, I don't think France is Germany's primary object. I think her *real*

aim is Soviet Russia.' This, at a moment when the German Army
was streaming through France, when towns were being bombed
and people were fleeing in confusion from one end of the country
to the other.

Laval was not the only one: a good many other Frenchmen,
mostly Right Wing reactionaries, reasoned along the same
lines. When I returned to England from Italy, four days after the
German invasion had begun, I talked to a Frenchman who was a
member of the French Economic Mission in London. Already he
was pessimistic about France's chances of victory. 'In a few weeks,'
he said, 'France will be faced with the most difficult decision in
her history. She will have the choice of either being completely
annihilated by the Germans or making a peace that will reduce
her to a third-class power.' It was the first time I'd heard peace
mentioned; I remember how astonished I was. 'But you wouldn't
even be a third-class power,' I said. 'You would be just a German
province.'

'Oh no,' he replied, 'you cannot destroy France. England yes,
but not France. There will always be a *bloc* of French people on
the continent, and one day they will rise again and regain their old
power just as the Germans have.'

At the time I was so alarmed by this conversation that I repeated
it to a friend in the Foreign Office. He attached little importance
to it, believing such sentiments were held by only a small and
inconsiderable group of chronic defeatists. But it was the same
brand of reasoning that was gaining ground in Bordeaux that
Sunday. 'Cut your losses and drive the best bargain you can'; that
was how the Peace Party pleaded for surrender. In a desperate
effort to persuade the French Government to continue its resistance, whether from France itself, or her overseas Empire, the
British Government offered to conclude an act of union between

the two countries. A draft was sent to the French Government by the British Ambassador that fateful Sunday afternoon. This is what it said:

> At this most fateful moment in the history of the modern world, the Government of the United Kingdom and the French Republic make this declaration of indissoluble union and unyielding resolution in their common defence of justice and freedom against subjection to a system which reduces mankind to a life of robots and slaves.
>
> The two Governments declare that France and Great Britain shall no longer be two, but one Franco–British Union. The Constitution of the Union will provide for joint organs of defence, foreign, financial and economic policies. Every citizen of France will enjoy immediately citizenship of Great Britain. Every British subject will become a citizen of France.
>
> Both countries will share responsibility for the repair of the devastation of war wherever it occurs in their territories, and the resources of both shall be equally and as one applied to that purpose.
>
> During the war there shall be a single War Cabinet and all the forces of Britain and France, whether on land, sea or in the air, will be placed under its direction. It will govern from wherever it best can. The two Parliaments will be formally associated.
>
> The nations of the British Empire are already forming new armies. France will keep her available forces in the field, on the sea and in the air.
>
> The Union appeals to the United States to fortify the economic resources of the Allies and to bring her powerful material aid to the common cause. The Union will concentrate

its whole energy against the power of the enemy, no matter where the battle may be, and thus we shall conquer.

The leaders of France rejected the offer. They had too little faith in their cause, too little faith in the Third Republic. That night it was left to M. Mandel, a staunch and bitter anti-Nazi, to announce to half a dozen journalists in a drab and dingy room at the Prefecture that Reynaud had resigned and that Pétain was the new Prime Minister – the peace Prime Minister. I will never forget him standing there, small and white, his head high and his voice firm, speaking the words he had fought against speaking to the end – words that sounded the death-knell of France. As he was known to be unswervingly anti-capitulation, one of the French journalists asked him if he had made any plans to leave. 'Oh no, I shall remain here.' Then he added with an ironical smile, 'I'm just beginning to know Bordeaux a little.' (The following day Mandel was arrested as the leader of the 'pro-revolt' party, but at the insistence of Herriot and President Lebrun was soon released. He demanded a written apology from Marshal Pétain and gossip had it that, not satisfied with the old man's first draft, he said severely: 'This won't do at all. I will dictate a *proper* letter of apology,' to which the Marshal acceded, writing down the profuse and abject sentences which were given him.)

What had happened to the tough spirit of France? What had caused this complete and utter moral collapse? Innumerable and conflicting explanations have been given: I leave it to the experts. But of one thing I am sure: that if the French people had had leaders of conviction and integrity, the debacle would never have happened. Reynaud, a sincere and accurate prophet, lacked the strong personality necessary to grip the popular imagination. His weakness became apparent when he finally threw in his hand and knuckled under to Pétain. Would Churchill have resigned? If the leaders had not lost faith in their cause, the people would not have lost faith in their leaders. German tanks might have penetrated the country's defences, but Paris would have been defended street by street; towns might have been bombed but there would have been no flow of hysterical refugees to spread despair like a contagious disease; the Government might have been forced abroad, but the French Fleet would be fighting at England's side now.

Instead, the people of France were betrayed and deserted. News was denied them and directions withheld from them. I think Gordon Waterfield, in his book *What Happened to France*, has summed it up in the following paragraph:

> It can be shown, I consider, that those who led France in her hour of trial bear nine-tenths of the responsibility . . . The Government kept on repeating that they would hold out to the last. 'Paris,' they said, 'is in a state of defence,' and a few days later they declared it an open town. 'We will fight from North Africa if necessary,' they proclaimed, and a short time afterwards they asked for the German terms. 'We will not,' they said, 'accept a dishonourable armistice,' and they gave Hitler a blank cheque. They were not only unfit to lead, but they deceived the people. It is the prosecutors of the Riom trial who should be in the dock.

* * *

We left for England on the following day on a British cargo boat. We motored to Le Verdon, a port on the mouth of the Gironde, about sixty miles from Bordeaux, where our ship was anchored in the harbour. There was a last-minute scramble among the journalists to get rid of their francs: everyone hurried down to the shops to buy whatever they could, most of them coming back with bottles of perfume to take home to their girlfriends.

The change of government was announced briefly in the morning papers, but the average French person hadn't yet grasped what it meant. It wasn't until midday that Pétain broadcast that France was asking the Germans for an armistice. Eddie Ward, Knickerbocker, Ed Angly and I were sitting at a small quayside café at the Pointe de Grave, a mile or so from Le Verdon. It was a wonderful day. Before us a hundred ships lay at anchor in the harbour; the white sand glistened in the sunshine, and the tall pine trees looked like splendid sentinels. Our waitress, a plump, smiling girl, filled up our wine glasses and took our order. A radio was turned on in the kitchen. Suddenly she heard Pétain's voice saying: 'It is with a heavy heart I say we must cease the fight. I have applied to our opponent to ask him if he is ready to sign with us, as between soldiers after the fight and in honour, a means to put an end to hostilities . . .' She came back in the room with tears streaming down her face, gasping: 'We can't live under the Boches. We can't. It is not possible.' Ed Angly tried to comfort her, but for the rest of the meal she served us red-eyed and sobbing.

The tender didn't appear until four that afternoon. At the last moment someone announced that no one was allowed more than one piece of luggage; there was a frantic commotion while people tried to decide what was most important. When we finally left the quay was littered with discarded hampers, bags and boxes – not to mention a long string of motor-cars that had to be abandoned. Among them were Tom Healy's valiant Chrysler, Gordon's Ford and Eddie's Citroen.

We lay in the harbour for over twenty-four hours. Every hour tenders steamed out towards us bringing more passengers until, finally, our small nine-thousand-ton cargo ship, the SS *Madura*, which normally carried a hundred and eighty passengers, was packed with over sixteen hundred people – the normal complement of the *Queen Mary*. There were bankers, officials, cabinet ministers, wives, children, soldiers, nurses, businessmen, invalid ladies, retired colonels, maiden aunts, and fifty or sixty journalists. Although most of the passengers were English, there were several hundred French people: many of them climbed on board weeping convulsively at the parting from their relatives and the uncertainty as to whether they would ever see their native land again. There in the harbour, with the sun streaming down and the peaceful outline of the French coast in the distance, it was hard to realise that France had come to an end.

Most people, however, had little time to meditate as to what it meant, for the immediate concern was to find a place to sleep: all the berths, tables and deck chairs had long since been snatched up. Everyone began hurriedly staking out claims on the decks and in the passageways. Soon it was so crowded there wasn't an inch of available space. Mr Comert, the French foreign press chief, made himself a bed on top of the ping-pong table. On the lower decks there was a detachment of Marines to keep order among the lascar crew (who were apt to panic in the event of danger); a group of marine artillery being transferred from Africa; thirty or forty nurses and ambulance drivers; and a number of wounded British soldiers.

The ship was so overcrowded that if it had been hit few would have survived. It was difficult to decide where to sleep, for although it was preferable below in case of bombs, it was wiser above in case of torpedoes. Eddie, Gordon Waterfield and I flipped a coin and put our blankets down on the top deck; soon afterwards we doubted the shrewdness of our move, for a German bomber dived out of the clouds and made a hit-and-run attempt at the harbour.

Our ship was armed and the guns in the stern burst into a loud rattle. We saw bombs fall in the distance and watched the water shoot up like a geyser. Then three French fighters roared overhead and we heard later that the German had been brought down. I don't know whether the events of the past few days had dulled everyone's sensibilities, but while all this was going on people were so indifferent that some of them actually sat in their deck chairs reading novels as calmly as though they were on a South Sea cruise. Later that night, while we were still at anchor, we had another raid warning but heard no bombs, and a few minutes later the all-clear sounded. The next day the German radio claimed we had been sunk.

We pulled out from Le Verdon on the afternoon of June 18th. We travelled on a parallel course only a few hundred yards from another refugee cargo ship and were escorted by a destroyer, a small but comforting speck in the distance. The Captain called for volunteers to stand lookout watches for submarines, and most of the journalists signed up. Each stood watch for an hour at a time, but the only excitement any of them had was when Bill Stoneman of the *Chicago Daily News* spied a small fleet of Spanish fishing boats. Other than that all was quiet and the Captain told us the only occasion any shooting had been done was when they made a mistake and blew a whale to pieces off the west coast of Africa.

The original passengers of our ship had had a tiring journey, to say the least. They were lost in the flow of refugees – none of us discovered which they were – but we were told they had boarded the vessel in East Africa for a two-week trip to England and had now been on it nearly two months. When they reached Suez, the Mediterranean was suddenly closed to British shipping and they were forced to go all the way back to Cape Town. They remained in port a week while the ship was 'degaussed' against magnetic

mines, then started once more on their journey. As they neared
the English Channel they received an SOS to put in at Bordeaux
and take off the refugees.

Although the Captain had been able to take on no extra rations
since Cape Town, the chef managed to provide all sixteen hundred passengers with two meals a day; for breakfast a cup of tea
and a slice of bread, and for dinner a piece of meat, some rice and
a potato. The native crew had a more substantial ration and were
only too pleased to share some of it with Knickerbocker and Ed
Angly in exchange for a handsome shower of silver. We had a little food left over from our Tours–Bordeaux trip – none of it very
practical – but plenty of caviar and pâté de foie gras which we
devoured hungrily for breakfast.

During the thirty-six-hour journey, news was picked up spas-
modically over the radio, typed out by one of the journalists, and
pinned to the billboard. All kinds of rumours swept the ship con-
cerning the German demands and the French replies. But the one
question that was on everybody's lips was the fate of the French
Navy. The French passengers were vehement about this. 'They
must never surrender it to the Germans; if they cannot turn it
over to Great Britain, they must scuttle it first.'

But whatever happened, one thing was sure: England was fighting on. On the same afternoon that our ship was sailing out of the
harbour of Le Verdon, and the coast of France was fading away in
the distance, Mr Churchill was saying in the House of Commons:

> What General Weygand called the Battle of France is over. I
> expect that the Battle of Britain is about to begin. Upon this
> battle depends the survival of Christian civilisation. Upon
> it depends our own British life, and the long continuity of
> our institutions and our Empire. The whole fury and might

of the enemy must very soon be turned on us. Hitler knows that he will have to break us in this island or lose the war. If we can stand up to him, all Europe may be free and the life of the world may move forward into broad, sunlit uplands. But if we fail, then the whole world, including the United States, including all that we have known and cared for, will sink into the abyss of a new Dark Age made more sinister, and perhaps more protracted, by the lights of perverted science. Let us, therefore, brace ourselves to our duties, and so bear ourselves that, if the British Empire and its Commonwealth last for a thousand years, men will say: 'This was their finest hour.'

Yes, England was fighting on and the people of England were already embarking on 'their finest hour' with that mild and unshakeable imperturbability so characteristic of them. When we disembarked at Falmouth, a group of motherly, middle-aged women brought us lemonade and sandwiches, fussing over us, saying what a hard time we must have had. 'Now you're safely back in England,' said one, 'everything will be all right.'

Yes, England was another world. A second woman volunteer handed me an emigration card, stamped 'Refugee'.

I protested: 'I'm not a refugee. I'm an American journalist.'

'Everyone,' she said firmly, 'who is not English, is a refugee.'

I nodded. I signed the card. I asked her what she thought of things.

'Improving, on the whole. At least, there's no one left to let us down.'

She said it not sarcastically, or bitterly, or reproachfully; but in a bright, rather pleased tone of voice.

Thank God for that maddening English insularity, I thought.

Part IX

ENGLAND FIGHTS ON

1

No Hour Was Finer Than This

The English will be regarded as the most valuable allies in the world so long as we may expect from their leaders and from the broad masses of the people that ruthlessness and toughness which are determined to carry through to a victorious end any fight which they have once begun without regard for time or sacrifices . . .

Adolf Hitler: *Mein Kampf*

Farmers loaded their shotguns. Soldiers barricaded the highways. Workmen stripped down the road signs. Villagers patrolled the country lanes. Volunteers flooded the Home Guard, the fire-fighting squads, the ambulance services. Eyes turned skywards as the nation waited for the German Air Force to strike with the full fury of its might. England was fighting on.

Eight sovereign states of Europe, disarmed, humbled and broken, lay beneath the grip of Germany; more were her vassals. Ports and aerodromes from Stavanger to Brest were in the hands of the Nazi Air Force. England, the last outpost of European civilisation, was alone. Her navy was engaged in the North Sea, the Atlantic and the Mediterranean, and there was the threat of new aggression in the Far East. Her guns, tanks and lorries lay scattered through Flanders and on the shores of Dunkirk. Her air fleet was only a third the size of Germany's. Would she be forced to bargain for peace? Her answer had already been given in the words of Winston Churchill:

We shall go on to the end . . . We shall defend our Island, whatever the cost may be; we shall fight on the beaches, we

shall fight on the landing grounds, we shall fight in the fields
and in the streets, we shall fight in the hills. We shall never
surrender, and even if, which I do not for a moment believe,
this Island or a large part of it were subjugated and starving,
then our Empire beyond the seas, armed and guarded by the
British Fleet, would carry on the struggle until – in God's good
time – the new world, with all its power and might, steps forth
to the rescue and the liberation of the old.

Ever since I was a child I had admired England. The first books
I remember reading were illustrated storybooks of the Knights of
the Round Table, of Alfred the Great, Richard the Lionhearted,
of Robin Hood and Drake. England seemed to me a wonderful
land where all men were very brave and wore splendid and beautiful clothes. My admiration increased rather than diminished
with time, and during the past few years it had sharpened with
a deeper understanding of what her long and persistent struggle
for freedom had meant: for the security she had brought to the
seas; for the law and justice she had spread to the dark corners of
the earth; for the reasoning and compassionate judgment she had
given to her people.

But I never admired her more than I did during those perilous
days of June and July. For the first time I understood what the
maxim meant: 'England never knows when she's beaten.' Not once
did I hear anyone talk of surrender. On the contrary, in the words
of Mrs Sullivan: 'After all the trouble 'Itler's given us, the least we
can do now is to win.'

Although the British leaders were well aware how precarious
the situation was they never faltered. There was no 'Peace Party'
to contend with in England. And as for the ordinary people, they
not only followed but actually took heart from the new situation.

All the way back from France I had wondered what the reaction would be. I was prepared for courage, but to find that the general public actually appeared to be invigorated by the collapse of their last ally was so surprising that it could only be described as 'typically English'. 'Now,' they said, 'we're all together again.'

Psychologically, the explanation was partly due to the fact that Englishmen have always regarded foreigners as strange and unpredictable, and took comfort in the knowledge that their own people were bound to prove more reliable; partly to the fact that the women felt a curious sense of relief that their sons and husbands were no longer going to fight on the continent. Through the centuries British soldiers had left their bones on foreign soil. They had been buried in the Crimea, in Africa, in India – in almost every country in Europe – but now the people of England were faced with the novel prospect of waging war in their own land.

I was more than impressed. I was flabbergasted. I not only understood the maxim 'England never knows when she's beaten'; I understood why England never *had* been beaten. On June 29th I broadcast over the BBC to the United States:

> Reports current in America that England will be forced to negotiate a compromise – which means surrender – are unfounded and untrue. Anyone who knows England knows just how untrue. The Anglo-Saxon character is *tough*. Englishmen are proud of being Englishmen. They have been the most powerful race in Europe for over three hundred years, and they believe in themselves with passionate conviction. Throughout English history the Guards regiments have fought to the death. When an Englishman says: 'It is better to be dead than live under Hitler,' heed his words. He means it.

The ordinary English person would have been amazed that anyone was speculating about Britain's determination – or, for that matter, Britain's chances of survival. I felt slightly embarrassed at even handing in my script to the BBC. Although the people knew they would be bombed, blockaded and besieged, their insularity, with its roots in nearly a thousand years of independence, was serving them in good stead; they were positive their island could not be invaded. They knew that England had once had few and very small ships and yet had beaten the Armada of Spain; they knew that Napoleon with all his armies and all his power had never succeeded in crossing the Channel. They had an unshakeable faith in the navy and no jibe pleased them more than the fact that Hitler was a landsman and knew nothing of the sea.

It was, therefore, not surprising that Hitler's peace offer of July 19th fell on deaf ears: 'I can see no reason why this war must go on. I am grieved to think of the sacrifices it will claim . . . Mr Churchill ought, perhaps, for once to believe me when I prophesy that a great Empire will be destroyed – an Empire which it was never my intention to destroy or even to harm. I do, however, realise that this struggle if it continues can end only with the complete annihilation of one or the other of the two adversaries. Mr Churchill may believe that this will be Germany. I know it will be Britain.'

England's answer was: 'Oh yeah?'

Although the situation was far more threatening than in the days of Napoleon, it offered such an extraordinary parallel that I rummaged through my books for a volume of Paul Frischauer's, entitled *England's Years of Danger*. It was a compilation of letters and documents during the long period of the Napoleonic invasion threat. I read it again, fascinated; here was history repeating itself almost event for event. Napoleon who, like Hitler, had the whole continent under his heel, also like Hitler, made offers of peace. They, too, were rejected. Although England was fighting alone, her navy struck out daringly in an effort to blockade the ports under his control. Napoleon, in pained surprise that the lone Island should defy him, wrote in a letter to Admiral Decres in June 1805 (exactly a hundred and thirty-five years before):

> When England realises the seriousness of the game she is playing she will be forced to give up the blockade of Brest. I really do not know what preventive measures she *can* take to protect herself from the terrible danger that hangs over her. How foolish is a nation that has no army and no fortifications, and yet risks invasion by a force of one hundred thousand picked men. That is the masterpiece of our flotilla. It costs money; but we need only six hours to be masters of the sea – and England ceases to exist.

A few months later Napoleon ordered Admiral Villeneuve, who was at Cadiz, to sail immediately for Brest and clear the Channel for a crossing of his vast flotilla of flat-bottomed boats in which army, artillery and horses were already established. His order to the latter was as follows:

> *Boulogne – 22nd August, 1805.*

> Admiral – I hope you have now arrived at Brest. Sail away. Do not lose a minute, but sail with the squadrons into the English Channel. England is ours. We are ready. Everything is on board. Only get there inside twenty-four hours, and the whole thing is accomplished.

The poor old Admiral, however, could not leave the harbour of Cadiz because the English force waiting outside was too strong. Once again the invasion was postponed. And how did the English react to this? Confident in the power of their fleet and the Home Guard of the day, they treated the attempts as a joke. Cartoons of Napoleon (of a 'You've missed the bus' category) appeared in the current newspapers. Frischauer reprints the following burlesque from a London periodical. It was written in the form of a Proclamation to be drawn up after Napoleon's victorious entry into London. The French Revolutionary calendar was used:

11th Thermidor.

ST JAMES'S PALACE.

Inhabitants of London, be tranquil! The Hero, the Pacificator, is come among you. His moderation and his mercy are too well known to you. He delights in restoring peace and liberty to all mankind.

No molestation shall be offered to the measures which the French soldiers shall be required to execute.

To the French Soldiers!

Soldiers! Bonaparte has led you to the shores and the Capital of this proud Island. London, the second Carthage, is given up to pillage for three days.

12th, 13th, 14th Thermidor.

London pillaged! The doors of private houses forced. Bands of drunken soldiers dragging wives and daughters from the arms of husbands and fathers. Flames seem in a hundred different places. Churches broken open, and the Church plate plundered – the pews and altars converted into stabling, four Bishops murdered.

15th Thermidor.

The houses of the principal nobility and gentry appropriated to the use of French Generals.

16th Thermidor.

Insurrections in different parts of the capital. Cannons planted at all principal avenues. Lords Nelson, St Vincent, and Duncan, Messrs. Addington, Pitt, Sheridan, Grey, and twenty Peers and Commons, sentenced to be shot. Sentence immediately carried out in Hyde Park.

The Island ordered to be divided into departments. The name of London changed into Bonapart-opolis – and the appellation of the country to be altered to that of La France Insulaire.

Hitler-opolis, that was an idea that wasn't coming off either. Once again people prepared for invasion. They did it with a certain amount of humour mingled with their determination, for the prospect of men dressed as bishops and curates dropping from the skies with sub-machine-guns struck everyone as extremely comic; however, no one was taking any chances. I motored down to the coast where the village people were blocking the roads with old carts and automobiles; where the farmers were sowing their fields with obstacles against troop carriers; where Home Guard volunteers were prowling through the country roads on the look-out for parachutists. Anne O'Neill, Margaret Douglas-Home and I spent a weekend with friends who lived near the coast. One night we were driving along an isolated lane when two men sprang out of the bushes, waving a lantern and shouting at us to stop. They poked their guns in the window, flashed their lights in our faces and asked us for names and destination. After a certain amount of questioning, one of them said: 'We might as well let them go. They don't look like parachutists.'

'Well,' said the other sceptically. 'You can't be too careful. From what I'm told they like to come down in skirts.'

We made a hurried exit before their doubts deepened.

The country people were not the only ones preparing for emergency. In every town and city thousands volunteered for the Home Guard. At Osterley Park, Tom Wintringham, backed by Edward Hulton of *Picture Post*, organised classes to train the men in guerrilla tactics. Asturian miners who had taken part in the Spanish war instructed dignified city clerks and brokers how to crawl through the grass on their stomachs, how to hurl grenades and 'Molotov Cocktails', how to stab, strangle and shoot. I drove out there one day with Eddie Ward. One mild little man, a floor walker in a department store, suddenly interrupted the instructor, a retired British Army officer:

'Pardon me, sir, perhaps you can tell me the quickest and most inexpensive way to kill a large batch of prisoners.'

The instructor was taken aback. 'Here in England we don't kill prisoners.'

The little man persisted. 'There might be an emergency. It might be awkward looking after them – you know, with more pressing things at hand.'

The instructor, still looking askance, acidly recommended the bayonet, and the little man nodded with immense satisfaction.

There was no doubt about it – England was becoming 'war-conscious'.

2

Per Ardua Ad Astra

One fine summer day in August, Knickerbocker and I drove along the coast from Dover to Southampton. An air fight had been taking place above our heads for over an hour. Although we could hear the engines, the planes were so high and the sun was so bright we could catch only occasional glimpses of the tiny silver wings, like the quick darting flash of minnows in a clear blue stream. It was still going on when we drove through the quiet town of Hastings – the town where the great battle of 1066 had been fought when the Norman invaders overran England. We thought it would be interesting to visit the battlefield. We saw three men sitting on a fence, their eyes strained towards the sky, and stopped to ask the way.

'The battle of 1066?' one of them repeated. 'Never heard of it.'

'Look at 'er!' said the second excitedly. 'She's on his tail now. Ooh! Look at 'em go.'

It was quite obvious no one was interested in the battle of Hastings, and as we drove on Knick said meditatively: 'Do you suppose one day, a thousand years from now, some bright young thing will write a book called *1940 and All That?*'

It was a startling thought, but one thing was certain: '*All That*' would take a good deal of describing. Ever since August 8th, Germany's great air armada had been grappling with the fighters of the Royal Air Force in a titanic effort to smash British resistance; then to lay waste to the Island and seal its doom with invasion. The quiet town of Dover, only twenty miles from the nearest German base, had suddenly become the world's news centre for the fierce and terrible battles taking place above the coast.

Hundreds of journalists and cameramen flowed through the lobby of the Grand Hotel – a provincial hotel on the waterfront which had formerly done most of its trade from special-rate holiday tourists en route for a weekend in France. I had seen the same journalists in hotels in Prague, Berlin, Warsaw, Helsinki and Paris, but this time it was different; this was the last stop. After this, there would be no other hotels to move on to.

Otherwise there was the same atmosphere journalists always seem to bring with them: excitement, confusion, activity. Although many people had been evacuated from the town, and the beach was a long, empty sweep protected by wire barricade to keep the pedestrians away, the streets were crowded with soldiers, sailors, balloon-barrage and ARP workers. The roller-skating pavilion in the small square next to the hotel was crowded with customers, the music from the gramophone blaring out gaily along the seafront just as it did in peace-time.

When the alarms sounded a red flag fluttered from Dover Castle on a hill high above the sea. You saw shop-owners bolting their doors, pedestrians running for cover, air-raid wardens taking their positions along the streets – the same scenes you had seen so often only this time slightly strange because it was England. Then you heard the far-away noise of engines, increasing until the drone was a mighty roar like the thunder of a waterfall, and the battle was on.

Some of us used to climb to the top of Shakespeare Cliff, about a mile from the town, and watch from there. The setting was majestic. In front of you stretched the blue water of the Channel and in the distance you could distinguish the hazy outline of the coast of France. Far below were the village houses glistening in the sun and the small boats and trawlers lying at anchor in the harbour; on the hill on the other side, the mighty turrets of the castle jutting into the sky; and, above all this, twenty or thirty huge grey balloons floating in the blue, flapping a little like whales gasping for breath.

You lay in the tall grass with the wind blowing gently across you and watched the hundreds of silver planes swarming through the heavens like clouds of gnats. All around you, anti-aircraft guns were shuddering and coughing, stabbing the sky with small white bursts. You could see the flash of wings and the long white plumes from the exhausts; you could hear the whine of engines and the rattle of machine-gun bullets. You knew the fate of civilisation was being decided fifteen thousand feet above your head in a world of sun, wind and sky. You knew it, but even so it was hard to take it in.

Sometimes the planes came lower, twisting, turning, darting and diving with a moaning noise that made your stomach drop; sometimes you saw them falling earthwards, a mass of flames, leaving as their last testament a long black smudge against the sky. Many of them fell into the sea and far below you could see the 'crash' boats racing out to the middle of the Channel to pick up the survivors. Often, when the German planes came down, the gunners on the cliffs shouted and cheered. No one had more respect for the fighter pilots than they. 'By God,' said one of them, 'you have to see those boys to believe how tough they are!'

I had seen them. Only a few weeks before, Knickerbocker and I had driven down to the aerodrome where the 601 Squadron was stationed. We stood on the field and watched the Hurricanes shooting off the ground like bullets, until a moment later they were only tiny specks in the distance. They had been sent up to intercept a group of German bombers approaching the coast near Brighton, but this particular occasion turned out to be a false alarm, for the raiders turned back and soon the Hurricanes were sweeping on to the field again.

As they were circling down for a landing, an airman who was conducting us around – a tall, dark, nineteen-year-old boy – asked me if I'd like to talk to one of the pilots in the air. He walked over to a plane near the hangar, connected the radio and told me to ask for X No. 1.

'But what'll I say?'

'Just say X No. 1, you're making a lousy landing. Repeat it twice very distinctly.'

Dutifully I did as I was told, then switched over for the reply. It came: 'You tell the controller to shut his Goddam face.'

My instructor guffawed with laughter. When X No. I came striding across the field, he greeted him warmly, and said: 'You must meet this lady. You were just talking to her over the radio.'

'Oh, I say,' mumbled X No. 1. 'I had no idea . . . I do hope . . .'

He was a painfully shy young man and by this time his face was crimson. He was wearing the DFC and I was told he had shot down eleven planes, but I didn't have an opportunity to learn any further details, for he promptly vanished and we didn't see him again for the rest of the afternoon.

The squadron was divided into three shifts: 'Readiness', which could be in the air within a few seconds; 'Advanced available', which had a ten-minute leeway; and 'Available', within call of an hour or two. The 'Readiness' pilots were billeted in small huts on the edge of the field and the Commanding Officer took us around and introduced us to a number of them. They had bright, keen faces and were wearing decorations they had won at the time of Dunkirk. They were extremely modest about their achievements, and if you had told them how wonderful you thought they were they would have been deeply embarrassed. In fact, when Winston Churchill made his speech, saying: 'Never in the field of human conflict have so many owed so much to so few,' one of them was reported to have commented awkwardly: 'I think he must be referring to our mess bills.'

Among the group were two Poles, newcomers to the squadron, who had yet to experience their first combat. As they knew only a few words of English, Knickerbocker addressed them in German, which they spoke fluently. 'If you don't mind,' said one, in a tone of gentle reproach, 'we prefer to talk English.' Although the conversation was almost unintelligible, I remembered the Polish pilots I'd seen in Romania, begging for a chance to have another go at the Germans, and I didn't have to be told what their feelings were.

Our day ended with tea in a garden at the back of an old farmhouse on the edge of the field. The farmer, frightened at living so near the aerodrome, had moved away and a group of pilots had taken over the house. They were as pleased about it as a lot of children. They made a special effort over tea, hurrying in and out of the kitchen to see if things were being done properly; bringing us platters of cakes and sandwiches and apologising profusely because we had come down to see them on such a slack day. They had been up only once, whereas they usually went into battle four or five times! I couldn't get over how young they were – little boys with blonde hair and pink cheeks who looked as though they ought to be in school. I sat staring at them as though they were slightly unreal: these were the men who were saving England. Each time they went up into the air it was a fight to the finish; either they died or the enemy. Just then one of the pilots interrupted my thoughts: 'You should visit one of our bomber squadrons one day.' And here his tone grew into one of awe: 'Now, those boys are *really* tough.'

For once I couldn't think of any comment to make.

* * *

A week or so later Knick and I took his advice and visited a bomber station in Lincolnshire. Although that was nearly a year ago, when England was still greatly outnumbered in the air, British bombers were already striking at Germany five times as vigorously as the Germans were hitting back. On August 15th official figures estimated that the Royal Air Force had dropped more than thirty thousand bombs on Germany to the latter's seven thousand on England. Since the invasion of Holland, three and a half months before, there had only been two nights during which enemy targets had not been attacked.

Knick and I stood on the aerodrome watching six gigantic, heavily loaded bombers taking off in the fading light for the long trip they had come to know so well. The picture was dramatic enough: the engines warming up, the signal lights flashing across the field, and the sudden loud roar as plane after plane swept down the runway and disappeared into the uncertain light. Soon the ground radio operator was talking to the pilots to test the wireless apparatus: 'Can you hear me? Can you hear me?' And from somewhere in the darkness, miles away, came the reply: 'Okay! Okay!'

The bombers were headed for oil refineries in the Ruhr. Each plane carried a crew of six: two pilots, two gunners, a navigator, and a wireless operator who was also a trained gunner. An hour or two before the flight was scheduled the 'briefing' took place. The Wing Commander called in his pilots and gave them their objectives: primary objectives, secondary objectives, and, finally, strict instructions to bring their bombs back home with them if they failed to locate their targets.

'Of course,' said the Wing Commander, 'if any of you happen to fly over the Skipol aerodrome (Amsterdam) and you still have your bombs with you . . .' Everyone laughed. The Skipol was an old favourite. For the next ten or fifteen minutes the pilots asked questions and checked up positions on their maps. They were a tough, keen, good-natured bunch of men. This particular squadron had averaged over a hundred trips a month to Germany during the past five months.

As they stood, their heads bent over their maps, plotting out their objectives, I was reminded of a story someone had told me about the time Sir Archibald Sinclair, the Air Minister, had visited a bomber squadron during a 'briefing'. Sir Archibald was anxious to say a few words to the pilots, so the Commanding Officer led him into the room where, he explained, the men were studying their instructions. He found the pilots bending over a table, roaring with laughter. In the centre was a huge package. When you unwrapped the outer layer there was another beneath it. When you unwrapped that there was still another. In the last package was a dead cat. The men had taken great pains to do it up to look like a strange and formidable bomb. Inside they had scribbled all sorts of ribald jokes and were planning to drop it in Berlin 'with love and kisses from the Air Force' – hoping of course that some serious-minded German would rush it to a laboratory for a thorough scientific inspection.

Knick and I waited at the aerodrome until the small hours of the morning for our bombers to return. Sitting there, hour after hour, wondering if they would all get back, I began to understand the strain of the long and gruelling trips that had come to be such a matter of routine. I thought of them flying through fog and wind, over miles of sea, and wondered how human endurance stood up to it night after night. The silence of the Operations Room seemed to add to the drama. Several men were studying enormous maps charting speeds and positions; the Wing Commander was working at his desk; the wireless operator was listening for messages. The only noise was the hiss of the tea-kettle which an orderly had set up on an improvised stove.

The pilots were instructed not to communicate with their stations until they were on the homeward lap lest the Germans discover their positions. About two o'clock in the morning there was a message from the first plane; then one by one the signals came in until they were all chalked up on the board. About half an hour later the drone of an engine penetrated the blackness. We ran outside and saw the airfield lights flash. The plane circled for several minutes and finally came down in a perfect landing.

Five of the bombers arrived within three-quarters of an hour of each other but the sixth was missing. The Wing Commander paced up and down anxiously for the boy's petrol supply was limited. One hour slipped away, then two and then three. It seemed unlikely that he would ever get back now, but suddenly headquarters reported that a bomber was not far off the English coast, and about half an hour later we heard the familiar drone of the Wellington engine.

The pilot came into the Operations Room, pulling off his helmet and unbuttoning his fur-lined leather jacket. He was red-cheeked and embarrassed. He explained that he had overshot his target and then got lost. Instead of reaching the coast of England he had suddenly discovered he was flying over Holland. His petrol supply had become so low he had been forced to unload his bombs in the sea and had just squeezed home with a quarter of a gallon to spare. The Commander asked him if his navigator had been at fault, but the boy shook his head emphatically: 'Oh no, sir, I must assume full responsibility.'

He went off still mumbling apologetically and the Commander said to us: 'I think he's covering up for his navigator. He's one of my best pilots and we've had trouble with the navigator before. But try and make him admit it!'

As each of the crews came in from their flight they were interrogated by an Intelligence Officer whose job it was to establish exactly what results had been obtained and what observations been made. Except for one pilot, forced to turn back because his rear gun had gone out of action, all had bombed their primary target.

They reported heavy anti-aircraft fire. One of the bombers had been struck several times by shells; a wing was torn and the right petrol tank punctured with holes. The pilot was a gay young man, with a large moustache which had won him the name of 'Handle-Bar Hank'. He had made over thirty trips to Germany and inspected the damage with the nonchalance of an old-timer. He said he thought he had heard a bit of noise, but he wasn't quite sure.

When all the questioning was over we went to the mess and had an enormous breakfast of bacon and eggs and baked beans. Everyone was in such high spirits it was difficult to realise they had just returned from an exhausting flight over enemy territory. One of the pilots who had made his first trip only a few days before, told me between mouthfuls of toast that what surprised him the most was the show the Jerries put on for them. He said there were so many bursts from anti-aircraft guns it was almost like Empire Day. 'When I realised they were going to all that trouble just for us, I felt as important as *Hell*,' he grinned.

Now, that was an angle that hadn't struck me before.

* * *

The Bomber and Fighter Commands were not the only Air Force groups striking at the enemy. Every morning at dawn the Coastal Command's heavily armed Sunderland flying-boats slipped out of their quiet harbours and roared into the mists of the Atlantic. Their job was to help the navy protect the great and vital sea routes of the British Isles. Sometimes the day's run was only hours of lonely patrol; sometimes it ranged anywhere from signalling the position of enemy ships and attacking submarines to rescuing U-boat victims, protecting incoming vessels and engaging enemy planes in combat.

One weekend I visited a station from which an Australian squadron was operating. During the previous six months, this particular squadron had established the startling record of flying as far as the moon and halfway back again. I asked one of the officers if there was any chance of my going out on a flight with them, and by a lucky slip-up somewhere (which caused the Air Ministry no end of indignation) I was signed on as an extra pilot and taken out on a thirteen-hour patrol of nearly seventeen hundred miles.

There were two officers – a pilot and an engineer – and a crew of seven. The officers were tough, experienced men with a long record of flying behind them; they seemed greatly amused at the bewildered looks the crew exchanged when I stepped aboard. 'I only hope you won't be bored,' one of them said anxiously. 'A ship was torpedoed off the coast of Ireland a few hours ago and Jim (one of the other pilots) has gone off to pick up the survivors, so maybe we'll run into some excitement, too.'

We left at six o'clock in the morning and flew at a speed of about a hundred and fifty miles an hour. Soon we were far out at sea with nothing but a solid blue stretch above and below and the sun sparkling on the waves. Everyone was very busy. The bomb racks were loaded and the gunners took their positions, scanning the brilliant horizon for enemy submarines. The engineer sat at the dual controls with the pilot; behind them the chief mechanic was sitting at his desk checking engine temperatures and pressures, the navigator was bending over his maps calculating speed and position, and the wireless operator listening for messages.

Our ship was two-decked and built entirely of metal. It carried petrol for two thousand miles and was armed with guns bow and stern, port and starboard. (The pilot said they spit fire from so many angles the Germans had dubbed them the *Fliegende Stachelschwein* – the flying porcupines.) It was also equipped with cameras for reconnaissance work, parachute flares for night landings, a collapsible rubber boat which expanded when it touched the water, and a cage of carrier pigeons. One of the gunners told me it had been so quiet lately the pigeons had been driven to laying eggs out of sheer boredom. But the most indispensable contrivance on the ship was an automatic pilot known as 'George'. George was an invention for long-distance flying; he kept the boat on its course so perfectly the pilot didn't have to use the controls for hours at a time.

We hadn't been in the air long before the wireless operator intercepted a message from the flying-boat which had set out to pick up the survivors of the torpedoed ship, reporting two enemy aircraft. They evidently weren't anxious for combat however, for a few minutes later we picked up a second message saying: 'Enemy out of sight.' During the next four hours the only object we saw was one small trawler, a Spanish fishing boat. Hundreds of sea-gulls were following in its wake – according to the pilot, the one indisputable way you could tell whether or not it was 'on the level'.

At ten-thirty we had breakfast: bacon and eggs, fruit, coffee, toast and jam. The front gunner, also an expert mechanic, had the triple role of cook. 'You can tell how busy he's been,' said the pilot, 'by how strongly the potatoes taste of petrol.' He was a good-natured, wise-cracking little man, proud of the fact that he'd learned to cook in the Australian bush. He said it was pretty difficult to feed ten people from such a small galley but on the other hand it wasn't supposed to be the Ritz. I asked him how he liked patrolling the Atlantic and he told me he'd like it better after he'd had 'a smack at Jerry'. He said he thought our flying-boat had a jinx, for it was the only one in the squadron which hadn't yet gone into action.

Shortly after lunch I thought we were going to have some excitement. The engineer was at the controls and the pilot and I were just finishing our tea when the ship suddenly swung off its course. The pilot jumped up and went to the window. We were banking steeply and far below there was a long patch of oil on the water. He muttered 'submarine' and scrambled up the ladder to the cockpit.

A second later a noise that sounded like an old-fashioned motor-horn resounded through the boat – the signal to man all guns. From the galley there was the sudden clatter of pots and pans, and the cook made a dash for the forward gun. We were turning slowly like a giant bird circling down to swoop on its prey. Suddenly it was all over. The all-clear sounded, the boat gained altitude and straightened out on its course. The cook came back to his dishes looking like a disappointed child. 'Just some old wreckage,' he grumbled. 'Thought we were going to unload a few that time.' He wasn't the only one who was disappointed. The chief mechanic shook his head gloomily. 'The trouble is, it's such a clear day the Jerries can see us for forty miles. It's always lousy fishing, this weather.'

The engineer apologised for the lack of excitement but said to make up for it he would put me into the rear-gun turret. This proved to be one of the most terrifying experiences I have ever had. The turret was a round, glassed-in cubicle which swung out over the sea. I suddenly found myself locked in, with the wind whistling ominously through the gun openings, and below me nothing but a sickening drop into the sea.

'Let me out!' I yelled.

'What's the matter?' grinned the engineer when I was back in the cabin once more. 'We were thinking of signing you up as our permanent rear gunner.'

This gave the engineer the idea of organising a little gunnery practice. The crew put on helmets, with wires and microphones attached, enabling them to communicate to each other from all parts of the ship. The engineer then broadcast an enemy attack with frightening realism: 'Now they're on our tail! They're diving towards the starboard! And here come two more! Port side!' After practising the movement of the guns, targets were thrown out and the gunners fired short bursts.

Soon it was all over, but two of the gunners forgot to disconnect their microphones. The pilot suddenly heard one of them saying: 'I wonder how long it's going to be before we're allowed to bring one of *our* lassies up on a hop?'

The pilot said: 'I advise whoever is doing the talking to remove his helmet.' There was a sharp click, then silence.

There were no further incidents that afternoon and we patrolled hour after hour with only sea and sky stretching endlessly before us. We landed in the harbour just as it was getting dark.

The sequel to the story is a sad one, for the next morning the little Australian cook who had longed to 'get a smack at Jerry' left on a flight for Gibraltar. His ship sighted and attacked a Dornier 18. Although the latter was put to flight, the cook, who played his part as front gunner, was seriously wounded and died a few hours later.

I felt as though I had lost an old friend.

3

Heigho, London Bridge Is Standing

Anne still kept open house, and every afternoon people drifted in for tea. It was so peaceful there, looking out on the green trees in the middle of the quiet square, that the war seemed a long way off. You had watched the air fights from the high cliffs on the coast and you knew the Battle for Britain was being fought hour by hour; even so, in London it was hard to take it in.

London still had its age-old air of tranquillity. Not that its appearance hadn't changed: only a year before, the thoroughfares had been crowded with traffic, the hotels filled with visitors from abroad, and the ballroom at Buckingham Palace glittering with more diamonds than any other room in the world. Now the streets were half empty. Entrances to government buildings were sand-bagged and protected by wire barricades, the parks were filled with anti-aircraft troops, and even the scarlet tunics and black bearskins of the Guards in front of the palace had given way to tin hats and khaki.

But in spite of the transition, the capital had lost little of its placid charm. To me, it still seemed a wonderful place to be. Life was more informal than it had ever been before – you even saw women strolling down Bond Street in slacks and sweaters, sometimes complete with picture hat and Pekinese. People lunched and dined Dutch treat, filled the out-of-door restaurants and went to cinemas, football matches and races. Occasionally the sirens sounded, but only a few raiders penetrated the capital's defences during the summer and people seldom bothered to take cover.

The first Saturday afternoon in September, Anne and I motored down to Mereworth, about forty miles south of London, to spend the weekend with Esmond Harmsworth. It was a warm, sunny day and we had tea on the lawn. Suddenly we heard the drone of planes. At first we couldn't see anything, but soon the noise had grown into a deep, full roar, like the far-away thunder of a giant waterfall. We lay in the grass, our eyes strained towards the sky; we made out a batch of tiny white specks, like clouds of insects, moving north-west in the direction of the capital. Some of them – the bombers – were flying in even formation, while the others – the fighters – swarmed protectively around.

One of Esmond's house guests, an old gentleman, near-sighted and hard of hearing, refused to believe it. To him, the world was a peaceful place and he was determined it should remain so. Even when the anti-aircraft shrapnel burst against the sky he insisted that it was only the guns on the practice range. During the next hour, Anne and I counted over a hundred and fifty planes. They were not meeting with any resistance and were coming in such a volume we realised they had probably already broken through the defences.

'Poor London,' said Anne.

'Rubbish!' said the old gentleman. 'You've been staying up too late. You'd better go and take a rest.'

That was Saturday, September 7th, the date that marked the beginning of the savage night attacks on London. From five o'clock that afternoon until the small hours of the morning, bombs rained down on the capital in the most furious air attack the world had ever known. While it was going on the German wireless broadcast hourly reports. The announcer said excitedly:

Bombs fall all over the place, and the fires flame up. Thick clouds of smoke spread over the roofs of the greatest city in the world. Explosions are detected as far up as the German planes. The efforts of the British anti-aircraft guns are unsuccessful.

Further waves of planes are constantly arriving, while a section of the German planes, which have unloaded their bombs, proceed on their homeward flight. The heart of the British Empire is delivered up to the attack of the German Air Force.

The Germans scored hits on dock buildings, factories, railway communications, gas and electricity plants. But it was the warehouses that made the greatest blaze. All night long they burned, millions of pounds' worth of wool, tobacco, rubber and sugar fuelling the most formidable fire London had seen since another September in the year 1666. Even where we were, forty miles away, the sky glowed pink.

The ordinary telephone service to London was disconnected, but Esmond had a private wire to his newspaper, the *Sunday Dispatch*; the editor had little new information except that the sky was more crimson than ever, planes were still coming, bombs still falling, and if the paper ever got to press no one would be more surprised than he. Even the old gentleman looked thoughtful. At nine o'clock we turned on the radio and heard the flat voice of the BBC announcer reading the Air Ministry communiqué:

Late this afternoon enemy aircraft in large numbers crossed the coast of Kent and approached the London area. They were heavily engaged by our fighters and AA guns, but a number of them succeeded in penetrating to the industrial area of East London. As a result of these attacks, fires were caused among the industrial targets in this area. Damage was done to the lighting and other public services and some dislocation of communications was caused. Attacks have also been directed against the docks.

That certainly didn't tell us much. It was so non-committal we became more apprehensive than ever. We could still hear the noise of engines overhead. Esmond said that in peace-time Mereworth had been on the direct route of the German civil pilots coming from Berlin to London, via Holland. Evidently they were keeping to the same course. As the steady drone kept up through the night we began to wonder if there was going to be anything left of the capital at all.

Shortly after we'd gone to bed there was a violent explosion as a thousand-pound bomb landed about a quarter of a mile away. Mereworth, a substantial eighteenth-century house, shook violently. A moment later we were out in the corridor asking each other what had happened. The old gentleman was missing. We went into his room and found him sitting up in bed reading, with the windows open and the lights blazing. We snapped them off, admonishing him indignantly, then went downstairs and walked onto the terrace. We could hear guns in the distance and the pink glow seemed to be growing brighter. We went into the drawing room and turned on the radio, hoping to hear some news, but all we got was a series of Hawaiian melodies from America. Anne cheered everyone up by saying that the dome on top of the house probably looked like a huge gasometer from the air and would certainly be taken for a military objective. With this thought firmly in mind, we all went gloomily to bed.

The next morning we learned that London was still standing. Miles of East End houses had been destroyed, however, and thousands of people were homeless. I was returning in the afternoon and had arranged to have tea with a friend in Brentwood on the way. To get there, I had to drive to Gravesend, about fifteen miles away, and ferry across the Thames; although it seemed doubtful that the roads would be passable, I started off about three o'clock in the afternoon.

The countryside had such a complacent look about it, it was hard to believe that anything out of the ordinary had happened. The first sign I saw was when I reached the ferry: great clouds of dark smoke were pouring down the estuary from the Woolwich docks. No one seemed disconcerted, however, for the Sunday afternoon scene was as peaceful as ever: the two ferrymen basking lazily in the sun; one of the dock-workers reading the morning paper; and the ticket-collector grumbling that the Huns were a noisy lot and he hadn't had a wink of sleep. From his bored tone of voice, you might have thought the disturbance had been caused by nothing more unusual than a cat on the back fence.

From Tilbury to Brentwood, another fifteen miles, I passed about half a dozen smashed buildings, and made several diversions where time bombs had fallen, but on the whole the area seemed surprisingly free of damage. When I arrived at the hotel I found my friend, an officer in an artillery regiment, in high spirits. I commented on the burning warehouses, but he waved my remarks aside, insisting that the Germans' primary aim was not the docks but to spread alarm and despondency by knocking out all the saloons and pubs. The bombers had been over again that afternoon, but the British fighters still had their tails up. He had just come from an aerodrome where a fighter squadron was operating, and said that many of the pilots were coming in doing the 'victory roll' – the signal that they had 'got their man'. One fighter did three victory rolls and the ground workers cheered.

I left for London, about twenty miles away, at seven-thirty. If I had realised the blitz of the night before was to be repeated, I would have taken care to get home before the sirens sounded. As it was, the mournful wail sounded a few minutes after I had started out. It was getting dark and I drove as fast as possible to make the best of the light. Although I was travelling through one of the most congested London suburbs (Stratford – a mile or so from East Ham), the streets were clearing rapidly; people were running for shelter in all directions, and buses and trucks were coming to a stop. Lines of tram-cars stood empty. Soon there was an ominous silence and mine was practically the only car on the road.

Two stranded soldiers waved to me and I stopped and gave them a lift. It was difficult driving in the semi-darkness and the quiet was oppressive. Suddenly, a few hundred yards ahead of us, we heard a sickening whistle and a deafening explosion. A bomb landed in the middle of the street and there was a shower of glass and debris from the houses on either side. The whistles blew and ARP workers and special police deputies were on the job almost immediately; it was too dark to see what damage had been done to the houses, but the street was covered with rubble.

The police warned us to be careful and detoured us round to another road. Soon we heard an ambulance siren ringing. Ahead of us the sky had lit up in a red glow and we could hear more bombs dropping in the darkness. We closed all the windows in order not to be hit by flying shrapnel (the wrong thing to do) and continued on our way. The soldiers were quiet. It was so dark I couldn't see them very well; they were just shapes in the back of the car. Occasionally one of them muttered: 'We'll get them for this,' but that was all. Their destination was London Bridge and, somehow, with the sound of the bombs and the guns, and the sky a deep fire pink, I couldn't help thinking of the old nursery rhyme: 'London Bridge is falling down'. They evidently thought of it too, for I heard one saying to the other: 'I'll lay you odds the old bridge *isn't* down,' and he was right, for a mile or so later it loomed up in front of us as solid and substantial as ever.

I then drove through the heart of the City, which seemed as eerie and deserted as a graveyard. I stopped to ask the way of an

ARP warden and he asked me to take two of his workers up to Piccadilly. The men hadn't had their clothes off for forty-eight hours. They had just come from a building where five people were dug out of the ruins. 'Three women and two children,' one of them told me grimly; then, almost under his breath: 'The price is going to be high for the Germans when the war is over.'

I finally reached Montagu Square and found Mr and Mrs Kinch (the caretaker and his wife) in the kitchen, calmly having their supper. Overhead you could hear the sound of the planes, and every now and then the house shook and the windows rattled as a bomb dropped somewhere in the vicinity. I asked them if they weren't afraid and Mrs Kinch said: 'Oh, no. If we were, what good would it do us?'

There was certainly no answer to that; although I had a sinking feeling in my stomach, I thought if they could take it I ought to be able to take it too, and climbed into bed hoping that if death came it would be instantaneous.

The next morning the sky was blue and innocent. If you hadn't seen the yawning craters and the wreckage, you might have thought that you had dreamt it. Traffic was normal, the shops were full, old ladies sunned themselves in the park, and soldiers and their girlfriends strolled down Piccadilly arm in arm. I lunched at the Berkeley restaurant and found it as noisy and crowded as ever. Suddenly there was a bang. The room shook as a time bomb exploded a few blocks away. A pretty girl in a saucy hat turned to the young army subaltern with her, and said, in a voice that rang across the restaurant:

'Did you drop something?'

* * *

You can write about the blinding flashes of gunfire and the long hiss of the bombs; about the deep roar of falling masonry like the thunder of breakers against the shore. You can write about the red glow of flames through the blackness, about the searchlight beams, the stars and the flares all mixed up together against the sky. You can write about these things, but it is improbable that they will convey the mixed sensations of the moment. The noise of the planes was the worst – an uneven, droning noise like the sound of a dentist's drill. Sometimes it grew so loud you held your breath, wondering painfully if the bomb racks would open. Once, Vincent Sheean stopped in the middle of a sentence and glared angrily into space.

'What's the matter?' I asked.

'Nothing. I'm just waiting for that bastard to get out of the room.'

That seemed to describe it best of all.

Everyone asked me how it compared with the raids in Barcelona and Helsinki and said: 'You're probably so used to this sort of thing you don't mind it at all.' Well, I wasn't. It was far worse than anything I had known before. Other air-raids had lasted fifteen or twenty minutes, then *ended*. These went on all night and there was no section of London you could go to to feel safe. Life turned upside-down while everyone scrambled to adjust themselves to an entirely new routine. Conversation was devoted to one topic only: where and how to sleep. The rich were no better off than the poor, for there wasn't a single shelter in London (including the shelter in Buckingham Palace) deep enough to withstand a direct hit. Everyone had theories on the subject: some preferred the basement, others said the top of the house was safer than being trapped under debris; some recommended a narrow trench in the back garden, and still others insisted it was best to forget it and die comfortably in bed. (Lord and Lady Camrose had the first argument of their married life. Lord Camrose said that since there was a shelter only a few yards from the house, it was ridiculous not to use it; Lady Camrose said that any concession, however slight, was a moral victory for the Germans. I think Lady Camrose won.)

During the first few nights, buses, street cars and taxi-cabs came to a halt. People were stranded all over London with no means of getting home. I ran into Eddie Ward of the BBC and asked him where he was staying. 'Nowhere. I just sleep wherever I happen to eat.'

A good many others did the same thing. Conventions went, and everyone doubled up wherever they could find a bed. A few people had their own cars and strangers besieged them for lifts. No one wanted to be alone, however, and you heard respectable young ladies saying to their escorts: 'I'm not going home unless you promise to spend the night.'

The hotel lobbies presented a strange picture, for besides the stray visitors sleeping in armchairs, many of the permanent guests, fearful of remaining on the top floors, brought their mattresses and pillows downstairs and made their beds wherever they could find a space. They wandered about in all forms of odd attire: beach pyjamas, slacks, siren suits, and some just in ordinary wrappers with their nightdresses trailing on the floor. Many of them sat up on their improvised beds, knitting, while strains from the dance orchestra echoed through the lobby and people thronged back and forth. Once I tripped over King Zog's sister, who was sleeping peacefully outside the door of the Ritz restaurant.

A few days later London's defences were strengthened. Every available anti-aircraft gun was dragged into the capital and all night long belched and roared in a deafening crescendo. On the first night of the barrage, a group of us were dining at the Dorchester Hotel, a few yards from the Hyde Park batteries; the windows rattled and for once even the wail of the saxophone was lost. At one point an incendiary bomb crashed on to the pavement. Someone pulled back the curtain and the window was a sheet of flame. The band grew louder and couples went on dancing. Vincent Sheean said it was so reminiscent of the scene in *Idiot's Delight* it made him feel self-conscious.

On this particular night Seymour Berry drove Anne and me home. There were a good many fires in the park and we overheard a woman saying, tearfully: 'Now Hyde Park is going. And I *did* love it so.' Outside, lights were flashing against the sky, and the noise was appalling. Anne and I were frightened, but Seymour, a captain in an anti-aircraft regiment, seemed to think the guns had a beautiful sound and insisted on driving along Park Lane at five miles an hour to drink in the full splendour of the moment.

'Do hurry, you idiot!' we said in exasperation.

'Now, you two pipe down. There's nothing to be alarmed about. Try to think of some nineteen-year-old boy flying around up there in the darkness twice as scared as you are . . .'

'Oh, shut up!' said Anne.

We finally got home and after that I took pains to drive my own car.

People accepted the odd situations they found themselves in not only calmly, but with a good deal of humour. On the night John Lewis's department store burned to the ground, a group of us were stranded in Claridge's Hotel, a few blocks away. The blaze illuminated the sky for miles and the Germans kept pounding at the brightly lit area all night long. I was dining with Basil Dufferin. About eleven o'clock we tried to leave. My car was parked around the corner and we had gone only a few paces when there was a whistle. An ARP man across the street shouted: 'Get down!' Basil was a soldier, but I put him to shame by the rapidity with which I responded. Luckily, it was a dud and didn't go off. I insisted on returning to the hotel. A tall, bespectacled soldier was standing in the middle of the hall, arguing with his wife about leaving. She said it was dangerous and he said it was nonsense; finally, he went out into the night by himself. Five minutes later he was back, looking like a ghost. He sank into a chair, breathing heavily; his wife fanned him with a magazine, and the waiter brought him a glass of brandy. As he was turning the corner, a bomb had fallen. The blast had hurled him across the street. He had turned two somersaults in the air and landed on the opposite pavement, by some miracle, still intact.

By this time the lobby was becoming more crowded than ever. Dozens of people were streaming down the stairs with their bedclothes over their arms. Everyone talked to everyone else, a round of drinks was ordered, and from the general merriment you might have thought an enjoyable (if somewhat odd) costume party was going on. Finally, an ARP warden came in and advised everyone to keep to one side of the hotel as a time bomb had fallen in Davies Street and was apt to go off at any moment. A few minutes later we saw an elderly lady coming down the stairs. She was wearing a long black coat, a black hat, and a pair of smoked glasses. We recognised her as Queen Wilhelmina of Holland. She was accompanied by three ladies-in-waiting and as she walked through the lobby a hush fell over the group. There was something very gallant in the figure of that old lady; she looked tough. You knew if she hadn't been ordered to evacuate, nothing would have induced her to go to a shelter.

In the meantime, Anne's friends had named Montagu Square 'Hell's Corner'. A good many bombs had fallen around her house, but she stubbornly refused to leave. 'Otherwise,' she said, 'where would we have tea in the afternoon?' That was a serious consideration. Mr and Mrs Kinch took their blankets and spent the nights in a shelter a few yards away, but since it was no safer against a direct hit than staying at home, Anne and I preferred the comfort of our own beds. We finally lost our nerve, however, when the house across the street was demolished. It was a macabre sight. Chunks of stone and bits of pulverised furniture gushed across the street: a red skirt, a blouse and a stocking fluttered from the tree-tops in front of our window; all day long workmen dug through the debris trying to recover the seven bodies pinned beneath. The only person who survived was the maid who was sleeping on the top floor; she fell with the wreckage and escaped with only a few cuts and bruises.

Anne closed the house, sent the furniture into storage and moved to a hotel. She went to the country for a few days' rest, but even there a stick of bombs landed on either side of the house. The maid came running into her room. 'Mr Harmsworth (Anne's host) is buried under four feet of debris.' Anne, by this time hardened and resourceful, replied: 'Whatever you do, don't put on the lights. We'll have to look for him in the dark.' As it turned out, it was all a mistake and Mr Harmsworth wasn't under the debris. 'But if I ever am,' he said acidly, 'you can at least look for me with a torch.'

In the meantime, I went to St John's Wood to stay with Freda Casa Maury. She had moved into a small house with white walls and mirror-topped tables. There was a mobile gun in the street and when it went off the curtains blew in, the chandeliers swayed, and the flower-vases invariably crashed to the floor. Somehow a power-ful field gun operating from one's front doorstep was so grotesque, it seemed comic. The noise was so loud you had to shout to carry on a conversation. On the first night I spent there, Vernon, the but-ler, came running upstairs at four o'clock in the morning, crying: 'There's a land mine on the hill. Get out as quick as you can.'

Five minutes later we were crammed into Freda's car – Vernon, the cook and myself, all in various states of undress – speeding down the hill. Vernon's nerves had been on edge and Freda suspected him of dreaming the whole thing, but the next morning we found it was true. A land mine, attached to a parachute, had floated down, and, by some lucky chance, settled gently in a vegetable bed without exploding. I learned from a friend who went to look at it that an officer and a group of soldiers had seen it coming and thought parachute troops were landing. They advanced with drawn revolvers.

'Halt!' cried the Major fiercely. 'Who goes there?'

When he saw what 'who' was, he bolted down the hill. I told the story to Basil Dufferin, who repeated it to an elderly officer in Bucks Club. The latter was not amused. No wonder. He was the same major.

* * *

Everyone had similar experiences. I don't believe there was a single person out of the whole eight million in London unfamiliar with the close whistle of a bomb. Thousands were killed, thousands were injured and thousands more were destitute. If I have not dwelt at length on the horrors of the ordeal it is not from lack of feeling. I leave the terror of the darkness, the moan of the ambulance sirens, and the cries of the injured to the imagination of the reader. The ghastliness and the suffering do not bear detailed description. Yet it was out of this awfulness that England reached up to claim her second great victory. British fighters had broken the back of the day attacks; now British spirit rose to break the back of the night attacks. It was the same spirit that had sent Britons to conquer the seas and explore the four corners of the earth; that had driven England's enemies from her shores time and time again and raised the Island to lead the greatest Empire the world has known.

There was no break in the dam here as there had been in France. Even the weakest link in the chain was reliable. From the highest to the humblest, each person played his part. Wardens, police, fire-fighting units, doctors, nurses, telephone operators, truck drivers, newspaper printers, factory workers, officials and hundreds of others stuck to their jobs and kept the huge organisation of the capital going. The co-ordination between government and people was a magnificent tribute to the solidarity and efficiency of English democracy.

Freda worked all day at her Feathers clubs, now crowded with people who had been bombed out. She ran five or six meals a day, helped hundreds of them to readjust themselves and find new places to live. She used to come home at night shaken by the things she had seen. 'When you see how wonderful human beings can be, it's hard to understand how such frightfulness can go on in the world.' I thought she was wonderful herself, but it was the last thing that would have occurred to her: everyone was impressed by the courage around them, but no one seemed to think that they themselves were extraordinary in any way. At times the standard of self-control they took for granted was perplexing. I remember the night a bomb fell on a hill not far away. Clouds of dust and smoke rose in the darkness and Vernon put on a tin hat and ran across the street. A few minutes later he came back with a caretaker and his wife, a soldier and a dog. The blast from the explosion had blown in the doors of their house, smashed the furniture and knocked down the plaster. They had managed to climb out unhurt except for a few cuts and bruises. Vernon took them into the kitchen and gave them some tea. The caretaker's wife looked pale and frightened. I'll never forget her husband saying severely: 'Don't look so upset, Elizabeth. Everything's all right. It's not like you to go to pieces.' From the way he spoke you might have thought the poor woman was having hysterics rather than sitting quietly in the corner.

The soldier had come home on twenty-four hours' leave and had dropped in to call on his friends. I couldn't understand why he had such a pleased expression until he told me he had never been bombed before – now he had a good story to tell when he got back to 'the front'!

The East End had been hit the hardest, but even here there was no weakening in the fibre. I went down there one afternoon with Eddie Ward. We drove for miles along the gutted-out warehouses near the docks and through congested areas where hundreds of workers' dwelling-houses had been destroyed by explosives and blast. It was about five o'clock in the afternoon and people were hurrying to their shelters before the darkness came. We stopped at a particularly desolate spot. The block of houses across the street were a mass of wreckage, and the ones opposite swept out by blast. I spoke to two girls who were walking along, their arms filled with pillows and blankets. I asked them if the planes still bombed this particular section, and one of them replied: 'Every b—— night! Cor! don't you know we're the front line?' They both laughed and went off to make their beds in a shelter underneath a pile of debris. What chance had Hitler to break the morale of people like this?

* * *

People soon readjusted their lives. The *Daily Express* ran a campaign: 'Don't Be a Bomb Bore'; shops put up their 'Business As Usual' signs (a barber shop next to a wrecked building posted up the notice 'Close Shave?'); and Florence Desmond sang in a wistful voice:

> I've got a cosy flat,
> There's a place for your hat;
> I wear a pink chiffon negligée gown

> And do I know my stuff?
> And if that's not enough,
> I've got the deepest shelter in town . . .

The mattresses disappeared from the hotel lobbies, street cars, buses and cabs began running again; shelter conditions were improved; the homeless were provided with homes; and a new routine was established. Crowds no longer gathered to peer at the craters in the streets – the novelty had worn off.

One night, Lord Londonderry came out of the Dorchester Hotel. It was unusually quiet. He asked the doorman if there was an alarm on:

'Yes, m'lord.'

'Have there been any bombs?'

'No, m'lord. In fact, if I may say so, up till now it's been a *very* poor show.'

People of England, *salaam*.

4

Invasion Weekend

Friday, September 13th, marked the opening of 'Invasion Weekend'. There was a full moon and a high tide. The ports across the Channel were swarming with German soldiers, and the harbours crowded with flat-bottomed troop-carrying barges; this was Hitler's last opportunity to launch an invasion before the equinoctial gales began. The British Navy doubled its watch-out patrols, the Army manned its guns, and the Air Force hammered at the enemy bases. England waited.

That same Friday, Knickerbocker and I drove down to Dover. We left London about eleven o'clock in the morning. Although the night blitz had been going on for nearly a week, we were surprised to find how little damage had been done to the main roads. On our way through the congested suburbs we were forced to detour only twice. We passed several houses looking like stage sets with the walls stripped off; workmen sweeping up the broken glass in front of a row of shops; and a group of people peering curiously down a crater in the middle of the street. But that was all. After the terrible pounding of the last few nights it seemed surprising that comparatively so little damage had been done.

Soon we were on the main highway with the country opening up around us. There was little traffic until we reached Maidstone, but from there to Dover – a stretch of about forty miles – the atmosphere turned into a military one. Army lorries, motorcycles, Air Force camions and light tanks hurtled past us at top speed. Would this road resound to the tread of armoured German divisions as so many other unlikely roads had done in their time? We stared at the insignificant green fields stretching out on either side of us, wondering if men would soon be giving their lives to defend them inch by inch; if one day teachers would bring their pupils – perhaps to that small hill in the distance – to see a monument marking the place where one of the great battles of 1940 had been fought.

These were the things we were thinking on that bright September morning. Knick said suddenly: 'Do you suppose one day we'll be driving like hell along the road to Norfolk, Virginia, or to Portland, Maine, or Los Angeles, or Chicago, to cover an invasion?'

'You may, but I'll be going in the other direction.'

'Well, it *could* happen. With the British and French fleets in the hands of Germany; with a hostile Japan; with South America and Canada under the Axis, it's exactly what *would* happen. Can you imagine what it would be like? Can you see the Nazi mechanised columns rolling over those long straight roads of ours? Can you see the Fifth Columnists sabotaging the power plants and cutting the telephone wires? Can you see the evacuees streaming out of New York and Chicago? And the planes swooping down, bombing and machine-gunning them? Can you see the panic? It's happened everywhere else – why not America? By God, I think I'll open up my lecture tour like that! What do you think of it?'

'Well, it ought to keep the audience awake . . .'

We stopped at Canterbury for lunch. Here the war seemed far away. The outline of the great cathedral took you back to another century, and even the food belied the fact that England was a besieged and beleaguered fortress. We had lobster mayonnaise, roast chicken, vegetable salad and ice-cream. Under the Sundaes we saw the heading: 'Knickerbocker Glory'. Delighted, Knick asked the waitress how they had happened to think of it. 'Oh, I

don't know. We like to give our sweets fancy names.' Knick paid
the bill with a five-pound note which called for a signature on
the back. The waitress was not amused; she gave him an angry
look, no doubt thinking it was an ill-advised American attempt
at humour.

On the last fifteen miles to Dover we passed a good many barricades and camouflaged blockhouses. The fields on either side were
cluttered with iron stakes, rolls of wire, and even old carts, to prevent German planes from landing. At one point we saw one which
had landed by mistake – a twisted mass of steel with a swastika
more crooked than ever. It looked like a Messerschmitt 109, but,
not being an expert, I asked the sentry standing guard.

'Can't say, miss,' he replied in a bored tone. 'There are so many
types scattered around here. It gets a bit confusing.'

I nodded understandingly and climbed back into the car. I
thought of the remark some American journalist had made:
'We mustn't exaggerate. Kent is not knee-deep in planes: only
ankle-deep.'

A few miles outside Dover the prohibited area began. A road
patrol stopped us and we showed our papers. My car had been
registered with the police several weeks before and the yellow strip
on the windshield with a Coastal Defence number on it permitted
us to drive into the town. From the top of a hill we saw the rugged
outline of the castle on the cliff, the sleepy houses far below, and
the blue waters of the Channel stretching out beyond. In the distance it looked the same as it always had, but when we reached the
waterfront we found that the lively atmosphere had given way to a
sombre, melancholy one. The Grand Hotel, where we had stayed a
few weeks before, was in ruins. Half its insides were spilt over the
square, and the roller-skating pavilion next to it had only the sky
for a canopy. The balloon-barrage soldiers were still billeted in a

house across the way. The windows had been blown out but the walls and roof were still standing.

We were walking around the square when O'Dowd Gallagher of the *Daily Express* and H. A. Flower of the *Daily Telegraph* drove up. They told us the bombing had taken place only a few days before and miraculously enough only two people had been killed. A couple of soldiers standing nearby said the bodies were still beneath the wreckage. Just then a bomber swooped out of the clouds, about a thousand feet above us. We looked at it, startled, but one of the soldiers said: 'Oh, that's a Wellington.' We went on talking. Suddenly I saw four small black specks falling from the undercarriage. They looked like a bunch of grapes and for a moment seemed to be hanging in the air.

'Bombs!' shouted one of the soldiers. 'Get down!'

We flung ourselves, face down, on the pavement. I buried my head in my arms and waited. It seemed interminable. Then the earth shuddered violently: one, two, three, four. We picked ourselves up, our clothes covered with mud. The bombs had landed on the beach and in the water fifty yards away. The plane was a Wellington all right – but one the Germans had evidently captured in France.

We tried to resume our conversation, but twice more lone raiders came out of the clouds and twice more we took cover – this time diving into a small brick shelter in the middle of the green. I'll never forget the fat girl with the black curls, who had been hanging around the square flirting with the soldiers, breathing heavily on my neck and saying: 'Christ, it's enough to ruin your digestion.'

It had certainly ruined mine. I decided I'd had enough of Dover Square. The men climbed into my car and we drove up to Shakespeare Cliff, where, three weeks before, we had watched the great air battles over the coast. We found Arthur Mencken, the photographer for *Life*, taking pictures of the harbour. There was a strong wind blowing and the Channel was flecked with white-caps. The coast of France looked clearer than usual and with the glasses I made out the lighthouse near Calais, the church steeple in Boulogne and the tall, thin monument which had been erected at the end of the last war in memory of the famous Dover Patrol.

'If only we could see some of those invasion barges!' said Knick. 'What a hell of a good story it would make . . .'

'I know,' said Arthur. 'Flash— As I was standing today on the rugged cliffs of Dover I saw the vast German flotilla hoisting anchor in final preparations for its death charge across the narrow straits . . .'

'Wait a minute,' said Knick, staring through his glasses. 'Who's that fat man I see over there with all the medals?'

'By God!' exclaimed O'Dowd. 'And the little dark hunchback one standing next to him?'

'Yes!' said Arthur. 'And the one with the crooked moustache?'

'You don't think it can be Charlie Chaplin?' said Knick.

It was obvious the bombs had had their effect.

* * *

It was a strange forty-eight hours of a weekend which will prob-ably go down in history as the weekend Hitler didn't invade. Opinion among the naval and military experts with whom we talked was divided as to the likelihood of the attempt, but it was generally agreed that any plan to send flat-bottomed boats across the Channel would first be preceded by an intense air and land bombardment; then, simultaneously, an effort to land parachute troops several miles behind the coast to attack in the rear and ultimately connect with the seaborne forces.

It was a strange atmosphere. Knick and I established ourselves in a country house only three miles from the coast, which a friend had lent us. After the London blitz the quiet was almost oppressive: no alarms, no droning planes, no burst of gunfire. Save for an occasional raider, or a few haphazard shells into Dover, the only display of fireworks was the show put on each night by the RAF. When the wind was right you could hear the bombs dropping across the Channel. One night we drove up to the seafront and saw the sky lighting up with bursts of shrapnel and the red glow of parachute flares.

Even though the army slept with its boots on and the civilian population went to bed each night prepared to hear the church bells tolling to tell them the hour had come, no one had any fear as to the ultimate result. When you talked to the local inhabitants about it, they laughed and said: 'Let him try it.' Although the countryside reverberated with the sound of lorries and motorcycles and fields were alive with military patrols, the villagers carried on their normal routine as though they were far removed from the war. At any hour their farms and backyards might have been turned into a battlefield, yet you saw children playing in the dusty roads and farmers calmly ploughing their fields. Some thought it couldn't happen; others thought it wouldn't happen; others never thought about it at all. When the maid brought me breakfast in the morning she asked me about the bombing of London.

'It must be very alarming,' she said. 'Did you come down here for a rest?'

In the meantime, Dr Goebbels was informing his countrymen that the English were trembling in their boots – just as the Paris *Moniteur* of 1803 printed despatches from Fifth Column reporters, calculated to please:

London Correspondence, 13th October: The well-to-do inhabitants of Dover and the neighbouring coasts have such a fear of the French that they have precipitately abandoned their habitations and have retired to Canterbury or London. It is agreed that the season of year and the long nights will be extremely favourable to the enemies' designs. . . .

The general opinion in London is that the expedition will take place between now and the middle of November.

London Correspondence, 18th October: A large number of workmen are at the moment employed in building locks on the River Lea by means of which a part of Essex could be flooded, if need arise.

From the Dover Correspondence: The alarms and consternation on the rumours of a visit from the other side of the water, with which we are menaced, increase here day by day.

. . . When fires were lit at Boulogne, in honour of the arrival of the First Consul there, the population of the English coast between Sandgate and Folkestone took fright and fled into the country.

A Convoy of a hundred ships arriving at Torquay from America was mistaken for the French Fleet and a panic ensued.

* * *

On Sunday, both in the morning and in the afternoon, the air was filled with the heavy roar of planes; it was that deep, throaty noise that meant volume; occasionally we heard the wail of an engine going into a power dive and the staccato rattle of machine-gun bullets, but low clouds prevented us from seeing anything. Even from Shakespeare Cliff there was no break in the solid grey curtain. In fact the only plane we saw all day was a nuisance raider. That was in the afternoon when we went up to Dover Castle to talk to one of the Intelligence Officers. The man we wanted to see wasn't there, but an elderly captain asked if there was anything he could do for us. When he heard Knickerbocker's name he glared at him angrily. 'You're the man who says the Germans are going to try to invade here.'

'That's the opinion in London.'

'Well, if that's what we pay our politicians to think, we'd better change the whole lot of them. Invasion? Nonsense! The Germans won't get over here unless we decide to build a bridge for them. Hitler's one big bluff.'

We were standing on a small promontory which jutted over the cliff with the long sweep of the Channel below us. The Captain had scarcely spoken his last words before a German raider dived out of the clouds and dropped a stick of bombs that seemed to whistle past our noses. Three hit the water and the fourth hit the end of the pier, about a mile away.

'I don't think *bluff* is exactly the right word,' said Knick. The Captain cleared his throat but made no comment.

Bluff or no bluff, no one was taking any chances, and for miles behind the coast towns and villages were honeycombed with troops. The three nights we were there Knick and I dined with some of the officers of the Queen's Westminsters, who were billeted only a short distance away from where we were staying. Tom Mitford was the adjutant of the regiment and persuaded the proprietress of the neighbouring pub to let us come in and cook our own dinner. Knick and I spent hours buying tinned food – everything from baked beans and vegetable salad to pickled onions and Californian pears. The boys provided eggs and butter, and, with the confidence that all men seem to have in their ability to cook, crowded into the kitchen offering to mix the omelette and warm up the beans. It seemed strange to see the young men you had dined and danced with now members of a shock troop regiment, waiting to meet the Nazi invasion. They appeared to regard it as a comic situation themselves, and when one of them expressed doubts as to whether the Germans would ever make the attempt, Anthony Winn said brightly: 'Well, if they don't I'm going to resign before hordes of angry bombed-out civilians start handing us white feathers.'

On Monday the order came that they could take off their boots when they went to bed. Things were relaxing. Knick and I started back to London with 'invasion weekend' fading peacefully into the background. What had happened? At the time it was difficult to draw any conclusions, but now, in the light of past events, the answer is more obvious. The Sunday we spent wandering about the streets of Dover buying our tins of baked beans and vegetable salad was September 15th – the greatest day in the history of the Royal Air Force. The actions which took place were described by the Prime Minister in the House of Commons as 'the most brilliant and fruitful of any fought upon a large scale up to that date by the fighters of the Royal Air Force'. The enemy lost one hundred and eighty-five aircraft.

This was the last big wallop the Germans took. When the score was chalked up on the night of the 15th, the Germans had lost 1,835 planes – over three-quarters of the total number they lost during the whole three months of their intensive daylight attacks.

That memorable day marked the turn of the tide. The back of the Nazi Air Force was broken and Germany had failed to establish the crushing superiority essential for a successful invasion.

According to the pamphlet published by the Air Ministry, *The Battle of Britain*, Germany's failure to destroy the British Fighter Force meant:

> . . . defeat of the German Air Force itself, defeat of a carefully designed strategical plan, defeat of that which Hitler most longed for – invasion of this Island. The Luftwaffe which, as Goebbels said on the eve of the battle, had 'prepared the final conquest of the last enemy – England', did its utmost and paid very heavily for the attempt. Between the 8th August and 31st October, 2,375 German aircrafts are known to have been destroyed in daylight. This figure takes no account of those lost at night or those, seen by thousands, staggering back to their French bases, wings and fuselage full of holes, ailerons shot away, engines smoking and dripping glycol, undercarriages dangling – the retreating remnants of a shattered and disordered Armada. This melancholy procession of the defeated was to be observed not once but many times during those summer and autumn days of 1940. Truly it was a great deliverance.

We left the peace of the English coast regretfully and headed back to London and the blitz once more. On the way, Knick said: 'I've been thinking over what that sour-faced captain at the Castle said. I didn't take to him any too well, but I'm beginning to think he's right. Hitler really *does* need a bridge.'

5

Only United Will We Stand

Here at West End Farm, thirty miles from London, the immediate problems of the day are preventing the ducks from catching cold, the pigs from catching swine fever, and the cows from gnawing the branches off the peach trees. This is where Maureen and Oliver Stanley live, and I have been staying here for the past few months writing this book. Maureen's life has altered greatly in the last year; *The Spectator* and *Harper's Bazaar* have been replaced by *The Feathered World* and *The Egg*; ambassadors are kept waiting on the telephone while she argues with the handyman about a new mash for the chickens; and we are all wise enough to know that the local auctioneer and the dairywoman must be treated with marked deference.

Maureen's London house, 58 Romney Street, was wrecked the first month of the blitz; shortly afterwards, she moved down here and turned her hand to farming. Every now and then she travels north to make a speech for the Food Ministry or the Ministry of Information. A few weeks ago, I saw on her calendar: March 25th: Four of the fattest pigs go to market – Maureen speaks at Queen's Hall. (Oliver's comment: 'Be sure you don't get the two things mixed.')

It is peaceful here in the country. At night you hear the German planes overhead, but so far this particular neighbourhood has had only one bomb. It landed in a pasture not far from the house. Duff Cooper was here for the weekend and village gossip insisted that was the reason why. I went out in the morning to look at the crater and found four cows staring at it with melancholy eyes. Cows don't understand that sort of thing.

During the winter I have gone to London once a week to work in the library. The streets are more deserted now and there are many new caverns where houses have stood, but the spirit is as firm as ever. The other day I went to see Mrs Sullivan. Her arm was in a sling and her leg was swollen from rheumatism (she had never been able to take up her ARP duties), but her morale was undaunted. When I asked her how long she thought the war would last she said it would be over this year.

'Why?'

'Oh, those Germans are always the same. They start big, but old Sullivan says in the end they always fizzle out. Besides, with that common trash 'Itler, where can they expect to land except in the gutter? But, I say, miss, wasn't that big blitz something! They *did* try to give it to us! I said to Sullivan it was just like someone sitting up there shelling peas. I went to bed with my clothes on. I didn't want to be turned out in the street like some people with only a nightdress on. And I don't mind telling you those whistles made me stop and wonder how good a life I'd led. But I suppose it's all in getting used to things. As old Sullivan says, you'll never hear the bomb what 'its you, so why worry?'

She beamed at me and I had a warm, comfortable feeling inside.

* * *

That morning I was on my way back to the farm. I remember it well, for when I passed through the village of Datchet and turned on to the country lane to Windsor the great castle on the hill loomed up with a breathtaking beauty. The grey towers rose out of a heavy white ground mist, as though they were floating in the heavens. I had made the same drive many times before and seen the castle at all times of the day: at noon, standing up boldly against a brilliant blue sky; in the evening, with its mighty contours mellowed by the fading light; in the early morning, glistening with a splendour that once occasioned Samuel Pepys to describe it as 'the most romantique castle that is in the world'. But I had never seen it more beautiful than on this particular morning.

As I drove along the winding road with the narrow stream of the Thames running through the fields and Windsor Park, guarded by its great craggy oak trees, stretching out before me, I thought of the long span of human history the castle had marked. The Doomsday Survey of 1086 mentions a castle on a hill, and it was there that William the Conqueror held his Court. Edward the Third built the Round Tower to hold the Round Table for his Knights of the Garter; Henry the Eighth and Edward the Sixth completed the building of St George's Chapel; Charles the First built the drawbridge and Charles the Second planted the trees in the park. It was from this castle that King John went forth to sign the Magna Carta; it was here that Queen Elizabeth spent her childhood, hunting in the forests attended by 'half a hundred ladies on hackneys'; it was here that Queen Victoria established herself and earned the name of 'the widow of Windsor'.

The ramparts of the castle have looked down on nearly a thousand years of history, during which no invader has succeeded in setting foot on the shores of England. Through this long span they have watched the nation meet many violent changes and survive many hazardous wars. But now, in the year of Our Lord nineteen hundred and forty-one, they rise out of the April mists to witness the most perilous moment of all.

Not only is England's existence at stake, but all the gain she has earned through the ages. On her victory the hopes of people in every corner of the world are pinned. I have seen some of them and they pass through my mind now in a long and vivid procession: the ragged soldiers fighting in the mountains near Madrid;

the weeping women in the streets of Prague; the tragic refugee streaming across the Polish frontiers; the Finnish patrols slipping through the ice-bound forests of the Arctic; the terrified flow of humanity choking the roads from Paris to Tours.

Although the consequences will be far more reaching than in any previous conflict, what is happening today is not new. All through history, tyrants have arisen with a lust for power which they have sought to satisfy by the enslavement of their fellow beings. All through history, men have struggled to keep their necks free of the yoke. With the teachings of Christ came the first great conception of the sanctity of individual life. On this conception the foundation of our civilisation has been laid. The stones have been added with blood, sweat and inspiration. Like Windsor Castle itself, the structure has been supplemented and rebuilt throughout the years with the splendour of each addition marking our progress.

But progress is not inevitable. We have progressed because we have met and defeated every challenge to our conception of life. Now we are faced with the threat of a savage retrogression. The tyrants of our time have borrowed their creed from the era of barbarism. They kill, plunder and torture; they deny man the right to claim his soul.

Although the great mass of civilised people are revolted by these precepts, science has provided the oppressors with such formidable weapons that should they gain the ultimate victory, human resistance will be broken with terrible finality.

Railways, roads, machines and wireless all play their part in the familiar pattern of corruption, devastation and subjection. Vast armies are set in motion, vast communities are destroyed, and vast areas held in subjection. If Napoleon had possessed the machinery of the present century with which to enforce his conquests, history might have told a different tale. Instead, the nations he roke rose up again like ghosts and, led by Great Britain, in the end destroyed him. Now no countries rise. When a conquest is accomplished, it is complete; only the dark night sets in.

How can such things have happened? Little over twenty years ago people all over the world were rejoicing in the Armistice. The war to end wars had been fought and won. 'On that November evening,' wrote Winston Churchill, 'the three men at the head of Great Britain, the United States and France, seemed to be the masters of the world . . . Together they had reached their goal. Victory absolute and incomparable was in their hands. What would they do with it?'

The three men laid the foundation for the first international court of justice civilisation has ever known. People had suffered badly and now peace was at a higher premium than ever before. Two decades later the structure was in ruins and amity had once more deserted the earth. The part I have seen of the collapse is small related to the whole, but I know that it was due less to neglect than to bewilderment in understanding how to preserve it. One by one, each of us preferred the expediency of the moment to the lasting pattern of the future. Although our pacifism provided the dictators with a powerful weapon and finally expedited the most terrible war of all, our widespread attachment to peace should not now be despised. It was a tremendous advancement in itself. If, when peace is reborn again, our devotion to it can be fortified with the wisdom to know how to guard and defend it from infancy onwards, there is every hope for the future.

Where did we fail? Today the metaphor is so simple even a child can understand it. The world was our village and we were the people who had struggled desperately to rid our community of bandits. When the fight was won we threw away our weapons joyfully, convinced we had settled the matter once and for all. The very fact that we were unarmed attracted more bandits. Even . we outnumbered them; if we had taken immediate and united action we could have destroyed them with little effort before they grew too strong. Instead, appalled by the prospect of more bloodshed, we locked the doors and bolted the windows, each one trusting that although his neighbour might be robbed and plundered, he himself would be spared. We failed to understand that our neighbour's misfortune was our misfortune; that we are all part of the whole; that when the bells toll they toll for us.

Even now, we, the people of the United States, do not seem to understand it. Already we bear a grave responsibility to history. Of the three great powers to whom the victory of 1918 belonged, we were the first to shrink from our obligations. We were the first to desert the whole. Because our house was removed from the centre of the community, we felt more secure than our neighbours. One by one their houses have been destroyed. Now, besides our own, only one strong point remains from which to resist them. We are still living on the outskirts of the village, but when the village has gone, even though our roof and walls may still be standing, we will be afraid to walk in the gardens and fields, or for that matter, even to take our pigs to market, for fear of being set upon. Our Isolationists still whisper to us to shut our eyes to the village fight; even though our children and our children's children will be denied all freedom of action, with no fields to work or play in, they advise us to think only of the preservation of our own life and property. But it is unlikely that we shall even be successful there. The other houses in the village are in ashes; why should ours be spared?

On March 15th, four days after the signing of the Lease and Lend Bill, President Roosevelt said in a speech:

The Nazi forces are not seeking mere modification in colonial maps or in minor European boundaries. They openly seek the destruction of all collective systems of Government on every continent, including our own; they seek to establish systems of Government based on the regimentation of all human beings by a handful of individual rulers who seized power by force . . .

There is no longer the slightest question of doubt. The American people recognise the supreme seriousness of the present situation. That is why they have demanded and got a policy of unqualified immediate, all-out aid for Britain – for Greece, for China, and for all Governments in exile whose home-lands are temporarily occupied by the aggressors.

Do not let us deceive ourselves. We are not giving 'all-out aid' to Britain. We cannot buy victory with our chequebooks. If we, at last, have come to realise that world progress is indivisible and that not only the future of European civilisation is at stake but the future of our own civilisation as well, why are our ships not fighting on the Atlantic? Why are our soldiers and airmen not defending our way of life? Our forebears gave us our heritage through the sweat of their achievements; they chained the mighty rivers and forests, blazed the trails west, and put down lawlessness in the deserted reaches of the continent. They shed their blood to establish the principle of justice and equality we take for granted. They fought their most savage war for the conception that has built us into the most powerful democracy the world has known: 'United we stand, divided we fall.'

Today, on a broader horizon, the same tenet applies. Divided we will fall. United – and only united – we will stand. With desperate conviction, I say: Let us recapture the virility of our forebears and rise up now, before it is too late, to declare war on the Nazi forces which threaten our way of life. Let us rise up now in all splendour and fight side by side with Great Britain until we reach a victory so complete that freedom will ring through the ages to come with a strength no man dare challenge.

Index of Persons